ANCIENT DRUMS, OTHER MOCCASINS

ANCIENT DRUMS, OTHER MOCCASINS

NATIVE NORTH AMERICAN CULTURAL ADAPTATION

Harriet J. Kupferer

Prentice Hall, Englewood Cliffs, New Jersey 07632

Library of Congress Cataloging-in-Publication Data

Kupferer, Harriet J.
    Ancient drums, other moccasins: Native North American cultural
adaptation / Harriet J. Kupferer.
        p.   cm.
    Bibliography: p.
    Includes index.
    ISBN 0-13-035478-3
    1. Indians of North America.   I. Title.
E77.K86 1988
973'.0497—dc19   87-18464
                                                      CIP

Editorial/production supervision and
  interior design: Joe O'Donnell Jr.
Cover design: Lundgren Graphics, Ltd.
Cover art: *Making Flint Arrowheads—Apache* by George Catlin,
  date: 1855, cardboard, 0.391 × 0.559 (15⅜ × 22 in. oval)
  National Gallery of Art, Washington, Paul Mellon Collection
Manufacturing buyer: Ray Keating

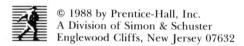

© 1988 by Prentice-Hall, Inc.
A Division of Simon & Schuster
Englewood Cliffs, New Jersey 07632

Printed in the United States of America

10 9 8 7 6 5 4 3 2 1

ISBN 0-13-035478-3 01

Prentice-Hall International (UK) Limited, *London*
Prentice-Hall of Australia Pty. Limited, *Sydney*
Prentice-Hall Canada Inc., *Toronto*
Prentice-Hall Hispanoamericana, S.A., *Mexico*
Prentice-Hall of India Private Limited, *New Delhi*
Prentice-Hall of Japan, Inc., *Tokyo*
Simon & Schuster Asia Pte. Ltd., *Singapore*
Editora Prentice-Hall do Brasil, Ltda., *Rio de Janeiro*

For Gene and Helen Outwin Kupferer,
their sisters, Min and Harriet,
and their kindred, including cousins of all degrees.

Contents

Preface

This book differs from others presenting a broad perspective on native peoples of North America, for I have discarded the culture area as an organizational concept. A *culture area* is a geographic region whose residents are thought to have more cultural affinities with one another than they do with people in other regions. Clark Wissler and Alfred Kroeber did the most systematic work in delineating culture areas for North America. With some modifications, the concept remains the basis for categorizing American Indian and Eskimo cultures.

It has its uses, yet it—like most other concepts—has shortcomings. The North American continent includes 8 million square miles. In this enormous land mass, Kroeber proposed only ten areas. Others who followed him identified one or two fewer, only occasionally more. Such gross demarcations result in grouping populations who may share only a small number of distinctive traits. In many regions the differences outnumber similarities. The southeast culture area extending from the Atlantic ocean to the Mississippi River is an example. Among many distinct populations speaking different languages were small coastal peoples subsisting on shellfish and game; successful gardeners; and the now extinct, highly complex and socially stratified Natchez. The situation in the great southwest is comparable.

An additional disadvantage of the concept is that rarely do classifiers agree on the number of areas, boundaries, or designations for them. Some have used geographic regions as culture areas; others employed primary food types to classify the culture area. A few were inconsistent with their nomenclature, using geographic tags for some and language for others.

To avoid these contradictions, I have chosen to group native cultures using major subsistence mode as the basis. The underlying approach is essentially ecological. The fundamental premise is that culture (never static) is, among other things, an adaptive system. In adopting this premise, no doubt other pitfalls have been created, yet it seems reasonable to look for likenesses as well as differences among peoples who make a living in the same general way regardless of where they do it. Native cultures were (perhaps still are) interrelated matrices of ideas and consequent strategies which enabled people to adapt, however effectively, to conditions in their environments.

Cultural ecology is not, however, simple environmental determinism, which held that specific cultural traits as well as such phenomena as intelligence were caused by the environment. It also goes beyond the "permitting" or "possibilistic" viewpoint. "Possibilism" contended that only the absence of traits could be explained by environmental characteristics, otherwise, there were always options from which to choose. Possibilists did recognize that there were complex interactions with environments and that specific histories and diffusions were also important influences. But, as Vayda and Rappaport observed, "these other influences were allowed to constitute a dark middle region between man and his environment in which almost anything could happen."[1] There was little attempt made to assess adaptive functions of religion and ritual, the effects of disease or the presence of enemies on settlement patterns, or the functional value of other traits.[2]

The ecological model stresses interactions between a number of factors, including natural resources, technology, social organization, and ideology. Causality is difficult to establish, consequently stress is often on explanation. As yet there is no widely accepted unified theory of cultural ecology or ecological anthropology, although Emilio Moran has attempted to synthesize various concepts and approaches to the study of human societies and their environments.[3] Without a unified corpus of thought or tested methodology, cultural ecology cannot rightly be called a discipline, though it remains a convincing point of view.[4] Because this is so, scholars differ in

[1]Andrew P. Vayda and Roy Rappaport, "Ecology: Cultural and Non-cultural," in *Introduction to Cultural Anthropology.* James A. Clifton, ed. (Boston: Houghton Mifflin Co., 1968), p. 483.

[2]Ibid., pp. 487–492.

[3]Emelio F. Moran, *An Introduction to Ecological Anthropology.* (Boulder, CO: Westview Press, 1982).

[4]Robert McC. Netting, *Cultural Ecology.* Cummings Modular Program in Anthropology. (Menlo Park, CA: Cummings Publishing Co., 1977), p. 1.

their approach to the "point of view." Different questions are asked, different relationships are sought, and a variety of research techniques are employed. Definitions differ too. It is likely that such divergences stem from theoretical biases.

Although Leslie A. White was far from a cultural ecologist, in his efforts to build a theory of culture evolution, he emphasized the importance of energy. Said White: "The basic function of culture is the harnessing of energy and putting it to work in the service of man."[5] Correctly, he noted that through technology energy was put into service; the more energy captured, the more complex culture became. In his scheme of cultural evolution, he ignored human creativity and downplayed the importance of habitat. White's Universal Evolution theory was challenged by Julian Steward who proposed the idea of multilinear evolution in which he stressed the role of environment in the shaping of specific cultures and institutions. He was also probably the first to use the term *cultural ecology*. Through it, he wanted to explain the origin of particular cultural features and patterns that characterize different areas by examining environmental adaptations.[6]

Their ideas have been "cussed" and discussed by their colleagues, but their key concepts—White's of energy and technology and Steward's of environmental adaptation—have been put to use in later work.

Yehudi Cohen combined both the concept of adaptive processes and energy in his theory of culture evolution. "Human adaptation," he said, "is the result of energy systems that are harnessed by a group and the organizations of social relations in the group that make it possible to use its energy systems effectively."[7] A human group has adapted to its environment when it has achieved, and continues to have, a workable relationship with its environment. Whether or not intended by Cohen, his definition omits any reference to the role of belief in effective adaptation.

Marvin Harris developed a broad theory to explain cultural similarities and differences not too different from Cohen's, calling it Cultural Materialism. The scheme, said Harris, is "based on the simple premise that human social life is a response to the practical problems of human existence . . . Cultural Materialism leads to better scientific theories about the causes of sociocultural phenomena than any of the rival strategies."[8] The two principal concepts of his theory are technology and environment. Harris argued that "similar technologies applied to similar environment produce similar arrangements of labor in production and distribution, and, that these in turn call forth similar kinds of social groupings, which justify and coordinate their activities by similar systems of values and be-

[5]Leslie White, *The Evolution of Culture.* (New York: McGraw-Hill, 1959), p. 39.

[6]Julian H. Steward, *Theory of Culture Change: The Methodology of Multilinear Evolution.* (Urbana: University of Illinois Press, 1963).

[7]Yehudi A. Cohen, *Man in Adaptation: The Cultural Present.* (Chicago: Aldine Publishing Co., 1968), Introduction, p. 3.

[8]Marvin Harris, *The Rise of Anthropological Theory.* (New York: Crowell Co., 1968), p. 4.

lief."[9] To understand a culture using his proposal, one must examine the material conditions (technology, economics) and environment.

Both Cohen and Harris were technological determinists, but they recognized the interrelationships between technology, environment, and social organization and, in Harris's case, between belief and values. Like White, each assigned the primary role in cultural development to technology and contended that it was the causal factor. Marshall Sahlins described this position as the "layer cake model." The model asserts that technology or modes of production are the underpinnings of a cultural system and that social organization and ideology rest upon it and reflect the material foundations.[10]

Other ecological anthropologists admit to the importance of technology but refuse to accept it as the major mover in cultural adaptations, arguing that other factors, both internal and external, may be equally as important. These people employ a systems framework. Its roots lie in the earlier functionalist theories that held that every human institution is related to every other one; together they maintain the culture or society, usually in a homeostatic equilibrium. Changes in one cause reactions in all the rest. No one institution is necessarily more significant than the others in the system. This theory—often referred to as "holistic"—was wed to concepts derived from biological ecology, most especially that of the ecosystem. An *ecosystem* includes an interacting group of organisms or groups of organisms in a dynamic relationship with their environment. Because humans were organisms, it was concluded that human behavior could be investigated using the ecosystem model. As Bennett pointed out, humans interact with one another, and the patterned interactions can be seen as systems. People also interact with environmental networks; these interactions within the group of organisms and its habitat "also can be considered to be a system—an ecosystem if you will."[11]

While not denying the importance of technology in interaction with environment, I am more comfortable with the "holistic" view. This book, therefore, is an effort to utilize it in discussing native American cultures. Congruent with this approach is the absence of formal paragraph headings. This may create difficulties for some, but their presence often tends to give a fragmented view of culture. I wish to stress the interrelatedness of cultural patterns and institutions.

Readers will discover that I have condemned white behavior as it affected Indians. Traders, missionaries, settlers, and emissaries of the federal government have been judged harshly. Although there were individuals

[9]Harris develops his position more fully in *Cultural Materialism: The Struggle for a Science of Culture*. (New York: Random House Vintage Books, 1980), Preface, p. ix.

[10]Marshall Sahlins, "Culture and Environment," in *Horizons of Anthropology*, 2nd ed. Sol Tax and Leslie G. Freeman, eds. (Chicago: Aldine Publishing Co., 1977), p. 218.

[11]John W. Bennett, *The Ecological Transition: Cultural Anthropology and Human Adaptation*. (New York: Pergamon Press, 1976), p. 36.

who tried mightily to mitigate the problems brought by whites and supported Indians in their struggle, the overall result of contact was noxious to both whites and Indians.

The matter of tense has been vexing: tribal accounts are set in the past although, in a few cases, significant culture patterns persist. Habitats are described in the present except for those that civilization has irrevocably altered.

ACKNOWLEDGMENTS

The people who have had a part in this volume are legion. Dr. John Gulick made possible my first visit to the Cherokee. Subsequent research was funded by a NIMH grant. Dr. Laura Thompson as well as John Gulick patiently advised me. Dr. John J. Honigmann provided the means for field work in the north. Before her death, Irma Honigmann read drafts of the first four chapters. Their friendship encouraged me for 25 or more years.

Without the research of men and women who pioneered in Indian and Eskimo studies, no volume of this sort would have been possible. I am in their debt. I am also grateful to later scholars upon whom I have relied for material.

The University of North Carolina at Greensboro was generous with its support. A leave of absence allowed time for the inception of the project. Departmental colleagues cheered me on. Dr. Mary W. Helms read a portion of the manuscript; her advice was incorporated into the final draft. Mrs. Pattie Barlow typed and typed. Departmental supplies were looted for a gross of yellow pads, pencils, and reams of paper.

The Academic Computer Center afforded the funds for word processing and the final copies. Humming Puccini, John Cary processed and reprocessed. The University Library staff was always willing to go the extra mile.

Dr. Jack Hidore, Professor of Geography, supplied all kinds of necessary information. His colleague Dr. Jeffrey Patton directed the preparation of the maps; Miss Patricia Burkart drew them. Dr. Elizabeth Bowles, School of Education, straightened out the grammar and solved the intricacies of punctuation. Maggie Bushnell helped with final details.

But it is to the Indians and Eskimos with whom I played and worked (in that order) that I owe the greatest fealty. Among the Cherokee: Amanda Crowe, Bill Crowe, Molly Owl Blankenship, and Wilbur, Lloyd, and Molly Sequoyah were significant. Lizzie and Frances Cucumber, Tom McCoy and his family, the Smiths and the Burgesses, and many others also played an important part.

At Rupert's House we were enlightened by Chief Diamond and his extended family; Rosie and Anderson Jolly; Isiah Salt; the Stevens; and the other Cree. The Euro-Canadians there—Maude Watt; the Hudson Bay Manager; and the Northern Nurses—made our stay more comfortable. Richard J. and Sara Preston III were good companions.

A small grant from NIMH funded the research in the southwest. While I must forbear mentioning their names, so many Santo Domingans took me into their lives. The adventures I shared with some are cherished memories. I hope I have remained true to their trust.

To all of the "First People," thank you.

Harriet J. Kupferer

ANCIENT DRUMS,
OTHER MOCCASINS

CHAPTER ONE

The
Beginnings

When Columbus landed his three caravels in the Bahamas in October of 1492, neither he nor his crew realized the significance of the event. Although the early Greeks had believed that the world was round, this knowledge had all but vanished in the Middle Ages. But Columbus, convinced of a round world, sailed westward from Europe and thought he had succeeded in his search for a sea path to the Asian Indies. Who the people of the Bahamas were or where they had come from did not trouble him because he had fully expected to find the land occupied. Not until later voyages proved that America was not Asia, did questions arise about the people in the new land.

Sixteenth-century writers pondered the origins of the American Indians. Were they the remnants of the lost island of Atlantis? Such a theory, first propounded in about 1552, still has its adherents.[1] The Rosicrucian Order and the Theosophical Society both believe fervently in the lost continent of Atlantis. Others proposed that an island in the Pacific called Mu sank in a cataclysmic occurrence, and those people who lived through it made their way to America. Both these fantasies saw savagery growing out

[1] Lee Eldridge Huddleston, *Origins of the American Indians*. (Austin: University of Texas Press, 1967), p. 24.

1

of civilization. After the island disappeared, the survivors, perhaps jolted into amnesia by the sudden disaster, lost all memory of their former idyllic civilizations and thus were forced to construct a new life far more primitive than the one they had previously enjoyed.[2]

Others linked the people of the New World to ancient Greece. After the fall of Troy, they believed Ulysses sailed westward over the Atlantic reaching the Yucatan peninsula, where he and his companions sired the stock from which the Indians sprang. The Lost Tribes notion was first put forth in Antwerp in 1576.[3] Like the Lost Continent theory, this thesis, too, still continues. It finds expression in the Book of Mormon and the Articles of Faith of the Church of the Latter Day Saints. Still others proposed Old Testament origins; Suarez de Peralta believed that the Indians descended from Canaan, the son of Ham; Canaan was cursed by Noah for his father's sin.[4]

Fanciful and romantic as these speculations are, the modern position on the peopling of the New World is even more exciting. The people we now call Indians descended from early men and women who moved slowly out of Asia into Alaska and from there, through the years, followed a beckoning horizon to the south, east, and west. On their long and arduous trek they encountered a terrain and a climate vastly different from that which exists today. The story begins in the Pleistocene, a geologic term meaning "ice age" or the epoch of the glaciers. Vast sheets of ice covered parts of Europe and America; these retreated and advanced four times on both continents. Between each advance and retreat came periods called substages or interstadials. While the names for each of the major glacial periods in the western hemisphere differ from those used for the European sequence, the dates of each are similar, the total time for the Pleistocene being reckoned at about 2.5 million years. The glacial periods in America are called Nebraskan, Kansan, Illinoian, and Wisconsin. The Wisconsin, thought to have begun between 100,000 and 70,000 years ago,[5] is critical to the story, for sometime between its beginning and 13,000 BC Asiatic nomads wandered into Alaska. (see Table 1-1).

The movement of the great ice sheets during the Pleistocene vastly affected the geography of the land and sea. Sea levels shifted and fluctuated repeatedly as ocean water, locked up in ice, bore down by its sheer weight on the land which supported it. Geologic evidence from the Pleistocene shows clearly that both the Asian and North American continents were very different from their present condition. Most notable for

[2]Robert Wauchope, *Lost Tribes and Sunken Continents*. (Chicago: University of Chicago Press, 1962), pp. 31–39.

[3]Huddleston, *Origins of the American Indians*, p. 34.

[4]Ibid., p. 37.

[5]Richard Foster Flint, *Glacial and Quaternary Geology*. (New York: John Wiley and Sons, 1971), p. 44.

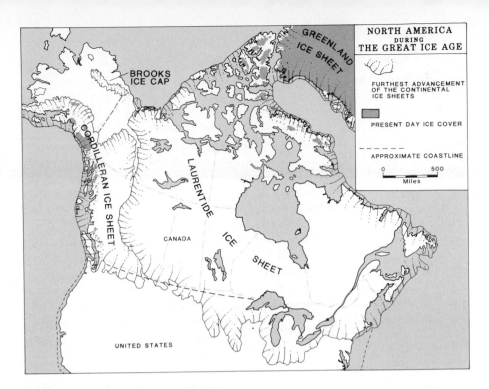

TABLE 1-1 **Wisconsin Glacial Sequence**

	Present		
Recent	Medithermal	2,500	BC
	Altithermal	5,000	
	Cochrane Advance	6,000	
	Valders Substage (Two Creeks Interstadial)	9,000 10,000	
	Mankato Substage (Interstadial)	12,000	
Wisconsin Glaciation	Cary Substage (Interstadial)	14,000	
	Tazewell Substage (Interstadial)	18,000	
	Iowan (Interstadial)	22,500	
	Farmdale Substage (Interstadial)	28,000	
	Altonian Substage	70,000	
Illinoian	Sangamon Interglacial		

From Gordon Willey, *An Introduction to Archaeology.* (Englewood Cliffs, NJ: Prentice-Hall, 1966), p. 28. Permission granted by Gordon R. Willey.

our story, no Bering Strait separated Alaska and Siberia. The two continents were joined by a land bridge. In fact, geologically, the term "new world" ought not to be used. It was new territory only to the venturesome fifteenth- and sixteenth-century Europeans; it was most certainly not new to the ancestors of the American Indians.

The land bridge resulted from the shifting sea level. The stored up ice exposed the floors of the Bering and Chukchi seas, which lay about 180 feet beneath the present surface of the water. William Haag suggests that, as the glacier grew causing the oceans to recede, a sea-level fall of 150 feet would have produced an entry to Alaska nearly two hundred miles wide.[6] At the maximum of the Wisconsin glaciation a much larger plain may have been uncovered, perhaps 1300 miles wide. The number of times a land surface entry to Alaska appeared underlies the arguments surrounding the dates of arrival of the Asiatic immigrants. Any time the sea fell below its present level, land would have surfaced. Therefore a land bridge probably existed between about 50,000 and 40,000 years ago and once more between 28,000 and 10,000 BC.[7] One may have even surfaced earlier than 50,000 years ago.

Along with the land bridge itself, the low-lying land of Siberia, Alaska, and part of the Yukon is known as Beringia. David Hopkins described the climate of periglacial Beringia.[8] Summers were short, warmer and drier than they are now; the winters were long, probably colder but with less snow than at present. The ground was drier and smoother, trees and large shrubs were rare, and the winds blew mightily. What is now tundra and taiga (the subartic forest) was arctic steppe.

In the times when North America was joined to Asia, a great variety of plants and animals adapted to a cool climate were spread across Beringia. During the Nebraskan glaciation, at least three varieties of mastodon, a type of saber-tooth cat, the camel, and the groundsloth inhabited the area, some of which became extinct during the following glacial period. In the middle of the Kansan glaciation came the mammoth, antelope, musk ox, and later the ancient bison. Most of these very large Pleistocene mammals survived until the end of the ice age and then became extinct. Others, more adaptable perhaps to the climatic changes, live on today, although somewhat modified.

Enormous ice caps to the east and south of Beringia almost isolated it from the land further east. These ice sheets are called the Laurentide and

[6]William Haag, "The Bering Strait Land Bridge," *Scientific American* 206(1962): 112–120.

[7]Hansgurgen Müller-Beck, "Paleohunter in America: Origins and Diffusions," *Science* 152(1966):1203.

[8]David Hopkins, "Landscape and Climate of Beringia during Late Pleistocene and Holocene Time," in *The First Americans: Origins, Affinities, and Adaptations.* William S. Laughlin and Albert B. Harper, eds. (New York: Gustav Fisher, 1979), pp. 15–26.

BERINGIA

the Cordilleran. The Laurentide, by far the larger, extended eastward of the Rockies, covering much of Canada, northeastern United States (including New England, New York, and New Jersey), and the middle west and Great Plains areas. The Cordilleran arose in the high western mountain ranges of Canada and penetrated eastward to the Rockies and westward to the Pacific coast. The two ice sheets came together, at least for a short time, along a front a hundred kilometers long in southern Alberta, and may have coalesced for some time in northeastern British Columbia; elsewhere they did not meet. Alaska and central North America may have been joined by a narrow ice-free corridor during most of the last glacial period. The corridor was perhaps blocked in southern Alberta and southeastern British Columbia for no more than a couple of thousand years. Although glaciation covered areas in Kamchatka and Koryak, most of Beringia remained unglaciated. Immense windswept plains and lower-lying lands extended from southeastern Europe across southern Siberia, down the Lean River

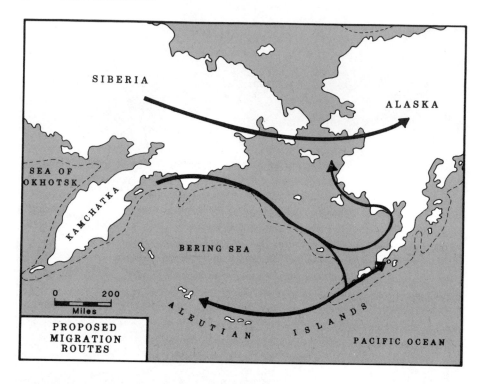

SIBERIA

ALASKA

SEA OF OKHOTSK

KAMCHATKA

BERING SEA

0   200
Miles

PROPOSED
MIGRATION
ROUTES

ALEUTIAN   ISLANDS

PACIFIC OCEAN

valley along the exposed continental shelf, and across the dry floors of the Chukchi and Bering seas into Alaska.[9]

South of the Laurentide glacier a narrow belt of treeless tundra may have stretched from southern New England all the way to the Rockies. A broad belt of coniferous trees bordered the tundra covering most of the Great Plains. Eastward this belt stretched from Illinois across the Appalachians to the Coastal Plains. The southwest, which is now desertic, was then dotted with lakes and streams; tall grasses covered miles of lush pasture land.[10]

Such was the country during the period of the Wisconsin glaciation, and it was to such a land that the newcomers came.

There is little about the coming of early man to America upon which anthropologists concur. Almost the only point of agreement is regarding the migration route through Beringia. At some time during the Wisconsin glaciation (or perhaps earlier) small nomadic bands moved out of Asia, crossed the connecting link between Siberia and Alaska, and filtered southward. Their meanderings were not deliberate; they did not know that a whole new land lay before them. Searching for food, following game trails,

[9]Ibid.

[10]Charles L. Matsch, *North America and the Great Ice Age*. Earth Science Paperback Series. (New York: McGraw-Hill, 1976), p. 81.

they wandered into Alaska. Much of Beringia was not glaciated, nor was it hostile to those who could withstand its challenges. Unsettled questions remain about the time (or times) of arrival and the routes taken as the migrants made their way southward. In the absence of extensive and unequivocal evidence, the whole subject of the peopling of the New World has been characterized by much speculation, educated guessing, and, too often, rancor among the experts.

The most heated disagreements turn on the matter of time of arrival. There are extremists on both sides of the argument, as well as a moderate view. To complicate the matter even further, those who accept the idea that Beringia may have been inhabited early—29,000 BP (before present) or before—are not sure that these people subsequently populated America south of Beringia. They may have died out, a not uncommon event in the history of animals and men, or, escaping the worsening weather, may have withdrawn back into Asia.[11] While the formation of an ice-free corridor during various periods is well accepted, some picture the latest corridor (13,000 BP) as boggy, terribly cold, punctuated by freezing glacial lakes, and lacking in plant food for both animals and men—not a very enticing path for travel.

George Carter,[12] an advocate of the earliest date for man in America, proposes a date of nearly 100,000 years ago. The Calico Hills site in the California Mohave desert, examined by L.S.B. Leakey, provided part of his support. Here lay broken, sharp-edged rocks and what appeared to be charcoal. The Calico material, according to Carter, is a blade-and-core type industry similar to that of the European middle and early Upper Paleolithic. Such assemblages are called a preprojectile-point stage. Critics of his interpretation contended that the finds Carter cited (material made by man) are not at all artifacts but were produced by the natural action of water. In reply, Carter contends: "The biggest myth in American archaeology is that nature breaks rocks by percussion and pressure and that this breakage reproduces human work." He has searched streams, creeks, and river beds and has yet to find fractured rocks of the sort present at the Calico and other sites. "Nature grounds and rounds, man bashes and smashes."[13]

San Diego, another area in California, is rich in archaeological sites. Here were found human skeletal material as well as Pleistocene faunal bones, including the horse which became extinct early in the new world. All of these bones, dated with a technique called protein racemization, are thought to be 50,000 years old. Carter believed that the horse was cooked

[11]Glen Cole, "Of Land Bridges, Ice Free Corridors, and Early Man in the Americas," *Bulletin of the Field Museum* Jan. (1979):19.

[12]George F. Carter, *Earlier Than You Think: A Personal View of Man in America.* (College Station: Texas A & M Press, 1980), pp. 96–98.

[13]Ibid.

and devoured by the first San Diego residents. He also reported extensive evidence for a blade-and-core industry there dating between 130,000 and 70,000 years ago.[14] To accept his dates we must admit to the presence of a Neanderthal-like group in California.

After studying sites in Washington, Oregon, Nevada, and Idaho, Charles Borden concluded that these areas were inhabited by hunting and gathering people when the interior regions of British Columbia were still buried under the Cordilleran ice cap.[15] How or when these hunter-gatherers got there remains to be discovered, but they must have arrived in areas south of British Columbia millennia earlier, at the latest before the formation of the Codilleran ice sheet of the last glacial maximum, when life in the Canadian plateau became unbearable.

The more moderate point of view, and probably the most popular at present, sets the date of migration between 42,000–27,000 BP just prior to the last flooding of the land bridge. MacNeish discovered crude stone tools and fossilized remains of the prehistoric sloth and horse in the Pikimachay Cave in Peru.[16] The dates established by radiocarbon range from 16,000 BP to 20,000 BP. Somewhat older sites are reported in Mexico (21,000–22,000 BP), but the material found was scattered, raising questions about the authenticity of the dates. Other early dates come from Santa Rosa Island off the coast of California. Here were charred bone fragments dated 30,000 BP. Many skeptics either do not accept the dates or do not believe that humans were on the island at the time. In Venezuela finds consisting of crude flakes and pebble tools were discovered in the company of mastodon and horse bones dated at 16,500 BP. If humans lived in Venezuela 16,000 years ago, their ancestors must have been in North America several thousands of years earlier.

Because early Americans used the Bering land bridge to enter the New World, evidence from Alaska and northwest Canada would be especially important. Some of it has been found in the area of the Old Crow and Porcupine rivers in the Yukon territory. Cole discussed the significance of the sites.[17] First, bones of a variety of later Pleistocene mammals occur in abundance. Along with these are bones that have been altered by human activity, either in the act of butchering, or in extracting marrow, or as raw material for tools. The bone tools have radiocarbon dates of 25,000–29,000 BP. Experiments with the mineralized bones show that modern Indians could not, many eons later, have made tools from them because they did not produce the kind of fractures present in the Old Crow material. Questions remain, but should the Old Crow data prove valid, a strong case will

[14]Ibid., pp. 161–206.

[15]Charles E. Borden, "Peopling and Early Cultures of the Pacific Northwest," *Science* 203(1979):964.

[16]Richard S. MacNeish, "Early Pleistocene Adaptations: A New Look at Early Peopling of the New World as of 1976," *Journal of Anthropological Research* 34:475–476.

have been made for the moderate position. In order to accept the 100,000-year or even the 40,000-year date, we have to be convinced that early migrants had the cultural wherewithall to deal with severe climates. There are hints that they did. Three hundred thousand years ago Peking Man survived under harsh circumstances, and, of course, Europe was occupied during the Wurm glaciation, the fourth European glacial period.

A few archaeologists will not admit to the presence of New World man much earlier than 13,000–14,000 years ago. Unwilling to accept very early dates, they argue that the sites were disturbed or that the material dated was contaminated. Only incontrovertible dates are recognized. The most famous and well documented of these are the Folsom and Clovis traditions, whose easily recognized fluted points are often found embedded between the bones of Pleistocene fauna. Folsom, the first point to be discovered, dated about 8500 BC, was found between the ribs of the ancient and now extinct bison. The Clovis point, a thousand years earlier, lay in mammoth skeletal remains in New Mexico. Widely distributed Clovis-type points appear in the midwest as well as the east. The people who hunted with Clovis and Folsom points are frequently called "Big Game Hunters," because all the sites seem to emphasize such a cultural focus.

C. Vance Haynes, Jr. most vigorously advocated the later dates.[18] It was clear to him that man was firmly established in the new world between 12,000 and 11,000 BP. Clovis points were, he thought, relics of the first major migration, and after it other cultural groups followed. A few anthropologists, he observed, insisted on purely conjectural grounds that man must have arrived 30,000 years ago or earlier, but Haynes questioned the sites — Calico Hills is one—used as evidence.[19]

The origin of the Big Game Hunters (people who survived on mammoth and mastodon) is clouded in mystery. There are two hypotheses: one, that Clovis points were brought from Siberian Beringia by the first migrants (Haynes' position); the other, that they arose in the new world, invented by some of the purported earlier folk and then diffused widely to other contemporary people. The latter idea rests on two beliefs: (1) that the dates reported for Mexico and Venezuela were accurate; and (2) that man, who had only arrived 13,000–14,000 years ago, could not have multiplied and traveled enough to have peopled the entire continent by 1400 AD. Paul Martin,[20] supporting Haynes, demonstrated through the use of a compli-

[17]Cole, "Of Land Bridges, Ice Free Corridors, and Early Man in the Americas," pp. 18–19.

[18]C. Vance Haynes, Jr., "Carbon 14 Dates and Early Man in the New World," in *Pleistocene Extinctions: The Search for a Cause*. Proceedings of the VII Congress of the International Association for Quaternary Research. (New Haven: Yale University Press, 1967), p. 284.

[19]C. Vance Haynes, Jr., "Ecology of Early Man in the New World," in *Geoscience and Man*, vol. XIII, Ecology of the Pleistocene. R. C. West and William Haag, eds. (Baton Rouge: Louisiana State University, 1976), pp. 72–73.

[20]Paul Martin, "The Discovery of America," *Science*, 179(1973):972–973.

cated population model that an entry time into Alaska need not have been earlier than 11,700 years ago to bring hunters to Arizona by 11,200 BP and to Tierra del Fuego by 10,500 BP. This brief summary of the contending positions illustrates how complex the dating problem is and points to the need for continued research and synthesis. We need not be discouraged by the lack of absolute answers; there is thrill in the search as well as in the final answer.

A discerning reader will also be alert to another puzzle. How many migrations were there, one or many? The evidence and conjectures surrounding this controversy allow more than one opinion.

Like the perplexity surrounding the dates of movement of people into Alaska, uncertainty abounds regarding the number of migrations which may have occurred. The very term *migration* is misleading and probably should not be used because it suggests intentional journeying. This was not the case. These ancient people moved ever so slowly, enduring the climatic challenges of summer and winter, led on by the search for food. The miles covered by each generation were likely few because a small band could eat for some while on the carcass of one mammoth and many of the miles they trudged may have been in a circle.

Separate migrations would depend upon the opening and closing of access routes to Alaska and upon whether each time the road was open, people followed it. In any case, some authorities postulated numerous separate incursions of wanderers; others, only two or perhaps three penetrations which took place toward the end of the Pleistocene. George Carter champions multiple migrations.[21] The race picture in America is complex, he observed, and includes middle and upper Paleolithic Australoids, Negroids, Europoids, as well as Mongoloids. He reasoned that there were many races entering America. The idea that one pure race entered and subsequently diverged in America is improbable. Neumann at one time proposed four or more migrations.[22] He examined the cranial material of large numbers of early Americans and from it identified a number of types. These types he thought migrated at different times. An Otamid, Iswanid, Ashiwid, Inuid, and a Deneid migration seem well established. The Walcolid and Lenapid varieties might have developed in the new world, but Neumann favored separate entry for them too. Later he revised his theory[23] suggesting that, after all, there may have been only two major streams, the older one he called the Paleoamerinds, the relatively recent.

[21]Carter, *Earlier Than You Think*, pp. 295–302.

[22]George K. Neumann, "Archaeology and Race in the American Indian," in *Archaeology of Eastern United States*. James B. Griffin, ed. (Chicago: University of Chicago Press, 1952), p. 33.

[23]George K. Neumann, "Origins of the Indians of the Middle Mississippi Area," *Proceedings of the Indiana Academy of Sciences* 60(1960):66.

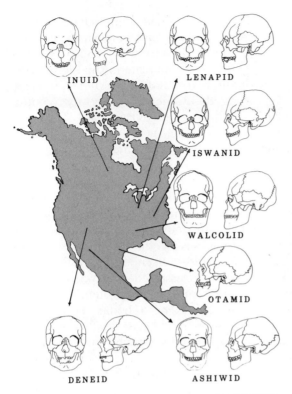

INUID   LENAPID

ISWANID

WALCOLID

OTAMID

DENEID   ASHIWID

CRANIAL TYPES FOUND IN NORTH AMERICA

the Cenoamerinds. A third group, the Mesoamerinds he believed evolved out of the Paleoamerinds.

James Hester also argued for separate migrations in order to account for the many different cultural entities which he saw in the North American archaeological record.[24] These began, he thought, between 25,000 and 35,000 years ago and continued to 8500 BC. The Clovis tradition would have developed from one of these migrations.

Marshall Newman took a conservative view with regard to migrations.[25] Although analysis of skeletal remains revealed different types of people, according to him, the evidence clearly shows that changes in body size and head form of a largely evolutionary nature occurred through time in the Americas. The tall present-day Indians in areas of colder climate evolved from shorter ancestors. Contemporary Indians in warmer climates

[24]James Hester, cited by Glen Cole in "Of Land Bridges, Ice Free Corridors, and Early Man in the Americas," pp. 23–24.

[25]Marshall T. Newman, "Evolutionary Changes in Body Size and Head Form in American Indians," *American Anthropologist* 64:253.

had taller ancestral populations. Turner examined dental characteristics and other genetic traits of paleoskeletal Indians and modern living Indians.[26] Because of the very low variability in these traits he concluded that the initial migration was singular, small, and came late in the Pleistocene.

While agreeing that the date of entry from northeastern Asia remains unsettled, James B. Griffin acknowledged but one major migration, population increases and physical variation having derived primarily from this early Paleo-Indian stock.[27] According to Griffin, there is no record of any later migrating groups influencing the life of the inhabitants of North America south of the arctic.

Others posit two migrations or at the most three. Early man or Paleo-Indian was one of them; the other comprised the ancestors of the Eskimo-Aleut group. The reasoning is based upon what are seen to be profound differences between Indians and Eskimo-Aleuts. These differences are manifested in red-cell antigens, haptoglobins, teeth, and a host of other characteristics. Work by Szathmary and Ossenberg questions the multimigration hypothesis. Their data, they asserted—derived from cranial and genetic markers (blood groups and serum protein systems)—demonstrated that Eskimo and the Na Dene (Haida, Tlingit, and Athabaskan Indians) were one population that began to diverge about 8000 years ago.[28] Despite the dispute over Eskimo-Aleut origins we may still infer only two migrations; the first, Paleo-Indian and the second, the base population from which came the Eskimo, the Aleut, and maybe the Na Dene Indians.

Resolving the debate would depend very much on ascertaining the general date of arrival. Should it prove to be very early in the Wisconsin, or during the interglacial period before it, multiple migrations would be plausible. The land bridge would have appeared and disappeared during the subsequent millennia, each group crossing it then would make up a discrete population flow. If, however, it is agreed that humans came late upon the scene, then it would be difficult to imagine more than one stream of Paleo-Indian nomads. The Eskimo-Aleut and perhaps the Na Dene would be the second group. Laughlin thinks that the first group, early mammoth hunters, moved across the land-bridge interior intermittently, and the second used the southern coast of the land bridge during its final presence.[29]

In the review of arrival times and the number of migrations, we have

[26]Christy Turner, cited by Glen Cole in "Of Land Bridges, Ice Free Corridors, and Early Man in the Americas," p. 24.

[27]James B. Griffin, "The Origin and Dispersion of American Indians in North America," in *The First Americans: Origins, Affinities, and Adaptation*, p. 98.

[28]Emoke J. E. Szathmary and Nancy Ossenberg, "Are the Biological Differences Between North American Indians and Eskimos Truly Profound?", *Current Anthropology* 19(1978):685.

[29]W. S. Laughlin and Susan Wolf, "Introduction," in *The First Americans: Origins, Affinities, and Adaptations*, pp. 1–2.

emphasized the idea that early people moved into the new world from Asia and that from them arose the various societies and cultures which were present at the time of European discovery. These include the high civilizations of Middle and South America, the hunting-foraging bands, and the part-time agriculturalists who were distributed over the entire continent. Not so, say some. Infusions of people and ideas from the Old World infiltrated long before the fifteenth century. These hypotheses are called Transoceanic Contacts.

The controversy about contact turns on the theories of independent invention versus diffusion. Some see no reason why the New World's complex societies could not have developed independently of Old World stimuli. New World accomplishments resulted from the interrelationship between environment and creative minds. The contrary position was propounded by Gordon Ekholm, who held that cultures or civilizations do not develop in isolation.[30] Isolation means stagnation; therefore, there must have been periodic contact between the areas of civilization in the New World and the Old.

Thor Heyerdahl is an ardent supporter of, if not the diffusionist position, the possibility of contact.[31] The voyages of Ra I and Ra II, reed boats common to the Old World and the New in Pre-Columbian times, proved that transatlantic trips were possible. The feat of Kon Tiki demonstrated the feasibility of Pacific crossings. Heyerdahl's work proved only the possibility of contact across the oceans; others insist upon the diffusion. They compare pottery, icons, and architecture of the Old and New Worlds to prove cross-cultural fertilization.

Chaman Lal links the rulers of Peru to the Ayar Brahmans of India; both the Peruvian rulers and the Brahmans were depicted wearing turbans and carrying stems of lotus and wheat.[32] Neither plant is native to South America. He found the arches of Mohen-Jo-Daro (an ancient Indus valley site) and Chichen-Itza (an elaborate Pre-Columbian city in Yucatan) to have the same structure, an engineering feat that he believed could not have been invented twice. He cites many other similarities and asserts that scarcely a Hindu god was unknown to the ancient inhabitants of Mexico and Peru. Lal's claims appear to be a little farfetched to most archeologists.

Analyzing Mesoamerican sculpture, Cyrus Gordon concluded that long before Columbus and the Vikings, extensive mingling of different populations had taken place in Middle and South America.[33] People

[30]Gordon Ekholm, "Diffusion and Archaeological Evidence," in *Man Across The Sea: Problems of Pre-Columbian Contacts.* Carroll J. Riley, Charles Kelley, Campbell W. Pennington, Robert Rands, eds. (Austin: University of Texas Press, 1971), pp. 56–59.

[31]Thor Heyerdahl, "Isolationist or Diffusionist," in *The Quest for America.* Geoffrey Ashe, ed. (New York: Praeger Publishers, 1971), p. 154.

[32]Chaman Lal. *Hindu America.* (New York: published by Chamon Lal, 1966).

[33]Cyrus H. Gordon, *Before Columbus: Links between the Old World and Ancient America.* (New York: Crown Publishers, 1971), p. 35.

crossed from both the Atlantic and the Pacific, he believed, with some of the most creative influences having come from the Middle East. Caucasians, African Negroes, Chinese, and Japanese—later joined by Semites, Etruscans, Romans, and many others—all placed their stamp on the high cultures of the Americas. Van Sertima saw evidence of an African contact in the sculpture of the Olmec civilization.[34] Some similarities are difficult to deny, the resemblance between parchisi and patolli (games present in both the Old and the New World) seems too close to have been by chance. Yet like Lal, Van Sertima greatly exaggerated his claims.

Still, sound evidence exists of European presence in the New World before the fifteenth century. The Norsemen undoubtedly reached Greenland in the late 900s AD. Fourteen ships carrying men, women, children, and livestock arrived in Greenland to establish a prosperous colony. From there explorations were made of Labrador and other parts of the North American coast. Yet with the possible exceptions of house types, the Norsemen had no demonstrable effect on the natives, whom they called *scraelings*. On the basis of material from legends and a work entitled *Navagatio* (author unknown), Geoffrey Ashe[35] concluded that St. Brendan and other Irish monks did perhaps discover America in about the sixth century AD. But if true, they, too, left no influence on native cultures.

There are traces of contact between northern Europe and North America in the late Archaic and early Woodland (periods in the archaeology of North America). Alice Kehoe noted similarities between tools, ceramics, and burial styles.[36] Moreover, although there is no documentation, it was possible for boats to cross the Atlantic at that time. *Curraghs* (hide boats)—excellent crafts for the Atlantic—were present in Europe from the eighth millenium BC, and seaworthy plank boats were in existence from about 1500 BC. Because ocean-going navigation was possible, and since similar cultural material has been found on both sides of the Atlantic, it is not unreasonable to argue for contact.

Other research supports a possible Pre-Columbian interchange between the Old World and the New. Pottery found in Ecuador termed *Valdivia* is very much like a type used in Japan in 2500 BC.[37] The bottle gourd indigenous to tropical Africa is found in Peru as early as 3000 BC or even earlier. Such gourds may have floated from Africa or Polynesia to the

[34]Ivan Van Sertima, *They Came Before Columbus*. (New York: Random House, 1976).

[35]Geoffrey Ashe, "Analysis of the Legends," in *The Quest for America*, pp. 157–172.

[36]Alice Kehoe, "Small Boats Upon the Atlantic," in *Man Across The Sea: Problems of Pre-Columbian Contacts*, pp. 276–280.

[37]Betty Meggers, Clifford Evans, and Emilio Estrada, *Early Formative Period of Coastal Ecuador: The Valdivia and Machallia Phases*. Smithsonian Contributions to Anthropology, vol. 1. Washington, D.C.: Smithsonian Institution, p. 1965.

New World, but more likely they were carried there by voyagers.[38] Maize also provides hints of contact. It is indigeneous to the New World, yet remains of maize found in Asia date from Pre-Columbian times. If maize entered China from the west, as is believed, that would validate a claim for transatlantic adventures.[39]

The assertions for Pre-Columbian contact range from compelling data to wishful thinking. The more fundamental issue centers on the effect contacts had on the developing cultures of the New World. Some scholars think it was negligible, but Betty Meggers contends that an increasing number of cultural complexes cannot be explained except by a theory of contact.[40] Many anthropologists think that transpacific meetings took place repeatedly at different times on different parts of the western coasts of the Americas. While these transpacific contacts did not contribute measurably to the gene pool, many argue they were influential in shaping the civilizations found by the Europeans. Reputed transatlantic contact—between northeastern North America and Europe—seems to have had a minor effect on the way of life of the New World inhabitants, however. We take up our story again with them.

By 11,000 BC the Paleo-Indians were clearly established in North America, some living on Pleistocene mammals as well as edible vegetation, others perhaps relying more on smaller animals and roots and seeds. The climate was slowly altering, as the glacier period was terminating. Huge continental ice sheets accelerated their retreat, and in their wake the vegetation which had been stable throughout thousands of years began a series of migrations and transformations that led to the current pattern of vegetation.[41] Another not inconsequential event was also taking place—the slow but inexorable disappearance of the large Pleistocene fauna upon whom many of the Paleo-Indians had depended for so long a time.

Between about 9,000 and 10,000 BP a whole series of large prehistoric fauna vanished; indeed this phenomenon is often used to mark the end of the Pleistocene in the Americas. The reason for their demise is not clear. Some claim the Paleo-Indians hastened their extinction. As Arthur Jelinek observes,

> Homo sapiens remains as a new element in the environment, with a formidable potential for disruption, whether directly as an extremely efficient and rapidly expanding predator group, against whom no evolved defense systems

[38]Thomas Whitaker, "Endemism and Pre-Columbian Migration of the Bottle Gourd," in *Man Across the Sea: Problems of Pre-Columbian Contacts*, p. 327.

[39]M.D.W. Jeffreys, "Pre-Columbian Maise in Asia," in *Man Across the Sea: Problems of Pre-Columbian Contacts*, p. 400.

[40]Betty Meggers, "Contacts from Asia," in *Quest for America*, p. 242.

[41]H. E. Wright, Jr., "Pleistocene Ecology: Some Current Problems," *Geoscience and Man*, vol. XIII, p. 10.

were available or indirectly as the source of profound changes in ecology already under the process of adjustment as a result of considerable climatic stress.[42]

Paul Martin also attributed the end of the mammoth, mastodon, and others largely to the work of man.[43] Yet others reason somewhat differently. A change in the extremes in temperature, both winter and summer, can have profound effects on animals even though the average temperatures change only slightly. The advent of wider temperature fluctuations probably caused the extinction of much of the megafauna in the interval between about 9000 and 7000 BP. A breakdown in reproduction caused by inflexible mating habits established under conditions no longer in effect seems a most logical reason for some of the extinctions. The North American continent, especially the southwest, did not offer a sufficient range of climates to allow many species to escape the climatic changes by migration.[44]

James Hester also explained the extinction by ecological variables. He preferred not to indict man as the major factor in the disappearance of the late Pleistocene creatures. He suggested that the animals were well adapted to the ecological circumstances present in the periglacial zone and adjacent vegetational zones south of the ice sheet. The slow waning of the ice, beginning 18,000–20,000 BP, resulted in widespread vegetational changes in ecological niches. Such changes brought selective pressures to bear on the animal populations. The ebbs and flows of the ice sheet border between 18,000 and 11,000 BP were of insufficient magnitude to restore the ecological balance, serving only to slow the inevitable fate of the magnificent Pleistocene animals.[45] The answer to the question of extinction is not a simple "either-or." The most fruitful conclusion sees the stress upon the animals by the changing environment taking place slowly, over several thousand years, combined with pressure on the herds from Paleo-Indian hunters. If the people failed to discriminate between male and female animals in their search for sustenance, if more females than males were taken, then the reproductive capacity of the herds would have been severely limited. This coupled with the stress accompanying the environmental changes might well have led to the passing of the great animals of the Pleistocene. Neither humans alone nor ecology alone destroyed them.

The Ellis Island for the New World was unquestionably Beringia. The wanderers—unencumbered by passports or baggage—searching for food,

[42]Arthur J. Jelinek, "Man's Role in the Extinction of Pleistocene Faunas," in *Pleistocene Extinctions: The Search for a Cause*. (Yale University Press: New Haven, 1967), p. 199.

[43]Paul Martin, "The Discovery of America," pp. 972–933.

[44]Bob H. Slaughter, "Animal Ranges as a Clue to Pleistocene Extinctions," in *Pleistocene Extinctions*, p. 165.

[45]James J. Hester, "The Agency of Man in Animal Extinction," in *Pleistocene Extinctions*, p. 189.

pausing for childbirth and for burying their dead, moved to follow the trail of game, to search for salt, and ultimately to find a place to repose. Just who the immigrants were and how many times they crossed over remain problems to be solved. What the effect was of others who may have stumbled onto the shores of North or South America is not clear either. The answers to these and other questions lie in the future. There are avenues to be explored and issues to be resolved. Whatever the uncertainties which attend the early peopling of the New World, Columbus and his followers did find a land filled with people. To these folk we now turn our attention, looking for answers to explain the development of New World culture.

PART ONE

FORAGERS

The relationship between the environment and culture is most readily seen among hunters and gatherers, or foragers as some call them. These are often societies that John Bennett describes as being in equilibrium with their environments.[1] Such groups constitute adaptive systems that have stabilized their internal affairs and their technology. Their supernatural beliefs, values, rituals, and social constraints allow and even encourage a harmony with the physical environment. Bennett notes that probably all American Indian groups are of this sort, but we may be sure that the foragers certainly fit the model.

In the chapters to follow we will consider several of the groups who were, at the time of their discovery, at least partially nomadic and totally dependent for their subsistence on the flora and fauna available in their territories. Most of these groups inhabited parts of the New World where agriculture was impossible for a number of reasons: too much or too little rainfall; soil infertility; average temperatures too low; or the growing season too short. All of these factors make cultivation out of the question. There were groups, however, who followed a hunting-gathering tradition for other reasons: either because their level of technology was insufficient

[1]John W. Bennett, *The Ecological Transition: Cultural Anthropology and Human Adaptation.* (New York: Pergamon Press, 1976), p. 137.

for agriculture under challenging conditions, or because their natural resources were sufficiently abundant to make farming unattractive or unnecessary to support the population.

Anthropologists have traditionally described hunters and gatherers as living close to starvation and spending all of their waking hours in a remorseless pursuit of food. The foraging life, it was thought, was "nasty, brutish and short." We have recently come to believe that for many foraging groups this unremitting struggle for existence was either erroneous or overstated for most groups. Sahlins goes so far as to assert that hunter-gatherers formed the original affluent society, arguing that an affluent society is one in which all of the people's wants are easily satisfied. "Hunters and gatherers often work much less than we do, and rather than a grind the food quest is intermittent, leisure is abundant, and there is more sleep in the daytime per capita than in any other conditions of society."[2] There is truth in Sahlins's remarks, but it must be recalled that one way of meeting this criterion of an affluent society is to maintain wants and needs in balance with supplies. Another factor which makes affluence possible is the ready presence of vegetable foods. Where these become less plentiful or absent, life becomes increasingly more demanding and fears of famine plague people. For two of our groups, the Eskimo and the Cree, vegetable foods were seldom part of the diet; for the other, the Washo, they provided a significant source of nutrition. Despite the environmental differences with which these groups coped, there were some similarities among them. Both similarities and differences can in part be traced to their environments.

We are not arguing that environment causes the form and content of a culture in a simple direct sense, yet as Julian Steward has remarked: "It is evident that the influence of subsistence patterns on the general form of socio-economic organization is great among the hunting and gathering peoples in areas of low productivity."[3] Environments do provide the conditions to which humans must adapt. These adaptations are accomplished through their technology, their social organization and, not least, through their belief and value systems.

[2]Marshall Sahlins, "Notes on the Affluent Society," in *Man the Hunter*. Richard B. Lee and Irven DeVore, eds. (Chicago: Aldine Publishing Co., 1968), p. 86

[3]Julian H. Steward, "Determinism in Primitive Society," in *Cultural Ecology: Readings on the Canadian Indians and Eskimos*. Bruce Cox, ed. Carleton Library Series. (Toronto: McClelland and Steward, LTD., 1973), p. 212.

CHAPTER TWO

The Netsilik Eskimo of the Central Arctic

To think of the arctic is to visualize great uninterrupted sweeps of land and water blanketed by snow and ice; to picture high winds bringing blizzards threatening all in their paths; and to recall men who explored it, some losing their lives and their ships in the search for the northwest passage. Our notions of the arctic are no more extreme than the reality. It is a region of harsh seasons challenging to life, both plant and animal. Yet life exists there: plant and animal life flourish through biological adaptations, human life largely through ingenious cultural strategies for survival.

The arctic circle does not include all the territory called "arctic." Tundra and barren lands result not from latitude but climate. Consequently, the arctic is defined by a line drawn through those places where the average temperature in the warmest month (July) is 50° F. This boundary, which excludes a major portion of Alaska, also marks the transition from the boreal forest to the tundra. The region is a vast, relatively homogeneous territory. Long cold winters last nearly eight months, January–February temperatures average − 22° F. The sun barely appears, night and day blend into one. During clear periods there is almost no humidity and sounds are audible at great distances. The aurora borealis fills the sky, spreading and contracting, sending great rays of color—red, yellow, and green. It fades, only to begin again with glittering rivers of silver. Violet and pink shadows

21

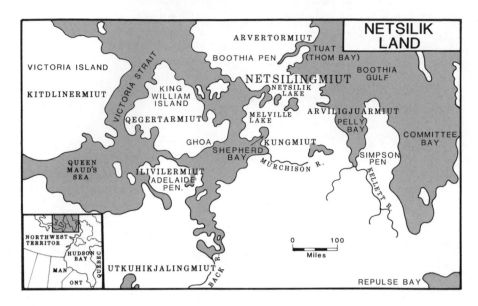

delicately tint the snow. During overcast periods, the temperatures rise slightly. Winter blizzards are dangerous, and it is often difficult to know whether fresh snow is falling or whether the wind is whipping up dry sandlike snow already deposited. Precipitation in the arctic is not heavy, averaging less than 200 millimeters a year.

Spring comes suddenly, snow melts on the tundra leaving it boggy and filled with streams and rivulets. Vegetation appears including tiny flowering plants. Arctic hare, fox, and ptarmigan lose their protective white coloring, changing to brown to match the sodden land. Temperatures rise to 40° F, daylight hours grow longer, the eider ducks return to nest. In bays and lakes ice melts and sometimes disappears, but in larger bodies of water it may never completely vanish, remaining as floes. Unexpected blustering snowstorms may yet scourge the land. Spring yields to summer, temperatures rise (average daytime temperature is 40–50 degrees farenheit), and daylight hours grow even longer, so that in some areas it is never wholly dark and the midnight sun glows softly. To mar the brief summer, plagues of mosquitoes torture people and beasts. Early summer brings fog along coastal areas, damp gray mist hovers, endlessly condensing and dampening clothes and spirit alike. Plant life slowly fades with autumn, nights lengthen and days shorten; ice reforms on the lakes, early September snows do not melt. The migratory birds and animals leave, and the weather becomes increasingly stormy. Once more the arctic yields to winter.

Despite the rigors of the far north, animal and some plant life thrive. Vegetation is xerophytic, growing with a minimum of moisture. Mosses and lichens carpet the tundra and the barren lands; here and there a few edible berries hug the ground. Dwarfed willows, birches, and alders barely rise above land. Dominant land animals were the caribou and musk ox. The migratory caribou arrived in the far north in the spring and returned to the forests with fall. Arctic fox, hare, wolverine, and wolves roamed the area. The ringed seal, bearded seal, several species of walrus and whale inhabited the seas. The polar bear spent most of this time roaming the pack ice, coming to land only occasionally. The most important fish were arctic char, lake trout, and tomcod.

This country was home to the Eskimo, more properly called Inuit. Inuit, meaning the People, spread over this desolate land from Alaska to Greenland. Kaj Birket-Smith estimated the pre-historic population at 40,000[1] while Kroeber thought it 89,000.[2] The Eskimo language has two major divisions. The Inuit from northern Alaska to Greenland speak Inupik, with some dialectical differences. Yupik is the language of the people of western Alaska and the islands off the coast.

Although the arctic appears homogeneous and the Eskimo had a common lifeway, which we call Eskimo culture, major regional environmental differences were related to substantial diversity. Birket-Smith[3] devised three major categories from seventeen separate groups: the Alaskan Eskimo, the Central Eskimo, and the Greenland Eskimo. Only the Central Eskimo used igloos exclusively for their winter homes. Within the central Canadian branch were many separate peoples. Often the term *tribe* was used to describe these units, but it must be understood that "tribe" does not imply any overarching structure nor political authority of any sort. Among the major groups within the Central Eskimo subculture area were: the Copper Eskimo, the Netsilik, the Caribou, and the Iglulik. In 1945 Birket-Smith used the term Northwest Passage Eskimo to designate the Copper and Netsilik. The Northwest Passage embraced all the groups living between Committee Bay on the east and Dolphin and Union Strait on the west coast of the mainland and on the offshore islands, particularly King William and the southern portions of Victoria Island.[4] Most of this area lies north of the arctic circle and poses some of the most difficult living conditions in the entire polar region.

THE NETSILIK

Within the Netsilik were the following named bands in the mid- to late-nineteenth century: Arviligjuarmiut, Netsilingmiut, Ilvilermiut, Killirmiut, and the Qiqiqtarmiut. The suffix *miut* means dweller; Arviligjuarmiut were

[1]Kaj Birket-Smith, *The Eskimos*. (New York: E. P. Dulton & Co., 1935), p. 8.

[2]Alfred L. Kroeber, "Demography of the North American Indians," in *The North American Indians*. Roger C. Owen, James J. F. Deetz, Anthony D. Fisher, eds. (New York: MacMillian Co. 1967), p. 43.

[3]Birket-Smith, *The Eskimo*, p. 225–226.

[4]Kaj Birket-Smith, *Ethnographical Collections From the Northwest Passage: Report of the Fifth Thule Expedition* 1921–1924, vol. 6, no. 2. (New York: AMS Press, Reprint 1976), p. 9.

dwellers of the Great Whaling Place, Pelly Bay. The total population is estimated to have been slightly over 400, but it is likely that there were more.
Franz Boas[5] provided no total figures, but his accounts of various settlements and camps suggest that 400 was too low. In any case males outnum-
bered females by a goodly margin, a consequence of Netsilik female infanticide. The Netsilik–People of the Seal–lived in large groups of forty or
fifty during the winter. Spring and summer found them dispersed with
fewer people dwelling together. Winter and summer settlements were not
always in the same locations. The availability of food dictated their movements and camps.

Netsilik country included great land masses: Boothia and Adelaide
peninsulas, King William Island, Simpson Peninsula, and the hilly area between Sherman Inlet and Pelly Bay. Smaller islands lie off the coast line,
which is indented by ocean inlets. Some of the land is rocky and covered
with gravel, but much of it is flat. Lakes, ponds, and rivers, abound. The
land supports only lichens, mosses, and various grasses, rarely a low-lying
tree. Driftwood, a valuable resource, is very scarce in Netsilik country. As
Birket-Smith observed, "Among the Netsilik a sledge of wood is of such
value that it is sufficient to pay for a wife."[6] Vegetation was important to the
people only because of its effect on the distribution of caribou and musk
ox. Caribou, seal, and to a lesser extent musk oxen, were the mainstays of
life. The climate was and is formidable. Ice begins to form on the seas in
late September, by December it is 6 feet thick and will not disappear until
the last days of July. Average January temperatures are $-20°$ F; seldom in
the short summer does the temperature exceed 50° F. The Netsilik were
able to live here only because of the animal population. Caribou—nineteenth-century writers referred to them as deer—traveled in herds of varying numbers migrating in predictable patterns. In the spring herds of cows
moved northward from the boreal forest to the tundras followed later by
the bulls. In September they returned south to feed on the browse in the
woodland. Eighteenth- and nineteenth-century observers described seas of
caribou moving over the barren lands, tens of thousands at a time.
Whether such numbers ever frequented the Netsilik area is not recorded,
but there were enough of them for the people. Earlier, musk ox roamed
parts of this vast remote land but were not as eagerly sought as caribou and
seal. Occasionally the people took polar bear, but only incidentally. The
most important animal, the ringed seal, thrived throughout the Central
Arctic. The bearded seal, a much larger animal, was present too, although
not in great numbers. Whales could not live in the shallow waters. Game
birds were of little importance, although ptarmigan and some water fowl
were hunted, both for food and for their skin and feathers.

[5]Franz Boaz, *The Central Eskimo*. (Lincoln: University of Nebraska Press, 1964), pp.
44–50. Originally published as part of 6th Annual Report of the Bureau of Ethnology, Smithsonian Institution, Washington, D.C., 1888.
[6]Birket-Smith, *Ethnographic Collections from the Northwest Passage*, p. 10.

Central Canadian Eskimo with dead caribou, 1931.
Smithsonian Institution National Anthropological Archives.

Fish provided the Netsilik with a change in diet and a food resource when sealing was difficult. Arctic char, a pink-fleshed delicious member of the salmon family, was the major species. Like all salmon it migrated to the sea in July, returning upriver to lakes in August. People caught other fish, largely lake trout, and took tomcod and polar cod only when food was scarce. This implacable land supported the Eskimo only because they developed a sophisticated and elaborate technology enabling them to make extensive use of the resources for food, shelter, and clothing.

A most outstanding characteristic of Eskimo culture was its technology, especially true of the Netsilik. From bone, stone, skin, some wood, and snow, were fashioned all the necessities for survival, and they were many. The Danish National Museum has a collection of 577 objects from the Netsilik, and this is not comprehensive.

Balikci,[8] a contemporary cultural anthropologist, divided the Netsilik technology into four types: the bone complex, the skin complex, the snow and ice complex, and the stone complex. Bone was the most important resource, from it were produced tools, weapons, and other essentials, for clothing, shelter, and food. Using simple tools men did all the bonework. Bear bone was the hardest, muskox pliable, but caribou antler was the most versatile. It was shaped, drilled, spliced, and whittled into a vast array of implements: harpoons, spears, bows, and fish hooks. For use in the home antler was made into snow shovels, snow beaters, snow knives, drying racks, and men's and women's knives. It formed part of sledges when wood, a scarce item, was not available. Wood was sought for kayak frames, tent poles, and spear handles.

Snow and ice, an almost ever-present part of the landscape figured prominently in Netsilik life, most importantly for building. The Netsilik

[7]Ibid., p. 20.

[8]Asen Balikci, *The Netsilik Eskimo.* (Garden City, NY: Natural History Press, 1970), pp. 5–12.

and the other central Canadian Eskimos used the snow house exclusively for winter dwellings and interior furnishings. Men and their wives constructed the igloo. Only snow with certain properties was appropriate. Using a snow probe the men searched for a proper site. Drawing a large circle, using a *pana* (snow knife), blocks were cut from within the circle and placed on its perimeter. Each succeeding row overlapped to form a parabolic structure. The last few blocks completing it were placed with utmost care. While the men laid the blocks, the women tossed loose snow on the walls using their snow shovels (*poalrit*), filling in cracks to make the dwelling air tight. When the main house was finished, the builders added a porch, a much smaller structure of the same shape, and finally a corridor leading to the outside. A kitchen table and a sleeping platform of snow were constructed inside the dwelling. Caches, wind barriers, and latrines made of snow were scattered near the igloo.

As important to the Eskimo as caribou antler was its hide. Without the peculiar properties of caribou fur, light and soft with dense hollow insulating hair, the people could not have withstood the extremes of the arctic winter. Men and women shared the long and tedious preparation of caribou skin. Men skinned the animal and women spread the fresh skins, hair side down, on the ground to dry. Much later the accumulated skins, perhaps thirty to forty needed by a family, were cured. Inner clothing required fine soft skins. To prepare these, husband and wife bedded down under the raw skins flesh side down. Over these they placed their sleeping furs. The heat from their bodies softened the raw skin so that it could be worked. In the morning, the wife scraped and further softened the skins using a caribou scapula and other scrapers; she then dampened them and placed them outside to freeze for a day or so. Further scraping removed all remaining tissue. Her husband completed the work by thinning the skin, a job demanding strength. Skins dressed this way were sewn by the women

Central Canadian Eskimo building a snow house, circa 1913-1918.
Smithsonian Institution National Anthropological Archives.

into winter inner garments, pants, and shirts worn with the hair next to the skin. Skins intended for outer clothing or bedding material underwent simpler curing processes.

Seal skin was stronger and more durable than caribou skin and was waterproof, a useful characteristic. Preparing seal skins for whatever purpose was exclusively woman's work. Curing processes varied with the intended use of the skin. Preparing seal skin for kayak covers and for waterproof summer boots and soles was especially taxing. It required removing the hair and chewing the skin, both to rid it of any remaining fat after scraping and to make it pliable. Women made all the seal-skin objects: kayak covers, coats for kayakers, and summer tents were but a few of them. The caribou and seal as well as other animals afforded the raw material for many other useful items. Depilated seal skins were made into water bags and dippers, fish skins and bird skins became bags, bladders and stomachs were used as containers, and willow and straw were used to make crude coiled baskets.[9]

Most migratory people do not weight themselves down with pottery or heavy objects, but circumstances demanded that the Eskimo have cooking pots and lamps. Husbands made them of soapstone and gave them to their wives. Soapstone was quarried in the eastern portion of the Netsilik territory. Working with picks, drills, and adzes, men shaped the soapstone lamps and pots. Lamps were shallow, flat bottomed, slightly oval-shaped vessels. Wives filled the lamps with blubber they pounded; a burning wick of twisted moss fed by the oil lighted and warmed the igloo and boiled the food. Cooking pots were carved out of a single block of soapstone; rectangular and varying in length they were suspended over the lamps by thongs passed through holes drilled in the four corners.

The migratory habits of some game and human technological limitations compelled the Netsilik to adopt a migratory life. The game supply was mobile, irregular, and to a large extent seasonal. Seal did not migrate but the Netsilik had no means to hunt them in open water. The major arctic seasons—winter and summer—determined the people's movements. Summer and early fall found them inland fishing and hunting caribou. Winter brought them back to the sea. Local life and group activities also changed with the seasons and food supplies. Life inland and on the coast required different adaptations.[10]

Arctic spring arrives in late June or early July. The changes it brings are rapid: sea ice melts quickly; hazardous fissures appear; and water covers the rotting ice. Sled travel was difficult and perilous; to fall into still frigid water meant probable death by drowning and freezing. The land brightens as the snow melts, forming rivulets which course toward the

[9]Birket-Smith, *Ethnographic Collections From the Northwest Passage*, pp. 101–102.
[10]Balikci, *The Netsilik Eskimo*, pp. 24–90.

thawing lakes and rivers. Mosses and lichens appear, and in some areas blankets of low colorful flowers cover the tundra. Such changes cause the water birds to return to the barren land, the caribou to leave the taiga for the tundra vegetation. Most important, the arctic char school and swim downstream to the sea; the large lake trout congregate alongside the cracks in the lake ice.

The coming of these changes signaled the Netsilik that the move inland was near. Men and women busily prepared for the move to the spring fishing camps. New seal skins had to be cured, seal oil accumulated and put in skin containers, and equipment sorted and packed on the sledges. When all was completed and before the breakup of sea ice, the Netsilik, with heavily laden sledges drawn by a few dogs and men, trudged away from the sea ice overland to establish the first camp near a likely fishing site. Early arrivals erected storage platforms and caches for unneeded equipment, extra clothing, and sledges. There was an air of haste. The women repaired the old tents or made new ones for it was still cold. Although they brought seal meat with them, the men hurried off to fish for lake trout and migrating salmon. Everyone looked forward to a change in diet and with enthusiasm ate the first fish raw. Surpluses, if any, were dried and stored for the winter.

With summer imminent there was much to be done now. The women sewed dog packs, waterproof sealskin kamiks (boots), and kayak covers. The men brought to the camp their kayaks which had been stored near the caribou crossings. Ribs were replaced, the frames spliced, all the work of men. In August the people burdened with summer gear moved further inland to other fishing sites. Small children peered out from packs on their father's backs. Women, older children, even the aged, and dogs, struggled along the slow and tedious trek to the new place where fishing weirs had been constructed long ago. Tents were rapidly erected and put to right by the wives while their husbands built and repaired the weirs and traps for the first salmon run upriver.

The composition of the summer camps varied, often two or three extended families—twenty or thirty people—settled together. Someone from the group constantly watched the weirs. A shout "fish are coming" caused men and women to gather at the tent of the oldest competent man. At a sign from him all rushed pell mell to the central basin, the men plunged—pantless—into the chilling water to spear the fish. Using no system each man speared as many as he could, stringing them on a thong. The Danish explorer and ethnographer Knud Rasmussen[11] observed that "it was always a riddle to me that in this scuffle with the leisters [spears] incessantly darting in and out of the water, apparently at random, the people pre-

[11]Knud Rasmussen, *The Netsilik Eskimos: Social Life and Spiritual Culture: Report of the Fifth Thule Expedition.* 1921–1924, vol. 8, nos. 1–2. (New York: AMS Press. Reprint 1976), p. 65.

served their toes unscathed; there was never anyone that got so much as a scratch on leg or foot." Dragging their stringers of fish from the water the men spread them near their tents for the women to clean and dress. Some were stored but some were eaten raw. For communal meals fish was boiled in soapstone pots. Men ate together, women and children ate apart. Large pieces of fish passed from hand to hand, each person taking a bite as it came to him. The summer fish camps while busy places were happy ones. Feasts for a little boy's first fish, practical jokes, and endless games were played. By the end of August, as the runs decreased, great quantities of fish were stored safe from predators. Tents were pulled down, and people and dogs heavily ladened trudged to the caribou crossings.

The caribou grazed in small herds in summer and only a few were hunted. In early September large herds formed to move south. This was the time for the great hunts; the animals were fat and their skins prime. The men, often assisted by women, hunted in several ways. Beaters drove the caribou through artificially constructed paths toward concealed hunters who unleashed a volley of arrows at them. The Netsilik were not skilled bowmen so often the kill was not great. At other times camps were pitched where the animals forded rivers and lakes. As soon as the lead animals entered the water, the senior hunter signaled the start of the hunt. Men crawled quietly and quickly to their kayaks, launched them, and paddled swiftly among the swimming animals to spear them. Some reached shore only to be turned back by howling women and children. The hunters made large kills, and each dragged his animals roped together to the shore to butcher and skin them. Women took the skins and sinew to dry. Choice sections were joyfully eaten raw, the rest cached. Later communal meals of boiled meat were the occasions for gossip, games, and relaxation.

The spring and short summer slipped quickly away; autumn arrived with cold winds and early snow. Ice formed on inland lakes and rivers and the tundra hardened. Daylight hours grew shorter, and by November the arctic winter arrived releasing a Pandora's box of weather. Sea ice grew 7 feet thick by December or January. Gusting winds blew the snow high against hills. Blizzards tormented the land. In the height of winter the "gloaming" prevailed (sun barely above the horizon), and the caribou were gone. It was time to move.

Enroute to the sea ice, the people split into smaller groups and paused at some fishing spots to jig for fish through holes cut in the ice. This time of year—late fall—was the busiest period of the annual cycle for women. Forbidden by taboos to sew during hunting, now they wasted no time in preparing new winter clothing. Each adult required inner and outer pants and coats, at least two pairs of stockings, several pairs of double-soled shoes, and mittens. While the women tailored, the men moved back and forth from cache to camp bringing in meat and fish and repairing tools, weapons, and sledges in anticipation of winter. It was an industrious time, but much of the work was done in the company of others, allowing for storytelling, reminiscences, gossip, and feasting. Yet the weather could be severe and unsettled, and gale winds and snow portended the coming of winter. Rasmussen observed,

> that the approaching darkness and long stormy nights affected the nerves and the minds of the Eskimos. Almost every evening the camp was scared by the imaginary visits of spirits which, they said, could only be heard or felt, and with which the local shamans—we had no fewer than two female and three male shamans—were consequently compelled to combat incessantly.[12]

If there were sufficient food, people moved to sealing grounds in February, but often they had to go earlier. Through the frozen arctic desert they traveled, sledges piled high. Women led the sleds shouting directions, the men helped the one or two struggling dogs drag the load around crevices and obstacles. Only the smallest children rode atop the baggage; older people labored painfully and slowly behind the entourage, often arriving hours—if they arrived at all—after the camp was established.

Winter settlements held up to 100 people although a camp of 50 was typical. The location depended upon several factors: the presence of clusters of seal breathing-holes, a supply of old sea ice for drinking water, and snow of appropriate quality. Upon finding a good spot men and women hurried to build the snow houses, snow platforms, and latrines, a tiring chore because it followed immediately upon the long journey. Later, after the households were in order, the villagers gathered to build a large communal dance house. The preparations complete, seal hunting began.

A number of men worked together, each maintaining a breathing hole. Breathing-hole hunting demanded skill, patience, and ingenious tools: harpoons, snow probes, breathing-hole searchers, breathing indicators, and wound pins. Talking excitedly and leading the dogs, men gathered. The oldest skilled hunter conferred with the others and decided where to hunt. Once at the grounds the hunters moved off alone with dogs who smelled out the holes in the snow. Preparing the hole, setting the indicator, placing his harpoon on rests, and standing on his fur hunting bag, each man began his long lonely vigil. Hours might pass before an animal was harpooned. Success brought other nearby men to enjoy a small feast of liver. While the men were gone the women tended to household chores, fixing lamps, melting ice, drying clothes, or chewing boots. Between these tasks they wandered from igloo to igloo to visit. Often young wives joined children in play in the snow, and so passed the time until someone announced the return of the hunters.

Upon a man's return, seals were given to the hunter's wife who happily butchered them; blood dripping down her hands and arms, she carved the carcass into portions. The hunter fatigued and aching, wearily re-

---

[12]Ibid., p. 84.

moved his outer garments, and hung them on the drying rack. The evening meal was made ready, men and boys eating on one side of the igloo, women and children on the other. Before bed the men gathered in small groups to talk animatedly of the day and plan for tomorrow's chase. Slowly the lights in the igloos were lowered and the family burrowed naked under the caribou skins; the day was ended.

Winter camp life was not all *sturm* and *drang*; games, dances, and shamanistic seances brightened the long evenings. Gradually the sun rose higher in the sky, the cold diminished and the igloos became damp. Large winter camps broke up and smaller groups moved closer to shore for spring sealing. By July the ice was treacherous, and the families packed and moved to land.

It might appear that despite the hardships, challenges, and risks, the Netsilik were well fed; this was not always the case. During the winter when the caribou were gone and many hunts were fruitless, people might starve. Samik, a good hunter and shaman, told Rasmussen:[13]

> There are many memories of hunger in our land, memories new and memories of bygone days. . . . Many years ago winter did not come. The caribou trekked out of the country and the birds flew away too, but the sea ice did not freeze over and the people had to stay at their summer places. . . . Many people died of hunger . . . we did not leave them out in the open as we always do but put them under stones just as we hide meat and fish . . . when there was nothing else to eat they were brought out.
>
> Need has compelled many people to eat human flesh; they had to do it to save their lives when their long suffering had affected them so much that they almost lost their senses. . . . So we never condemn those who have eaten human flesh; we have only pity for them.

Life was indeed hard, and Netsilik knowledge of their land and their exploitive technology were not sufficient to ensure survival. Their social life and faith in the supernatural were also adapted for survival.

An important Netsilik unit was the nuclear family. Although the nuclear family might travel alone or spend some brief time apart from others, it was always embedded in a larger group of relatives. Most dwellings sheltered additional kinfolk, forming an extended family composed of at least three generations with the authority vested in the oldest man. Many Netsilik followed this pattern. The extended family was formed by the operation of a patrilocal rule of residence. When a hunter's sons married, they brought their wives to their father's home. If the man were fortunate enough to have more than one or two married boys, only the younger stayed with the parents; others camped close at hand in separate dwellings. The men cooperated in most undertakings with leadership provided by the father. As he declined in ability, the brother bonds grew stronger and the elder brother assumed the mantle of leadership. As time passed this unit

[13]Ibid., p. 136.

might divide because of death, conflict, or other exigencies, and new extended families were formed. There were variations on this pattern. Occasionally an extended family formed when the newlyweds lived with the wife's family, most often because she had no adult brothers. Other young men joined the houses of uncles. Not all large households contained extended families. Some of them included two brothers-in-law with their wives and children; others, a hunter and his male cousin or an adopted person. Such permutations on the extended family are best called "expanded families." All of these closely knit groups were called *ilagüt nangminariit*—"own relatives in proper." These expanded families were the major economic units, camping together in the spring, summer, and fall, and sharing food. In the winter they joined with other such units to form the large sealing camps and, in so doing, relinquished some of their autonomy. Leadership, whether in the extended family or in the winter sealing camps, was indirect, nonforceful, and concerned primarily with hunting decisions.

Although the large winter camp seemed filled with jovial, amiable cooperating people, Rasmussen[14] and Balikci[15] reported that tensions and hostilities seethed below the surface between kinsmen and nonrelated fellows alike. Minor or trivial events produced quarrels and often ended in violence and murder. In this respect the Eskimo differed sharply from the Cree and Washo who went to great lengths to avoid violence. Causes of conflict were many. Sexual access to women was a major one. Failure to give a girl promised for marriage; wife stealing; jealousy arising from wife exchange; and polyandrous unions were examples. Other resentments and envy led to trouble. Successful men were vulnerable to sorcery performed by the less competent. Lazy hunters contributed to friction; they were barely tolerated and often ostracized, until an opportunity arose for a quarrel. Stingy people also provoked trouble. To manage these discords, the Netsilik resorted to mockery, derision, and gossip. Should they go too far, the victim often retaliated and produced more trouble. Not only shamen but all Netsilik had a ready arsenal of sorcery and magic techniques. The fear of being assaulted by them also kept quarreling parties in check.

Other devices to resolve clashes were fist fights, drum duels, and approved execution. In a fight the combatants exchanged blows. When one had enough he gave up and the quarrel was settled. The song duel required more preparation. Each man secretly composed a long song accusing the other of sexual impotence, incest, weakness, clumsy hunting, and the like. The songs were sung by their wives accompanied by their husbands on a drum. The whole community gathered in the communal house to enjoy the performance. The more sarcastic and amusing the ridicule, the

[14]Ibid., pp. 203–205.
[15]Balikci, *The Netsilik Eskimo*, pp. 163–193.

more it was enjoyed with shouts of approval and laughter. When lampooning ended the audience did not judge guilt or innocence, but it was made clear, however, who was the better satirist. The duels were no doubt cathartic but did not always reduce acrimony, and the opponents sometimes engaged in a fist fight to settle the matter.[16]

Execution was a serious undertaking and one of last recourse. Only a person who became so dangerous to others because of insanity or so obsessed with hatred that he could not be otherwise contained, was killed. The decision was made by the extended kin group and conveyed to the others in the camp. A close relative carried out the assignment, thus precluding revenge. The lack of institutionalized authority does not mean normlessness. Netsilik norms were concerned with the good of the group. If the peace and stability of the community were threatened by troublesome members, there were means to restrain them and preserve village and camp constancy.

The Central Canadian Eskimo had a bilateral kinship system. Although some preference might be given the father's side because of patrilocal residence, in general relatives of mothers and fathers were equally important. Netsilik kinship system was complicated and the terminology so complex that we can give only an overview. There were separate terms for father, mother, son, and daughter. Older and younger siblings were called by different terms. Paternal aunts and uncles were labeled differently from maternal ones, and the same terms applied to others in that generation. For example: father's brother and father's sister's husband were called *akka*; father's sister, father's brother's wife, and mother's brother's wife were called *atsa*. *Anga* was the word for mother's brother and mother's sister's husband, and mother's sister was *arnaviq*. All children of these combinations were cousins. Cousins of the same sex were called *idloq*; cousins of the opposite sex called each other brother and sister. This was a peculiar phenomenon because the Netsilik preferred cousin marriage, so one's sister could become one's wife. At the great-grandparent generation all relatives were called by the same term, and often distant relatives were considered cousins, a useful practice when one was searching for a spouse.

This system of kinship stressed the importance of the nuclear and extended family as significant kinship groups; the importance of age in determining authority; and the solidarity of persons of the same sex. Moreover, as Balikci reported, the extension of terms to collateral relatives reflected the nomadic ways of the people:

> Frequently a man or his family had to take long trips and risk meeting strange people in distant settlements. Since travelers were thought to be dangerous, possibly carrying evil spirits, they were often at the mercy of their hosts. The

[16]Ibid., p. 189.

best way for a traveler to secure the cooperation of the community was for him to establish kinship links with one of the people."[17]

Marriage was a simple matter and free of ritual; the bride had only to collect her goods and move in with her husband's family. Finding a wife, however, was not always simple for the Netsilik boy. If he were fortunate, his mother or grandmother had betrothed him in infancy to a newborn girl or one yet to be born, usually a first cousin. Often such arrangements could not be made, so the young man searched for a wife among other close bands, occasionally stealing a married woman and sometimes murdering her husband to do so. The scarcity of potential brides derived from the practice of female infanticide. In 1902 there was a ratio of 48 girls to 100 boys. Twenty years later of 96 births from 18 marriages 38 girls were killed.[18] Parents or grandparents decided the fate of the infant before she was named, but a betrothal or adoption might save her. From the Eskimo perspective female infanticide was ecologically adaptive. All children were loved, but boys were preferred for they would remain home and become hunters. Girls contributed less to the family and would leave it. While a mother was nursing she probably would not conceive; therefore nursing a female baby postponed the birth of the hoped-for boy. In an environment where starvation was imminent and hunting arduous, the baby girl, especially if she was the firstborn, would be discarded.

Newlyweds quickly became an economic unit. The man was the toolmaker, the house builder, the food supplier. The woman, the butcher, the homemaker, and a helper on the trail; but her major value lay in her skills as a skin processor and seamstress. A man could if forced, cook and butcher—but sew, never. The marriage based on division of labor soon became more than that as ties of affection built. The arrival of children further strengthened the union. Infants were a tremendous source of pleasure to parents, and babies were always in close body contact with adults who held, fondled, and nuzzled them. Toddlers strutted around the igloo to the indulgent amusement of all. As they grew older they began to imitate adult activities. Traditionally when a little boy was about 5, the father-son relationship deepened, and by 10 he was his father's helper and companion. Little girls soon learned women's work, but as they grew older the overt affection of their father diminished. Here no child was spanked nor scolded; teasing and mocking sufficed to control behavior. Age shaped the relations between brothers. The older received affection and respect from younger ones; sisters, on the other hand, were much more intimate as they played and later worked together. Brothers and sisters treated one another with reserve and reticence.

There were no formal rites of passage for Eskimo children; however,

[17]Ibid., p. 101.
[18]Ibid., p. 148.

sometimes the first feats of little boys were celebrated. Rasmussen describes such an event:

> ... thus I one day happened to see Pagutaq catch his first fish. The boy was no more than six years old, so that it was his mother that had to do most of the catching. He was too small to wade out in the river so she had to carry him. ... There he had to hold the leister himself but had to be assisted in spearing the fish. ... But as soon as this was done she broke out into loud joyous cries. ... Later on the day was celebrated with a great feast, consisting of all the trout possessed by the family.[19]

While in theory the husband was master of his home and could do as he liked, in practice his wife was very assertive, lively, and outspoken, and exercised considerable authority. Squabbles did occur, usually over trivial matters. Traditionally should a quarrel continue "the woman's brain always seemed to work more quickly than the man's, and her sallies would fall with such ready wit that they either left the husband entirely speechless ... or compelled him to clout her."[20] But the general air of an Eskimo home was one of affection, cheer, and cooperation.

The closeness of the members of extended families was not sufficient to protect them from the potential disasters of arctic life. The Inuit, therefore, worked out other cooperative relationships which afforded additional support and also increased cohesion. These were partnerships between men and in some instances between women. Partnerships were formal sharing arrangements between nonrelated or very distantly related people. The operation of this institution was seen most clearly in the winter sealing camp. After the successful hunter had given the seal to his wife, she placed it on a cover of clean snow and cut it into fourteen named parts. The first twelve she presented to the wives of her husband's meat-sharing partners, each of whom always received the same cut. This practice guaranteed the distribution of specific portions of meat to the partners. The remaining two and the skin belonged to her. Usually the partners were chosen by the man's mother when he was an infant; should one die, a partner's brother took his place, or if two adults were partners their sons became partners too. Other dyadic bonds (bonds between two people) including joking partners often occurred between men of the same name. In addition to exchanging jokes, they swapped gifts of identical objects or of equal value. Partners exchanged wives too. While this practice may have enlivened the lives of the participants, it had a pragmatic function. Should a hunter's wife be unable to travel with him, his partner's wife went along to do woman's work, while his mate remained in the settlement with his partner.

Life in the remote polar zone was often fierce and unpredictable. Exploitive skills and social networks did not assure survival; despite hu-

---

[19]Rasmussen, *The Netsilik Eskimos*, p. 66.
[20]Ibid.

mankind's best efforts, the unforeseen happened and so the Netsilik turned to the supernatural. Their beliefs explained the world, influenced human relationships, and reduced fear. Supernatural forms permeated every facet of Netsilik life. In their view the universe was peopled with a vast array of spirits, ghosts, and strange creatures affecting human fate. Of these, human and animal souls were vital to Eskimo welfare.

A person's soul provided a Netsilik with strength, courage, and decisiveness. The hunter waiting hours at a breathing hole pelted by wind and cold could do so because of his soul. A woman's soul was the force enabling her to endure the rigors of her life. While the personal soul was the wellspring of life and health, it was always in jeopardy. Evil spirits or malignant shamans attacked it, bringing serious illness. After death the souls continue their existence for eternity in an afterworld. But should survivors fail to observe proper death taboos, the soul changed into a malevolent spirit who lurked near the living causing all manner of calamity. Personal names also had powerful souls which protected their bearers from misfortune. It was not surprising, then, to find people with a great many names. "Pack ice," "leister," "the one who is partial to woman's genitals," are three of twelve names by which one Netsilik woman was called.[21]

Seal, caribou, and bear had powerful souls which demanded respect. Failure to observe the strict taboos or perform the rituals at the kill of an animal transformed its soul into a vengeful spirit. Dead seals must lie on fresh snow in the igloo because their souls would be offended if they lay where women had walked. Though dead, they thirst and must be given water. Seals demanded even more of the people. In preparation for the arrival of a newly killed seal, all old blubber had to be removed through the window. While an unflensed seal was in the house, the wife could neither sew nor process skin, and her husband refrained from work with bone or stone. These reverential acts pleased the seals and they allowed themselves to be caught again. Caribou souls too required special attention. No sewing or tanning of hides could be done during the great caribou hunt. Mixing of seal meat and caribou meat was absolutely forbidden. The ritual treatment of caribou, seal, as well as bear, and to a lesser extent salmon, emphasized the significance of these animals in Netsilik life. The sharp distinction between caribou and seal was symbolic of the major migrations in the Eskimo year.

A third category of spirits resided in amulets which all men, women, and children wore. Some ensured hunting success; others afforded health and vigor; while a third group protected the wearer from evil. Individuals wore an amulet throughout their lives as it grew in power over the years. People often inherited especially potent ones.

These congeries of spirits were presided over by three dieties,

[21]Ibid., p. 219.

Nuliajuk, Narssuk, and Tatqeq. Nuliajuk was the mother of all animals and mistress of land and sea. Living in the depths of the sea, all knowing and all powerful, she gave game or withheld it if taboos were violated. Narssuk was the master of snow, wind, and rain. Breaking menstrual taboos infuriated him and caused him to loose blizzards in the land. The female moon spirit, Tatqeq, a much less forbidding personage, brought luck to the hunters and fertility to their wives.

Interdictions and ritual surrounded life crises such as birth and death. The Netsilik spiritual universe was a capricious one and had to be dealt with by careful observances of rites and taboo, by wearing protective amulets, and speaking magic words. When these failed, and they often did, shamans intervened with the spirits on behalf of the people. In dramatic seances in the dark of winter camp they descended to the depths to mollify Nuliajuk and flew up to confront Narssuk. They exorcised evil spirits who caused disease and visited misfortune upon delinquents.

To become a shaman a promising young boy was apprenticed to an elderly *angatkok*. He abstained from eating the head, liver, and intestines of game and eschewed sexual relations. Sleeping little, he soon experienced visions. Then, his teacher taught him an esoteric vocabulary and shamanistic techniques. The elderly *angatkok* climaxed his instruction by presenting his apprentice with a protective spirit (tunraq) which he must learn to control. With experience the novitiate became a full fledged shaman as powerful as his master.[22]

Netsilik religious beliefs and practices reflected clearly their primary concerns: food, birth, and death, and interpersonal relationships. The taboos differentiated between land and sea animals; they were psychic defenses against physical hazards, and when breached explained misfortune.

This account of Netsilik culture is abbreviated, but we can see that the major dimensions of the culture were directed toward individual and group survival in a razor-edged environment. Without their elaborate technology and their flexible social system, the Netsilik would have found life in the polar zone impossible; their religion explained the vicissitudes and protected against uncertainties that plagued this very small group of people.

EPILOGUE

In the 1920s and 1930s whites established small trading posts in Netsilik land. With them, the Eskimo traded pelts for steel traps, canoes, rifles, and fish nets, items which were to have drastic consequences for the Inuit. Because men could shoot seals at the edge of the ice or along fissures in it,

[22]Asen Balikci, "Shamanistic Behavior Among the Netsilik Eskimos," *Southwestern Journal of Anthropology*, 19(1963):382–383.

breathing-hole sealing disappeared. The cooperation between hunters, imperative for traditional sealing, was no longer necessary. Sharing and trading partnerships and similar institutions faded away. In canoes men sought seals in the open water of summer, an entirely new enterprise. Caribou fell to the rifles at any time and place. Fishing nets replaced the stone weirs. The collaborating, extended family yielded to the nuclear family in importance.

Seasonal migrations halted and families settled in permanent camps. While women and children remained in the camp, men left to hunt or fish. On occasion a number of people deserted the base camp and congregated around the trading posts for extended periods.

Within Netsilik land itself, at Pelly Bay, a Catholic missionary constructed a small church adjoined by a trading post in 1936. Drawn by the mission and post, people clustered around the mission; the permanent camps were abandoned. Only men traveling alone left to hunt and trap. The disintegration of the traditional socioeconomic system was completed.

Even more important than the missionary's economic activities were his efforts to convert the people to Christianity. By preaching, teaching, and exhorting, he eliminated female infanticide and senilicide. The sex ratio gradually balanced; it was no longer necessary to steal or share wives or to betroth infants. He excoriated polygyny and sex outside of marriage. Changes equally as deep occurred in the aboriginal magicoreligious system. Taboos were ignored, amulets disappeared, and the shamanistic practices, regarded by the priest as satanic, were suppressed. The Netsilik became good Catholics.

Until the 1960s the missionary had complete authority over the lives of the people. He was the religious leader, teacher, trader, and government agent. The Canadian government then, through its Department of Northern Affairs, changed the situation.

To implement its goal of bringing the Inuit into the "mainstream" of Canadian life, materials were freighted in to build a town. Eskimos, working under the direction of Euro-Canadians, built a day school, a nursing station, low-cost houses for their families, and other community buildings. Generators were installed to provide electricity to all structures; a sewage disposal plant took care of human wastes. An air strip and radio telephones facilitated contact with the outside.

An insatiable demand for western goods developed: snowmobiles—which replaced traction dogs—tape recorders, radios, and motorcycles were imported. People exchanged western clothing for all but a few items of aboriginal garb. Except for caribou and fish, the native diet changed as tastes for bread, eggs, and sweets increased.

Fishing and hunting continued and some men were able to earn a modest living at them. Others worked in maintenance and service jobs for the town. Skilled artists produced soap stone carvings for sale in the south; older men produced replicas of traditional tools for collectors.

The aboriginal social, economic, and religious life vanished, apparently without much regret. Yet the community is not self-sustaining. If government subsidies, services, and oil and gasoline deliveries were cut off the people would be set adrift. The once-nomadic Netsilik have become wards of the government.[23]

[23]Asen Balikci, "The Netsilik Inuit Today," *Etudes/Inuit/Studies* 2(1978):111–119.

CHAPTER THREE

The
Cree Indians
of the Subarctic

The North American subarctic is a vast remote expanse of land, a broad swath of forest lying just south of the tundra and reaching from Alaska through northern Canada to Labrador. It is an area of glacial debris covered primarily by spruce, balsam, larch, and the hardwoods of birch, poplar, and aspen. Interrupting the endless miles of boreal forest and partially separating Ontario from Quebec are Hudson Bay and James Bay. Willow and alders border the banks of the numerous rivers, streams, and lakes which dot the subarctic. A significant topological feature is muskeg, a boggy spongy turf, the breeding ground of the ubiquitous northern mosquito. The southern boundary of the boreal forest generally coincides with the northern limit of aboriginal agriculture. Except for the mountainous areas of the west and parts of Quebec, the boreal forest is only slightly elevated. The climate is spectacular for its deeply cold winters and short, warm summers with occasional hot days. The two events which have enormous importance for the dwellers in the subarctic are freeze-up—when in the lakes and rivers the ice becomes thick enough to support the weight of people and equipment; and break-up—the amazingly short and violent period when the ice breaks free from the shore and the current carries the floes from lakes, down streams and rivers, into larger bodies of water. In its

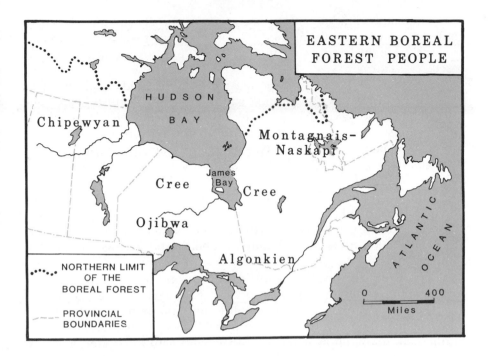

broadest aspect the subarctic is a conspicuously uniform ecological zone, yet within it are smaller ecosystems each with its own characteristics.

In the eighteenth century, west of Hudson Bay to interior Alaska lived the northern Athabaskans. To the east were the Algonkians divided into Ojibwa, Cree, Montagnais, Naskapi, and Algonquin. Differences in language and dialect rather than significant variations in behavior distinguished the groups. The Montagnais lived primarily in Quebec in the forests extending north of the Gulf of St. Lawrence to the James Bay watershed. The Naskapi occupied the Labrador Peninsula. The Cree inhabited the area west of the Montagnais, south and east of James Bay and curving northward to the southwest coast of James Bay. Their nearest Athabaskan neighbors were the Chipewyans. These Cree are often called the Swampy Cree which differentiated them from the Plains Cree.

The Cree exploited an enormous stretch of territory. The population was divided into small bands united by kin ties and language, although dialect differences distinguished the Cree east of James Bay from those who lived west of it. The bands comprised small groups of related nuclear families, probably no band consisted of more than fifty adults and children. In so far as it is known the microbands, as John Honigmann[1] called them,

[1]John J. Honigmann, "Indians of Nouveau-Quebec," in *LeNouveau Quebec*. J. Malarie and J. Rousseau, eds. (Paris: Mouton, 1964), p. 332.

were unnamed.[2] Traditionally in late spring and early summer the bands gathered at a river for fishing and for conversation, gossip, and courtship. Late in the fall the bands broke up into smaller hunting groups, usually kin based.

Whether the families composing the hunting bands held territories for their exclusive use is a question which has sparked much heated and learned anthropological debate. Frank Speck[3,4] observes that the exclusive family rights were an original response to the resources of the boreal forest—especially beaver. Since beaver were a major subsistence item, sustained-yield harvests would have been advantageous; the take could only be controlled, he argues, by families exploiting their own territory. The opposing point of view claims that territories were not in the exclusive domain of microbands and families nor would such a practice have been adaptive. Animal populations fluctuated and families changed their size and composition thus necessitating flexibility and change in hunting grounds.[5]

The Cree did not own land in the European sense. In fact they scoffed at the idea that man can own land; it was said to belong to the animals. Specific hunting groups did utilize the same regions for years, yet there was no notion of trespass. An individual or family might join any hunting group by simply making arrangements with the leader, and so in effect, it might hunt anywhere so long as it was done in the context of a hunting group. We may conclude that there were use rights associated with specific family groups, but there was also opportunity to change hunting territories.[6]

In general most Cree bands were similar to one another, despite local cultural differences. Fisher linked the differences to the variability of the ecological niches in the Canadian shield-muskeg bush regions inhabited by these seminomadic, eastern microbands.[7] The descriptions to follow (of life in the late-nineteenth century) are based on the Cree living east of James Bay, especially the Misstassini and Rupert's House Bands.

[2]Presently Cree bands take their names from the posts or sites where they gather for the summer. The bands are administrative units for the Canadian Government Indian Affairs Branch.

[3]Frank Speck, "The Family Hunting Band as the Basis of Algonkian Social Organization," *American Anthropologist* 17(1915):289–405.

[4]Frank Speck and L. C. Eiseley, "The Significance of the Hunting Territory Systems of the Algonkian in Social Theory," *American Anthropologist* 41(1939):269–280.

[5]Rolf Knight, "A Re-examination of Hunting, Trapping, and Territorality Among the Northeastern Algonkian Indians," in *Man, Culture, and Animals*. Anthony Leeds and Andrew P. Vayda, eds. (Washington, D.C.: American Association for the Advancement of Science, 1965), pp. 40–41.

[6]See Adrian Tanner, *Bringing Home Animals*. (New York: St. Martin's Press, 1979), pp. 201–202, for an elaboration of this point of view.

[7]Anthony D. Fisher, "The Cree of Canada: Some Ecological and Evolutionary Consideration," in *Cultural Ecology: Readings on the Canadian Indians and Eskimo*. Bruce Cox, ed. Carleton Library Series #9 (Toronto: McClelland & Steward, Ltd., 1973), p. 132.

The country the Cree inhabited is relatively flat. Flying over it at low altitudes in spring one sees numerous lakes, ponds, and rivers, which divide into smaller meandering streams. These waters provided the Cree with fish and also means of getting around in both winter and summer. The climate is continental characterized by long, cold winters and short summers. The coldest months are December, January, and February. While not common, a temperature of $-56°$ F has been recorded just before sunrise. Daytime temperatures of $-18°$ F are typical. The short summer daytime temperatures range between $40°$ and $90°$ F. Frost may come in September, and by the end of October the ground is often covered with snow, accumulating in 3- to 5-foot depths in the winter months. By December the bodies of water freeze completely. Break-up starts the latter part of April and is completed by the end of May.

In this land of spruce, balsam, fir, and some hardwoods, roamed caribou, moose, black bear, beaver, otter, mink, muskrat, marten, fisher, fox, wolf, wolverine, and hare, each making its own use of the environment. On these animals the Cree depended for food, clothing, and often shelter. Ptarmigan, grouse, and the migrating water birds, Canada goose, snow goose, and ducks, were another source of food. Fish were common: mainly trout, whitefish, sturgeon, burbot, and pike. Never a source of subsistence, spring and summer insects made life difficult. Black flies, deer flies, moose flies, and mosquitoes savaged hapless victims, attacking head, face, and other exposed parts of the body. No doubt the climatic and environmental conditions seem unduly rigorous to the outsider. But the Cree considered the climate neither harsh nor mild. In fact, in winter they frequently complained about the weather being too warm, and most weather magic rituals were designed to lower the temperature during mild spells in winter.[8]

There was little or no solidarity among the Cree bands, and no chiefs or strong political figures existed with power to coerce or govern. Leadership resided in the head of the family or the head of the small winter hunting group, and his authority was limited. A good man, wise in the ways of the people or skilled in the hunt, had informal influence. People often sought counsel from him, but he had no way to enforce his decisions or advice.[9] Honigmann suggested that, "ambivalence characterizes thinking about leadership. Indians regard firm leadership as desirable yet no pleasure comes from exercising power. Too great evidence of power is resented and feared by those whom it affects."[10] The Cree type of social structure was called atomistic. In the atomistic type society there was no political authority, leadership was informal, and the family unit was the most

[8]Tanner, *Bringing Home Animals*, pp. 27–33.

[9]Harriet J. Kupferer, "Impotency and Power: A Cross-Cultural Comparison of the Effect of Alien Rule," in *Political Anthropology*. Marc J. Swaratz, Victor W. Turner, and Arthur Tuden, eds. (Chicago: Aldine Publishing Co., 1966), p. 62.

[10]John J. Honigmann, "Interpersonal Relations and Ideology in a Northern Canadian Community," *Social Forces* 35(1957):369.

significant in the lives of the people. Rites and rituals were largely individual- or family-based. People rarely came together for big ceremonies. There was a psychological dimension to atomism too. People were slow to show feelings, either anger or overt affection; emotions were muted.[11] Preston describes the trait among the Cree as reticence: a wariness, a wait-and-see attitude on the part of the Indian when he or she encountered a stranger, respect for the autonomy of others, and a dislike for the effusiveness of the non-Indian.[12]

Despite the atomistic quality of Cree society most people conformed to the appropriate norms. But like folk everywhere some, for whatever reason, stole or killed or otherwise violated accepted standards of behavior. Traditionally in the absence of formal power and authority to punish or to correct, other means of social control were employed. One of the most common was gossip; another, in the case of serious violations, was resort to a conjuror or medicine man. The aggrieved, if he lacked such powers himself, brought his case to the shaman, describing his grievance in an informal way. If after some time the circumstances continued, he went again to the conjuror who then sent his spirit helpers to bring misfortune to the accused. It was expected that the miscreant would either sicken or suffer severe misfortunes. As a Cree has told this writer, in the old days conjurors were their only "support"—meaning there were no other means of social control. She continued with a story:

> A long time ago there was a bunch of families on the Pontax (a river). A fellow from Misstasini was mad at them (over a marriage) and he was going to send something to get rid of the man. The people, the men and women, were already out at goose blinds. Old Peter Trapper sensed that something was wrong. He saw tracks that looked like wolf tracks but much bigger. Then he saw a lion. The lion had come to get the girl; the people tried to shoot him but they couldn't. Peter was a magician; he said he was going to stay out all night. Next morning the lion was found dead under a rock. . . . Peter Trapper killed the lion, he was a medicine man, he was a very strong man they say.[13]

Honigmann has observed that the ever-present threat of sorcery was a significant factor in maintaining the deferential relationships in subarctic Cree society.[14]

The Cree recognized no clan or lineage system. They traced descent bilaterally, that is, both mother's and father's relatives were of equal importance. These people formed a kindred. Traditionally polygyny was

[11]Arthur J. Rubel and Harriet J. Kupferer, "Perspectives on the Atomistic-type Society," *Human Organization* 27(1968):189–190.

[12]Richard J. Preston, III, "Cree Reticence and Self Expression: A Study of Style in Social Relationships," *Proceedings of the Seventh Algonkian Conference*. W. Cowan, ed. 1976.

[13]Harriet J. Kupferer, unpublished field notes, 1963.

[14]John J. Honigmann, "The Attawapiskat Swampy Cree: An Ethnographic Reconstruction," *Anthropological Papers of the University of Alaska* 5(1956):78.

Summer dwelling of Ruperts' House Cree, 1963.
Harriet J. Kupferer

permitted, but its actual frequency is hard to ascertain and probably was low as it would have taken a very successful hunter to provide for more than one spouse and her children. Parents often arranged marriages, the couple usually accepting the parents' choices. Cross-cousin marriages were permissible and probably preferred. In some areas the cross-cousin marriage was bilateral; in others only the sons and daughters of father's sisters were potential mates.[15] Should a wife die, often the widower was given her unmarried sister as a wife; the practice is called the sororate. The marriage rite was simple. A prospective groom presented his chosen bride with game. She prepared it for a small feast. Thereafter she lived with him, most likely in his father's group after a period of bride service in hers.

The family lived either in dome-shaped lodges covered with skin or in conical shelters erected on a four-pole foundation covered with hides, bark moss, and earth. The floors were carpeted with fragrant spruce boughs, laid down by the women. Some dwellings held only the married couple and its children. In others perhaps an elderly person or unmarried brother of the husband joined the group. During the winter when the hunting bands were formed, more than one commensal unit (those who eat together) might live in a larger dwelling, but each family organized its own domestic space and ate separately. Whether a multiple-family or a single-family dwelling, the interior space was organized by sex. Tanner described the arrangements. Each dwelling had a fire near the center; behind the fire and opposite the entrance was the living space where each person had his or her own private place. People slept with their heads against the rear wall and their feet toward the fire. The interior of the shelter was divided in half from front to back; to the right facing the door was the woman's side, while hunting and trapping equipment was kept on the men's side. We can

---

[15]Regina Flannery, "Cross Cousin Marriage Among the Cree and Montagnais of James Bay," *Primitive Man* XI(1938):32.

see this as a clear symbolic ordering of that which the Cree regarded as men's work and women's work. Sex and age ordered the sleeping arrangements. The married couple slept side by side, each on his or her division. Children and others attached to the group were arranged from the same-sexed parent in order of increasing age. Boys lay in between the father and the oldest unmarried male, while girls were sandwiched in between their mother and the oldest unmarried woman.

Days were busy in the winter camps. Each family consumed great quantities of wood. Men felled trees and brought them near the camp; women most often split them. The exhaustion of a wood supply could be a major reason for moving a camp. Women worked on hides, preparing them for clothing and other needs. They also snared rabbits and shot grouse and ptarmigan. Men spent the days hunting and trapping. Depending on the type of camp, they might return at night, or sleep on the trail returning every three or four nights with the game. If the men stayed in camp at night, they spent their time repairing hunting and trapping equipment or making snow shoes and toboggans. Conversations centered on the game, the weather, and other domestic topics of immediate concern.[16]

To say that traditionally among the Cree there was women's work and men's work is not to say that the women were thought to be inferior to men, or that their contribution was devalued. Men did not lose caste if they assisted in what was considered women's work, and older women, widowed or childless, often had the reputation of being good hunters. Women had the right to dispose of the game their husbands killed. Wives were never considered the property of their husbands and married women were free to come and go as they pleased. Divorce was equally easy for both sexes. The status of women depended upon their judgment, skills, and the way in which they shared food with others.[17]

The Cree valued children, treating them with quiet affection and respect. Physical punishment was rare. Children learned through imitating adults and were praised when they succeeded; failures were ignored, or at the most, only gentle efforts were made to correct their mistakes. Traditionally children of both sexes underwent a ritual called the "Walking Out."[18] As soon as the child could walk, he or she was led by parents along a path covered by spruce boughs to a small decorated spruce tree. A boy carried a bow and arrow, a girl a small ax. Mimicking adult activities, the boy shot an animal (whose body was placed earlier under the tree). The girl chopped a pile of firewood also previously prepared. The toddlers then cir-

---

[16]Tanner, *Bringing Home Animals*, pp. 69–76.

[17]Regina Flannery, "The Position of Woman Among the Eastern Cree," *Primitive Man* 13(1936):81–86.

[18]Tanner, *Bringing Home Animals*, pp. 90–91.

Cree woman with child in cradleboard, circa 1927. Smithsonian Institution National Anthropological Archives.

cled the tree clockwise carrying the results of their labor. Led inside the tent they again circled clockwise and were greeted by the others present. They gave their burdens to the same-sexed parent or grandparent. A small feast was held using the material provided by the children; during its course, they were praised for providing such excellent help.

As the children grew older they learned through association with adults and by participating in the tasks which men and women performed. At menarche the girl was secluded in a small shelter apart from the family hut. Aside from the vision quest there were no clearly defined rites of passage for the maturing young man.

The traditional belief of the Cree in regard to a single supernatural being or entity was not clear and reports are conflicting. The lack of a well-articulated ideology was probably related to the general absence of a complex social structure. We have noted that Cree bands were small and seminomadic. Only in the summer did people come together in large numbers. This kind of situation precluded the development of an elaborate theology upon which all people agreed and which they understood in the same way.

The spiritual concept of Manito reflects this lack of agreement. Some Indians described it as a power but not a personalized supreme being. Others recognized a bad and a good Manito. The writer Diamond Jenness reports that the Manito of the Cree Indians was the father neither of gods nor men and could not be charged with causation of all things.[19] It is best to

[19]Diamond Jenness, *Indians of Canada*, 7th ed. (Toronto: University of Toronto Press, 1977), pp. 188–189.

view Manito as a spiritual potency associated with an object or natural phenomenon, an all-pervasive force infusing everything in nature, which can be made responsive to humans through the appropriate ritual. Traditionally, to gain power boys and many girls withdrew from their families; waiting in solitary in the bush, they sought visions. These came in the form of animal or other natural objects which spoke to the young petitioners. The recipients kept the details of the vision secret but knew that they had a power which increased with the years.

The beliefs are best understood as they were acted upon in the daily round. The economic and subsistence life of the Cree was so inextricably bound up with their beliefs about nature and the supernatural that it is impossible to discuss the one without reference to the others. The beliefs were reflected in rituals many of which were performed by solitary individuals and were often barely discernable. But Tanner has observed that these beliefs were parts of a system having the purpose of "controlling, predicting and explaining behavior of game animals and the behavior of imaginary beings which are believed to influence the animals, or are identified with particular natural phenomena."[20] Daily Cree life, then, especially in connection with winter, combined empirical knowledge of game habits and magicoreligious activities intended to control the unknown and thus ensure success. The Cree believed that animals, wind, and other phenomena were like persons. They understood and were understood by men. Or, as Harvey Feit has cited: "Causality is personal rather than mechanical or biological . . . in return for gifts the hunters have the obligation to act responsibly; to use completely what is given and to act respectfully to the bodies and souls of the animals."[21]

The two seasons most important were winter and summer, and thus it is not surprising that there were magicoreligious means to affect the weather. The two seasons had spirits, and winds especially were thought to be embodied by or to be associated with spirits. Other spirits had local influence causing sudden storms or catastrophes. To the Cree, winter was the time between freeze-up and break-up. Most often winter magic was employed to produce colder weather by means of various techniques which had to be performed by a person born in the winter. A common one was to make a snow model of a hare facing toward the west. Another was tying witches' broom (a parasitic growth on spruce trees) to the tail of a dog, setting it on fire, and turning the dog loose to run on the ice. The few techniques to make the weather warmer in winter were only used should the movement of men and animals be constrained by extreme cold. The elaborate and complex symbolism in winter rituals made sense according to the

---

[20]Tanner, *Bringing Home Animals*, p. 126.

[21]Harvey Feit, "The Ethno-Ecology of the Waswanipi Cree; or How Hunters Can Manage Their Resources," *Cultural Ecology: Readings on the Canadian Indians and Eskimos*, pp. 120–121.

Cree view of the world. Summer rites most often appealed to spirits in specific localities. Tobacco figured importantly here; placed on the ice it hurried break-up, and scattered in rivers and lakes it prevented sudden squally weather when people were traveling.[22]

Hunting rituals paralleled the activities of the hunt. One had to know where to hunt to achieve success in killing game and in bringing it back. So rituals were performed in a sequence: divination, killing rites, and ritual treatment of the dead animals. Divination consisted of efforts to gather information about the unknown.

Perhaps the most spectacular divining ritual of the Cree was the "Shaking Tent." The differing descriptions of it reflect the period in which it was observed or the particular hunting band which conducted it. Flannery observed the event in Rupert's House in 1938:[23] "Six poles—two of each of three different kinds of wood—are placed in a circle about four feet in diameter. They are lashed in place by a hoop near the bottom and another at the top. The conical structure was covered by canvas tenting. The shaman or medicine man entered it soon to be followed by spirits." Both Flannery and Tanner[24] reported that the major spirit, Mistaapew or Mistabeo, entered first and acted as master of ceremonies and spoke in the human tongue. Other spirits—those of fish, clawed animals, and others—followed. They uttered noises, whistles, and sounds, which Mistabeo translated. As each spirit entered, the tent shook violently, and seldom during the performance was the tent not moving. Old men asked most of the questions concerned with hunting. Mistabeo answered some and others he did not. The ceremony was not completely serious or occupied with divining. Mistabeo often told jokes and those which produced the greatest amusement were scatological and often directed at women. He had a prodigious appetite for tobacco and during the evening men slipped some under the side of the tent; it was gone when the tent was taken down. The shaking tent amused as well as divined.

The Cree also forecasted through scapulomancy. The scapula of an animal was heated over a fire until it cracked and created patterns. Older men with the requisite knowledge and spiritual power read and interpreted the lines. Advice of the oracle was sought to determine the location of game or beaver houses, the success of the hunt, and perhaps the number of animals to be killed. Dreams, too, predicted the future, although often weeks or months elapsed before the events dreamed of came to pass. Other objects, strangely shaped, might augur the future.

Tanner has written that "divination is a rite which involves two levels

[22]See Tanner for an extensive explanation of the ideology which governs both winter and summer ritual, pp. 96–107.

[23]Regina Flannery, "The Shaking Tent Rite among the Montagnais of James Bay," *Primitive Man* XII(1939):11–16.

[24]Tanner, *Bringing Home Animals*, p. 113.

of communication. First its explicit purpose is to receive communication from animals and the entities that control them. But secondly it is like any other rite; it is a symbolic performance in which materials and actions, in the context of cultural knowledge, make statements of a more general nature, and of ideological significance."[25] To that might be added that, in divination, confidence is built for an undertaking of great importance to the people.

Ritual and symbolism surrounded the killing of animals.[26] The hunter carried or wore amulets; decorated weapons and special cords for dragging game were used; rites preceded the killing and guided the disposal of the animal. The bear hunt illustrated excellently the merging of religion and hunting. Prior to killing a bear the hunter spoke to it believing that the animal heard and understood. After the kill, he placed tobacco on its chest and hung a necklace on the bear. During the hunt no other game was sought and the women at home kept the camp clean.

Other ritual precautions were observed during the hunt. For example, should the spirit of the north wind, conceived to be the Master of the Winter Animals, come upon a kill site and find it soiled with blood, he would be offended and retaliate by sending a severe storm. All of the many hunting rites and symbolic behaviors underscored the Cree idea that humans and animals were in a reciprocal relationship. With appropriate deferent behavior on the part of the hunter, animals would "give themselves" to be killed.

Such observances did not end when the kill was returned to camp, butchered if it were a large one. Norms guided the distribution of meat and the disposition of the inedible portions of an animal. All these norms expressed the respect which the Cree showed to the animals and the importance of their social life. When the hunters returned to camp they did so quietly, never boasting about the catch nor engaging in loud talk; people in the camp were dignified and greeted the men solemnly. In a subdued atmosphere people silently admired the catch. All of the meat was taken into the dwelling of the man who killed it; there it was placed in the rear, with the head of the animal facing the entrance. The meat was distributed to others in the camp following rules of age and relationship to the hunter. Whether at feasts or at ordinary meals, meat offerings were put into the fire, an expression of gratitude as well as of the hope that future hunts would be successful. Certain cuts of bear and beaver were thought to be men's food or women's food. At Rupert's House women could not eat the head of the bear nor its forelegs.

After all the edible parts of the animals had been eaten the remains

[25]Ibid., pp. 132–133.
[26]The following descriptions are drawn from Tanner, pp. 145–148 and my field notes, Ruperts House, 1963.

Cree man calling moose, circa 1927.
Smithsonian Institution National
Anthropological Archives.

were treated according to rules. Skulls or antlers of large animals were placed in trees or on platforms, as were the forelegs of the bear and beaver, and painted or decorated with ribbons. Other bones were also treated ritually. No remains could be eaten or molested by dogs; remains of water animals were returned to the water while those of land animals and birds were laid on an elevated platform. Some portions might be retained by the hunter. The head and neck of the first goose killed by a youth was stuffed and decorated with beads by a woman. The chin skins of bears were often kept, beaded, and strung together and thereafter hung in the dwelling.

The behavior accorded game animals reflected the ideology forged over centuries of living in the bush, exploiting it for subsistence with unsophisticated weaponry. It was a belief system consonant with the exigencies of the northern forests. The interpersonal relationships, too, can be seen to be a correlate of the bush. People maintained their social and emotional distance, which functioned to prevent most overt hostility, for in an area where physical interdependence is a necessity and generosity obligatory, overt aggression would be highly destructive.

EPILOGUE

In the 17th century, a few white men drawn by the prospects of fur trade entered Cree territory. Following closely on their heels were Anglican and Catholic missionaries. Apart from exchanging guns and traps for fur, the traders had little effect upon the Cree. They continued their traditional life, made somewhat easier by the new weapons. Because they maintained their annual cycle, missionaries had little opportunity to begin conversion to Christianity.

With the passage of time fur trading rapidly expanded. Independent small traders gave way to the Hudson Bay Company. By the late eighteenth century the company had established well-stocked trading posts throughout the region which acted as magnets for the Indians. Several small bands gathered at each in the summer creating larger native aggregates. Eventually these bands became permanently associated with the posts and took their name from the location. Most people converted to the Anglican faith. (Catholic missionaries were present but were restrained from proselytizing by government edict.) Although nominally Anglicans, the subtleties and nuances of the doctrine escaped them and they preserved their native religion and ritual.

To obtain the material goods afforded by the post—western clothing, flour, lard, tea, and ammunition—the people returned to the bush each fall to trap the valuable beaver. But much of the traditional life remained intact.

By the end of the 1920s the animals were dangerously imperiled. In 1932 James and Maude Watt, the manager of the Hudson Bay Post and his wife, persuaded the provincial government to create a beaver preserve in western Quebec. Trapping was curtailed and hunters were assigned quotas. Gradually the beaver increased and quotas were adjusted upward. During this period Hudson Bay post managers consolidated their power and authority over the Cree. Few significant actions were taken without their approval.

Before World War II families traveled to bush in canoes. Several hundred pounds of flour and other staples, dogs, ammunition, and people almost overburdened the small crafts. After the war canoes were built with square sterns to accommodate outboard motors. Bush air lines maintained a regular schedule to each post (weather permitting!). Affluent trappers often chartered the planes to transport their families and equipment to the trapping grounds. White sportsmen flew in to hunt and fish, providing employment for guides.

The Indian Affairs Branch opened day schools and nursing stations at some of the more populated settlements. Promising students were sent south to boarding school after they completed the local school curriculum. To stimulate population growth the Canadian government instituted a family allowance plan for all its citizens. Allowances were based upon the number of children per family. Fur money, allowances, and guiding wages provided most of Indian income. After the accounts were settled at the company store, little remained. Yet the Cree were not in severe straits. Many were able to leave their old people and school children in the settlement during the winter without undue concern for their welfare.[27]

Thus despite these westernizing developments, Cree life remained stable and predictable until about 1976. Responding to a perceived need for electric power, the Canadian government proposed a series of dams to

---

[27]John J. Honigmann, "Indians of Nouveau-Que'bec," pp. 345–365, and Kupferer, field notes, 1963.

generate hydroelectricity in the Cree area. The plans threatened trapping territories as well as jeopardizing some of the post settlements. Several of the small towns north of the Rupert river were relocated because of impounded water.

Faced with the possibility of severe disruptions in their social and economic life, the Rupert's House people organized to negotiate changes in their status. They managed to obtain self-government at the local and regional level, which included operating their own school and creating medical and social services boards. Most important, they secured an income-security program for trappers.

The entire region along the east coast of James Bay, and for some distance inland, has been modernized.[28] Yet the Cree persist, adapting as they always have to their changing boreal forest environment.

[28]Richard J. Preston, III, personal communication, 1986.

CHAPTER FOUR

The
Washo
of the Great Basin

From the eastern edge of the Sierra Nevada to the western foothills of the Rockies—or more specifically to the Wasatch Mountains of central Utah—lies the region called the Great Basin. Its north-south boundaries are less easy to define; to the north it gives way to the Columbia plateau, to the south it fades into the southwest desert. Called a high dry steppe by geographers, most of the land is above 4000 feet. Winters are long and cold; snow falls frequently, accompanied by periods of freezing temperatures. Summer mornings are cool, but as midday approaches the heat becomes intense, then diminishes with sunset. Yearly precipitation, including both snow and rain, averages 4 to 11 inches, most of it falling during the colder months. From April to November the skies are cloudless and there is almost no precipitation. If it should rain, the fall is torrential, causing dry stream beds to gush with water only to dry up again within a few hours.

A series of mountains extending north to south and rising a few thousand feet above the valley floor interrupt the vastness of the Great Basin. Most are no more than 75 miles long and 15 miles wide. The rivers with headwaters in the flanks of these mountains drain into the land below; few of them flow year-round. Those that do are edged by verdant strips. In the enormous stretches of almost waterless wasteland, Julian Steward estimated the population density to be one person for every 50 to 100 square

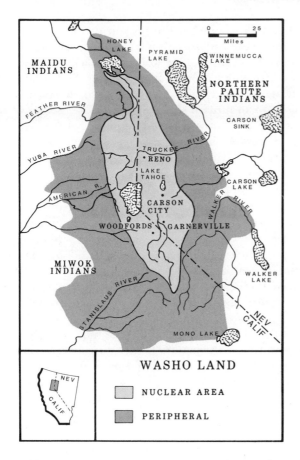

miles.[1] Sagebrush and greasewood, two drought-resistant plants, grow in infinite abundance. Their muted colors of gray and dull-green provide a monotonous scene in every direction. The arid, dull mountains, too, do little to enliven the vista.

Distinct ecological zones in the Basin afforded somewhat different resources to indigenous Indians of earlier times. In the valleys edible roots and seeds lined the infrequent permanent streams. Other edible plants in the empty lands depended upon the rain, which varies 5 to 20 inches from year to year and from place to place. Such floral resources provided only limited food for both humans and game. Traditionally the animals of greatest importance here for Indians were antelope and rabbits. Smaller species such as rodents, snakes, lizards, and insects—mainly locusts and grasshoppers—supplemented their diet.

At about 6000 to 9000 feet on the mountain slopes grew pinyon and

[1]Julian Steward, *The Theory of Culture Change.* (Urbana: University of Illinois Press, 1955), p. 103.

juniper. The juniper provided only wood, but the pinyon produced pine nuts, a food of inestimable value to the Indians. More rain fell in the mountains and so more seeds, grasses, roots, and game were available, especially the mule deer. But the short growing season at high altitude limited the food resources. Some of the mountain ranges thrust upward more than 9000 feet, providing sanctuary for mountain sheep and deer. These game were hunted when the area was free of snow. The varied biotic zones of the Basin supported animal and vegetable life, but as a consequence of the fluctuations of rainfall the location and quantity of the food resources were inconsistent from year to year. A district that was very productive one year might offer little or nothing in another. Never was sufficient food present in one place to allow permanent settlements. The northern and southern Paiute, the western Shoshoni, and the Washo roamed this empty expanse each keeping to its own region. Described by early visitors as wretched, poor, and miserable, they nevertheless through extensive and intimate knowledge of their land and its resources endured until the westward movement of whites destroyed them.

The Washo, who lived in the western area of the Basin, were probably always a small population. Estimates of their number vary from 1500 in 1770 to 3000 in the middle of the nineteenth century.[2] The mobility of the people and the dispersed nature of their settlement patterns prevent agreement on population figures. Moreover, Indian agents in the nineteenth century paid little attention to the Washo because they caused few problems and offered little resistance to American intruders and settlers.[3] Agents were unaware of the distribution of the people and ignorant of groups that remained isolated.

The language of the Washo was a member of a widely scattered phylum known as Hokan. Within this stock fall a number of both language families and language isolates that cannot be grouped into families. Washo is a language isolate. Aztec-Tanoan is the other phylum present in the Great Basin. One of its major families includes the languages spoken by the Shoshoni and the Paiutes.[4]

Like the Cree the Washo exhibited a minimum of political organization. Lowie reported three distinct groups, but these seem to have had little internal coherence and were identified primarily by their location.[5] One

[2]James Downs, *The Two Worlds of the Washo: An Indian Tribe of California and Nevada.* Case Studies in Cultural Anthropology. (New York: Holt, Rinehart and Winston: 1966), p. 4.

[3]Warren L. d'Azevedo, ed. *The Washo Indians of California and Nevada.* University of Utah Anthropological Papers #67, 1963.

[4]Harold Driver, *Indians of North America*, 2nd ed. (Chicago: University of Chicago Press, 1969), p. 44–45.

[5]Robert H. Lowie, *Ethnographic Notes on the Washo.* University of California Publications in American Archaeology and Ethnology, vol. 36, no. 5, p. 301, 1939. Permission to quote from Robert H. Lowie's work is granted courtesy of the Lowie Museum of Anthropology, University of California, Berkeley.

Washo woman in front of dwelling, circa pre-1900.
Smithsonian Institution National Anthropological Archives.

was associated with the area of today's Woodfords, California, one with Gardnerville, and the third was located near Reno. The territories were not owned in any sense and people moved from one site to another. Within these ill-defined territorial groups the Washo lived in small family groups; probably no more than four houses constituted a settlement. Although neighbors might be nonkinsmen, they were most often relatives.[6] The settlements were in no way permanent as the quest for food dictated a migratory life.

Washo country was more bountiful than other regions of the Great Basin further east. Its center was a chain of a fairly well-watered valleys at the eastern slopes of the Sierra Nevada from Antelope Valley in the south to Honey Lake in the north. Rigid boundaries are difficult to draw, but the Washo viewed their territory as a series of layers which included the valleys and had at its center Lake Tahoe.[7] East to west their range extended from the Pinenut Mountains in Nevada to an area several miles west of the main crest of the Sierra Nevada in California.[8] The Carson and Walker Rivers were never dry; other streams originating in the Sierras course eastward terminating in the lakes and sinks in the low parts of the valley. The edges of the lakes (often saline) and sinks and banks of the rivers and streams supported lush vegetation. But away from these green areas the land was typically Basin, drab in appearance and blanketed with sage brush and greasewood. A rich variety of animals occupied the valley floors, some spe-

[6]Stanley A. Freed, "A Reconstruction of Aboriginal Washo Social Organization," in *The Washo Indians of California and Nevada*, p. 18.

[7]Downs, *The Two Worlds of the Washo*, p. 5.

[8]John Price, "Washo Prehistory: A Review of Research," in *The Washo Indians of California and Nevada*, p. 77.

cies widespread, others found only in well-defined niches. Rodents such as sagebrush chipmunk, ground squirrels, pocket gophers, kangaroo rats, pack rats, and multitudes of mice scurried through the sagebrush feeding on the vegetable and large insect population. Pygmy rabbits were limited in distribution. On the other hand black-tailed hares commonly called jackrabbits were everywhere. Like all deserts the Great Basin hosted toads, lizards large and small, and snakes, including a species of rattlesnake. Bobcats, badgers, and coyotes were the important carnivores. The sole grazing animal of the sagebrush land was the pronghorn, often called antelope. In the summer it roamed in small bands, while in the winter it gathered in larger herds.

The mountains on the western edge of Washo land rose precipitously from the valley floor to heights of 8,000 to 10,000 feet. The sides covered with cedar and yellow pine presented a formidable obstacle in reaching the alpine valleys which lay beyond the eastern palisades. In many of these valleys were a myriad of mountain streams and lakes, including Tahoe. Deer were plentiful; squirrel and other rodents and fur-bearing animals such as beaver, fox, bear, mink, and weasel made their home here. At higher elevations mountain sheep abounded. Eagle, hawk, and falcon soared over valley and mountain. Fish leaped in lakes and streams; the most useful were trout, whitefish, and a variety of sucker. The moist and fertile soil produced berries and abundant wild vegetable food.

The animals of the arid steppe, valleys, and mountains were part of a food chain for one another and for the human inhabitants sharing the land with them. This land of the Washo was more hospitable than that of the Shoshoni and Paiute, yet life was a challenge and starvation often a threat. Skilled exploitation of all the biotic zones was critical to Washo subsistence and survival.

Washo culture developed largely through continued efforts to make the most efficient use of local resources. Because they grew no food, the Washo had to develop an intimate knowledge of the habits of wild plants and animals, a technology to secure them, a flexible social organization sufficient to permit group life and to respond to seasonal demands, and supernatural beliefs to sustain them through good and bad times. Because the seasons dictated so much of Washo life, it would be useful to follow them through the yearly cycle.[9] Each season required different activities and prompted different behavior.

When the Basin winter drew to a close the stored seeds and meat were almost exhausted and spring had not yet arrived with its edible bulbs and grasses; it was a time of potential famine and death for the susceptible—the young and the elderly. But as milder weather returned, snow melted in the

---

[9]See Downs, *The Two Worlds of the Washo*, pp. 12–37, for a detailed account of the annual subsistence patterns.

foothills and optimism returned to the people. Young men and boys and unmarried girls moved into the mountains toward Lake Tahoe. Here they caught whitefish, gathered edible plants, courted, and played. Some of the young men returned to the winter camps with food so that those left behind might recover from the ravages of late winter and prepare for their journey to Tahoe. Each family moved independently of others. Decisions to depart or to delay departure were based on the abilities of family members to tolerate the weather and the travel.

By June, however, all the Washo groups were camped on the shores of the lake awaiting the abundant runs of trout and sucker. It was a time of gossip, of catching up on events of the winter when people had been separated, of dancing and contests. But when the fish appeared a period of intense work began. Many wading in the cold water, gathered the teeming fish in baskets, then tossed them up upon the banks where others filleted and hung them to dry. Had the Washo known of the technology of smoking fish they might have lived most of the winter on the fruits of the spawning, but sun-dried fish spoiled quickly in the warm lowlands and so they provided food only for a brief period. When the fish runs diminished many families moved further into the higher mountains near smaller lakes and in alpine valleys. Here fishing continued, but as an individual activity with spear, net, or hook and line, and gathering became more important. Women and girls used digging sticks to collect edible plants and filled burden baskets strapped to their backs. Very few of these plants were preserved for the winter season.

As summer gave way to fall, families gradually moved back to the lowlands drawn by the knowledge that the grasses were maturing and their seeds had to be reaped and stored. Autumn was, in addition, a season for hunting large game; fishing, however, never completely ceased. While the days at Tahoe were a time of large gatherings, the late summer and fall collecting was undertaken by individual families. Women now assumed great importance in provisioning families, for the collecting provided the bulk of the winter food. Poor harvests could mean disaster and even death for members of the family. Plants were abundant but widely dispersed; therefore, people wandered widely but not aimlessly in the search for vegetables and seeds. Where plant life was to be found and how it was to be prepared depended upon the women. This knowledge was gained through years of experience, and older women were significant persons in this quest. Very few seeds or plants could be consumed without preparation. Most seeds had to be husked and winnowed, in special baskets made by the women, and then cooked; many had to be ground before cooking. Some plants required leaching to rid them of bitter tastes or harmful ingredients.

To gather a sufficient supply of seeds, roots, and berries, families traveled almost constantly, often not staying in one place long enough to build shelters; but despite their energy and diligence never could they collect an amount sufficient for the winter. As the days grew shorter and October approached, the people turned toward the east traveling to the mountains where the pinyon trees grew. It was the pinyon nut that made life possible in the Basin. The groves were unique in that they were considered private property and were inherited. No other food-producing lands were claimed by individuals or families, nor were there norms pertaining to their use. Spouses were permitted to pick nuts on the property owned by their parents, and a husband might harvest his wife's plot and she his, but with the death of either, the privilege was withdrawn. The time of the pine-nut collection brought the people together, but unlike the congregation at Lake Tahoe not all bands gathered. The northern groups worked the hills north and west of Reno; the southern bands focused on the area near what is today Gardnerville.

Men harvested the nuts by knocking the cones to the ground with long poles while others picked them up and put them in large baskets. In less than a month, a family would have gathered and prepared thousands of pounds for winter storage. The pinyon harvest was also a time for ritual and great sociability. Once more the people were together, but now they were well fed and there was the promise of food enough for all. The gatherings at which the rituals were held were called *gumsaba*. Following the harvest, families trudged slowly, burdened by the great quantities of nuts, to their winter quarters along the eastern border of the Sierras. With supplies sufficient for the winter the days were passed in basket making by the women and the preparation of weapons by the men who hunted when the weather made it possible. The staples of the Washo diet were mainly seeds, tubers, and pine nuts, but game was also a conspicuous contribution to the larder. Except for the severest days of winter and early spring when game animals were apt to be emaciated, hunting continued until the winter snows. Hunting was man's work just as gathering was woman's, although as we have seen, men took part in the pinyon-cone harvest and women participated in some kinds of hunting. Hunting demanded extensive familiarity with the ways of the prey, skill in stalking, and expertise with the bow. To ensure success in the venture the hunter needed to know and to practice correctly the rites so necessary to hunting. Acquiring the arts of hunting occupied most of the time of young boys. They were guided first by old men, and then as their skills increased they joined their fathers in the quest.

Although hunting was usually a solitary activity or engaged in by only a few working together, there were several exceptions. One such was the rabbit hunt. Washo country abounded with fat jackrabbits in the fall. After the pinyon-nut crop was cached and people had moved to the low country, they undertook communal rabbit hunts. Led by a secular rabbit chief, as many as 200 people might take part. It is not clear whether this leader inherited his position from his father or was appointed by the people, but he set the time for the hunt and notified the people to assemble. Each family brought its own rabbit net fabricated from sage fiber. When these were joined together, they stretched 100 or more yards wide and were about 4 feet high. The animals were driven into the nets by shouting and clapping men, women, and children. Some rabbits were killed on the way with bow and arrow, but most were dispatched entangled in the nets, their necks wrung, their temples squeezed or clubbed. The hunts continued for several days, the nets being moved to different sites until the entire area was emptied of rabbits, or the rabbit chief announced the end of the hunt saying, "We stop today, we have all we want today. Let us go home."[10] It was a time of great activity and urgency. The rabbits broiled and not eaten immediately were skinned and hung up to air dry. The skins were cut into strings, twisted into long pieces and dried. These would be woven into blankets, an item necessary to withstand the rigors of winter. Rabbits were also run down by single hunters in the spring and summer, but the fall hunt yielded the bounty for the cold of the year.

Like the rabbits, deer were hunted communally or by one or two men. Women and children were not part of this effort. The group hunts took place most often in September. Parties of six to eight under the direction of a leader who decided to organize the expedition assembled at his calling. Such a man might say to others: "Get together; we'll try to kill a few deer."[11] The men gathered, prepared to be away for several weeks. Some days each might hunt alone, but more often, two or three would lie in ambush along a well-defined deer trail. The others moving quietly troubled the creatures so that they came within the range of the hunters. These hunts resulted in great quantities of game which were butchered and dried. The meat was shared among the men, and at the conclusion of the hunt each packed home more than 80 pounds.

The pronghorn, often called antelope, was also hunted communally. The pronghorn hunt was likewise under the direction of a leader. But while the others were secular leaders, the antelope shaman, as he was sometimes called, achieved his position through dreaming, and any man who had prophetic dreams might organize the hunt. Lowie in 1926 secured this account of the activity of the Antelope Chief.

> The Antelope Chief sees some antelope in a dream. He reflects about it and goes to the place dreamt about. . . . He sees two or three head, then he knows his dream is true. He begins to talk to them. He does not tell anyone yet. . . . He continues dreaming three or four times. . . . Soon he tells the people to come together and says, "My people, I have dreamt truly or falsely. . . . If I dreamt truly, you'll see them there this morning." He sends two boys to the place as scouts . . . they see ten or fifteen head feeding there together. They

[10]Lowie, *Ethnographic Notes on the Washo*, p. 327.
[11]Ibid., p. 326.

go back and tell the chief. . . . He dreams again and tells his people. . . . The people answer: "Yes if you dreamt right, we'll have meat, we'll try tomorrow to go after them."[12]

A sage brush enclosure was constructed and the leader standing behind the trap smoking his pipe talked to the animals, saying,

Do not get scared, antelope, come easily, creep up, come right into your home. Don't be afraid. We made your home, listen to me . . . don't get scared of anybody.

While the chief exhorted the antelope, the men and others urged them into the trap. When the herd entered, it was closed and the animals slaughtered. The largest was killed first and given to the shaman. The others were divided among the participants, who carried them back to the winter encampments.

The Washo could not afford to ignore other sources of food and sought different creatures as well, among them the desert bighorn and mountain sheep. Waterbirds nesting along the sinks and rivers were gathered by hand, net, or bow and arrow. As they flocked together the birds of sagebrush and greasewood, quail, sage hen, and prairie chicken, were easy targets for the bow. The Indians also set snares and traps to catch them. Small animals—squirrel, rodents, and occasionally lizards—often taken by women and young boys supplemented the diet. Like most residents of arid lands the Washo collected grasshoppers, locusts, and caterpillars. These they roasted and ate immediately or dried and ground into meal to use later.

The food quest of the Washo shows their flexibility in exploiting the land. Each item of their diet, often associated with the seasons, required various cultural adaptations to their ecosystems. These actions were not, however, independent of other dimensions of Washo life. We turn now to a consideration of Washo society and culture.

The significant unit in Washo social organization was the nuclear family which lived in a single dwelling called *galesdangl*, the winter house. This group was frequently augmented by single or widowed relatives. Polygyny was permitted although its frequency is not recorded.[13] The husband normally headed the household, but the influence or even dominance of wives over spouses varied with individuals. During the winter after the pine-nut harvest, families returned to winter campsites adjacent to water and fuel. Several households—perhaps related—were located in the same vicinity. These settlements were small, few having more than four or five households. The anthropologist James Downs has called these winter camps

[12]Ibid., pp. 324–325.
[13]Freed, "A Reconstruction of Aboriginal Social Organization," p. 17.

"bunches."[14] They might vary in membership from year to year, a consequence of local environmental factors or incidents in the lives of members. Leadership in these groups was informal, the position of chief or headman carried no power. Wisdom, patience, and good humor characterized these men, and they were frequently loath to take on the role. Their advice was sought by others, and counsel was given quietly, sometimes reluctantly. Lowie reported that chiefs occasionally delivered hortatory speeches to the bunches. In 1926 he recorded the following:

> Behave well, do not fight, play. If you lose, do not get angry. Play ball, some win, others lose. Play the basket game. Shoot rabbits, eat them. Make soup and eat it. After a while, shoot deer. Shoot grouse, sage hen, mountain quail, ground hogs, ground squirrels, meadow squirrels, small squirrels, mice. . . . Spear fish.[15]

These statements were not commands but advice delivered as part of the chief's responsibility to his people. Others assumed leadership roles for special events. These positions—the rabbit chief and deer chief, both secular, and the antelope chief, a position achieved by dreaming—were temporary, and at the conclusion of the hunt the men resumed their daily routines. Some bunch leaders might also be rabbit chiefs or organize a deer chase although this was not necessarily the case.

Although Washo normative behavior was deferent and unaggressive, not all the Washo, like people the world over, always conformed to the cultural ideal. This created the potential for interpersonal conflict. Because the chiefs had no governing power nor did they adjudicate disputes, social control had to be effected by other means. Aside from gossip and teasing and the right to punish someone poaching in a pine-nut grove, the major forms derived from the fear of ghosts and the presence of shamans among the people.

In the Washo view people were either kinsmen or nonkinsmen, and both could be dangerous. The fear of ghosts was the compelling force in maintaining harmony among relatives. At the death of a person his spirit was thought to go to the east (some said south), but often it would remain in the area to cause illness in a living relative with whom the departed had a grievance. In fact no ghost was welcomed by its survivors regardless of its qualities or intentions. The ghost often clung to some piece of his property which had not been destroyed at his death and was in the possession of a relative.[16] As part of a typical death ritual relatives mourned at the side of the body, crying:

[14]Downs, *The Two Worlds of the Washo*, p. 45.

[15]Lowie, *Ethnographic Notes on the Washo*, p. 303.

[16]Stanley A. Freed and Ruth S. Freed, "A Configuration of Washo Culture," in *The Washo Indians of California and Nevada*, p. 45.

You are dead now. I'll never see you again. I don't want to see you anymore. . . . Don't make any noise outside our house. You live under ground. We don't want to see you anymore."[17]

The deceased's name was never mentioned again.

Attempted suicide was institutionalized among the Washo indicating the importance of ghostly power. Relatives who could not be persuaded in other ways to correct their behavior were threatened by a suicide attempt, an awesome act, for, if successful, the ghost could then visit disaster on the offending kinsman and there was little that could be done to prevent it. The common method for suicide was eating wild parsnip, a slow-acting poison. The delayed effect of the toxin allowed time to save the victim's life by forcing an emetic on him and provided the offender an opportunity to mend his ways before a ghost overtook him; a situation which worked out well for both of them.

Ghosts never harassed a nonrelative. Hostilities among acquaintances were controlled through fear of shamans. Shamans—male and female—controlled power. Their skills were often used for curing or other benevolent ends, yet most of them could cast spells. Anyone could enlist the aid of a shaman to avenge himself on another person. Therefore, most Washo strove to comport themselves in a manner which did not give offense. Fear of an accusation of sorcery also limited Washo behavior, for shamans were sometimes killed by a victim's angry relatives. Moreover if a sorcerer became too wicked, a group of people often concluded that the magician must be killed, sometimes even with the consent of his relatives and friends.

Without well-developed secular means for social control Washo sanctions were visited upon the people by the supernatural. Fear of ghosts and shamans encouraged maintaining appropriate behavior toward one another.

Like many other foraging societies, the Washo had no clan or lineage organization. Children regarded mother's and father's relatives to be of equal importance and inherited from both sides. In the case of the Washo, only pinyon-nut trees were inherited, all other property was destroyed at the death of its owner. The Washo, like the Cree, had a bilateral kinship system. In all kinship systems relatives or classes of relatives are referred to by specific terms. Societies may vary in the number of terms they use; the Washo, for example, had at least fifty-four separate labels for their kinsmen. Their system was complex, much more so than ours, and we will sketch out only the more important features.[18]

The Washo called children of their parents' siblings by the same terms they used for their brothers and sisters, and they distinguished by age; thus

[17]John A. Price, "Some Aspects of Washo Life Cycle," in *The Washo Indians of California and Nevada*, p. 113.

[18]Stanley A. Freed, *Changing Washo Kinship*. University of California Anthropological Records, vol. 14, no. 6, 1960, pp. 356–357.

the terms for older brother and sister were different from those of younger brother and sister and were extended to their cousins. No single category of aunts and uncles existed; there were distinct terms for father's brother, mother's brother, father's sister, and mother's sister. But the greatest number of terms occurred in the group used by people when referring to their grandparents, their grandchildren, their great aunts and uncles, and their great nephews and nieces, eighteen in all. There were also separate labels for in-laws and great-grandparents. This proliferation of kinship terms that a Washo baby had eventually to learn was not a capricious cultural trait. It was a system well adapted to the Basin habitat and Washo subsistence. Washo land was not always beneficent and, despite all efforts to provide, there were good and lean years, and there were dreadfully harsh seasons. Having a great number of people whom an individual considered his relatives and to whom he could turn for help was useful. As he and his family wandered from place to place he was certain to come upon his own or his wife's kinsmen, who would show him generosity and hospitality. Generosity was expected of Washo, most especially toward relatives. The taxing life of hunters and gatherers left men and women less able to provide as they aged. The kinship system protected them from the vicissitudes of decreasing abilities. Washo terminology defined very specifically the relationships between alternate generations and so made clear the responsibility toward the elderly.

A Washo belonged to a vast network of relatives with terms for each, and from them he anticipated support from infancy to old age. A related function of the kinship system was the identification of potential mates. The Washo could not marry any person who was identified by a distinct kinship term. Thus there was no cousin marriage among them nor any other form of consanguineal marriage. As a Washo told Robert Lowie: "Indian people don't do that, they would spoil themselves. . . . If a person marries a kinsperson they say, shame on you! You are spoiling yourself."[19] After the third generation there were no kinship terms, and children who shared the same great-great-grandparent were free to wed. By excluding almost every kinsman with the exception of some in-laws from marriage, the Washo increased sources of support when they married, for the couple shared no relatives in common. This was useful in a small population dwelling in a rigorous area.

Parents usually arranged their children's marriages. At the *gumsaba*, the fall festival, or perhaps at the Lake Tahoe congregation, parents looked for eligible mates. Having found one or having been prompted by a son or daughter, they called upon the parents of the prospective spouse bringing with them a gift, most often of food. During the visit the subject of marriage was not directly approached; talk might concern the weather, the

---

[19]Lowie, *Ethnographic Notes on the Washo*, p. 309. Whether any stronger sanctions were ever invoked against the people who violated the marriage rules has not been reported.

pine-nut crop, or other topics of interest. To be too direct in these matters was not the Washo way. The gift was left with the in-laws. If they accepted it and offered one in return either then or a few days later, the young people were engaged. If the gifts were left untouched by either set of parents there would be no nuptials. Frequently engagements lasted a year, during which time the courtship was closely monitored by the parents to avoid undue intimacy. Marriage took place when the parents consented to the children living together. It was formalized by the couple dancing side by side under a single rabbit-skin blanket. It isn't clear whether virginity was expected of the bride, but it was unlikely. There were many opportunities during the year for young people to come together without parental surveillance. Not all marriages were arranged, some children bypassed parental control and began to live together, a situation not fully approved of by the older generation.

Lacking an arbitrary rule of residence, circumstances largely dictated the choice of postmarital dwellings. Stanley Freed has noted that most Washo spent the greater part of their lives near the parents or close relatives of either the husband or wife. Neolocal residence, where newlyweds settle down independent of either set of parents, occurred but was usually of short duration.[20]

For marriages that took place later in life—either polygynous or polyandrous unions, or invoking the levirate, where the dead husband's brother marries his widow, or sororate—no formalities took place. Divorce was easily attained. A discontented wife suggested that her husband take himself off, or a husband gathered his effects and moved out.

The young married pair began their life together in a conical structure made of limbs with a low door and a smoke hole in the roof. It was sometimes covered with dirt. The *galesdangl*, as it was called, was the winter house, and to it the family returned after its spring, summer, and fall migrations unless a death had occurred in it. Should this have happened, however, the structure was burned and the people moved to another location. The young couple was above all a functioning economic unit—he a skilled hunter and fisherman, she a basket maker, food preparer, and expert gatherer—and could easily sustain itself. But when a child was born and the mother's activities were temporarily curtailed, another woman was welcomed into the household. She might be a sister of the wife or an aged parent of either the husband or wife. The extra hands made child care easier and posed no extra burden for a good hunter, as they too contributed to the larder. Downs observes that the Washo family simultaneously satisfied a number of roles:

> [It was] a biological unit, conceiving, producing and nurturing children; an economic unit, gathering and hunting the food needed by its members; and

[20]Freed, "A Reconstruction of Aboriginal Washo Social Organization," p. 16.

an educational institution wherein was learned all the basic behavior patterns of Washo life. In as much as there was little authority in Washo life, the family might also be considered a minimal political unit as well, allying to and cooperating with other such units but bound by no laws or to follow any desires other than its own.[21]

A child was born in the *galesdangl* attended by a midwife or an older female relative. Details of the ritual surrounding birth varied. This is to be expected, for the Washo, like the Cree, lived in small groups and so some practices became localized. There were, however, some general customs. During the late states of labor a short speech was made:

Hurry up. Crawl out. I'll see you soon.
Hurry up. Crawl out. I'll see you soon.
Hurry out so I can see you.
For sure that's the way.
Hurry up, that's the way. I'm going to see you.[22]

The infant was bathed and laid in a winnowing basket. The afterbirth was wrapped and buried, upside down if no more children were wanted. The mother lay in a shallow pit filled with warm sand for perhaps a month. During this time she was forbidden meat and salt and drank warm water; the father hearing of the birth ritually bathed and left a deer skin near the stream for anyone to take. He too observed his wife's dietary restrictions during her confinement. During the time the mother reclined on her bed the father was expected to be exceptionally busy, hunting, cutting firewood, and remaining awake as long as he was able. These activities were intended to insure that the child become an energetic adult. About a month after birth a baby feast took place. The mother bathed for the first time and she and the baby had their hair cut. The winnowing basket—the baby's first bed—was filled with food and valuables. After the mother chewed some of the food mixed with sage and spat it out, the food and valuables were distributed among the guests. The baby's hair was wrapped in buckskin and hung on the cradle board. All restraints were now lifted and life continued as before.

The Washo dealt gently with children. Physical punishment was very rare. Misbehaving children were warned that wild beasts would carry them off if they continued to disobey. The fear of ghosts lent additional support to the Washo notion of childrearing. If a parent dealt too harshly with his child, the ghost of a relative from the family of the other parent would make the offender sick, or even worse, cause the death of the child who, returning as a ghost, plagued his punitive parent. Children were taught to respect their elders, to avoid fighting, to play quietly, and to refrain from

[21]Downs, *The Two Worlds of the Washo*, p. 42.
[22]Price, "Some Aspects of Washo Life Cycle," p. 96.

stealing, lying, or boasting.[23] Such teaching occurred by precept, story, and myth. Permissiveness characterized childrearing. Babies' needs were attended to immediately; no infants wailed in their cradleboards very long.

The major ritual in the lives of Washo adolescents was the girl's Puberty Dance. The celebration of the first menses and the instruction accompanying the ritual emphasized the significance of Washo women in the life of their people. Again accounts differ in their details, but the general outlines are similar. Fasting and working diligently were the primary elements. From the time the girl first menstruated she drank only water sweetened with sugar-pine leaves. The fast, it was said, would make her live longer and grow properly. Working hard for 4 consecutive days, picking berries and collecting vegetables, remaining awake at night busy with domestic tasks, she shaped her life. Whatever she gathered or produced was given to others, stressing the importance of generosity. During this period of intense activity she was accompanied by another girl who had already undergone her Puberty Dance. Each of them carried a staff, the initiate's decorated with red paint. The latter's was never to fall, break, or be put down, lest she not be straight and tall. When the 4 days of fasting and work were over friends and relatives gathered for an all-night dance and feast. The celebrant began the ceremony by lighting four fires on a nearby mountain. She then raced her companion back, a race which she must win. If she did not, all she had sacrificed within the prior 4 days would have been in vain. After the race the two girls put their poles in the ground, linked arms, and started the dance. The attending women joined them, followed by the men completing the circle; the dance continued until daybreak. At sunrise the sponsor of the girl daubed ashes on her face and down her arms and legs, admonishing the girl:

> Be lively; don't be lazy, don't eat meat, fat, or salt during your menses; wash your face gently at this time or you'll have wrinkles.[24]

Water was poured over the girl, and the waterbasket was tossed toward the women who rushed to get it. The girl was annointed once again, this time with red paint. The men took her pole to the vastness of the mountain where it was hidden upright, should it remain unharmed she would remain straight and tall for life. After the men had left, the initiate broke her fast by chewing pine nut and meat mixed with sage which she then spit out. A feast concluded the ritual, and any foods not eaten were taken home by the guests.

No event of similar magnitude marked the maturation of the Washo boy. For years he trained to hunt, starting first with small animals—squirrels, woodchucks, and rabbits. All the game he caught he gave to oth-

---

[23]Philip E. Leis, "Washo Witchcraft: A Test of the Frustration Aggression Hypothesis," in *The Washo Indians of California and Nevada*, p. 62.

[24]Freed and Freed, "A Configuration of Washo Culture," p. 53.

ers and, like his sister, he learned to be generous. When he killed his first buck deer, his father or grandfather ritually bathed him, and naked he attempted to crawl through the antlers of his deer. If he succeeded, the deer was a large one, and he made the transition from boy to man. He was not, however, ready for the responsibilities of marriage.

The Basin world was an uncertain one. Despite a hunter's best efforts, game sometimes eluded him; a sufficient pine-nut crop was not a surety; illness and death struck unexpectedly. There was little people could do unaided to prevent or control these perils, nor could they always be logically explained. The Washo, therefore, turned to the supernatural to aid, to give meaning to, and to order their world. Most hunting and gathering groups lacked a comprehensive and integrated ideology, and the Washo were no exception. Their rituals and beliefs centered on life's major concerns and most often were carried on in small groups or by individuals. The most significant concept in the Washo cosmology was *wegeleyu*, power.

Wegeleyu resided in some men and women but they did not seek it. No vision quests, no masochistic rites conferred power among the Washo. It came unbidden from dreams and could not pass from one person to another. Water, waterbabies, rattlesnakes, blood, eagle, and bear were sources of power. To dream of one or more of these was to be visited by power. The dreamer must either accept it, learn to control it lest he fall ill, or rid himself of it. Many were reluctant to receive power and resorted to a shaman to remove it. Should a person admit the *wegeleyn*, he or she became a shaman whose power was used to cure. Illness came from a ghost, the violation of a taboo, or the work of a malevolent shaman.

A shaman labored 4 nights to cure, beseeching his personal power, chanting songs which belonged only to him, and smoking Indian tobacco. During this time he fell into a trance, and in this dream state he identified the cause of the illness and attempted to effect a cure. The shaman's cures depended upon the source of the disease. His performance was attended by relatives and neighbors, who by their presence reassured the victim and showed their support and concern. The successful medicine man was paid in goods and foods. Shamanistic power was impartial, the shaman decided whether to use it for good or evil, either to satisfy his own ends or those of another. The Washo regarded shamans as potentially malignant, and fear of them was an important source of social control.

Although only a few possessed *wegeleyu*, evidently all people and probably plants and animals had a general power. In humans this increased with age so that elderly people were treated cautiously and some were thought to be witches. Witches did not intend to harm, but could do so inadvertently. Children were most vulnerable and were kept away from unrelated old folk. The notion that power increased with age tended to ensure that the elderly were cared for, however reluctantly, as their physical abilities declined.

When an individual's attempts to hunt deer failed, he resorted to a shaman who purified him. Like all major Washo rituals, this required 4 days of prayer and incantation. When the animal was finally slain, the hunter gave the meat away. A shaman also facilitated the deer hunt by locating a medicine root which he alone could find; this medicine root would put deer to sleep. Before gathering it he washed and prayed; once obtained, he gave pieces of the root to hunters who placed it in a deer track. When the frustrated hunter overtook the animal, he found it sleeping and killed it easily.

Individual magicoreligious activities preceded almost all hunting trips. Weapons were avoided by menstruating women. Of course, some hunters were more successful than others and their ritual songs provided them with good medicine. These men did not brag of their prowess and guarded their secret closely. The bones of food animals were sacred and were treated with extreme respect. Most often they were sunk in a river or deep stream where no harm would come to them; thus the animals would continue to permit themselves to be killed.

Usually little ritual surrounded a gathering quest; it was not a chancy enterprise but required only knowledge and endurance to find the food. The Washo, as we have seen, ritually prepared their young women for this gathering in the Puberty Dance. The emphasis on activity, on walking and running great distances, on carrying a straight tall staff were ceremonial attempts to guarantee future success in the prosaic task of collecting. The pine nut, however, was the staple of the Washo diet; crop failure would condemn the people to near starvation. It was not surprising, then, to find ritual and taboo attached to this important resource. Tree limbs must never be damaged. A pine cone soaked in water and placed in a grove by an old man brought sufficient rain for a good crop. The most important pine-nut ceremony, however, was the *gumsaba*. The most complex of all Washo rituals, it brought together the largest number of people.[25] Both secular and sacred activities were woven together in an elaborate 10-day period.

The event was organized and conducted by a pine-nut leader, an elder who had dreamed about the nuts and prayed for them. At his summons the people congregated in the vicinity of the groves. As the people assembled, communal rabbit and deer hunts were carried on for 4 days. While the men hunted, the women who had a ritual bath each morning gathered fallen nuts and vegetables. The leader fasted and prayed for successful hunts and harvests. The hunts over and the gathering completed, the next 4 days were given over to games during the day and ritual and dancing at night. Teams of men played a form of hockey and the women played shinny, a form of stickball. Hand games were also played. The Washo, dedicated gamblers, bet on the outcome of all of them. The dancing was slow and decorous, the people singing as they moved in a great

---

[25]Ibid., pp. 34–36, and Downs, *The Two Worlds of the Washo*, pp. 22–24 provide detailed descriptions of the event.

circle carrying the tools used to gather and prepare the pine nuts. While they danced, the leader circulated among them, praying and urging the people to be kind to one another. At the end of the fourth day the game and vegetable foods were distributed among the families and a great fast was held. At its conclusion all bathed again and the leader declared the nuts ready to pick. The harvest then began in earnest and families spread through the groves to find their own trees.

The simple social and political organization, the desired interpersonal relations, the systematic search for food were all buttressed by the Washo belief system, reinforced in ritual. It served them well in their vast territory with its varying resources, no single one of which could sustain life. Their culture was the result of their ingenuity in deriving a living in challenging circumstances.

EPILOGUE

White adventurers appeared in Washo land in the early 1800s. Their initial impact was minimal; the Washo continued their foraging cycle wary of the newcomers. Perhaps as some historians suggest, the Washo guardedness of whites was heightened by their knowledge of the cannibalism to which members of the tragic Donner party were driven in 1846.

News of gold in California altered the situation. Attracted by prospects of riches, thousands trekked through the Great Basin on their way to the fields. Enterprising men built trading posts; others abandoned the gold quest and took over the most fertile land to farm. But in the vast territory there were perhaps 1000 intruders at most; Washo contact with them was limited and change was slow.

In 1858 silver was found in the mountains east of Washo land. California treasure seekers poured into the area. Mines were opened; towns sprang up. Theaters, saloons, opera houses, and prostitution flourished. In fewer than 3 years 10,000 head of live stock grazed on Washo land, and thousands of acres were cultivated along the Carson River. Washo traditional culture was doomed; game vanished, wild plant foods grew scarce, pinyon trees were cut for mine timbers and fuel, and sacred Tahoe waters were invaded. Washo adapted by laboring for whites, receiving payment in flour, beef, and other comestibles. White junk piles were gold mines for the Indians!

Ultimately the Washo settled part of the year in small communities adjacent to large farms or towns, becoming enmeshed in the white economy. Farming, mining, and lumbering depended upon Indian labor. For the Washo these were prosperous times, furthermore, most of the wage work was seasonal, allowing many to follow the traditional foraging cycle.

Circumstances changed again: wheat and cattle replaced vegetable culture. Sheep husbandry intensified. Opportunities for farm labor decreased and the Washo did not have adequate skills for the cattle and sheep industries. Indians and their labor became unnecessary to local whites. During this period recommendations to create a reservation were ignored in Washington. Life was precarious in the small Washo settlements. In the middle 1930s the peyote religion spread among the Washo, mitigating perhaps some of their despair. Although the cult was resisted by the Bureau of Indian Affairs and some of the Washo, it became firmly entrenched. What had lingered of the traditional belief vanished, and peyote became the dominant supernatural for the Washo.

Little remains of traditional Washo economics. Wage labor is their major source of security, and many travel miles searching for jobs. when the job ends they return to their barren communities. Some families have escaped the distressing hardships, but poverty and alcohol menace others. Yet, some basic themes persist. People share money and food; the land retains its mystique; and power endures in the universe.[26]

[26]The account of contemporary Washo life comes from Downs, *The Two Worlds of the Washo*, pp. 99–110.

Conclusion:
Part One

Traditionally the Cree, Washo, and Netsilik lived in harsh regions, deriving their subsistence from hunting, fishing, and gathering. Economic systems such as these are called either hunting-gathering or foraging. The Cree did little vegetable gathering, the Netsilik none. The Washo, on the other hand, relied heavily on wild vegetable foods and supplemented them with hunting and fishing. To make the most efficient use of their food resources, the three followed a migratory pattern. In none of the three groups was the wandering desultory. For each society there was a predictable cycle of movement varying with the seasons. To adapt to an environment by wandering required a flexible social organization; each of the three had this trait and were similar to one another in some respects. Leadership was informal and nonauthoritarian. The Washo and Netsilik had leaders for specific activities, a result, in part, of the need to organize large groups for hunting or fishing. Social control was diffuse and often based on supernatural beliefs and practices. The nuclear family or extended family was the only significant kinship structure. Fission and fusion characterized the three as large groups formed and then dispersed. The greatest difference among the three was the Netsilik's sophisticated technology.

The content of the belief systems varied, but the forms were similar.

There were no well-articulated theologies, no full-time religious practition-ers, and few large religious ceremonies. Individual ritual and taboo domi-nated and centered on life's major concerns.

We pointed out that the Cree were structurally atomistic and, to some degree, emotionally atomistic. With some qualifications of the concept the other two were also atomistic. The similarities among these three groups were the consequence of strategies to adapt to different but hostile envi-ronments.

PART TWO

PART-TIME GARDENERS

In aboriginal North America some populations combined hunting and gathering with agriculture. Their gardening was never as intensive as full-time agriculturalists, nor did it always feature the elaborate storage and preservation skills common to the latter group. For many of these part-time gardeners, the combination of farming with hunting and gathering required migration; cultivation was carried on in one location, foraging in another.

In the following chapters we will examine three tribes who combined hunting and gardening and journeyed between two zones in so doing. Why this mode of adaptation was followed is not always clear, nor were each tribe's reasons always the same. In two instances horticulture may have been grafted to a basic foraging economic system, a result of diffusion and culture contact. In the other circumstance, farming was likely an old subsistence pattern, but the people were close to an excellent game source too useful to ignore. In none of the cases did one type of subsistence totally supplant the other. The reasons for this we shall explore.

For two of the groups—the Havasupai and the Western Apache, both in Arizona—the farming appeared to have been borrowed from their long-time agricultural Pueblo neighbors and superimposed on their earlier hunting-gathering tradition. The other—the Mandan, living along the

Missouri River—combined more skilled agricultural techniques, suggesting a long-time practice, with bison hunting, another trait of great age. The latter skill became even more important with the Mandan's acquisition of horses.

These cultures participated in a mixed economy, two of them in the southwest, the other on the prairie. While their subsistence modes were structurally similar, they differed substantially in many cultural aspects, a consequence we shall argue of different environments and of different cultural history and tradition. Unlike the hunters and gatherers these folks were nowhere so closely bound by the limitations inherent in their ecosystem.

CHAPTER FIVE

The Havasupai of the Southwest

The American southwest—including southern Utah, southern Colorado, New Mexico, Arizona, and extreme west Texas—is a spectacularly beautiful land of endless variety. The Colorado plateau in the north is a vast windswept region; gashing through it are great canyons, and rising above it are jagged red cliffs and strange rock formations sculpted by cutting winds. Buttes thrust upward, like surrealistic monuments interrupting the boundless space. The surface is sliced by gulches, washes, and arroyos, dry most of the time, but always dangerous because of flash flooding during summer storms. Air, clean and thin, distorts distance. This ancient plateau vibrates with colors; red, purple, blue, and yellow fade into one another as dawn gives way to dusk. To the east of Grand Canyon in Arizona lies the Painted Desert and the Petrified Forest.

The only areas in the plateau below 5000 feet are the valleys and canyons cut by rivers and streams. The San Francisco Mountains, south of the Grand Canyon, rise above 12,000 feet. Further to the south the Mogollon Rim, nearly vertical cliffs of 1000 to 2000 feet, borders the plateau; the Rim, too, is visually startling and ecologically diverse. Rugged brush-covered mountains rise abruptly from the plains extending from the northwest to the southeast. Between them are dry valleys, some sparsely covered

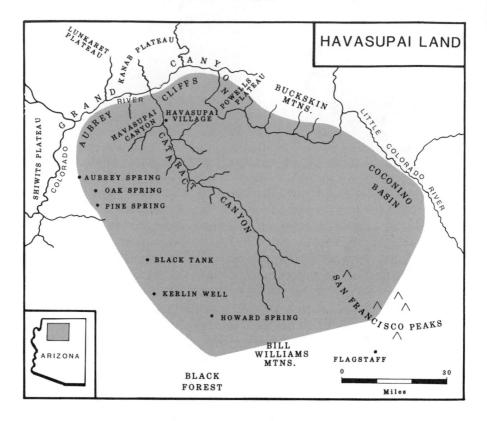

by arid vegetation. Others, nearly badlands, are littered with rocks small and large and sparse plant life. The central mountain area grades into the American desert, a great empty land of striking contrasts. Death Valley in California, almost a lunar landscape, is its most desolate portion. East to Arizona are the Mohave, the Colorado, and the Gila Deserts. Although they support somewhat different vegetation, they are similar in landscape. Open, flat, like a great sea, mountains always on the horizon, they are areas of mirage, of stinging sand storms and drying winds cracking lips and searing skin.

Through the southwest flow famous rivers: the Colorado, the Rio Grande, the Red, the Gila, and Salt. Others, smaller, flow intermittently fed by fearfully violent summer storms, or more gentle winter rains. In Arizona temperatures, precipitation, and humidity are largely the consequence of altitude. In general, rainfall is light and the humidity low. Summer daytime temperatures soar, but drop sharply at night. Winter cold ranges from 32° F in the desert to well below zero in the mountain and plateau region. Total rainfall varies from 2 to 5 inches in the desert to 25 to 30 in the mountains. A trace of snow may appear on the floor of the Grand

Canyon while 70 or more inches fall on the plateaus and mountains around it.[1]

Altitude also governs the vegetation, which ranges from subtropical to subalpine. If rain is abundant in December and January, desert, plateau, and mountain are awash with color in the spring. At high altitudes grow lupine, geraniums, violets, gentians, saxifrages, and hosts of other plants, some of them medicinal. Saguaro, cholla, Joshua trees, and other yuccas bloom in the desert spring joined by low-growing cactus. Always there are green shrubs, cacti, and sagebrush to color the desert regardless of season. Subalpine forests of spruce and fir grow on the San Francisco Mountains and the Kaibob plateau. Ponderosa pine stand below the subalpline forests, especially along the Mogollon Rim and on some of the taller central mountains. Pinyon and juniper are at lower dryer elevations. Chaparral, composed of a variety of small deciduous trees such as scrub oak, manzanita, and others, grows in lower altitudes. Gallery forests include water-seeking trees—cotton wood, mesquite, and willow; these follow along stream banks in the desert and low grassland areas.

White tail and mule deer wander the grassy areas of the Colorado Plateau, and smaller variants of them can be found in the less hospitable basin and desert areas where they are joined by herds of pronghorns. Mountain lion prey upon deer in the north. The southwest night is filled with cries of the coyote and, in the mountains, the timber wolf. Black bear roam the highlands, and peccary, sometimes called wild pig, root in the desert. Jackrabbits, cottontails, and an amazing array of rodents, the food of bobcats, are everywhere. The huge grizzly bear formerly haunted remote mountain wilderness. Slithering along the ground of plateau, basin, and desert are several species of rattlesnakes. They are joined in the desert by countless forms of lizards. The Gila monster and the edible chuckwalla are two of the best known.

Wheeling and gliding over mountain and desert were the California condor, the voracious and useful vultures, and golden and bald eagles. Prairie falcon and red-tailed hawks still search the land below for rodents and reptiles. Horned, barred, and screech owls fly silently through the night hunting nocturnal creatures. Wild turkeys, grouse, and western quail are game birds.[2]

This colorful land, both beneficent and harsh, is home to many Indian groups. Pima and Papago are in the desert areas, Navajo, Apache, Havasupai, and Yavapai wander the higher plateau country. Hopi, Zuni, Acoma, and Laguna live in villages ringed by cultivated acres. Many other

---

[1] Henry G. Alsberg and Harry Hansen, eds. *Arizona* (New York: Hastings House, 1966), pp. 9–11.

[2] Charles Vorhies, "Important Birds," in *Arizona and Its Heritage.* University of Arizona Bulletin VIII, 1936, pp. 83–97.

Pueblo villages are strung along the Rio Grande in New Mexico. In the past some groups were full-time farmers, others pastoralists, and others combined farming and hunting. As the land is one of great diversity and contrasts, so were its Indian peoples.

Living in northwest Arizona the Havasupai were a small population (300 in 1869) who combined foraging and gardening. They, like the Walapai and Yavapai, spoke a Yuman language belonging to the Hokan family. Precisely who the Havasupai (Blue Green Water People) were or where their origins lay are not entirely clear and scholars disagree.

Leslie Spier considered them separate although closely related to the nearby Walapai.[3] Linguistically they were almost identical and intergroup relationships were close; intermarriages were frequent and they held common viewpoints. He suggested that the Havasupai were an offshoot of the Walapai who took up agriculture and settled more permanently in Cataract Canyon. Despite their gardening, Spier argued that their culture was fundamentally a Great Basin variant with only a minor inclusion of Pueblo traits including farming.[4]

Henry Dobyns examined all available historical documents pertaining to Pai and Havasupai. He found that before the Anglo-American intrusion into the southwest there lived, in northwestern central Arizona, a group of Indians calling themselves Pai (The People).[5] Speaking one language, following common customs, and practicing tribal endogamy—marrying within a specified group, for example a tribe, village, caste, or race—they conceived themselves to be one people. Torn apart by the United States government, only two of several bands remain, the Havasupai and the Walapai. Dobyns observed that not only the Havasupai but all the Plateau Pai practiced canyon-bottom agriculture. Moreover, in many respects—social organization and leadership, hunting-gathering techniques—they differed sharply from the Basin people.[6]

The anthropologists Dobyns and Spier both recognized close connections between the Havasupai and the Walapai. Dobyns asserted that they were remnants of a much larger population. Spier viewed the Walapai as the parent body which probably did not engage in farming. The more important disagreement is in their diverse views on the relationship of Havasupai culture to others in the southwest. Spier saw it as closely related to the Great Basin—Shoshoni, Washo, and others—while Dobyns contended that Havasupai culture shows affiliations with the southern Yumans

---

[3]Leslie Spier, *Havasupai Ethnography.* Anthropological Papers, courtesy American Museum of Natural History vol. 29, 1928, pp. 97–98.

[4]Leslie Spier, "Problems Arising From the Cultural Position of the Havasupai," *American Anthropologist* 31(1919):217.

[5]Robert Manners, Henry F. Dobyns, and Robert C. Euler. *Havasupai Indians.* (New York: Garland Pub. Co., 1974), p. 183.

[6]Ibid., pp. 253–269.

and the Arizona Pueblo peoples. There yet are no definitive answers to the puzzle. Perhaps close attention to the implications of the historical data reviewed by Dobyns and the cultural material collected by Spier may guide readers to their own conclusions.

Havasupai territory lies in the Arizona Grand Canyon region, an area of terracelike plateaus separated from each other by faults and gorges. The highest is the Kaibob plateau, north of the Canyon and the Colorado River. West and north of the river are the Kanab, Uinkaret, and Shivits plateaus. South of the canyon and the river is the Coconino plateau bisected by a narrow canyon deeply worn by Cataract Creek[7] flowing north through rugged narrow canyon walls to join the Colorado. In traditional times, the Havasupai ranged over the plateau from the Colorado River gorge south to Bill Williams Mountain and the San Francisco peaks, west to Aubrey Cliffs, and eastward to the Little Colorado River. Their farmlands lay on the floor of Cataract Canyon. In the canyon are walls within walls. Red sandstone rises from 300 to 600 feet; about these walls and behind them thrusting upward is the outer canyon, a recalcitrant wasteland of white limestone, ascending to join the plateau.

Closed in by towering palisades the village was in the widest section of the canyon—in fact, it is still there—about one-half-mile wide across the 6 rugged, nearly impassable miles from the confluence of Cataract Creek and the Colorado. South of the village the creek explodes from springs in the canyon floor, careening for 2 or more miles through the village. The green fields irrigated with the intensely blue water, and the clumps of willow, cotton wood, and low growing plants bordering it, form an oasis contrasting vividly with the red and white precipices towering above. Access to the village was by way of a few narrow, tortuous, serpentine trails twisting and winding down through canyon walls from the plateau.

Average precipitation at Supai, largely rain, is 8.89 inches, the heaviest rains falling in February, July, and August. Canyon temperatures are 10 degrees higher year-round than those on the plateau, which average 30° F during the winter and 70° F in the summer. One-hundred-degree summer heat has been reported at the village, and Carma Lee Smithson observed that canyon humidity makes the warmer winter temperatures (40-50° F) uncomfortable.[8]

Botanically, the canyon floor and the plateau demonstrate extremes within the Sonoran Life Zone. Lower elevations on the plateau support sagebrush, yucca, mescal, and other edible seed plants. At higher levels grow juniper, cedar, and pinyon trees. Pine, fir, and spruce appear nearer

---

[7]Cataract Creek and Cataract Canyon are also referred to as Havasu Creek and Canyon in some literature.

[8]Carma Lee Smithson, *The Havasupai Woman*. Anthropological Papers, Department of Anthropology, University of Utah, vol. 38, 1959, p. 12.

the mountains. At lower reaches and on the canyon floor desert plants flourish: accacia and mesquite, Morman tea, agave, prickly pear, yucca, cacti, salt brush, and seed-bearing grasses.[9] Rabbit and rodents would have abounded near the Havasupai village, but most game animals—antelope, deer, mountain sheep—dwelled on the plateau. Although not often used for food, predators such as mountain lions, bobcats, coyotes, fox, and bear, competed with the Indians for food. While they were not always benevolent, plateau and canyon were home to the Havasupai, and hardships did not occur often. Havasupai technology and social organization were designed to make maximum use of the land, and belief in their gods supported them in the effort.

The Havasupais' mixed economy required two locations. From early spring until October the people occupied the canyon village, planting, cultivating, and harvesting crops. After the harvest most of them departed in family groups for the plateau's semipermanent camps. Until snow fell, they gathered wild plant foods and pinyon nuts. Hunting improved with the coming of the snow, for tracking animals was easier. When the temperatures rose and the plateau country began its spring bloom, they returned to the village.

Two types of village houses were constructed: a circular, dome-shaped thatched structure, sometimes dirt covered, or a rectangular one with thatched sides and dirt-covered roofs. Nearby were rectangular open-walled shades. Here people carried on sedentary work. Construction of houses and shades was men's work although women often helped with the thatching. The householders slept in slight depressions in the sand on cedar bark mats and rabbit-skin blankets with their heads toward the east. In this position they rested soundly free from troublesome dreams.[10] Close by the dwellings were sweat lodges, small conical airtight structures holding about four adults at a time.

During heavy rains when the dwellings along the creek were threatened by floods, people moved to small caves and rock shelters along the cliffs at the top of talus slopes. Here also were rodent-proof granaries and storage houses chinked and plastered with guano and sand mortar. It was here, also, that women and children fled to escape attacks of marauding Yavapai and Apache, constant threats to the serenity of canyon life.

Most of the arable land surrounding the village was cultivated and irrigated by ditches leading from dams on Havasu creek. The ditch and dam system was a simple one maintained by individual users. No regulations governed the use of water because the supply was ample and demand light. Two days before each corn planting fields were irrigated. When the crop was 6 or 7 inches tall it was watered, and watered once more when the corn tasseled. Men, women, and children worked together to sow the fields, each

[9]Ibid., pp. 12–13.
[10]Spier, *Havasupai Ethnography*, pp. 178–179.

Havasupai storehouses in canyon wall, circa 1900.
Smithsonian Institution National Anthropological Archives.

family planting as much corn as its fields allowed. Using a planting stick the farmer scratched a hole into which he dropped the seed, saying: "Grow good: when your stalk grows, grow tall: grow like the mythic corn." Chewing another kernel he blew it toward two white marks on the canyon wall which represented the two original ears given the people by culture heroes long ago.[11] The remainder of the field was sown in somewhat erratic rows. Between the corn hills people planted beans which climbed on the corn as they both grew. Other foods were squash, melon, and sunflower.

To break the monotony of a diet of dried foods, some green corn was picked, boiled, and made into bread, or roasted, but the main harvest commenced when the corn was hard and ripe. Women walked through the fields breaking off the ears and tossing them into burden baskets on their backs. In this they were assisted by other members of the family. Yards, the roofs of shades, and houses were crowded with drying corn, soon to be husked and some ears shelled. Much of it was stored in the granaries. Seed corn was carefully preserved in anticipation of another spring. Beans and squash not eaten also were dried and put away.

Summer days were not, however, inevitably filled with work; leisure time was plentiful after planting and before harvest. Families gathered at the creek to swim; men assembled at the sweat lodges to visit and gossip. Women settled under shades weaving baskets or shelling corn, but the more important reason was to comment on village affairs. The middle of

[11]Ibid., p. 102.

Havasupai women planting, circa 1900.
Smithsonian Institution National Anthropological Archives.

the afternoon found younger men and women engaged in gambling games, betting enthusiastically, the children scuffling and playing around them. Many young men raced their horses or trained young ones for competition. When dusk descended, families had their evening meals and the elderly retired. The young remained awake longer, but few walked very far abroad for fear of ghosts.

Before the villagers left the canyon, they held an annual harvest dance, usually at the end of August or September. Preparations for the dance began with singing practice. Most of the young men and some of their elders gathered at the dance ground as the moon rose. The older men sat around a fire while the younger stood in a circle around them and sang. One or more of the listeners called out advice or if satisfied commented, "Good." A day or so later the band chief ordered the dance grounds cleaned, and volunteers hurried to do it. Shades, too, were erected under which the women would cook. The first day of the dance people gathered in the late afternoon, more men than women arriving. While the women cooked, younger men and boys ran foot races or raced horses. Lineage headmen spread the food for the men; later more food was laid out for the women. Until the dancing began lineage headmen, the eldest male of each family line, delivered admonitory speeches to the assembled folk, who may or may not have listened attentively. Accompanying the moral discourses of which the headmen were fond, were prayers: "My ground, ground hear me, let us always live, I want always to live well, ground hear me."[12] Dancing began after dark. Despite the coaxing of the drummer and dance leader many people were hesitant to begin, but ultimately people rose and formed a circle. Girls held back until urged on by older women. They moved in a circle, three times with the singing, stopping in the original position, then beginning again. When the evening drew to an end, the people and tired children drifted back to their houses. The activities started again the fol-

[12]Ibid., pp. 263–264.

lowing afternoon with feasting and dancing. Again the chief and headmen exhorted the group to follow the way of the people. Suddenly, late in the evening, burst a masked figure from the bushes wearing short black pants, his torso and legs painted in white and black stripes. Carrying cottonwood branches in each hand, he whipped the laggards urging them to join the dancing which continued until after midnight. In the afternoon of the third day, young men again raced their horses, Hopi and Navajo visitors traded goods for buckskin, and the affair concluded with dances until dawn.

The harvest in, the dancing over, the families moved to the plateau. Trudging along the tortuous trails out of the canyon, they carried a supply of dried corn to supplement the wild foods they would collect throughout the fall and winter. Plateau houses were built in cedar thickets, facing south. Dwellings were similar to those in the canyon, but perhaps more thoroughly weatherproofed. Women and children searched the land for the great variety of edible plants: mescal, prickly pear cactus, mesquite pods, and yucca fruit. These ripened at different times and required extensive preparations to make them palatable. Pinyon nuts were valued, too, but unlike the Washo, the Havasupai had no ritual nor regulations attending the harvest.

Hunting, done all year-round, was far more important during the plateau phase. That it was viewed as important and its outcome uncertain was underscored by supernatural activities bound up in it. A highly useful but scarce amulet was a calculus (bladder stone) found in the stomach of a deer. Reported an experienced hunter:

> I always carry this . . . when hunting deer, antelope or mountain sheep, in order that they stand looking at me unsuspecting while I approach. When I have this I can secure plenty of big bucks; I need many buckskins. . . . Perhaps other men have them but I do not know. Not all deer have these in their paunches. I do not know how they are formed.[13]

Before a group of hunters departed for deer, a ritual was performed which had its charter in a myth of long ago. The big chief issued orders:

> We are all going to hunt. One of you should go a long way . . . just before it is daylight. There you should gather some old deer droppings in a pile and set them alight until they are entirely consumed. When the ashes are cool we will all go there.[14]

Upon arriving at the spot each touched his finger to the ashes and made a mark at the corner of his mouth. Turning to the rising sun the chief prayed:

[13]Ibid., p. 109.
[14]Ibid., pp. 109–110.

Sun, my relative, look at us, that is why I am here. You should give us your domestic animals, let us see them quickly, we want to kill some.

Sexual intercourse before a hunt condemned the venture to failure, therefore, hunters abstained for several days and bathed before the pursuit. Game drives were common; bowmen hid while others forced animals along narrow trails to be ambushed. Rabbits were also driven, but without the elaborateness typical of the Washo. Smaller animals were trapped or hunted individually. Men also hunted alone on the precipitous ledges and trails of the canyon, often a dangerous and sometimes fatal activity.

Economic and social life was embedded in the Havasupai family. The nuclear family, occasionally polygynous, was rarely apart from a larger group of relatives unless a specific subsistence activity dictated it. The larger group of kin was a patrilocal extended family composed of parents, their unmarried children, and their married sons. Married daughters, after briefly living near their own parents, moved to the homes of their husbands. Other people moved in and out of both the nuclear family and the extended family so that often a household did not fit the model. The extended families were grouped into patrilineages;[15] they and the extended family were the units in which individuals spent almost all their time. Women wandered about collecting together, gossiping, and sometimes bickering. Under the shades during the summer, they wove baskets and made pots. Men formed the larger hunting parties, made trading trips together to the Hopi or Navajo, and helped one another tan buckskin. All of them worked their landholdings together. A headman guided the communal activities of the lineage both by admonition and persuasion, and, in some cases, by command.

The position of headman was inherited, preferably from father to son. If however, there was no son or he did not demonstrate qualities of wisdom, courage, and oratorical skills, brothers or nephews were likely to succeed. In Pai society lineages were united into bands, all of whom took their names from the geographic areas which they inhabited. The Havasupai was the largest of them. The band chief came from the ranks of lineage headmen. He possessed to a greater degree all the character traits necessary for leadership. Spier stated that men became chiefs by prestige and renown based on their prowess in war, their prominence in intertribal relations, and their wisdom displayed in council.[16]

Trivial disputes or minor delinquencies were handled by informal means: gossip, teasing, or ostracism. Occasionally neighbors intervened: "When two men quarrel over a woman, bystanders interfere before either

---

[15]A lineage is defined as a group of people who trace their descent from a common ancestor, a male if patrilineal, a female if matrilineal.

[16]Spier, *Havasupai Ethnography*, p. 236.

comes to grief."[17] More serious conflicts were settled by headmen. "My father had two wives at once. One ran away with another man. The matter was taken before the chief, and he decreed that the seducer should pay my father a mare plus some money."[18] There were no reports of attempts to influence behavior through sorcery. But in a small population with authority vested in leaders, magical techniques are not apt to be a prominent device for social control.

In a band as small as the Havasupai, everyone was related in some way to almost everyone else, but only a fraction of the folk were recognized as blood relatives because most of the people sought mates within the band.[19] There were twenty-nine kinship terms which the Havasupai toddler mastered. A child referred to his mother's younger and older sisters by separate terms; for father's sisters there was only one regardless of age and it was distinct from maternal-aunt labels. Father's older and younger brothers were called by different terms. For mother's brothers regardless of age there was one term, and it differed from paternal uncles. Older and younger brothers were terminologically distinct as were younger and older sisters. The terms for parallel cousins were merged with brothers and sisters, distinguished by age and sex. Cross-cousins carried a different tag from parallel cousins. A child's father's parents and mother's parents were labeled differently. There were other kin distinctions to be learned, but these did not include most in-laws nor any people connected to him beyond his grandparent's generation, nor any of their descendants.

To find a mate, Havasupai looked outside of their patrilineage because blood relatives were tabooed. It is not at all clear whether cross-cousins wed. Dobyns asserted that cross-cousin marriage was preferred, but Spier did not record the practice.[20] That parallel cousins and cross-cousins are terminologically distinct suggests that cross-cousin marriages, most probably matrilateral, were permissable. If a suitable partner could not be found in the band, Walapai spouses were preferred; in much fewer numbers, mates came from the Hopi and Navajo. Often these marriages were brief.

Marriages were commonly instigated by the boy asking his father to broach the matter with his chosen's family. If her parents agreed and she was persuaded, the matter was concluded by a gift—buckskin, a horse,[21] or meat. Some young men, bolder than others, slipped silently at night into a girl's home, and unless she shrieked and rejected him, he stayed the bal-

---

[17]Ibid., p. 253.
[18]Ibid.
[19]Spier, *Havasupai Ethnography*, pp. 213–214.
[20]Manners, Dobyns, and Euler, *Havasupai Indians*, p. 240.
[21]Horses are reported to have been acquired in the late 1700s.

ance of the night. If her parents accepted the situation they were husband and wife. He later presented her family with a gift and moved in for a brief period of work or until a child was born. Eventually the young family settled with his people. Havasupai patrilocality was related in part to land ownership and control vested in the men and inherited through the patrilineage. Divorced or widowed women were, however, entitled to use of their paternal lands.

While there was a division of labor by sex it was not unduly rigid, and in many chores husband and wife assisted each other.[22] Hunting, however, was confined to men, and only they tanned hides and made them into clothes and moccasins for their families. Pottery and basketry were the province of women. Ideally the husband was the head of the house, but a wise spouse was rarely domineering. Husband and wife both delighted in the prospect of children and shared in observing ritual taboos. Neither ate meat in the later stages of pregnancy; they avoided looking at any grotesque human or animal lest the child resemble it. The expectant father never injured the legs of any game, nor did he kill a snake for this would cripple his child. A woman's husband and older women aided her in giving birth—often a trying experience—by applying pressure during each contraction. The baby delivered, mother rested on a bed of heated sand for 4 days. The new father slept with his head on a rock for the same period so that he awakened early to hunt or work his fields.[23]

As soon as the baby was washed, it was put on a cradle board made by its grandmother. Here it stayed most of the time until ready to take its first steps. Dangling from the rim of the cradle board was a cloth bundle containing its first hair and the dried umbilical cord. Until the child exhibited some personality characteristics, often not until age 5 or more, it had no name. Sooner or later a grandparent bestowed the first of many names it would carry during its lifetime.

Children learned largely through precept, although some sporadic instruction was given in hunting for boys and basketry and cooking for girls. But most of the teaching was contained in long speeches enjoining them to be industrious and wise.[24] To a girl it was said:

> When growing things are ripe you must gather them. That is what a woman does. When you are grinding for the first time, look for the rat's burrow and observe how he has piled up dirt at the entrance; then when you grind corn make your pile of meal a little larger than that. . . . When you marry do not loiter about the house, but bustle around gathering plenty to grind so you will not starve. . . . When you are married and have a camp of your own, do not be

[22]Smithson, *The Havasupai Woman*, pp. 124–125.
[23]Spier, *Havasupai Ethnography*, p. 322.
[24]Ibid., pp. 322–323.

Havasupai woman with child in gathering basket, circa 1890-1900.
Smithsonian Institution National Anthropological Archives.

angry if someone comes to your house, and do not fail to give them some of whatever food you have. Do not be angry with your husband's relatives. . . .

To a small boy:

You will have to gather armsful of wood or collect water when you are playing about, do things just as you will when you are grown. You should now hunt rabbits so that later when you are older and hunt deer, you will be able to kill them. . . . If you are lazy you will not have anything; you will be poor. . . . Do not sleep after dawn; wake as soon as the sunlight appears. Run toward the dawn. . . . Do not walk, run. . . . If you do not wash every morning you will miss seeing a deer. . . . If you live as we tell you, you will live to be an old man. . . .

Quiet affection and fondling were also part of an Havasupai child's life, and grandparents were exceptionally indulgent and talented tellers of tales. Punishment, rare, was reserved for extreme unruliness.

Rituals associated with adolescence were most pronounced for girls. At the beginning of the first menstruation, a girl's mother bathed her, washed her hair, and painted her face and body. Wearing a buckskin dress made especially for the occasion by a man, she ran toward the sun at dawn returning to a shelter built for her by her father. Here she lay on a bed of blankets over heated sand and stones. At sunset she arose and raced to the west. During the night an elderly woman sat with her singing and talking to keep her awake. This routine continued for 4 days and nights, during which she ate no meat, refrained from scratching with her fingernails, and at her mother's command got up to perform assigned tasks so that she not become shiftless. In subsequent menstrual periods the meat taboo and interdictions against scratching were observed, and women avoided smiling. To smile would encourage premature wrinkling.[25]

Only a minor custom was celebrated for the maturing boy, connected with hunting. When he killed his first deer alone and unaided, he left it and sought out his grandfather. The old man returned to the site with him, skinned the deer, butchered it, and packed the carcass home. There grandfather consumed the cooked liver. These ceremonies—which were not public events—marked a step on the way to maturity, although at least for the boy marriage was 5 or more years away.

Havasupai life, while not entirely free from difficulty and uncertainty, was not stressful. Crop failure was rare, and preservation and storage techniques were sufficient to provide supplementary food during the winter hunting and gathering cycle. Insecurity and distrust did not pervade interpersonal relationships. Yet they had questions and fears about dimensions of their life which they were not always able to control, and so supernatural beliefs, rituals, and shamans provided answers and attempts to influence events. Havasupai religious ideology was not highly systematized, however, nor was there always agreement among the people on the nature of the supernatural.

Some ritual, as we have seen, attended deer hunting; gardening also evoked ceremony, both individual and group. In addition to the harvest dance and planting rites, men participated in masked dances. These—held for good luck, rain, and for prosperous crops—could be organized by any man who felt the need, and others joined him. But group rituals were not as prominent in Havasupai life as were individual ones. Men prayed to rocks, trees, water, air, and wind, saying: "We wish to be like the earth, or rock, to live to be old." At sunrise they beseeched the sun:

> Sun, my relative, be good coming out, do something good for us, make me work so I can do anything I wish in the garden I hoe, I plant corn, I irrigate. You, sun, be good going down at sunset, we lay down to sleep, I want to feel good while I sleep. You come up. Go on your course many times, make good things for us men. Make me always the same as I am now.

At the source of springs on the plateau and upper levels of the canyon men placed prayer sticks encircled with corn meal and prayed:

> Spring I drink, plenty more come, I feel glad I use it to drink. Prayerstick feathers I put in spring, look at it plenty more come.[26]

When crises occurred which the Indian was ill equipped to handle or

[25]Smithson, *The Havasupai Woman*, p. 73.
[26]Spier, *Havasupai Ethnography*, pp. 285–286.

his own efforts had failed he had recourse to shamans. Shamans received their power through inheritance and dreaming and had spirits to assist them in their undertakings. Havasupai shamans were specialists: some controlled the weather, some cured, and others dealt only with snake bites, fractures, or wounds. The curing shaman was by far the most important for it was in this realm that people had the least control. Illness was caused by spirits: The creator of the deer went into a man who was profligate with deer; that of a dead shaman entered the body of one who mocked him; hawk spirits penetrated the body of an unborn child. Ghosts and taboo infringements also brought about sickness.

Relatives of the sick person called in the shaman. Kin and friends crowded into the house of the afflicted. There they shouted encouragement while the shaman sang accompanied by a gourd rattle. Later he sent his spirit into the victim's body to uncover the cause of the malady. Once revealed, the shaman waved an eagle feather over the patient and sucked out the offending spirit. Such curing ceremonies often lasted for 4 nights. Should he fail to effect a cure another shaman was engaged. Spier describes such a situation:

> Little Jim sucked Jess' chest and neck. Although he made no incision he spat out blood. He said Jess was suffering from a spirit sent by the being who made everything, deer, rabbits, and mountain sheep. Later that summer Dr. Tommy announced the same opinion, for he too sent his spirit into Jess. . . .[27]

However effective shamans may have been, people died. Their souls which resided in their hearts left and went to the north, drawn by the mythical being *Pagiy'ga*. The deceased, placed with his head toward the northwest, was washed; a relative painted his face and dressed him in good clothes. People congregated the second day to wail, lamenting his passing. A funeral party bore him to a pyre where he was cremated; his belongings were burned with him, and one or more good horses killed. The house in which he died was also burned; his survivors built another not too distant from it. Farmlands used by the departed lay idle for a year. People avoided referring to the dead by name, resorting to circumlocution to talk of them. Should they be careless in this, souls might return as ghosts, portents of calamity.

The Havasupai lived in an environment in which they practiced a mixed economy. While the fall migration was eagerly anticipated and no doubt added variety to life, Manners and others have concluded that it was necessary because the farm produce was not sufficient to sustain them year-round.[28] The necessary transhumant existence (the practising of one economy in one place, then moving to subsist somewhere else) affected sev-

[27]Ibid., p. 280.
[28]Manners, Dobyn, and Euler, *Havasupai Indians*, pp. 84–91.

eral aspects of their culture in significant ways. Village life fostered tribal cohesiveness and identity; land use encouraged some sort of lineage or extended-family structure. That it was patrilocal instead of matrilocal is not so easily explained; it is possible that the hunting cycle encouraged patrilocality. Familiarity with a territory in which a hunter grew up probably ensured greater success than he would have had in the more distant and unfamiliar region of his spouse's family. While nonaggressive foragers managed well without centralized power, orderly village life required stronger authority, so we find lineage headmen and a chief. That the Havasupai were often victimized by the Yavapai is an additional reason for institutionalized leadership. Religious ritual centering around subsistence was present but not highly elaborated, a phenomenon related to a reasonably reliable food supply. With effective techniques to farm and irrigate, skill in hunting and collecting, Havasupai culture was well designed to make good use of two environments. Their life was sustained through this dual environment until white incursions substantially altered it.

EPILOGUE

Until the 1700s Havasupai had few contacts with whites. Their canyon home held no attraction and the plateau seemed infinite. Yet the isolation was temporary. With the end of the Civil War and the Apache "pacification," the Arizona territory beckoned whites in search of land and freedom from eastern restraints. Cattle ranching gradually encroached upon the Havasupai tableland and eventually affected their traditional winter rounds. But it was not until the late nineteenth century that major changes started. The first, and the one with the most lasting consequences, was the establishment of a reservation in Cataract Canyon with only a few square miles of plateau territory.

Soon a farmer and a school teacher were dispatched by the federal government to instruct the people in farming techniques and the children in basics like literacy. Cultural transformation was inevitable; school kept the children in the canyon for the winter and the plateau restrictions further discouraged the exodus. The traditional subsistence patterns eroded, and the Havasupai came to depend more and more on economic forces beyond their control.

In later years the National Park Service built a village near the Grand Canyon Park. Havasupai employed by the Park Service or lessees live here during the summer season. Some men raise cattle on the limited reservation range. The U.S. Forest Service issues annual grazing permits for the Kaibob National Forest. Cattle raising is not very profitable, and except for a small number of men employed year-round by the Park and Forest Services, tourism is the main source of cash for the people.

Mounted precariously on Havasupai horses and mules, stout-hearted tourists follow Indian guides down the twisting serpentine train to the canyon village. Once there, however, there is little to buy; traditional artifacts are few and accommodations poor. They return without having spent much more than the cost of the trip.[29]

The Havasupai are not utterly destitute, but they live in severely straitened circumstances, surrounded by the beauty of the land that once was theirs.

[29]The description of contemporary Havasupai life comes from Bertha P. Dutton, *The Rancheria, Ute, and Southern Paiute Peoples.* (Englewood Cliffs, NJ: Prentice-Hall, Inc., 1976), pp. 48–50.

CHAPTER SIX

The Western Apache of the Southwest Desert

The origins of the Apachean people lie in the far North, sometime between 1000 and 1500 AD. Athabaskan-speaking people wandered south from the boreal forests of central and western Canada. The routes they followed and the time spent reaching the southwest are yet to be established. But by the end of the sixteenth century they had fanned out from central Arizona through a small portion of New Mexico to northwestern Texas and northern Mexico. Who first called them Apache is not clear, but during the turbulent period of Anglo incursions into the southwest, troups and settlers alike dreaded the fierce and implacable Apache. Descriptions of their truculence abound in history books, some factual, some exaggerated; however, little attention is paid to Apache reasons for resisting "pacification." Moreover, texts do not distinguish among all the groups who were labeled Apache. Grenville Goodwin separated them into six divisions based upon territorial, linguistic, and cultural differences: Jicarilla Apache, Lipan Apache, Kiowa-Apache, Mescalero Apache, Chiricahua Apache, and Western Apache.[1] While the Navajo are usually considered a distinct group, Goodwin classified them as Apache because, linguistically and culturally, they were similar. Based on linguistic analysis, anthropologist Harry Hoijer

---

[1]Grenville Goodwin, *The Social Organization of the Western Apache*. (Chicago: University of Chicago Press, 1942), p. 1.

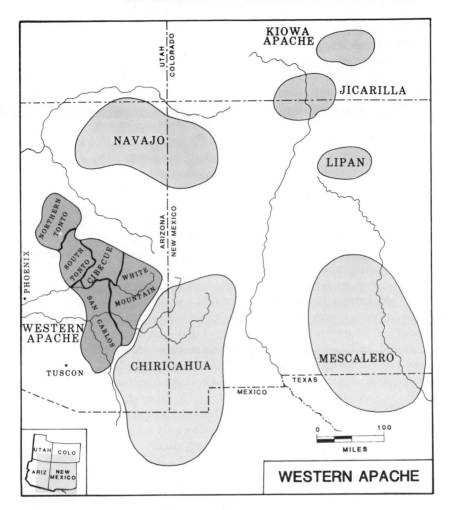

established two major divisions: The Eastern group included the Jicarilla, Lipan, and Kiowa-Apache. The Navajo, Chiricahua, Mescalero, and Western Apache comprised the Western.[2] The Western Apache were further subdivided into five groups occupying contiguous territories in eastern and central Arizona.[3] Keith Basso has stated that altogether the Western Apache exploited a region of nearly 90,000 miles and numbered about 4,000 people.[4]

The subtribal groups, as Basso calls them, were the White Mountain

[2]Harry Hoijer, "The Southern Athabascan Languages," *American Anthropologist* XL(1938):86.

[3]Goodwin, *The Social Organization of the Western Apache*, pp. 2–8.

[4]Keith Basso, *The Cibecue Apache: Case Studies in Cultural Anthropology.* (New York: Holt, Rinehart and Winston, 1970), pp. 1–2. Copyright © 1970 by Holt, Rinehart & Winston, Inc. Used by permission of CBS College Publishing.

Apache, the San Carlos Apache, the Cibecue Apache, the Southern Tonto, and the Northern Tonto Apache. The eastern-most unit was the White Mountain Apache who traversed an area between the Pinaleno Mountains to the south and the White Mountains on the north. The San Carlos people occupied the foothills of the Santa Catalina Mountains and both sides of the San Pedro River. North of the Salt River to above the Mogollon Rim and bounded on the west by the Mazatzal Mountains lay the territory of the Cibecue. The Southern Tonto roamed the Mazatal Mountains. The Northern Tonto lived along the northern waters of the Verde river and ranged north from there.

These subtribal groups, although they intermarried occasionally, regarded themselves as distinct entities and never formed a united political body. Each group protected its clearly delineated hunting land and killed or expelled intruders. Relationships with other Indian groups varied. They traded with Zuni and Hopi, and perhaps the Yavapai, and they raided the Pima, Papago and, Maricopa.

The Western Apache lived in the ecologically diverse land common to the Great Southwest: Jagged mountains thrust upward; serpentine canyons divide plateaus; and arid deserts contrast with well-watered valleys. In some areas winter temperatures reach zero; summer heat can top 100 degrees. Animal and plant life vary with terrain and elevation.

Like the Havasupai the Western Apache practiced a mixed hunting-gathering and horticulture economy; their environment and farming technology did not permit sole reliance on crops. Unlike the Havasupai, however, they had no permanent villages, and much of the year found them on the move. The nearest thing to permanence were home localities, areas adjacent to farming sites. Only farms were individually or family owned; all other band territory was considered communal and was open to all members for hunting and collecting. Farms could be loaned to others and were inherited by sons or daughters and from either parent's side of the family.

Seasonal activities shaped the life of the people and caused fission and fusion within local groups.[5] In April gathering parties formed to harvest mescal, often traveling great distances. After they had collected and prepared it, they trudged back laden to home localities. Early in May a chief bestirred himself and lectured the people in camps around him: "You should go to your farms. Build up your ditch and dam well, and put in your corn carefully."[6] He often went to his farm, providing an example for his followers. People were free to follow his urgings or to ignore them for the chief did not command, he advised. Usually within 10 days all the families arrived at their farms and set about preparing for planting. Irrigation ditches were cleaned and repaired by all who used the water, often under

---

[5]The material on yearly cycles is adapted from Goodwin, *The Social Organization of the Western Apache,* pp. 155–160.
[6]Ibid., p. 156.

the direction of "ditch bosses," old men who possessed agricultural ritual and were skilled farmers. In early July when the corn was 6 to 8 inches high, some departed to harvest saguaro in the Gila River valley. A few old people remained at the farms to care for the crops.

The most important wild food, acorns, ripened in late July, and at this time all moved north to the acorn grounds frequently under the direction of their local chief. For 4 or more weeks they gathered acorns; after each family had a sufficient supply it either waited for others or returned alone to the home locality and the farms. Some people moved back south for mesquite. Domestic crops ripened in September, and the chief spoke again leading his people back to harvest crops. After they were in, pinyon nuts and juniper berries growing not far from home sites were ready to be collected and stored. Although men hunted sporadically all year, late fall and early winter was the time for deer hunting—usually along the foot of the Mogollon Rim and the White Mountains. Some families wintered near their farms, while others moved south to escape the harsh winter temperatures; all occasionally traveled to visit relatives.

The Apache and the Havasupai were transhumants; each farmed in one location and each left their farms for a major part of the year to hunt and forage. The Apache, however, saw another source of meat—raiding— and exploited it vigorously. Five to ten men would form parties to steal domestic animals from the Mexican settlements in southern Arizona and northern Mexico. Pima and Papago livestock were also taken; less often the Apache preyed on the Navajo for sheep and goats. Horses, the main animals taken from the Mexicans, were used for food as well as transportation. Apache raided when the food supply of a local group was nearly exhausted, usually at the urging of an older woman.[7]

> Our people used to go on raids down into Mexico to bring back horses, mules, burros, and cattle. This is the way we used to take the property of the Mexicans and make a living off them. There were no white people to take things from in those days. . . .
> Besides going to Mexico, sometimes we went over towards Mogollon Mountain where we fought with the Navajo and took their sheep and horses.[8]

The five western subtribes were divided into bands, usually not more than four, each having its own hunting land, and only under extreme conditions of hunger did they trespass on other's land. The bands were composed of the most important constituents of Apache society, local groups. Basso has explained that "each local group had exclusive rights to certain farm sites and hunting localities, and each was headed by a chief who di-

[7]Grenville Goodwin, *Western Apache Raiding and Warfare*. Keith H. Basso, ed. (Tuscon: University of Arizona Press, 1971), p. 16. Permission to quote given by University of Arizona Press.

[8]Ibid., p. 43.

rected collective enterprises such as raiding parties, food gathering expeditions, farming projects and activities involving other local groups and tribes."[9]

Two to six family clusters or *gotas* made up the local groups. These were large matrilocal extended families comprised of nuclear families, each held together by the presence of a female member who was a sibling or descendant of an older woman in the family cluster. A matrilocal rule of residence prevailed but there were often departures from it. Frequently a married son continued to live in the company of his mother or sisters. Often the family cluster was augmented by the presence of a son-in-law's widowed parent. In addition to matrilocality the Apache observed a matrilineal rule of descent; therefore, the *gota* contained a matrilineage which belonged to one of the many Apache matriclans. Said Grenville: "The Apache readily identifies a family cluster by its nuclear clan and will often say, 'the people in that cluster are of such and such a clan,' although it may be composed of members of several clans. He is correct, for by mentioning the nuclear clan of the unit he emphasizes a bond holding the unit together, a core about which it is built."[10]

The nuclear and extended family was the bastion of security for Apaches. Nuclear families seldom lived apart from the *gota*. Individuals were reluctant to travel very far alone because enemies or dangerous animals might beset them or accidents and injuries befall them. Women always gathered wild foods in concert and solitary men never hunted. Cooperation between households made the labors of obtaining food lighter and ensured sharing of resources. Grenville observed that ". . . the unfortunate were carried along by the fortunate, the unskilled by the skilled, the lazy by the industrious, the unfit by the fit."[11] The apprehension of the Apache at being alone is easily understood when viewed against these values of cooperation, support, and sharing. In speaking of Anglo residential habits an Apache said:

> It maybe all right for white people to live that way; they seem to like it. But it would not do for us. We can't live off alone. It isn't right. Other people would talk and say there was something wrong with a family who did this; that they must be trying to conceal something or they were doing something bad.[12]

A *gota* was led by a headman, usually not a member of the core clan he most often had married in. As he matured and demonstrated leadership qualities, he assumed the status. Acting on his advice and directions, members engaged in farm labor, food gathering, or other activities necessary to

[9]Basso, *The Cibecue Apache*, p. 5.

[10]Goodwin, *The Social Organization of the Western Apache*, p. 128. Much of the ethnographic data on Apache social and domestic life are drawn from Goodwin, pp. 123–569.

[11]Ibid., p. 123.

[12]Ibid., p. 124.

existence. He also arbitrated disputes, reviewed prospective marriages, and lectured his followers:

> Do not be lazy. Even if there is a deep canyon or a steep place to climb, you must go up it. Thus, it will be easy for you to get deer. If any of you go out hunting this morning, tomorrow, or the following day, look after yourselves while you are alone. When you trail deer you may step on a rock. If the rock slips from under you, you may fall and get hurt. If there is a thick growth of trees ahead of you, don't go in it. There might be a mountain lion in a tree ready to attack you. Always go on the upper side or the lower side of such a clump. If there is thick brush ahead, there may be a bear or some wolves in it. Go above or below it. When you trail a deer and you come upon him, if he should start to run, don't run after him for a deer can run faster than you, and you cannot overtake him. You women who go out to gather acorns and walnuts, don't go alone. Go in a party of three or four. Look after each other. If you get a mescal head ready to cut off, don't stand below it while you cut, it will roll on you, and its sharp points will stick into you. If you cut it off and are about to chop away the leaves from the head, don't open your eyes wide. Close them halfway so the juice won't get in them and blind you.[13]

While a headman could and did command, his control depended upon people's willingness to listen to him, for he lacked any real authority. A portion of his influence derived from his wealth. Affluence and the dignity associated with his status freed him from some kinds of menial work. Others whom he paid worked his land; poor relatives looked to him for support. Most people deferred to him. Wives of headmen shared the respect accorded their husbands. Some women, almost invariably the wife or widow of a subchief or headman, were subchiefs. A female subchief was a paragon of virtue. Unlike her husband, however, no task was beneath her. She industriously engaged in household chores: child care, basket making, farming, and gathering. Because of her energy she, too, became wealthy and thus generous. Both were requisite to her position. While she seldom addressed the people, she spoke at war dances encouraging the men in the undertaking. Other women followed her on collecting forays and, however patiently, suffered her lectures on the need for diligence in all domestic affairs.

Family clusters, we noted, formed the local groups. These were headed by a chief called a true chief if he held the position by virtue of inheritance; if selected from a group of headmen, he was the chief but enjoyed less prestige. Regardless of the path to chieftainship, the incumbent had to demonstrate qualities of leadership. Older men observed the behavior of boys to identify future leaders. Speaking of a chief a man told Goodwin: "He was a chief even while playing with other boys."[14] When the years exacted their costs in fading mental and physical strength, the chief's

[13]Basso, *The Cibecue Apache*, p. 9.
[14]Ibid., p. 173.

Western Apache elder, circa 1882.
Smithsonian Institution National Anthropological
Archives.

prestige diminished: Seeing this, he accepted the need for a successor, say-ing:[15] "My people, I am too old, too weak, I am just about to go. You should pick out one of yourselves to be the next chief. I have done well for you, but my life has almost passed by." The new chief was chosen by subchiefs, headmen, women chiefs, and other prominent men and women. An older wise man counseled him on the duties of the office and instructed him in the holy powers required, horse and cattle power, and war and enemy power. Installation of a chief lasted 4 nights featuring feasting and speeches. A shaman sang particular songs over him as a blessing:

> My maternal uncle became chief this way. They talked for four nights and put him in. A man spoke to him, saying, "Be smart, treat people well and give to the poor. Help the men along. Always talk well to them. Help the women and kill a horse for us every so often." Then a rich man gave him a bundle of arrows, saying, "Keep these. Other men have arrows, so you shall have them."
> Another gave him a lance, and another a blanket.[16]

In addition to being exemplary a chief had numerous and arduous responsibilities. He gave to the poor, sponsored communal ceremonies, and arbitrated quarrels. Anyone undertaking an important activity—economic, social, or religious—consulted the chief. As a rule a chief re-

[15]Ibid.
[16]Ibid., p. 176.

mained somewhat apart from the people and maintained his dignity by his reserve. He and his wife taught their children to comport themselves with dignity and confidence. His daughters were composed and unafraid. His sons were fearless, dignified, and self-confident. Some children, of course, were not as talented or skilled as their chiefly parents or their siblings.

All Apache belonged to one of sixty-two named matrilineal clans. These were not, like the bands, local groups, and *gotas*, geographically distinct. Clan members lived in such units all over Apache territory. Clan members assisted one another, avenged insults or murder, and controlled marriage. Intraclan marriages were forbidden although young people were sometimes encouraged to select a mate from their father's clan.

The Apache clans were grouped into a larger category called a *phratry*.[17] The phratry included clans the Apache recognized as closely or distantly related. Members of closely related clans could not marry and were expected to extend help to one another. Closely related clans were identified as a section. Related clans belonged to another section; again intermarriage was proscribed and mutual obligations were characteristic. Distantly related clans usually meant that each was related to a common third clan. Members might marry and were not as obligated to one another for support.

This somewhat elaborate social organization established relationships among all the Western Apache regardless of where they lived. It guaranteed mutual aid and perhaps checked any divisive tendencies inherent in the local group isolation. Moreover it enlarged the potential number of participants in activities requiring the cooperation of large numbers of people.

Marriage and family formed the root of this social organization. For an Apache not to wed was inconceivable. Men needed women to gather wild foods, to prepare farm products, and to provide them with children. Without a husband, a woman had no meat, no horses, or other prizes from raids, and no children to add to her lineage.

Apache adolescents were characteristically self-conscious and remained so until marriage. They seldom looked at or spoke to one another: ". . . When together, young people of opposite sex even refrained from scratching their bodies, and both (especially boys) would rather sit in great discomfort than excuse themselves to urinate."[18] Most often girls made the initial overture toward courtship; occasionally a more courageous young man took the first steps. Any sort of physical liberties were highly improper and a girl who allowed them was immodest. Young people often received lectures from their elders admonishing them to exhibit proper decorum:

[17]The description of the phratry organization is based on Basso, *The Cibecue Apache*, pp. 9–11.

[18]Goodwin, *The Social Organization of the Western Apache*, pp. 285–286.

> You are at that age now and getting old enough to marry. We want you to behave and not act crazy, running about after boys. If you don't do this, you won't be worth anything. But if you behave yourself, then some man, the one who will marry you, will treat you right, and you will have plenty in your own camp and live well. This is what will happen if you do as I tell you and do not let anyone touch your body.[19]

Grandparents offered additional advice warning their grandchildren not to flirt with their own relatives. Through this and other ways youths became aware of eligible mates. Doubtlessly it occurred, but the Apache distinctly disapproved of premarital sexual intercourse and there was a special term for those who had engaged in it.

If young people after a long time of subtle gestures to one another at dances or parties became serious, they employed their cross-cousins to carry messages back and forth and to set up assignations. Go-betweens attended early meetings but soon departed, leaving the courting pair sitting several feet apart smiling at each other. In subsequent meetings they lost their shyness, flirted, and perhaps spoke of marriage.

Marriages between blood relatives or clan members were viewed with extreme horror, and all knew that disaster would befall anyone who breached these exogamous rules. Whether the marriages were arranged by the parents or resulted from courtship—both occurred—gifts between the two families were exchanged and other relatives were consulted for advice and approval. They, too, offered gifts to the girl's family: a gun, horse, or blankets. These varied in value and depended in great measure upon the social status of the families. Her kinsmen, if they approved, provided items for return gifts to his family. Fathers often solicited local chiefs for counsel with respect to the forthcoming nuptials of their sons or daughters. Occasionally consent was withheld either by relatives or a chief (gifts were then returned to the donors).

No elaborate ritual accompanied the marriage. When all parties were agreed, the girl went to the boy's camp at dark accompanied by his mother or sister; she most often slept with them. Leaving at dawn she returned to her home to spend the day, going once more to his camp at dusk. This coming and going continued until her mother built a *wickiup*, a conical dwelling made of grasses and shrubs, for the newlyweds in her *gota*. Some couples moved into their *wickiup* alone, but more often a young man and woman (cross-cousins of the wedded pair) accompanied them to ease the disquietude they would have endured at being alone. Sleeping together, the bride lay by the wall, next to her lay the female companion, the male next to her, and on the outside edge of the bed slept the bridegroom. This arrangement might continue for several weeks. Only after their companions ceased to join them at night was the marriage consummated, and often

[19]Ibid., p. 289.

Western Apache family in front of wickiup, circa pre-1891.
Smithsonian Institution National Anthropological Archives.

not immediately. As Goodwin records it: "Parents advised their son not to try this for the first few nights but to wait until she was more at ease with him. Both would be almost paralyzed with shyness, but it was the youth who was expected to attempt the first advances and who was advised concerning them, not the girl."[20]

Gradually the couple grew accustomed to one another and moved into the status of adult members of the family cluster as they formed an economic unit. The husband hunted with weapons he had made, skinned and butchered the game, and brought it home. He went on raids and fought in battles. To him his wife and children looked for protection. She occupied herself with domestic tasks: collecting wild food, preparing meat and storing it, gathering firewood, as well as building the *wickiup* and *ramada* (a rectangular structure used as a shade in summer for domestic activities). In this task her husband helped with the heaviest labor. Each of them owned the "tools of their trade." The house belonged to the wife as well as did most of the food. The Apache husband was titular head of the family, but the degree to which either spouse dominated was a consequence of individual personality.

Of course, not all marriages lasted, and divorce was easy to obtain. Either spouse could leave—often after a quarrel—not to return. Frequently families encouraged or forced divorce, taking the action because they judged that the marriage was not succeeding. Because a wife owned the dwelling she could force her husband to leave by placing his belongings outside of it, but only a strong-willed woman could effect this. Most often the wife repaired to her parents' home, waiting until her husband collected his belongings and departed. The husband, too, by decamping on a hunting trip and taking all his essential equipment—bows, arrows, and ceremo-

[20]Ibid., p. 328.

nial property—but leaving horses and cattle, indicated that the marriage had ended. Children of divorce most frequently stayed with their mother. Unless the partners were old or in some way undesirable they remarried, but without the elaborate gift exchange which was a part of the first marriage (and without the reserve and embarrassment).

While not frequent, polygyny was practiced largely by rich men who seldom had more than four wives. Many however were satisfied with one wife. The Apache did not disapprove of the institution but it amused them and practitioners of polygyny were often teased. An old man, the husband of six women, used to stain his face. Seeing this people said:

> "Well, you must be out after another woman again." To which he would good naturedly answer, "The time was when I visited all six wickiups every night, but now I only visit four. I am getting old. I'm sort of going downhill now. . . ."[21]

But for newlyweds, Apache spouses were nondemonstrative in public. Holding hands or embracing was avoided for fear of appearing ridiculous. A man never showed affection for his wife or used endearing terms; such sentimentality was counter to everything he had been taught. For a woman to engage in public affection was also unseemly as she would humiliate her husband. Yet on occasion such decorum was suspended, and a wife might put her arm around her mate's waist; but only if he yielded in pleased embarrassment.[22] Although restraint marked much of marital comportment, the death of a partner occasioned less inhibited behavior. In fact people, especially in-laws, expected a proper display of sorrow. Survivors cut their hair off, wore old and shabby clothing, avoided parties and, most especially, ignored the opposite sex. Men mourned for almost a year. Women grieved for one or more. Lamenting showed one's grief and exhibited respect for the deceased's kinfolk, who carefully monitored the activities of the bereaved. At the close of the mourning interlude the widow or widower was expected to remarry into the maternal lineage of the departed. Irresponsible conduct caused a widower to be shunned by his in-laws; a widow suffered such indignities as having the tip of her nose cut off

Apaches recognized six life stages—babyhood, childhood, youth, young adulthood, middle age, and old age. Marriage conferred the status of young adulthood; it was further affirmed by the birth of the first child. There seemed to be no preference for the sex of the firstborn, yet a family without girls suffered for there was no one to bring son-in-laws and gifts to the family cluster.

Newlyweds were under constraints of a variety of taboos during their first year. Entering a field of growing squash would cause the fruits to

[21]Ibid., p. 352.
[22]Ibid., pp. 336–337.

wither. During this first year leg-muscle meat of game was forbidden; to eat it was supposed to cause cramps during pregnancy and danger to the fetus. Young people, married or not, were enjoined against eating quail eggs or jackrabbits. Consuming the eggs caused their children to have freckles. The rabbit flesh made children susceptible to an illness which abided in the animal.

Babies were not named until they survived the first several months. It was not prudent to name an infant who might yet die. Children often received names from grandparents or other older interested people.

> Names bestowed by old people and by those who have lived free from misfortune and sickness all their lives are considered lucky, for the child may be likewise blessed. On the other hand, a name offered by a person who has suffered ill health or been otherwise unlucky is tactfully refused by the child's parents. . . . No payment is received for a good name but the child's parents may show their appreciation on some later occasion by a gift. . . .[23]

Babies until they were toddling spent most of their time on cradleboards. The first, regarded as temporary, was made by a maternal relative of the mother. Fathers, relatives, or even the mother made the permanent carrier, which was larger and sturdier than the first. Amulets dangled from the hood. A squirrel tail guaranteed ability to climb; a striped pine cone assured protection from injury when falling from a tree. A bear paw—a source of great power—kept all illness at bay. After the umbilical cord sloughed off it was wrapped in turkey down or buckskin and fastened to the inside of the carrier close to the baby's head. Later the mother buried it, if it were a boy's, in the track of a horse or deer. He would then, when older, obediently go for horses or become a skilled hunter. Placing a girl's in a mescal plant or depositing it in a cornfield encouraged diligence in preparing mescal or in farming. These practices were symbolic of a sexual division of labor as well as pointing to significant economic enterprises.

Like most Indian children everywhere Apache young were quietly cherished. Parents often worried if they thought their child was slow in learning to walk. This concern was a natural one, for the people's life required mobility. When abilities were critical to activities of a society, rituals often surround them; so it was with the Apache. There were a number of rites employed to hasten the motor development of babies. Some performed by shamans, others by girls undergoing puberty rites.[24]

> When my son was a baby, he was only crawling about by the time he should have been walking. A girl was having a puberty ceremony then, so I took my baby to her. She led the baby, making it walk to the four directions: east, south, west, and north, just a few steps. Then I told her. Let him walk today.

[23]Ibid., p. 258. Material on children comes from Goodwin, *The Social Organization of the Western Apache*, pp. 434–443.

[24]Ibid., p. 443.

Western Apache women with child, circa 1892. Smithsonian Institution National Anthropological Archives.

Tell the Sun to let this baby walk today, so the girl said, "Let this baby walk today." It was summertime, and the corn was getting ripe. I took my baby home, untied him from his carrier, and left him to sit on the ground. Then I went after some roasting ears in the field. When I came back, I saw him standing up, holding to his carrier. In a little while he started to walk toward me. When he reached me, he put his arms about my neck. He has never been sick since that time, because he obtained luck from that pubescent girl.

Mothers amused their babies by talking and laughing with them. While not ignoring them, fathers played with them less. Although grandparents occasionally allowed young children to lean against them, bodily contacts were usually uncommon between adults and children as they grew older. After age 7 or 8 children were no longer treated as babies and became more distant and shy. Apache children seldom cried.

One man's reply to the question, What do you do to a child that cries all the time, shows how seldom this problem was encountered. "We don't do anything to the child. We hire a shaman to cure it, for, if something is not wrong it would not cry that way.[25]

People were patient with their children and seldom interfered in their activities unless they severely disturbed adults. Then a sharp remark subdued the child or caused it to play elsewhere. Discipline, when required, was direct command, threats of supernatural intervention, or teasing. Physical punishment was least desirable; boys most often were the victims.

[25]Ibid., p. 453.

Young Apache, through direct and indirect coaching by parents and relatives, were taught the intricacies of their kinship organization: the terms for all of their relatives, both blood and by marriage, and the expected behavior associated with the kin statuses. A total of thirty-one kin statuses existed, and by the time they were adolescents they had assimilated all of them.

Basso explains the Western Apache kin system in a way that simplifies what to us seems a complicated maze.[26] Children addressed their parents by separate terms but the father's siblings, irrespective of sex, were classed together. Mother's sisters and brothers, however, were labeled by distinct terms. They used different words for brothers and sisters and extended these to include all of their parallel cousins. Viewing their cross-cousins as different from parallel cousins, they employed different terms for them. Sons and daughters were distinguished from one another and from the offspring of brother's and sister's. They called a sister's children, regardless of sex, by the same term and applied a different one to brother's children. Maternal grandparents and their brothers and sisters of both sexes were identified by a single term; paternal grandmother and her sisters were differentiated from paternal grandfather and his brothers. Grandparent terms were applied to grandchildren. Kin terms denoting close biological relatives were extended to all clan and phratry members even though exact genealogical relationships were vague.

In-law labels were different from those used for biological relatives. Mother-in-law and father-in-law were classed together as were grandparents-in-law and spouse's siblings. There was a single term for any man marrying a person's blood relative and another for a woman marrying one.

As complicated as the Apache kin nomenclature was, by far the more important aspect of the system was kinship behavior. Three behavior types—authority, obligation, and restraint—governed the Apache. Individuals had authority when others conformed to their wishes. Obligations were of two types: symmetrical or reciprocal, and nonreciprocal or asymmetrical. Restraint involved interdictions against touching or joking with specific classes of kin; in its most extreme form certain relatives avoided one another. Such was the case between an Apache man and his mother-in-law:

> They must not look upon each other for it is believed that to do so may cause one or both to sicken or die. They must not come close to each other, and to be in the same dwelling at the same time is impossible. Ordinarily, they cannot address each other, and when talking to each other, must use the polite form of the verb. . . . These behavior patterns are regarded as demonstrations of the deep respect which the two are supposed to have for each other because of their affinal relationship.[27]

[26]Basso, *The Cibecue Apache*, pp. 11–15.
[27]Goodwin, *The Social Organization of the Western Apache*, p. 251.

The two lived in the same family cluster because of matrilocality; in order to facilitate their daily activities their *wickiups* were placed so that entrances faced in opposite directions. Proper decorum was still observed in the case of accidental meetings. If they encountered one another, the woman immediately covered her face with her blanket and he turned tail quickly and rushed off in the opposite direction. Anthropologists interpret this institution as functioning to reduce conflict between the two, each of whom has a vested interest in the same woman as daughter or wife.

The strongest reciprocal obligations bound members of the same matrilineage. Young men and women regarded their mother's siblings as especially important. Equally significant were their own brothers and sisters as well as their maternal parallel cousins. Members of this group offered support to one another, cooperated in various enterprises, and shared goods. Except for one's father, obligations toward paternal kinsmen were tenuous at best. The most important relationship outside of the nuclear family existed between maternal uncles and their nephews and nieces. They showed interest in them and often took over their support should their father die.

The close bond with a maternal uncle was especially important for a boy, who almost invariably sought out his mother's brother when in need of advice, aid in an undertaking, or the loan of property. The maternal uncle in need of a young man to help him, to send on a trip, or to take his place in an undertaking the uncle did not wish to complete, turned to his nephew after his son.[28]

A woman needing assistance received it from her maternal uncle too. His horses, food, or other possessions were hers to use. He did not expect the same sort of succor from her, largely because she often was unable to supply it, but she helped in other ways, preparing feasts or running errands.

Restraint characterized the interactions between children and their parents, between brothers and sisters, and between parallel cousins of the opposite sex. Brothers and sisters did not touch one another, nor did they stand or sit close together; never was there joking or familiarities between them. To breach these norms would cause suspicions of incest, an abhorrent act to Apaches. Despite these restraints brothers and sisters helped one another, and normally there was deep affection between them. Brothers, while observing far fewer restraints, avoided physical contact; they neither shook hands nor embraced, yet their relationship was exceedingly close. Cross-cousins—who, of course, were not of the same clan—had few inhibitions toward each other. They joked and teased, often in a ribald fashion, and were the closest of friends.

Restraint and nonreciprocal obligation were mandatory between a

[28]Ibid., p. 211.

man and his parents-in-law. He worked for them, hunted for them, the booty from raids was to be given to them:

> So pressing are these obligations that a man often feels it necessary to inform his father-in-law before he leaves on any undertaking which will keep him absent several days. A man who never gives his parents-in-law anything is not only disliked by them but is also disrespected. Parents-in-law cannot compel him to live up to his obligations but they may take their daughter from him if he does not. The man who gets on well with his wife's parents, who treats them as he should, is the good man, the one worth keeping in the family, and his parents-in-law are proud of him.[29]

These kinship expectations, as well as others, guided the Apache's life from birth to death. Observation of them provided support, solace, loyalty, and friendship.

If the people followed the dictates of kinship norms, life went smoothly in the family cluster and local bands. Moreover when they exhibited the proper demeanor in the company of strangers or nonkin, danger of conflict was minimal. A major dimension of this comportment was maintaining silence in situations which Apache viewed as uncertain. For example Apache, when in the company of strangers, did not speak to them. Basso describes such a circumstance reported to him by an informant:

> One time, I was with A, B, and X down at Gleason Flat working cattle. That man, X, was from east Fork (a community nearly forty miles away from Cibecue) where B's wife was from. But he didn't know A, never knew him before, I guess. First day, I worked with X. At night when we camped we talked with B but X and A didn't say anything to each other. Same way second day. Same way, third. Then at night on the fourth day, we were sitting by the fire. Still, X and A didn't talk. Then A said, "Well I know there is a stranger to me here, but I've been watching him, and I know he is all right." After that X and A talked a lot. . . . Those two men didn't know each other, so they took it easy at first.[30]

Yet Apache, of course, did not always behave as they should. Family members quarrelled; murder occurred; women were occasionally raped; witchcraft and incest—two heinous crimes—were committed. To control antisocial behavior or rectify such wrongs people turned to leaders. The headman—leader of a family cluster—attempted to solve difficulties within his family. Together, several of them arbitrated disputes among different *gota*. Band chiefs settled arguments if asked. Neither sort of chief, however, had absolute authority nor the power to punish miscreants. Their abilities

[29]Ibid., p. 250.

[30]Keith H. Basso, "To Give Up on Words: Silence in Western Apache Culture," in *Apachean Culture History and Ethnology*, Keith H. Basso and Morris E. Opler, eds. Anthropological Papers of the University of Arizona #21, 1971, p. 153. This incident and others took place 20 or more years ago. There is, however, no reason to think that such behavior is not ancient.

to eliminate friction rested entirely on their wisdom and persuasive power and the consequent respect they enjoyed; they were not always successful.

Like some other Indian groups Western Apache lacked strict means to control interpersonal behavior outside of kin groups, or, in some cases, local settlements. And like them, they had other cultural means which were adaptive in managing behavior among unrelated people. The major device was their belief in witchcraft and their fear of being accused of practicing it.[31] Apache did not doubt that some people had the requisite power to effect illness and death—for both people and livestock—or to cause strange accidents such as the breaking of a strong saddle girth. They protected themselves from the possibilities by carrying turquoise beads, cattail pollen, or eagle breast feathers. When these amulets were overwhelmed by a stronger power, the victim sought relief in curing rituals. Bear, snake, or lightning ceremonials were the most effective. Medicine men conducted these using their power and chants to negate the witch's power. When they succeeded, the witch often sickened or died and the victim recovered.

This entrenched belief clearly served to govern behavior among strangers or unrelated people, for only they were likely to be accused of such malfeasance. Kinfolk were seldom, if ever, alleged to be witches. The belief was sufficient cause for the suppression of actions and utterances suggestive of hostility or hatred.

An informant explained it to the researcher Basso this way:

> With people who are old and you think can have it (power) you have to be careful. If you get angry, or make stories, or bother around with their women, they will start to hate you for it is the same way. If you get angry, or get into fights, or talk bad, they will think you can have it and think you hate them and want to use it to make them sick. . . . The best way is to act good to all these people. . . . That way no trouble.[32]

From Apache perspective the best way to avoid being a victim or accused of witchcraft is to refrain from provoking others.

Throughout the foregoing discussion of witchcraft the idea of power figured prominently. It was central in the Apache world view and belief.[33] While their religion was not based on a formal theology and did not dichotomize strictly between natural and supernatural characteristics typical of western doctrine, the Apache did conceive a category of things called *holy*. This category was one of three. The second category included all things capable of self-movement: people, animals, fish, and insects, as well as flora. We would classify this as *animate*. *Immobile* objects or those dependent

---

[31]Keith H. Basso, *Western Apache Witchcraft.* Anthropological Papers of the University of Arizona #15, 1969, pp. 38–54.

[32]Ibid., p. 51.

[33]This discussion of Apache beliefs and religion relies upon Basso, *The Cibecue Apache*, pp. 36–44.

on external forces for movement and all topographical features comprised the third. The *holy* category was made up of ceremonial ritual paraphernalia, celestial bodies, rain, thunder, wind, lightning, mythic beings and ghosts, and the most important varieties of power. Power defies precise definition although Apache were clear about what it did and what possessed it. Basso in 1966 described it as:

> "Power," in its *dinyih* meaning, is a supernatural force which men may obtain under certain conditions from all phenomena of the Apache universe, including mythological figures, animals, plants, stones, shells, etc. When used properly, *dinyih* serves as a vital tool, not only as an aid to the individual in his day to day existence, but also as a safeguard against the very source from which it is derived.[34]

Power then is a dimension of phenomena said to possess it, and there were many. A sample of them were: Water Power, Fire Power, Thunder Power, Wind Power, Moon Power and Sun Power; Bear Power, Eagle Power, Snake Power, Mountain Lion Power, Deer Power, Elk Power, Lizard Power, Pole Power, and Hoop Power. Changing Woman Power, a female mythological figure, and Gan Power, a set of male deities who in ceremonies appeared as masked dancers, were the only two forms of power residing in humanlike beings.

Each of these powers was in an inexhaustible supply, and a limited amount of it could be acquired by men and women. The balance remained free to behave as it willed. Moral sanctity was not characteristic of power, and the Apache did not necessarily regard power as benevolent. Moreover, were it to be offended by improper human behavior it could become malevolent. Although power and the other things called "holy" were no less real than the things in the other classes, they did have access to supraterrestrial regions barred to humans. However, they often appeared in the human world and frequently meddled in its affairs. Because such powers were believed to follow the rules guiding human behavior, they were addressed and treated as if they were people.

While powers were available to all, most Apaches did not have them. A major obstacle to acquiring a power was the cost in time, goods, and effort; most could not afford these. Other compelling reasons were the responsibilities inherent in possessing powers and the envy and fear they often generated in others. Although power was owned by a few, it had a critical role in the lives of Apache. Life's major events—illness, death, war, luck, and social relationships—were suffused with it. Apaches had to deal with power continually. Shamans of course possessed one or more powers, using them for others usually in diagnosing and curing sickness. Other people might also have a power which they employed for personal benefit:

---

[34]Keith H. Basso, *The Gift of Changing Woman.* Bulletin of the Bureau of American Ethnology #196, Washington, D.C., Smithsonian Institution, 1966, p. 150.

finding lost objects; predicting the future; enhancing chances for success in hunting, war, gambling, or raiding.

Power also protected its owners and insulated them from misfortune and calamity if they behaved appropriately. Apaches showed it the same courtesies, respect, and deference shown to human companions. Never did they command it; they spoke softly and obeyed its instructions, however troublesome they might be, with a good heart. Owners thanked a power with prayer and chants. Power could not be taken for granted, to keep it demanded vigilance and polite interaction. Not to display the proper conduct toward a power resulted in its loss, leaving an Apache desolate, afraid, and vulnerable to attack by the angry power.

Apaches gained a power either by seeking it or by being sought out by one. People sought by a power were viewed as especially deserving and reputable folk. A person sought by a power (most often men) usually learned of it through a dream in which the power source, a bear for example, appeared telling the dreamer that its power was available and that to manipulate it he must learn the appropriate chants and prayers. Basso recorded such a dream:

> Long ago it happened this way. I lay down in my wickiup and saw a big mountain. Only I didn't know I was sleeping. It was all covered with spruce, that mountain, and I thought I really saw it. Then, on the top I saw something, so I went up, and it was a bear. I was sure scared. But then that bear talked to me. At first I didn't know what it was saying, but then I started to understand. It wasn't the words we people use around here, so it talked some more and I heard it. After that I wasn't scared. I followed it to a spring and we drank some water. Then it talked some more. I didn't say anything. Pretty soon that bear told me that if I went to a certain place I would find a black stone. That bear told me to get it. After that, the bear went away. And I tried to follow it but it didn't leave any tracks. Then I woke up. I was sure scared when I knew what I had been dreaming. I wondered about it. Then in the morning, I went over to the place where that dream I had told me to get the stone. I found it right away, and then I knew that I could get some of that "Bear Power."[35]

People to whom powers had been proferred seldom refused them. To have done so would likely have turned the power into a vengeful one ready to retaliate on the hapless dreamer. The reluctance to refuse power mirrored the behavior between humans. To refuse to accept a gift insulted the giver and angered him. Not all power came from dreaming. Some unexpected or unusual happening was often considered a sign that a power was close at hand and ready to make itself available when the proper chants and prayers were learned.

To actively seek a power—the other way of obtaining it—an individual decided upon the one he wanted and enlisted the aid of a shaman to learn the requisite prayers and chants. Often such a person learned only a

[35]Basso, *The Cibecue Apache*, p. 41.

few of the great array of chants. Usually a power obtained in this way went to work immediately, yet there were cases when it failed to respond. The new owner recognized then that he was on trial; the power was not altogether certain that he was worthy. Until the power gave aid, sometimes after a long interval, no Apache was confident that he truly had it.

Learning the body of chants and prayers associated with each power was long and arduous. For example, Black Tailed Deer Power required memorizing fifty-five or sixty chants. Each of these likely had twenty or more separate verses, and each verse required a half an hour to sing. The chanter had to be letter perfect. An error in a word, line, or verse, or order of chant, nullified it and even worse insulted the power. To learn all the chants required weeks, even months, of intense effort, a prodigious memory, and physical vigor. The medicine man (shaman) who taught the neophyte demanded food, horses, and other stock. The amount of payment depended upon the number of chants he taught and the time required for the instruction.

While some learned only a few chants, sufficient to control a power for personal or family needs, others memorized an entire corpus of one or more power chants. Such people became medicine men, enjoying the respect and sometimes awe of their fellows. It was they who performed the ceremonials for curing or bestowing protection against illness and good fortune in war or raiding.

Improper behavior to holy things the Apaches believed caused serious maladies. Specific sickness struck when one violated the taboos surrounding things in which power dwelt. Boiling the deer stomach, eating its tongue, or cutting the tail from the hide offended Deer Power and invited disaster. Stepping on a snake's trail was dangerous, so was resting against a tree which had been struck by lightning. One did not urinate in water or defecate near a corn field—these latter two may have had practical value. Most of the taboos—there were hundreds—apparently did not. Some of them were relevant only to men and their activities; others affected only women. They all, however, defined respectful and safe deportment with respect to the powers. The Apaches by observing the taboos kept order within their universe. But there were so many that sooner or later a man or woman ran afoul of one; malaise or sickness could follow. When this occurred, a medicine man was hired to diagnose and cure the victim.

A curing ceremonial was a community affair. People gathered at dusk; the medicine man or another wise person told myths describing the origin and history of the ritual. A skilled teller made the story come alive and recalled for the listeners their connection with the ancient world and so reaffirmed their faith in the rituals. Curing ceremonials were dramatic events: fire burned, casting shadows in the background; the camp resonated with the sounds of drumming. The medicine man entered, sat in the glow of the fire light, and began to chant. In the distance a coyote yelped.

The patient sat motionless on the other side of the fire. The medicine man chanted constantly for over 2 hours, sweat trickling down his face. The drums beat monotonously disturbing the silence of the desert. Suddenly the chants ended; the chanter walked wearily to a *wickiup* for food and *tulpai* (a native liquor made from fermented corn). People rested, all sound was stilled, the patient struggled to remain awake. At about 3 AM the drummers and the medicine man resumed. He sang four chants from the lightning corpus, two from the Gan, and four from the Black Tailed Deer. When the stars vanished from the sky, he ceased and walked to the patient, sprinkling cattail pollen on his shoulders and his head, and stroked his forehead with lightning grass. Although exhausted the medicine man returned to his seat to sing two final chants. As their notes faded the people gathered up their children and blankets and left. The patient went slowly to his *wickiup* to fall asleep immediately. The ritual had ended.

Medicine men often directed the activities of war or raiding parties. In 1932 a man, then over 85, described the events surrounding a war party bent on revenge for the killing of seven Cibecue chiefs by Navajo.[36]

> Some time after this happened a woman was talking to her brother, a chief. She said, "You remember our chief who got killed up in the Navajo country. You are a man, and a man ought not to stand for that. If your relatives get killed, you ought to do something about it." That chief started to think this over and then he decided to notify the Pinal Band, the San Carlos band and the Apache Peaks band about what was in his mind. So he set out for the country of these bands and talked with their people. They made a plan for everyone to meet at the head of the Seven Mile Wash near Apache Peaks. . . .

The bands gathered at the meeting place; one was led by a powerful medicine man called "Hears Like Coyote."

> Then early in the morning a woman began to talk to all the people there and said, "I am glad you are going up there to fight those Navajos for what they have done to our chiefs." She kept talking from then on till noontime, praising them for going. . . . There was a very big group of men there, and they all stood still while she talked. Then they said, "All right, we will go."
> Then "Hears Like Coyote" got up and spoke. He said, "We are going to the Navajo country to help because these chiefs have been killed. That's what they want us for." Then he stepped to one side to make medicine and find out what was going to happen. He took his cap off and looked inside it. No one knew how he did this. Inside it he saw children, women and men. Then he said to the people, "We are going to kill fifteen women and fifteen men first, but we are not going to kill the one who killed our chiefs till the sun goes down." . . . Then "Hears Like Coyote" walked right to where that woman who spoke was and told her, "All right. We are going to do the way you want and kill all the Navajos who killed those seven chiefs. . . . The woman said thanks

[36]The following narratives describing a war-party raid are from Goodwin, *Apache Raiding and Warfare*, pp. 85–91.

to him. Then they said they would put up a dance here and everyone agreed, so they did.

The groups moved to Salt River where they camped and held another dance. From there they continued on to Cibecue where other men joined the war party. The people danced that night and then again the following morning.

The raid was a success; the Apaches ambushed a Navajo camp killing thirty people and capturing women and children. They returned to Cibecue with the captives and a flock of Navajo sheep.

All the people stayed at Cibecue for quite a while. "Hears Like Coyote" took a good rest there. The people kept dancing every night. . . . This all happened long before the White people came here, and the men who took part in that war against the Navajos are all dead now.

Curing ceremonials and war rituals were paramount in Western Apache life, but there were others; childbirth, planting and harvesting, and hunting required minor rites, and people performed private rituals to control or keep in touch with their powers. But the singular most prominent and elaborate ceremony was held at the onset of puberty in girls.[37] Rich in symbolism and expressive of Apache values it involved a large network of kin and nonkin. Its charter lay in the myth of Changing Woman thought to be the founder of Apache culture. Changing Woman conceived one son by the Sun and another by Water Old Man. Together they rid the world of much that was evil.

Immediately following a girl's first menstruation her parents selected a group of wise people to help in planning for the ceremony. With their guidance, the parents chose a medicine man to officiate and, most important, elected a sponsor for their daughter at this momentous time. Finding a sponsor required a knowledge of all the clan affiliations of the initiate. The sponsor, an eminent principal in the ritual, could not belong to the girl's clan, nor to her father's, nor to any other to which these two were at all related. After eligible women were identified, one wise woman was nominated because of her stirling virtues and wealth. Astride his horse the father arrived at her camp one morning before sunrise to ask her to serve. If she accepted the responsibility, he gave her an eagle feather and cattail pollen. By agreeing, she and her husband and the girl and her parents entered a binding relationship carrying reciprocal lifetime obligations similar to those required through kin links.

Preparations were many and had to be carried out according to tradition. To deviate offended the powers and angered the medicine man. Relatives and friends of the family cleaned the site, constructed shelters for the

[37]This account of the puberty ritual is drawn from Basso, The Cibecue Apache, pp. 53–72.

girl and her family, for the sponsor and hers, and for the medicine man. *Tulipai* had to be brewed, a sweat bath constructed, and food collected. When all was ready, after a week or 10 days, the sponsor and her entourage arrived to assist in the final phases of preparation. Two days before the event the girl's father fetched the medicine man and his wife.

The day prior to the start of this great communal ceremony two significant events occurred. In the first, male relatives of both the initiate and her sponsor joined in a sweat bath; the medicine man also attended and prepared the ritual accoutrements necessary to the occasion. He decorated a staff with which the girl would dance and which she might use as a walking stick in later life. The decorations were highly symbolic, consisting of two eagle feathers to afford protection against power illness, and several oriole feathers, these because the oriole was the most amiable of birds, a trait highly valued in humans. The medicine man also made a drinking tube and a scratching stick. For the next four days the girl drank through the tube (to do otherwise eventuated in unsightly facial hair) and scratched herself with the stick. Had she touched herself with her fingers she would have incurred disfiguring sores. After the ritual paraphernalia was ready the sponsor presented the girl and her folks food sufficient for a large feast; they reciprocated after the ceremony concluded, so cementing the two groups together.

The great drama unfolded at sunrise with an address to the audience exhorting them to pay attention and behave well. Escorted by a female relative and carrying the staff the girl appeared. For the next 4 or more hours all eyes focused on her as she participated in the age-old ceremony. It was divided into eight distinct parts, each separated from the other by a brief recess. In the first the two women took their place on a large buckskin and faced the rising sun. Eyes down, modest, and expressionless, the young woman danced to the pulsating drums. Soon the power of Changing Woman entered her body, and she knelt to pray.

The sponsor replaced the first companion in the second phase and remained with the initiate for the duration of the puberty celebration. Kneeling, the girl swayed from side to side to rhythmic chants as she gazed at the sun. It was the reenactment of the myth of Changing Woman's first menstruation and her impregnation by the sun.

In the third part the sponsor massaged the girl as she lay supine on the buckskin, legs together and arms at her sides. Because of the Changing Woman's presence in her she was especially pliant.

A medicine man explained:

Changing woman's power is in the girl and makes her soft like a lump of wet clay. Like clay, she can be put in different shapes . . . and Changing Woman's power makes her grow up that way, in that same shape. . . . She will grow up strong and never get tired.

Sponsor rubs her legs so she will never have any trouble walking long ways. Also, so she can stand up for long time and never get tired. She rubs her back so that when she gets to be really old age she won't bend over and not straighten up. Her shoulders . . . so she can carry heavy things for her camp and never get tired doing that. . . .[38]

It is evident that Apache placed great value on the contributions of women to the welfare of the tribe. We might see this symbolism as indicating a life of drudgery; it was not always so, and Apache women were not without influence in the affairs of their *gota* and band, and were proud of their abilities.

To start the fourth phase of the ceremony, the decorated cane was placed about 15 yards east of the buckskin. With the start of the first chant the girl ran, circled the cane, and returned to the skin. Her sponsor followed, retrieved the staff, and restored it to the girl who then danced until the end of the chant. This procedure was repeated three more times, but in each the staff was placed farther and farther away. These runs were mirrors of the girl's life: the first, and the shortest, her infancy; the last, the longest, her old age.

Of this a woman commented:

For the girl, that is the most important part. That is where she prays for long life. She has the power to make herself very old when she runs around the cane that way. Each time she runs around the cane that way she will live to be that age. That way, after she makes the last time—when it is far away—she will live until a very old lady. She goes through her life running around that cane. Changing Woman did that one time and it made her very old. The girl has her powe. to grow up to a long age.[39]

Running was also featured in phase five. The cane was first set in the east, and the girl and sponsor circled it. Then it was placed in the south, the west, and last in the north; each time the pair ran together circling the staff.

After she runs around the cane in the four ways, she will never get tired and will always be able to run fast. Changing woman gives her power to the girl and this is why it happens this way.

She runs in the four ways so she will never get tired. Changing woman ran fast long time ago, they say. That is why the girl runs so fast around (the cane). She wants to be like Changing Woman and run good.[40]

To begin the next part the medicine man blessed the initiate by sprinkling cattail pollen over her head, shoulders, and on the cane. Baskets of food had been prepared earlier. He poured the contents of one of these over her.

After he pours it over her head, everything in all the baskets gets holy. Not just the stuff from the basket he pours over her. All the baskets, even the big

[38]Ibid., p. 66.
[39]Ibid., p. 67.
[40]Ibid.

ones near the buckskin. Because it is holy, all those things, everybody wants it.
. . . If you take one of the corns home and plant it, you have plenty of corn to
bring in later on. . . . The girl's power makes all those things holy and good to
have.[41]

In order for all to share in the good fortune contained in the food and
goods, male relatives of the neophyte moved through the crowd urging all
to take as much as they could.

After a brief recess phase seven began. The sponsor and her young
charge danced in place to the beat of the drums, while adults lined up and
repeated the blessing that began the prior phase. This was vital; by doing
this they enlisted the power of Changing Woman to grant their wishes.

The long ceremony finally drew to a close with the pubescent girl
shaking the buckskin and tossing it to the east. To the other three directions she threw blankets.

> She does this for two reasons. She throws the blankets so she can always have
> blankets, plenty of them in her camp when she gets old. She shakes them out
> like if they had dust in them, so her blankets and camp will always be clean.
> The buckskin she throws so there will always be deermeat in her camp, and
> good hunting for everyone.[42]

With this the ritual ended, the girl and her family withdrew to their
wickiup, and the people, satisfied that all would go well, drifted away. The
girl, however, was still host to Changing Woman. For 4 days people sought
her out to cure sickness and bring rain. Remarked a medicine man:

> At that time she is just like a medicine man, only with that power she is holy.
> She can make you well if you are sick even with no songs. Anyone who doesn't
> feel good can come to her, it doesn't matter who it is. Sometimes, if there's
> been no rain, they put that cane in the ground inside (a wickiup or shade) and
> ask her to sprinkle water on it. That way she can make it rain. I've seen it.[43]

The puberty ceremony encompassed the most salient Apache values.
Living to be old, to be healthy and free from hunger, to be wealthy were all
ritually expressed. Qualities of strength, endurance, and forbearance, so
closely associated with women's economic importance symbolically were
exemplified too. Life in adult society demanded a good nature and a generous and even disposition. The ceremony bestowed these qualities upon the
pubescent girl; she became the model of proper deportment. But why the
maiden? Why she and not her brother?

While it is impossible to trace the creation of significant supernatural

[41]Ibid., p. 67.
[42]Ibid., p. 68.
[43]Ibid.

beings in a society lacking a written history, clearly the selection of adolescent girls rather than boys to emphasize cherished qualities stemmed from abiding faith in Changing Woman. She embodied all the Apache ideals. And, of course, the Apache organized their society around women. The matrilineage and matriclan were the most significant social institutions in Apache world. From matrilineal kin came emotional and physical security. Women continued the lineage through their children; because of them, society endured. Through the ritual they learned to deal with power and from it they received the beneficence of Changing Woman; through them it was promised to the men of the matrilineage. Males were physically stronger, encouraged to be dominant, and were the heads of local lineage segments; yet without women, central to the clan and lineage, men would be adrift in a sea of hostile strangers and powers.

Like the Havasupai the Western Apache inhabited an area which permitted a mixed economy: farming and collecting; hunting; and later raiding. The people entered the southwest between 1000 and 1500 AD, formed local groups, and each became somewhat isolated and adapted to local ecological niches. They established relationships with other tribes, some hostile, some friendly, and some distrustful. When the Spaniards settled in villages, the Apache saw in them a source of additional food and, most important, horses for transportation.

Because of the singular history of the Western Apache we cannot explain their cultural development solely in terms of the interplay between the environment and their technology. What sort of culture they possessed when they intruded into the southwest, cannot be stated with confidence because they encountered many groups during the long course of their migration. But few of their northern Athabaskan "relatives" had unilineal kinship structures.[44] Although some of the Athabaskan groups were located in areas permitting part-time village life, the subarctic in general did not foster enduring settlements nor did it permit minimal cultivation. Athabaskan beliefs about the supernatural and rituals, while different in content, were in a general way reminiscent of the Boreal Forest Cree.

Nevertheless, by the middle of the eighteenth century the Western Apache were organized into groups (Cibecue, White Mountain, and others). These were subdivided into bands, and bands into local groups. Characteristic of their kinship system were matriclans, composed of matrilineages whose members were scattered all over Apache land. They lived in matrilocal extended families. Deities most important to them were Changing Woman, her two sons, and the Gans (usually associated with farming), and always the ever-present powers. Roaming seasonally

[44]See James Van Stone, *Athapaskan Adaptations: Hunters & Fishermen of the Subarctic Forests.* (Chicago: Aldine Publishing Co., 1974) for an excellent portrayal of various Athapaskan societies.

through several distinct biotic zones, they camped in winter below the Gila and Salt Rivers and during the summer farmed in uplands south of the Mogollon Rim. Men hunted most often during the fall and winter; it was then, too, that they plundered the settlements of Spanish colonists' descendents in Mexico as well as other Indian groups: Papago, Pima, and Yavapai.

The culture of a group is influenced by the environment in which the people live and their ability to sustain themselves in it, but we must recognize that "cultural borrowing" often plays a part in the ultimate result. This is certainly the situation in the case of Western Apache culture. The original subsistence depended upon hunting of both large and small game and collecting fauna. To this was added farming. The Papago, Pima, and Pueblo peoples were full-time cultivators; some were skilled irrigationists. From one or more of them the Western Apache adopted farming, but they never farmed as intensively. In fact Goodwin estimated that only 25 percent of their food resulted from cultivation.[45] We might speculate that the earlier hunting pattern continued because it satisfied some implicit emotional need, for they perhaps could have farmed as skillfully as others did. Adopting part-time horticulture augmented their food supplies and permitted a continuation of their earlier economy. Because it is improbable that clans and lineages were brought from the north, we must conjecture that they developed from contact with early Pueblo people, the Anazazi,[46] or from congress with the matrilineal Hopi and Zuni Pueblos. Apache clans resembled these but without the presence of a female clan head. Because Apache clans were not territorially based, it is understandable that a single clan head—either female or male—was impractical. Just when or how Changing Woman became enshrined as the chief supernatural is unknown, but the likelihood is strong that she, too, was borrowed from the Pueblos and recast into a personage compatible with the Apache world view. Katsinas (important Pueblo supernaturals) were similar to Apache Gans in that both were portrayed in major rituals by masked male dancers.

More might be said about the probable influence of the Pueblos—and perhaps others too—on Western Apache culture. Here we have highlighted only some of the most visible effects of cultures in contact. However, Western Apache culture was not a mechanical mixture of original traits plus borrowed ones. They modified some of their early cultural behavior to fit their new environment and wove indigenous southwestern cultural elements into it, producing a coherent, functioning cultural system different from both their original culture and those of their neighbors. This hybrid culture allowed them to prosper in the southwest deserts and

[45]Grenville Goodwin, "The Characteristics and Function of Clan in a Southern Athapascan Culture," *American Anthropologist* 39(1937):394–407.

[46]The term Anazazi refers to the ancestors of the historic Pueblo people.

plateaus. Their social organization provided support as they wandered across the land. Changing Woman, her offspring, and the Gans assisted them and supplied answers to fundamental human questions. Powers, when properly controlled and served, kept them well and aided their economic endeavors—until the southwest was invaded by troops of the United States government. Despite valiant and often violent attempts to maintain their freedom and to roam the land, the Apache were ultimately defeated and confined to reservations in Arizona and New Mexico.

EPILOGUE

After decades of conflict, United States troops finally subdued the Western Apache. In Arizona two reservations—San Carlos and Fort Apache (sometimes called White Mountain)—were organized in traditional Apache territory. While confinement to them was onerous, the land held all that was dear to the Apache. Much of traditional life, particularly sacred beliefs and kin organization, endured. Many people followed traditional subsistence patterns; government rations supplemented their efforts.

Later the Bureau of Indian Affairs built agencies in selected sections of the reservations. Schools, trading posts, and missionaries soon followed. Drawn by them, various bands wintered in and around the agencies, interrupting the customary winter activities. But as late as the 1930s most Western Apache still engaged in some aboriginal subsistence pursuits as well as raising cattle. Cattle became especially important on the San Carlos reservation,[47] but with the passing of time game grew scarce and the Apache were made to follow hunting regulations. Some continued to farm but earned little from it.

By the 1950s the Western Apache had become ineluctably caught up in a cash economy. Money came from wage labor—not always readily available—cattle sales, and government subsidies; many families were perpetually in debt to traders. Cash weakened the kinship relationships; to share deer or corn with relatives was one thing, sharing money was quite another. As a consequence the nuclear family became the primary economic unit. Yet in some conservative settlements the old ways, somewhat diluted, are still valued.[48]

A number of Western Apache live a "hand to mouth" existence, but despite their financially precarious circumstances the people as a whole are less demoralized than some other reservation populations. Those who, in one way or another, follow the "faith of their fathers" are psychologically

[47]Harry T. Getty, *The San Carlos Indian Cattle Industry.* Anthropological Papers of the University of Arizona, #7, 1963.
[48]Basso, *The Cibecue Apache,* p. 22.

sustained by it. Attending summer Indian Powwows in Flagstaff, Arizona and Gallup, New Mexico adds to feelings of worth and Indian uniqueness.

True, alcohol produces some violence and is often disruptive. Most adults, however, have behavior patterns to deal with it. The difficulty lies with young people who have not internalized the older generation's norms about drinking and consequent behavior.[49]

[49]Michael W. Everett, "Drinking As a Measure of Proper Behavior: The White Mountain Apache," in *Drinking Behavior Among Southwestern Indians*, Jack O. Waddell, M. Everett, eds. (Tucson: University of Arizona Press, 1980), pp. 172–173.

CHAPTER SEVEN

The Mandan of the Northern Plains

In western Montana within sight of the northern Rockies rises the Missouri River, the longest in North America. Winding its way eastward into North Dakota not far from the Little Missouri, it bends and snakes southward. Never a placid, peacefully flowing river, it twists through the Dakotas, Nebraska, and Missouri, gouging out new channels, building treacherous sand bars overnight, falling and rising with the seasons, laying clear or innundating its bottom lands. The vast area it drains is appropriately called the Missouri Valley, a part of the Great Plains physiographic province.[1] It empties into the Mississippi near St. Charles, Missouri, after traveling over 4000 miles and dropping 7000 feet or more from its source.

Father Marquette discovered the Missouri in 1673. First the French, then later the Spanish, paddled north on the river to trade for furs with Indians living along its banks and to search for the elusive "passage to India." Diseases which began the ultimate decimation of the Indians accompanied these voyagers. President Thomas Jefferson, eager to know the land bisected by the Missouri and to locate the riverine connections to

---

[1]Nevin M. Fenneman, *Physiography of Western United States*. (New York: McGraw-Hill, 1931) provides an excellent description of Great Plains physiography. For a history of the region see Rufus Terral, *The Missouri Valley: Land of Drought, Flood and Promise*. (New Haven: Yale University Press, 1947).

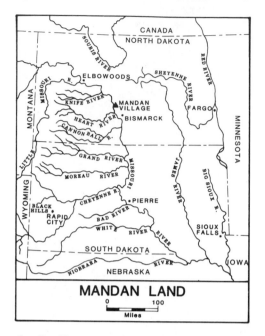

MANDAN LAND

the Pacific, commissioned Merriweather Lewis and William Clark to lead a transcontinental expedition to explore it, to describe the resources of its drainage, and ultimately to discover the water passage to the west coast. Men of John Jacob Astor's American Fur Company plied the river, swapping, among other things, whiskey for furs. George Catlin in 1832 and Prince Maximilian with Karl Bodmer in 1833 sailed north on company boats beckoned by the land and by a fascination with its native peoples.

The river from its mouth meanders west and north through Missouri, Kansas, and Iowa, coursing through bottom lands covered with willow and cottonwood. Hardwood grow on higher river terraces, slowly giving way to grassy, high rolling, verdant prairies. Stands of timber interrupt the open vista. North of the mouth of the Kansas river more open land appears; trees are fewer and flourish closer to the river. In this part of the Missouri drainage lived the Kansa, Oto, Iowa, Omaha, Ponca Indians, and others. To the west were the once-powerful Pawnee. The semiarid treeless plains begin north of the Platte river. Willow, cottonwood, and other moisture-loving shrubs grow along the bottom lands of the river; islands in its shallow, broad expanse support similar growth. Hardwoods stand where banks are stable. Above the flood plain loom high cliffs, and beyond these stretch the northern plains, a panorama unrelieved by trees; differences in elevations are barely discernible as the land reaches west toward the Rockies. Eastward from the river the land rolls toward the northern reaches of the Mississippi. Geographers use the ninety-eighth meridian to mark the eastern boundary: to its west rainfall is 20 inches or less; to the east of the meridian, moisture increases. Standing on a bluff overlooking the confluence of the Missouri and White Rivers, Lewis eloquently described his first view of the lower edge of the plains:

> The shortness and virdue [sic] of grass gave the plain the appearance throughout its whole extent of beautiful bowling green in fine order, it's aspect is S.E. a greater number of wolves of the small kind, halks and some pole-cats were to be seen. I presume those anamals feed on the squirril. I found the country in every direction for about three miles intersected with deep revenes and steep irregular hills of 100 to 200 feet high; at the tops of these hills the country breaks off as usual into a fine leavel plain extending as far as the eye can reach. from this plain I had an extensive view of the river below, and the irregular hills which border the opposite sides of the river and creek. The surrounding country had been birnt about a month before and the young grass had now sprang up to the hight of four Inches presenting the live green of the spring . . . this senery already rich and pleasing and beautifull was still farther hightened by the immence herds of Buffaloe, deer Elk and Antelopes which we saw in every direction feeding on the hills and plains.[2]

North of the White river the country becomes less fertile and more arid. Grasslands are punctuated with stretches of barren dessicated soil. Pelting spring and summer rains erode them into the river below, choking the water with sand and driftwood and leaving starkly carved bluffs above.

But for spring and summer an absence of rain is typical of the northern plains; less than 20 inches fall annually. Equally as characteristic of the land is the incessant wind. With few trees to divert it or hills to diminish its velocity, it blows unobstructed; although it is hot in the summer, numbing, bone chilling, blinding blizzards are one of its winter consequences. Winters are deeply cold and come early. Lewis and Clark on October 12, 1804, leaving the mouth of the Grand River headed north on the Missouri,

> found the wind had grown so strong that the men were forced to resort to hauling boats with towlines that remained slick and stiff with ice until mid-morning. The cotton woods along the river had already acquired their pagan hues and were now dropping their leaves, and the party experienced several of the short but intense snow storms that are euphemistically called "flurries" in the northern plains.[3]

Wintering near the Mandan villages, they recorded the winter's first snowstorm on November 25; for many of the succeeding winter days they were tormented by arctic blasts and temperatures of minus forty degrees.[4] In

---

[2]Quoted in John Logan Allen, *Passing Through the Garden: Lewis and Clark and the Image of the American Northwest.* (Urbana: University of Illinois Press, 1975), p. 200. Permission granted by the University of Illinois Press. To be accurate, he was gazing at the Missouri plateau province.

[3]Ibid., p. 205.

[4]Ibid., p. 213.

this country, in any year, gales scour snow off the land and combine it with sand that whips into the faces of animals and men. By the end of November the Missouri River freezes solid, allowing foot passage across it.

Slowly in March winter loses its grasp on the plains. Buds on the trees swell, migratory birds return, and the river ice turns to mush—though the weather remains capricious (on June 19, 1833, Maximilian remarked upon a clouded sky, a high cold wind, and a temperature of barely 60 degrees).[5] However late summer comes, its crystal air opens up an endless sea of land undulating under a vast blue sky. The wind, ever present, is now hot; summer temperatures may reach 114° F. Despite the implacable winters, the cold damp spring, the short summer and fall, the Missouri Valley has always been an abundant land, teeming with game grazing on the thick sod of the plains. The fertile river bottoms were easily cultivated by the traditional Indian dwellers; sufficient timber provided winter warmth and—when used with sod—shelter. Here until the early nineteenth century lived the Arikara, the Hidatsa, and the Mandan. To their south and west were the Dakotas, who were often hostile. To the north roamed the nomadic Assinboins, Plains Cree, and Crow, with whom Mandan traded despite animosities which sometimes flared.

The Mandan and their near neighbors the Hidatsa were Siouan speakers living on the bluffs overlooking the Missouri. There is some archaeological evidence to suggest that Mandan ancestors migrated to the Missouri from the east, perhaps from Minnesota or the eastern Dakotas.[6] In any case they were living along the river by the fourteenth century. In succeeding years they moved their communities upstream, perhaps because of menacing groups or perhaps because of the better agricultural opportunities. How large the villages were before the 1800s is not certain, yet they were surely larger prior to 1804 when Lewis and Clark visited them. Abandoned villages dot the area south of their 1804 location. Studies of the sites suggest populations of over a thousand living near the Heart River in six or seven fortified towns.

Alfred Bowers has reported that the Mandan at that time were divided into five bands, each occupying one or more villages and speaking three dialects.[7] These were reduced to two by the time of Maximilian's arrival—as were their villages then located near the present city of Bismarck, North Dakota.

[5]Bodmer, Karl, *People of the First Man: Life Among the Plains Indians in Their Final Days of Glory*. Thomas, Davis, and Karin Ronnefeldt, eds. First published, 1976, in the United States by E. P. Dutton. All rights reserved under International and Pan-American Copyright Conventions. Reprinted by permission of the publisher, E. P. Dutton, a division of New American Library. (New York: E. P. Dutton and Co., 1976), p. 36. This work is an edited account of Prince Maximilian's expedition up the Missouri River, 1833–1834.

[6]Roy Willard Meyer, *The Village Indians of the Upper Missouri*. (Lincoln: University of Nebraska Press, 1977), pp. 5–12.

[7]Alfred W. Bowers, *Mandan Social and Ceremonial Organization*. (Chicago: the University of Chicago Press, 1950), pp. 24–25.

In the early eighteenth century the Mandan were a prosperous people. Their gardens produced surpluses which they traded to other Indian groups for products originating great distances from their territory: obsidian from the west, copper from the east, and shell from the Gulf Coast. The arrival of horses in the middle 1700s added to their wealth. Roy Willard Meyer conjectures that after this period, "they became involved in an even more complex web of trading activity. Well before any Mandan saw a white man, they were receiving—and presumably trading—European made goods."[8] In these times they were at the apogee of their cultural development, but their commercial activities contained the seeds of their own destruction. From the late years of the eighteenth century, periodic plagues of virulent disease enfeebled them: In 1837 smallpox struck; at the end of the epidemic, no more than 150 anguished Indians survived!

The Mandan between 1800 and 1830 lived along the Missouri in North Dakota, a beneficent environment encouraging both horticulture and hunting.[9] Like the Apache and the Havasupai the Mandan combined the two technologies, but the resources of their land and their ability to utilize them produced an affluence unknown to the others. The river, in its irregular winding through the upper plains, created fertile bottom lands lying several hundred feet below the towering bluffs marking the edge of the plain. These alluvial bottoms were easily tilled with simple tools. Quick maturing corn prospered there, as did beans, squash, and sunflowers. The short-grassed plains hosted countless bison; herds were estimated to vary in size from 500,000 to 4 million head.[10] In September the silence of the plains was shattered by the bellowing of rutting bulls. Pronghorn mingled with the bison to graze. Wolves circled the herds waiting for the young or the infirm. The giant grizzly bear wandered the area. Prairie dogs built their villages in the soil; jackrabbits and other small animals scuttled about. Overhead soared the great raptors—hawk, falcon, and eagle—searching for prey. The prairie rattler and other reptiles wriggled through the grasses, also hunting small creatures. Migratory fowl, Canada geese, snow geese, as well as many varieties of ducks, fed in and along the water. Traveling up stream from the villages in 1833, Maximilian and his companions lived almost entirely on the bounty of the land for 33 days. Meticulously he recorded in his diary the following:

Buffaloes–54; Elks–18; Bighorns–2; Bears–9; Blacktailed deer–13; Common deer–26; Antelopes–2; Bears–9; Wolves–1; Skunk–1; Porcupines–1; Hares–2; Eagles (bald)–6; Horned owls (big)–5; Prairie hens–3; Wild geese–10; Prairie dogs–10; Rabbits–1.[11]

[8]Meyer, *The Village Indians*, p. 16.
[9]The description of Mandan culture and land are as they were in 1830 and the years immediately preceding.
[10]Prescott Webb, *The Great Plains*. (Boston: Ginn and Co., 1931), p. 44.
[11]Bodmer, *People of the First Man*, p. 86.

In the winter, tempestuous winds roared over the territory; snow whipped into a frenzy swept across it; cold crept through dwellings and clothing. Clark entered in his log the following: "Little work done today it being cold etc. . . . The weather is so cold today that we do not think it prudent to turn out to hunt in such cold weather. . . . As the end of December approached the party was so ennured of frigid temperatures that a reading of −9 was not considered Cold."[12]

Spring seemed to appear only to vanish; temperatures rose giving hope, then tumbled. Yet in March or April trees budded, grasses changed from brown to green—the land still threatened by late snows—and eventually summer came. Rivers of grass rippled in ever-present warming winds. Bison and pronghorn moved from the shelter of the bottom lands to the uplands. Calves capered beside their mothers signaling the end of winter. Formidable though the land was, the Mandan flourished (until they were ravaged by disease and alcohol, both gratuities of gluttonous white traders).

The people lived in fortified villages on promontories overlooking the Missouri. At the end of October or early November, the Mandan abandoned them and moved to winter villages in the Missouri's timbered bottomlands. In early November of Maximilian's trek through the region, he observed: "Every day we saw inhabitants of the summer villages removing, with much baggage, laden horses and dogs."[13] The winter villages provided protection from the frigid plains wind. Wood was available for warmth; horses fed on cottonwood bark, and bison sheltered there. With the ebbing of winter in mid-March, the villagers returned to their summer locations.

Each village was an autonomous ceremonial and economic unit, owning its own gardenlands and controlling its own affairs including the summer buffalo hunt. While the Mandan were not nomadic they were only semisedentary; not only did they leave their summer villages annually, they also left them for weeks at a time during the summer to hunt bison on the plains. It was not uncommon also for villages to be moved to another site when gardens lost fertility, game became scarce, and wood supplies were exhausted. Moving was never a simple affair. People, largely the women, had to agree on an appropriate location. A suitable site was one protected by natural barriers—or one which could be easily fortified—and with gardenlands close by. Hundreds of people transported their belongings by dog and horse to new lodges. Building them required considerable work, and clan members assisted one another in their construction. A new ceremonial lodge was erected. Caches for food storage were dug, corn-drying platforms were raised, and, soon, nearby the village scaffolds for the dead were built.

[12]Allen, *Passing Through the Garden*, p. 217.
[13]Bodmer, *People of the First Man*, p. 177.

Mandan chief's lodge, 1833.
Smithsonian Institution National Anthropological Archives.

Early in Mandan history the population was probably divided into bands, each with its own village and speaking one of three dialects.[14] Every village was almost a replica of the others. Each had a round, open ceremonial plaza 100 or more feet in diameter. At its center, religious leaders had set a cedar in the ground and enclosed it in a wooden circle. The cedar was the symbol of the culture hero—Lone Man; the enclosure symbolized the wall he built to protect his people from the flood. North of this area stood the large Okipa ceremonial lodge. Prominent or affluent families built their lodges facing the ceremonial center on the perimeter of the circle; such families owned medicine bundles vital to the Okipa ritual.[15] Other folk constructed lodges grouped closely together making it difficult for prowlers to find their way around; an additional hazard was the number of deep storage caches into which the unobservant might tumble.

Political organization centered in villages, each independent of the others. Influential men, owners of tribal bundles, composed a council. From the group they selected two leaders whose talents for making war or keeping peace were acknowledged. He who had excelled in battle became war chief. The second was a prudent man of generous disposition, possessing significant ritual bundles, whose wisdom and ability to ameliorate disputes were superior. These two complemented one another: The war chief repelled the enemy; the peace chief held the welfare of the village

[14]Bowers, *Mandan Social and Ceremonial Organization*, pp. 24–25.

[15]Ibid., p. 24. The succeeding description of Mandan life derives largely from Bowers whom I have paraphrased. Direct quotes are acknowledged.

uppermost, giving feasts, settling quarrels, and greeting visitors. At council meetings, peace talks with neighbors, and various social events, they were resplendent in headdresses of buffalo horns and ermine. Yet their authority was constrained.

A chief persuaded the council to accept his judgments through his eloquent oratory. Dressed in his finest, speaking and gesturing at the meeting, he outlined his accomplishments and his successes to underscore his devotion to the village. Following the recitation of his deeds, he offered his advice on the wisdom of the proposed action or policy. Absence of village dissension was the mark of an eminent leader. When people no longer accepted his opinions to the exclusion of others, his power waned. While not demoted or removed, "others younger who had been distinguishing themselves merely replaced the older man in public esteem."[16]

The Mandan had a number of ceremonial and other events as well as a system of secular societies for both women and men. Leadership of these was widely distributed among community members. A leader in one activity was a follower in others. Spreading leadership responsibilities among many contributed to community integration and perhaps prevented a few from consolidating power.

Members of the Mandan nation belonged to one of thirteen exogamous, matrilineal clans present in each village. These were divided into moieties, or roughly equal halves; one sat on the east side of the Okipa lodge, the other on the west. Clans were not equal in status. The WaxiKena clan enjoyed the highest prestige as the culture hero Lone Man had belonged to it in mythic times and because members owned the most important bundles in the Okipa ceremonial. Each clan selected a wise, good, and esteemed man to lead, but like the chiefs, his role was primarily advisory.

In addition to regulating marriage, clans owned property, gardenlands, lodges, ritual bundles, and names, and each was the custodian of one variety of corn. The WaxiKena controlled bluish-green flint corn; the Tamisik, the red corn. Yellow flint and dent belonged to the Prairie Chicken clan. "Crows Heart," an informant of Bowers', reported the following: " 'Hides-and-Eats,' an old woman who lived in his lodge, told him that, when she was young, people of one clan were not permitted to raise corn belonging to other clans without first securing the rights and that each clan claimed to be the preserver of its own corn."[17] Frances Densmore, in the 1920s, described a ritual which illustrated clan custodianship of corn. The principal in the rite was the Corn Priest who every spring distributed seed:

> . . . The Corn Priest kept a supply of every variety of corn and knew what variety each family usually planted, for he noticed the scaffolds in the fall

[16]Ibid., p. 35.
[17]Ibid., p. 31.

with their braids of drying corn. If by any chance he forgot the variety, he asked the woman who made the request. . . . No one knew where the Corn Priest obtained his seed corn but he always had an abundance. The request for seed was always accompanied by a gift, and he gave each woman a few kernels which she mixed with her own corn thus rendering it productive.[18]

People expected and received all manner of support from fellow clan members. Childless elderly were cared for. Women adopted orphans into their lodges. Successful hunters gave meat to old people. Clan leaders advised the young; members gathered goods so that a young man might purchase a ceremonial bundle or perform a ceremony. They avenged wrongful deaths. Most of the matriclans included several matrilineages. Clans cut across villages; lineages almost always resided in the same community. Generally after marriage the couple lived with the wife's people in lodges owned by the women. Occupants of the lodge made up a matrilocal extended family or in some cases a small lineage. A typical lodge sheltered a senior woman, her husband, her sisters, some of whom may have also been her husband's wives, their married and unmarried daughters, single sons, and grandchildren. A prolific family might soon outgrow a lodge. Should this happen part of the family refurbished and moved into an abandoned one owned by the clan; if none were available they and their maternal relatives built a new one.

While there was little ceremony associated with constructing a new lodge (an elderly woman of the family sang a song and prayed for the family), there was plenty of labor involved. The ground within a circumference of 40 to 60 feet was excavated to a depth of 2 feet, the dirt tossed up on the edge of the circle. After the earth was packed down, men, who did only the heaviest labor, set up four huge cotton wood posts in the center and, on the perimeter, a ring of shorter posts topped with cross beams. Leaving a smoke hole from the center posts, they ran rafters to the outer post ring. Women and older children lay thick willow branch mats over the roof and outer wall; finally the entire structure was covered with layers of earth and sod. The entrance opened upon a passage slanting upward to ground level. The passageway, high enough to admit a horse, was closed with a stiff rawhide door. To deflect chill winds, the men set up a row of vertical planks and poles immediately inside the entrance. The tops of the lodges, often flattened, gave space to dry corn; householders relaxed there in the summer—gossiping and observing the business of their neighbors—and, most important, viewed the elaborate ceremonials. Well adapted to the plains environment the earth lodge was cool in the summer and relatively warm in the colder months. The generous interior easily accommodated the enterprises of the inhabitants. They slept on furs in boxlike rawhide beds

[18]Frances Densmore, *Mandan and Hidatsa Music*. Bureau of American Ethnology, Bulletin 80, 1923, p. 37, Smithsonian Institution. By permission of Smithsonian Institution Press.

placed on platforms around the left and rear walls. Behind the cubicles lay stored many of their possessions including their most prized clothing. Close by the fire pit were pottery vessels, heavy wooden mortars and pestles, and other cooking utensils. On the right side men kept their weapons; here, too, was an altar and a place for the ceremonial bundles.

During the cold months the women worked inside cooking, preparing skins, or grinding corn, while the men reclined on bison robes talking, repairing their weapons, planning raids or ceremonies. From here they received guests. Through it all babies crawled or tottered about. Wealthy families had space enough inside to stable their valuable horses. Maximilian described his visit to Yellowbear's winter lodge:

> The beds, consisting of square leathern cases were placed along the insides of this spacious hut, and the inmates sat around the fire variously occupied. The Yellow Bear, wearing only his breech cloth sat upon a bench made of willow boughs, covered with skin, and was painting a new buffalo robe with figures in vermilion and black, having his colours standing by him, ready mixed in old potsherds. In lieu of a pencil he was using the more inartifical substitute of a sharp painted piece of wood. The robe was ornamented with the symbols of presents he had made, and which gave the Yellow Bear much reputation and made him a man of distinction.[19]

Two clans were paramount for the Mandan. While social and economic cooperation and harmony characterized relationships among clan members, a Mandan depended upon his father's clan mates for ritual support. From his own clan and lineage an aspiring young man collected goods and food and feted members of his father's clan. These men—sometimes called "clan fathers"—and to a lesser degree women advised him on ceremonial affairs and prayed for him when in danger; at his death they prepared his body for the scaffold. If he died far from the village they brought his skull home. And his return from a first successful raid was a celebrated occasion, for then they bestowed his permanent name on him.

Marriage affiliated the people with still another set of important folk, their in-laws—technically called affinal relatives. Rarely did a Mandan fail to marry; only such circumstances as severe physical or mental impairment precluded it. Mandan lineages and families enjoyed differential prestige; therefore methods of acquiring a mate varied with social position. Important families, those owning or controlling important tribal bundles who had material wealth, carefully selected partners for their daughters. They called these arranged marriages "choosing a son-in-law." While young men avidly courted girls, mothers kept a wary eye on their daughters; when it appeared that matters were becoming serious, they cautioned against any impulsive action. Daughters were not to marry without a significant exchange of wealth. To do otherwise would disparage the family. As a Man-

---

[19]Bodmer, *People of the First Man*, p. 182. Winter lodges were usually smaller than summer ones.

dan informant told Bowers: "People would say that a daughter was no good if little was received at her wedding."[20] Families possessing valuable ritual bundles worked at marrying their children into families similarly situated. A household was exceptionally fortunate were it to acquire a son-in-law who was a member of his father-in-law's clan. Not only would related bundles remain in the lodge; there was every reason to believe the two men would get on better if they were of the same clan. The ideal son-in-law was a scion from an important family and a successful warrior and hunter.

After the girl's parents selected a worthy candidate, they purchased a white buffalo robe at a great cost in horses, robes, and corn. With it in hand they pointed out to the girl the young man's virtues and the wisdom of the match. If she consented—daughters usually did—the young man at the father's invitation entered the lodge and the proposition was put to him. If he agreed—and he usually did, for this did not come as total surprise to him or his parents—he and the young woman sat together on another robe with the white robe over their shoulders. If the prospective bride had younger sisters, they joined the couple, for they too would become his wives as they grew up. After consuming food fixed by her mother and accepting horses from her brothers, the young man left the lodge and climbed to its top. There he proclaimed that the white robe had been offered. Hearing this his father's sister arrived to receive the robe and care for it. The couple was now married, but a final elaborate ceremony was yet to come. Assisted by his wife, her sisters, and brothers, his age-grade society, and his younger clanmates, he collected great piles of bison robes as well as other goods. The Okipa lodge was prepared, and on the day of the ceremony the goods were displayed there. Prominent among them all was the white buffalo robe. Relatives of the pair—who included most of the eminent people in the village and some from other villages—crowded in to admire the gifts, to feast, and to participate in the final ritual. Singers directed sacred songs. At the end of each song an older participant received a gift from the young couple, and reciprocated by presenting them with an article from his sacred bundle and prayed to the white robe for their success. When the gifts were distributed, the songs ended, and the food eaten, the ceremony was over. The newlyweds took up residence in her father's lodge.

Less prestigious families married their children through a gift exchange. The young man's parents chose a girl acceptable to their son, usually one he had been wooing. To gain approval from her parents they offered horses. When the four parents agreed, the horses were tethered in front of her lodge; the girl gave them to her brothers who in turn gave her an equal or larger number. Four or 5 days later her mother and her brothers' wives carried great quantities of food to her prospective husband's lodge where his relatives were gathered. Each of his female relatives had brought gifts. After the meal was finished the women of her lodge re-

[20]Bowers, *Mandan Social and Ceremonial Organization*, p. 75.

turned to collect the empty vessels and took the gifts for themselves, and the nuptials were official. The bride remained with her husband in his lodge, assisted with the domestic chores, and was subservient to her female in-laws. However, she would never become a co-owner of it the husband's lodge. Usually after a short time her parents prepared a section of their lodge for the couple, presented the groom with a horse or two, and persuaded them to move in.

Young men who married in either of these two ways also married their younger sisters-in-law as they matured, giving each a horse on the occasion. Parents supplied additional leather beds in his part of the lodge. Bridegrooms never spoke directly to their mothers-in-law, who also avoided the young men. Lodges were sufficiently commodious to allow the avoidance. As time went on many a young man removed the taboo by bringing his mother-in-law a scalp:

> When returning from a successful war expedition, he would go directly to his wife's lodge instead of to his sister's, which was the usual practice, and give the scalp to the oldest mother-in-law in the lodge. Usually there were a number of females in the lodge who were treated as "mother-in-law." In this group would be those whom the wife addressed as "mother," "grandmother," or "father's sister." The oldest mother-in-law took the scalp, sang the victory songs, and danced toward each woman who was treated as a mother-in-law. When the scalp dance was performed on the succeeding day, she danced while carrying the scalp and singing her new "son's" praises. She then treated him as a son . . . while the son-in-law treated her as he would his own mother. . . . He could then interfere in a quarrel between a group of women which included his mothers-in-law.[21]

On occasion people married without consulting with their parents. This was called "marriage by mutual agreement." Usually a girl, disliking her sisters' husband and wishing to avoid becoming his wife, encouraged the attentions of a would-be swain. When she accepted his gift of several horses and moved to his lodge, their marriage was recognized. If the lodge were not already occupied by her husband's sisters and their spouses, she would remain to care for her parents-in-law and to inherit the lodge and its belongings at their death. If sisters were entrenched she searched for a household of old women of her clan to join. There the couple remained and, when they died, she inherited the lodge, goods, and garden.

Mandan marriage varied in methods of acquiring a mate and was often ritually complex. Family prestige, personal likes, and lodge demography, caused the differences, a situation not too dissimilar from ours. While matrilocality was the ideal, peculiar circumstances often dictated the young couple's choice of a home.

Once married and at home, wife and husband settled into centuries-old domestic routines. She gardened in the lowland plots using simple

[21]Ibid., p. 56.

tools—digging sticks and a hoe made of a bison scapula hafted on a handle—and harvested the produce. Looking ahead to the long winter, she and the other women of the lodge dried and preserved a large portion of it. When the lodge needed repair, she and the others undertook it. On the summer buffalo hunts the women butchered the carcasses dragged in by the men. When her husband engaged in rituals, she played her part in them. Her husband hunted, raided, and protected the village. Each owned specific property, with the other women the wife owned the lodge, its contents, the garden, dogs, and mares and foals. Men owned their weapons, clothing, pipes, stallions and geldings. The ownership of horses by sex and age underscored, in part, the separation and importance of sex roles. If the lodge housed sacred tribal bundles, they were held collectively by the married pair. Although men and women were expected to carry on separate economic and domestic affairs, joint ownership of sacred bundles illustrated clearly that in sacred matters they were a ritual unit.

Divorce was common and easily accomplished. To divorce a mate, a woman asked him to leave the lodge with his belongings. If she were residing with his family, she took only her clothes and the children—if there were any—and went home to mother, and so ended the marriage. An unhappy husband divorced his wife by leaving her lodge. Should a married woman with children elope with a married man having children, she created a great commotion among a number of people. The aggrieved husband hearing of the event might retaliate by killing their horses. Because brothers and sisters were responsible for the behavior of their siblings, they took horses and other property to the rejected spouse to forestall the slaughter.

> My Mandan informants enjoyed relating instances when the brothers and sisters, learning that a brother had eloped with another man's wife, had reached the lodge before the wife was missed. They would come to his lodge in a group leading the horses. Seeing the people with horses, he would hurry into his lodge or go through the village calling for his wife. People considered it very humorous to surprise a man that way, and it was the subject of gossip for quite a while. He was expected to accept the horses and forget his wife. . . . When a prominent man lost his wife, he would usually organize a war party or go out alone against the enemy. He could disregard his former wife, and those most concerned with public opinion usually did. However, a man of position usually called her into his lodge when she returned from her elopement, painted and dressed her, mounted her on a good horse, and took her back to her new husband. Those who cried because a wife eloped or who attempted to take her back or agreed to let her return if she requested it were considered weaklings and not worthy of respect.[22]

For a man to marry his brother's widow was an honorable act although it required him to live between two households. Not wanting to

[22]Ibid., p. 80.

share a husband with women of a different clan and lodge, the widow seldom accepted the offer if she had brothers to provide for her. In the death of a wife, a widower could ask for one of her younger sisters who usually agreed if there were young motherless children. While the levirate and sororate were institutionalized, their practice depended in great measure on the residence of the survivors, the presence of children, and personal inclination.

Mandan marriages were seldom born of romantic love. Parents usually arranged them, and respect for their parents sustained the tie between spouses; children further strengthened the conjugal bond. Since most women lived in their mother's lodge, their babies were born there; those who did not returned home for the birth. At the first indication of labor the old women ordered everyone else out of the dwelling. Darkening the lodge by closing the smoke hole and covering the entrance, they then placed a robe on the floor for the straining girl to rest. Murmuring quietly in the shadows thrown by the fire they comforted the mother. When the labor was unduly long one of them slipped out to call her father's sister. Only she could concoct a potion from sacred plants contained in her brother's bundle to hasten the process. Should the birth not go well, a prominent medicine man or woman specializing in "obstetric" problems entered the dim lodge to attend to the final stages. The senior woman took charge of the newborn, disposing of the placenta and greasing and powdering the infant to prevent chapping. In a soft-tanned hide the baby was swaddled and laid in a leather cradle.

Ten days later the lodge would give a naming feast; before the feast the unnamed infant belonged to the "baby home" from which it had come; only a name established it as a member of society. Should the child die before being named, a paternal grandmother wrapped it in hides and placed it in a special tree and its spirit returned to "Baby Hill" to be cared for there by an old man. Barren women often made pilgrimages to the hill to pray for children, carrying clothing and a ball if they hoped for a girl, a tiny bow and arrow for a boy. Although they were not entirely certain on how frequently it happened, the Mandan believed in rebirth; a child resembling a dead relative was no doubt the reincarnation of the deceased.

The naming feast was an occasion for an eminent family to enhance its social position. A father—an already established Mandan and an owner of a major tribal bundle—named his child or asked that his sister do it. A less important or young father requested the favor from one of his clan members. Any brothers and sisters of the baby and members of its clan brought robes, skins, and gifts to the ritual. An abundant display reinforced the family's prestige. In a burst of pride the father often gave horses away. People of the father's lineage and clan received the gifts. Common folk had to content themselves with a less ostentatious celebration.

The baby entered a world peopled by kin; people to whom it must learn to apply the appropriate terms and to behave toward them in a prescribed fashion.[23] Terms and behavior differed in some respects depending upon whether the child was a boy or girl. More important though than terminology was the patterned behavior of relatives to one another. Each Mandan, man or woman, knew that toward a particular category of relatives specific comportment was expected. Yet, of course, real behavior did not always correspond with the ideal. Mothers (and other women classified with mothers) were the most important adults in the lives of children. A mother taught her daughters to garden, to dress hides and make robes, to weave baskets and make pottery. To her little sons she told stories about the good men of the clan and taught them to revere the sacred bundles and to turn to their fathers for advice. The little ones repaid mother for her nurturing with a few beads; thus they were instilled early with the notion that knowledge must be bought. Affection, although not always demonstrated, was deep between mothers and their children. Brothers and sisters also maintained a close bond for life. To his mother's lodge a son brought meat and valuable mares. When he grew older, he taught his sister's children, disciplined them, and prepared them for the ritual life to come; and in his middle years he became the leading male of the lineage. His sisters named his female children, and assisted him in acquiring property necessary for important ceremonials; to his children they were "little grandmothers."

Brothers—including half-brothers and male parallel cousins, called brothers too—formed a tight group. Older ones taught little ones to care for horses, to wrestle, and encouraged them to fast. Together they provided for their mother, her sisters, and their own sisters. Sisters forged a similar bond; usually their lives were lived together in the same lodge and eventually they frequently shared a husband. Older sisters mothered younger ones, and they nurtured each other's children.

Until they became too old or cranky, grandparents living in the lodge played with their grandchildren and, in the darkened lodge at night, told them stories of the ancients and how the world came to be as it was. On the long summer buffalo hunt a grandfather watched over his grandsons while grandmothers took care of little girls. Grandmothers indulged them, putting up with little ones jumping on beds and flinging belongings around until they could tolerate it no longer. In spite of hands old and gnarled, grandmothers worked skins for their clothing and grandfathers produced toys. For these favors children paid them as best they could. Father's mother, not a member of their lodge, "spoiled" them even more, probably because she didn't have them under foot constantly. Father's father and all his male clan members, also called "grandfather," played important ritual roles. After little girls approached puberty their "grandfathers" treated

[23]Bowers recorded twenty-three different kin terms. Ibid., pp. 40–43.

them with utmost decorum and to avoid gossip were never alone with them again.

Children—so long as father remained with mother in the lodge—treated him with respect. He advised them on important matters, encouraged his sons to fast, to learn to ride, raid, and hunt. He supported his wife in her child-rearing efforts; eventually he approved their marriages. While he did correct little ones, his authority over the children was limited. His wife's brother disciplined his children while he trained his sister's offspring.

Behavior among sets of in-laws was normative too; terms for some of them matched those used for blood relatives, so labels applied to biological kin were widely extended to others in the group (technically this is a classificatory system).[24] A Mandan, therefore, was never uncertain about appropriate conduct and obligations. With these people life was lived. From some a young person learned economic responsibilities; from others ceremonial behavior. When boys and girls joined age-graded societies they assumed a new set of fictive kinfolk and incurred additional duties.

These societies were graded in a sequence correlated with age. For men there were ten societies, for women four. Entering one was not a simple matter; while age was a factor, collective purchase and negotiations were more important. Edward Bruner reported that transferring the rights in a society from its current members to the younger aspirants was grandiose, lasting perhaps for a month or more and culminating in a public event.[25] When parents decided that the time had come for their son or daughter to join a group, or in their wanderings about the village heard that boys or girls of an eligible age were organizing to "buy" a society from present members, they urged their child to join. Collecting the goods, robes, food, horses, bartering and bargaining with members, the boys or girls bought the first of the societies they might join in their lifetime. For the young girl membership committed her to additional responsibilities. She prepared robes or clothing for husbands or brothers of a society member who needed them for ceremonial purposes; she, of course, received the same services when she needed them. As she moved through the society system, each move costing much in goods and time, her ceremonial importance increased.

Young girls joined the Skunk Society by purchasing rights from current members whom they called "mother."[26] To them fell the responsibility, and no doubt pleasure, of praising victorious warriors. At dusk led by a drummer, faces daubed with black and white paint, they moved from lodge

[24]Ibid., pp. 43–46.

[25]Edward M. Bruner, "Mandan," in *Perspectives in American Indian Culture Change*. Edward H. Spicer, ed. (Chicago: University of Chicago Press: 1961), p. 225.

[26]Densmore, *Mandan and Hidatsa Music*, p. 94.

to lodge singing to the exultant young men. In subsequent years the more successful bought rights into the ritually important Goose Women Society. The society held ceremonies from March until October to plead for a bountiful crop from the gods in concert with other women who had dreamed of corn. "When the weather was too hot, too cold, too dry, all those with Corn medicine rights met and the Goose Women's Society joined them to dance and pray."[27] Goose Women also influenced migrations of the water fowl. Densmore learned the following in her studies:

> When the geese went away in the fall a woman might say, "I promise O geese to give a feast for the Goose Women when you return in the spring." Such a woman began her preparations for the feast before the coming of the geese and several of her friends helped her. . . . This feast was held in connection with the ceremony of the Goose Women Society which took place in the spring of the year.[28]

When the women in the Goose society reached menopause, some of them, if not all, relinquished their rights in the society for appropriate payment and entered the White Buffalo Society. Scattercorn explained to Bowers:

> The rule was that a woman should not belong to this society until she was beyond child bearing age. This was the highest and last society to which women could belong. Women could not be members while they still had menstruation periods, as it was believed that the blood would drive the buffaloes away.[29]

Calf Woman spoke about her years in the society:

> Everything in buying is the same as with the Goose Society, and the sale is made in the late fall. They meet each night for sixty nights; during that time those who are buying the society bring in food for the society they are buying out. At the end of sixty nights, the older people give the clothing needed in the ceremony to the ones who are buying in. . . .
> We would meet in the wintertime when the days were the coldest, also in early winter when the days were shortest. The leader wore the white robe; they called her "white robe." MitE'atu'ki means "white robe." The third officer is "keeper of the incense." . . . They dance in the winter when they want the buffaloes to come and any other time, except when warm enough for crops to come up on invitation. When they sing the songs in the spring after the crops are in, the frost will kill all the plants, so they are afraid to sing or dance then . . .
> They always meet in the leading woman's lodge, in this case Otter's lodge. Otter had three daughters, three sisters, and a mother living in that lodge, and that way there were eight of them; they would hitch up their dogs and bring in wood and water for the ceremony. She had three sons and a son-in-

[27]Bowers, *Mandan Social and Ceremonial Organization*, p. 193.
[28]Densmore, *Mandan and Hidatsa Music*, p. 40.
[29]Bowers, *Mandan Social and Ceremonial Organization*, p. 325.

law, and they brought the buffalo meat. That was what they had when they danced. She was "Keeper of the Ceremony," and when they danced, she fed the whole society.[30]

Like the Goose Women's Society, the White Buffalo Society carried out rituals, the origins of which lay in myth, to assure the people of food. They held the ceremonies by request to bring the buffalo herds from the plains to the wooded river bottoms. While they carried out the ancient rites, the Black Mouth Society men patrolled the winter village silencing dogs and children; adults spoke in hushed tones.

Boys, too, joined a number of societies during their lives. Preadolescents entered the system encouraged by their parents. Learning that rights were to be sold in the first society "Foolish Dogs," parents would gather together goods to purchase the rights for their son. The seller, a member of father's clan, sponsored him and two or three other boys, guiding them through the intricacies of purchase and teaching songs, dances, and responsibilities. With this man the boys entered into a fictive father-son relationship. In all future society purchases buyer and seller became "father-son." If the boy was married his wife addressed the father as "grandfather" and the initiate offered her to his ceremonial father. Early white visitors to the Mandan regarded this, somewhat piously perhaps, as a scandalous practice. Not having a wife was no handicap, for the young man borrowed one from his brother or young clan members.

Maximilian described the purchase of the Crow or Raven Society by young men between age 20 to 25:

> . . . Frequently young people are in none of the bands for half a year or more. They then go to the band of the Crows, and say "Father I am poor, but I wish to purchase from you." If the possessor agrees, they then receive the raven's feathers, which the band wear on their heads, a double war whistle consisting of two wing bones of a goose joined together, a drum [*schischikue*], the song and the dance. Each of these bands has a leader called, by the Whites, the head-man, who decided on the sale of its rights and attributes . . . a festival then takes place in the medicine lodge, which is continued for forty successive nights. They dance, eat, and smoke there; the purchasers defray the expenses and give up their wives every night to the sellers, till the fathers, as they are called are satisfied, and transfer their rights to the purchasers, with which the festival concludes.[31]

Offering wives to Ceremonial Fathers also took place in crucial rituals. In the Red Stick Ceremony, a 4-day winter buffalo-calling rite, young men chose an old man (a clan member) to "walk with his wife." Bowers in a footnote mentioned that: "Mrs. Goodbear related that her ceremonial grandfather went out with her, all the while bellowing in imitation of a buf-

[30]Ibid., pp. 326–328.
[31]Bodmer, *People of the First Man*, p. 244.

falo bull." For a number of reasons, perhaps age was one, some "grandfathers" declined the invitation.[32]

> One time when Red Coyote was selected, he said: Stop right there, my "granddaughter." I want you to hold my medicine bundle now. Once I fasted four days in a ravine. While I slept, an owl came to me and said that I would be a lucky man and live to be old. I have killed an enemy, captured six horses, and struck three enemies. I pray you will live a long time, be healthy, raise many children, and keep free of diseases."[33]

Offering wives was connected to the Mandan view of "power" and how it was acquired. Power was controlled by the supernatural, but humankind could acquire it through fasting, noble deeds, mortification of the flesh, solicitude for the elderly, as well as purchasing or owning rights in sacred bundles. At each stage of a man's career, given proper demeanor, he obtained more power. When more powerful men had sexual intercourse with younger men's wives, some of that power was transferred through the wife to her husband. In the case of the reticent Red Coyote, the "granddaughter" obtained power by holding his bundle to her breast.

Reaching middle age (40 or more), a Mandan would ask his sisters, wives, and others to help him collect sufficient horses, robes, and goods to purchase rights in the Black Mouth fraternity. It, like the Goose Women Society, was founded in the mythical past by Good Furred Robe, a culture hero, and was one of the two most important male societies. The other was the Buffalo Bull Society made up of a select group of men well past middle age. After his ceremonial father instructed him in the esoterics of the group and the 40-day induction ceremony concluded, he and his companions began one of the busiest periods of their lives. Throughout the year they met two or three times a week to discuss their plans and carry out instructions from the village council. If an attack on the village was anticipated, they kept vigil allowing no one to leave it. Each had his own carved club with which he coerced recalcitrant villagers. Criers, members of the society, stalked through a village announcing sacred or secular events and demanded proper behavior. During the days of the magnificent Okipa ritual the Blackmouths were everywhere enforcing tradition. In combat they fought valiantly; to retreat was unthinkable.

The summer buffalo hunt too required the unswervable attention of the Black Mouth Society. The hunt so necessary for winter survival was held every summer. When the plants thrust upward in the garden, women and girls weeded and hilled them, providing a signal for the men to repair equipment, examine their best horses and dogs, and prepare for the village exodus. Scouts had been leaving daily, riding miles out on the plains to locate the great herds and to note their movements. The scouts—and warri-

[32]Bowers, *Mandan Social and Ceremonial Organization*, p. 318.
[33]Ibid.

ors, too, if they had been out on the unbroken sweeps—reported their observations to the hunt leader, who had been chosen by the council. A man who had been a member of the Black Mouth Society, or who had buffalo skulls as part of his sacred bundle, was elected; the Black Mouth crier announced his identity to the village. Gathering intelligence from the scouts and war-party leaders, he planned the hunt consulting nightly in his lodge with former leaders and Red Stick Ceremony members. Arrangements completed, the Black Mouth criers circulated among the lodges announcing the departure day and the nightly camping sites.

In the early morning hours villagers loaded buffalo hides, cooking receptacles, and other equipment on horse-and-dog drawn travois, long *tipi* poles lashed together and slung from the sides of the animals. The leader at the head, they moved out in a narrow column mounted or on foot to leave the village deserted for 8 or 9 weeks. Scouts and warriors rode ahead searching for both animals and potential foes. Black Mouth men trotted back and forth along the line urging stragglers to keep up. Seeing an area thick with wild turnips the leader turned to his assistant, a Black Mouth crier, to halt the marchers. All fell to digging the vegetables while the scouts roamed ahead alert for ambush; the Black Mouth attended the toiling diggers.

As the sun dropped low on the horizon, the call came to set up camp. The leader's family erected his *tipi* first using the travois poles and the buffalo hides. Other households in the line swung in behind him pitching their lodges in a circle. A watching Black Mouth man ordered any lodge taken down if it were out of place or not the proper distance from its neighbor. The circle complete, people tied ropes from shelter to shelter to make a corral for the horses. The success and welfare of all rested upon the hunt leader, and he relied upon the Black Mouth Society to communicate and enforce decisions.

Small groups of hunters under the direction of a leader who had fasted and prayed for them rode out of camp daily to surround the herds and fire volleys of arrows into the huge beasts. Danger was never far away, a stumbling horse, a charging cow protecting her calf, meant frequent disaster. Dismounting, they butchered the behemoth creatures and packed the meat back to men and women waiting in camp, who cut it into strips and hung it on scaffolds to dry. When the herd was decimated or had moved on, camp was broken and the column formed to move on until another was sighted. When the meat from the last animal was butchered and dried, the people, and their heavily burdened beasts, trudged the weary miles back to villages on the river bluff. The Black Mouth members alternately harangued or cajoled them to keep in line and maintain pace.

Mandan relationships with the supernatural were both individual and collective; medicine bundles, personal and tribal, symbolized them. Some people could never expect to own a tribal bundle nor to have partial rights in it. For them, both men and women, a personal bundle was a necessity if they were to achieve any success. The road toward acquiring a personal bundle was long and harsh and depended upon fasting to have a vision. Sequestered in an isolated spot, boys and young men fasted in search of a supernatural assistant. Little boys, advised by their parents, fasted for brief periods but usually did not expect a vision. Young men, however, through deprivation and self-torture, zealously sought a spirit guardian who would both protect and help them put together a personal bundle. As collected by Bowers, here Scattercorn narrates the story of Big Coat's search for a vision:

> When Big Coat was eight years old, the Nuptadi Village was destroyed by the Sioux, and he was taken prisoner. When he was older, he escaped with his mother and came back to the Mandan. Thinking of the treatment of his people, he vowed that he would get a guardian spirit that was real strong so that he could kill many Sioux. He first went out to fast when he was seventeen years old. At first he only fasted four days at a time, and many animals offered him help. Then he began to fast seven days to get still greater gods. All the people began to recognize his ambitions and say that he would surely be lucky and become a great leader who would do much good someday. He began to cut off his fingers and offer them to the Sun, Moon and big birds of the sky. He cut off three fingers of each hand, leaving only the thumb and middle finger of each hand which he needed to use the bow and arrow. He cut gashes in his legs and arms. He even cut off his flesh and offered it to the Holy Woman. [These were his father's gods.] Before he stopped fasting, he had nearly everything as a guardian. He was always successful when leading war parties.[34]

Mandan women fasted too in their gardens or on their corn scaffolds, but usually without self-flagellation. Because they, unlike the men, did not need as powerful guardians, they seldom renounced food and water for more than 24 hours. Concern for the men in a war party, however, might prompt a longer and more tortured abstinence. Here, Mrs. Good Bear describes her mother's fast:

> My mother, Stays Yellow, fasted in the woods in quest of a god. Just before daylight she fell asleep. In her dream she saw two old people doctoring a woman who was having difficulty bearing a child. She saw that they were using black roots [Black Medicine] which they dug up in the forest. The old people, a man and a woman, had a hide rattle decorated with white feathers. She listened to the song they were singing. At the same time they administered to the woman giving birth to the child they were doctoring to a number of dead watersnakes. The old woman chewed the roots and blew the chewed-up mass over the snakes; each time she blew on a snake, it came alive and squirmed away. The last of the snakes had young in her body and was slow to come to life. The woman blew the black root on the snake several times, and each time the snake gave birth to a young snake until all were born.

[34]Ibid., p. 167.

The old man and woman then instructed Stays Yellow that she could doctor women when they had difficulty bearing children. My mother never killed snakes after that; she always blew some of the medicine root on any snake near our lodge and then carried it away.[35]

Tribal bundles, each representing a sacred myth, were the most holy and revered. Some were more specific than others, but all contained a bison skull and a variety of other objects (some human skulls) pertaining to the myth. Each had secret songs and rites which dramatized the lore. Displaying bundle contents followed ineluctable tradition, and tradition guided behavior in their presence. Specific clans through constituent lineages owned and controlled tribal bundles. Through a system of inheritance—usually, although not always, from mother's brother to his sister's oldest son—they passed from generation to generation. Owners could sell rights to bundles four times to more distant clan relatives. Purchase was expensive, and lineages or, in some cases, households cooperated in collecting the goods for purchase including food for a feast. Both inheritance and sales required a large feast to legitimize the transaction. Sellers kept the original bundles and provided duplicates for the purchasers who then shared ownership in the secret myth and learned the bundle ritual. For a number of reasons, such as fertility, bountiful crops, hunting success, owners feasted their bundles. The single most important celebration for the bundles, however, was the Okipa ritual.

Of all Mandan ceremonials, the Okipa was the most holy and spectacular. Held prior to the summer buffalo hunt—and often after—it portrayed in a dramatic fashion the earth's creation and all beings on it, particularly the Mandan. Reuniting the people with their past and pledging the welfare of the tribe, 4 days of dance, drama, and severe self-torture were given over to its performance. While other white men may have seen parts of the ritual, only George Catlin witnessed and recorded the entire event. Maximilian in discussing it said: "I regret to say that I cannot describe it as an eye witness. I am, however, enabled to give a circumstantial description of it word for word, as it was communicated to me by men initiated in the mysteries of the nation."[36] Bowers' account derived from elderly Mandan who had been participants in the final Okipa and who explained it to him in 1930.[37]

Officers and members of the Okipa Society were responsible for the correct conduct of this most intense rite, and they—most of whom belonged to the WaxiKena clan—played the central characters in the enactment of the sacred myths, an important part of the affair. The two most

[35]Ibid., pp. 174–175.
[36]Bodmer, *People of the First Man*, p. 247.
[37]Bowers, *Mandan Social and Ceremonial Organization*, pp. 111–163.

important were "Lone Man" and "Hoita" who represented the "People Above." Men who had "given" the ritual in other summers also belonged to the society. The members planned the ceremony in meticulous detail and selected young men to pledge the ritual.

Only young men who had experienced a vision of buffaloes singing the Okipa songs were eligible, but not all of them were chosen. A youth told his parents of his supernatural episode. Realizing the painful demands of the ordeal and knowing their son's character and his wives' loyalty, they either advised him to abandon his goal or to seek approval from the Okipa Society. Encouraged by them he—through his wives and family—gave a feast in his lodge for the society. There he carefully recounted his vision. Meeting night after night the society members debated and discussed the virtues and abilities of the young men who had feasted them, choosing some, eliminating others. Those considered worthy (seldom more than two) were congratulated upon having supernatural benediction to perform the ceremony. They suggested to young men about whom they had doubt to fast often, feast older men, help the elderly, and go to war. In effect they were on probation and would be evaluated another year. After the society nominated a young man, a crier announced to the village that "a certain man will have the Bulls' dance when the next water willows are in full leaf."[38] If two were selected, one ceremony was held before the summer hunt, the other after the villagers had returned from the plains.

To become a Okipa maker or pledger demanded utmost courage, but courage alone was not enough. The pledger in order to meet his obligations had to accumulate at least 100 articles including robes, elkskin dresses, tanned skins, knives, porcupine twill decorated shirts, and men's leggings; and while he learned the mysteries of the ritual, he was obliged to feast the members of the Okipa Society. Collecting the property mobilized many people. His wives called on their relatives and their society sisters to help. The man entreated his mother and sisters as well as his clan "grandfathers" and "grandmothers" to contribute. They all gave willingly and as generously as they could, for by giving the Okipa he would bring honor and prestige to all his kinsmen.

To prepare for the ceremonial four men owning Holy Woman bundle rights swept the floor of the lodge, carried out ashes from other fires, and scattered sage over the floor. Each received a robe from the Okipa maker for his efforts. Four other men with rights in the Woman Above bundles painted the interior, and they too were rewarded with robes.

The rites began when Lone Man approached the village on the following sunrise to recreate his arrival from the supernatural world. The Keeper, shouting from the top of the ceremonial lodge, announced his advent. Catlin portrayed the scene:

[38]Ibid., p. 122.

In a few moments the tops of the wigwams, and all other elevations, were covered with men, women, and children on the lookout; at the moment the rays of the sun shed their first light over the prairies and back of the village, a simultaneous shout was raised, and in a few minutes all voices were united in yells and mournful cries, and with them the barking and howling of dogs; all were in motion and apparent alarm preparing their weapons and securing their horses, as if an enemy were rushing on them to take them by storm.

All eyes were at this time directed to the prairie, where, at the distance of a mile or so from the village, a solitary human figure was seen descending the prairie hills and approaching the village in a straight line, until he reached the picket, where a formidable array of shields and spears was ready to receive him. A large body of warriors was drawn up in battle-array, when their leader advanced and called out to the stranger to make his errand known, and to tell from whence he came. He replied that he had come from the high mountains in the west, where he resided, that he had come for the purpose of opening the Medicine Lodge of the Mandans, and that he must have uninterrupted access to it, or certain destruction would be the fate of the whole tribe.[39]

Dressed in a wolf skin, his body and face painted white and wearing a porcupine hair headdress on which perched a stuffed raven, he entered the settlement. In one hand he carried a wooden pipe, in the other an ash club with the moon and thunderbird on one side. The Morning Star and Sun were depicted on the other. Allowed to pass by the Black Mouth Society, the Lodge Keeper escorted him to the Okipa Lodge which had been prepared for his arrival. In it was an altar with a human skull and a buffalo skull on each side of it. Beneath it lay the tools to be employed in the succeeding days' activities. The Bull Dancers paraphernalia hung near by. Drums, rattles, and bundles lay in places dictated by ancient practice. Waiting for him in the lodge were the Okipa officers. In dramatic fashion, Long Man related to them the exploits and the deeds he had done in behalf of the Mandan. The Black Mouth prodded men, women, and children and their dogs to withdraw from the roof tops and to enter their lodges; quiet cloaked the village. The door of the lodge opened; Lone Man stalked the paths retelling the tales of his adventures to the silent people. On his way he stopped at the lodges of the young men who were to fast and participate in the ritual; there he demanded knives or sharp implements which would be used to cut open the flesh of the participants. Late in the afternoon he and the other ritual personages assembled in the lodge, and that evening the Okipa giver entered burdened by all the goods he had gathered. Following him were young men and boys ranging in age from 8 to early middle age; some came only to fast, others to participate in the torture thus validating their claim to manhood. Naked and painted, all entered solemnly carrying a bow, shield, and their father's bundle. With a buffalo skull for a pillow and sage brush for a bed, they sank down along the wall to

[39]George E. Catlin, *O-KEE-PA, A Religious Ceremony and Other Customs of the Mandan.* John C. Ewers, ed. (New Haven: Yale University Press, 1967), pp. 47–48.

begin the fast and await the start of the ritual. Lone Man initiated it by transferring his pipe to the Okipa maker and summoned Hoita to supervise every detail of the dance to follow. Starting immediately, the ceremonial figures danced in the shadows of the fire, and the fasters wept; the drama had begun.

At sunrise drummers emerged and sat at the east side of the sacred cedar. The pledger followed; grasping the planks enclosing the cedar, he prayed to Lone Man to answer the people's desires, to bring the buffalo close, and to avert misfortune. When he had finished the fasters appeared and danced before him. Suddenly the drummers increased the tempo and all returned to the lodge. Three more times this day the dance and prayer were repeated. As the fires were kindled in the lodge that night, small boys and some young men left. Others remained for the 4 days without food or water and to undergo torture.

Early the second morning while Lone Man once again walked the village receiving tribute from the people, artists painted and adorned the Buffalo Dancers. At noon, signaled by drums and rattles, the elaborately decorated and fearsome Buffalo Dancers burst forth from the lodge. People, now allowed out, clambered up drying scaffolds and crowded on rooftops to watch. Eight times during the day the Buffalo Dancers performed; the fasters performed only once, for they had to prepare themselves for their part in the ceremony. Before the Okipa began, each had asked a man from his father's lineage to cut the holes in his skin. While the Bulls danced, a young man stood before his clan "grandfather," who using the knife given to Lone Man made the incisions for the skewers. Catlin who watched, described the procedure:

> . . . One of the emaciated candidates at a time crawled up, and submitted to the knife which passed under and through the integuments and flesh taken up between the thumb and forefinger of the operator, on each arm, above and below the elbow, over the brachialis externus and the extensor radialis, and on each leg above and below the knee, over the vastus externus and the peroneus; and also on each breast and each shoulder.
>
> During this painful operation, most of these young men, as they observed me taking notes beckoned me to look them in the face, and sat, without the apparent change of a muscle, smiling at me whilst the knife was passing through their flesh, the ripping sounds of which, and the trickling of blood over their clay-covered bodies and limbs, filled my eyes with irresistible tears.[40]

By rawhide ropes attached to the skewers in the chest or back the young men were lifted toward the top of the lodge to dangle in midair. Buffalo skulls were skewered to the legs. As the Bulls returned after each dance they twisted the tormented victims. When each became unconscious he was

[40]Ibid., p. 63.

lowered to the floor to regain his senses unaided. Such visions which may have come during this agony were regarded as indeed rich and genuine.

The third day was called by the Mandan "Everything Comes Back Day." All significant creatures and mythic beings who had been on earth in ancient days and symbolized by bundles returned. Men painted to represent wolves, antelope, snakes, eagle and hawks, bears, as well as others poured from the lodge. Joining them were the Sun, Moon, and Holy Women (impersonated by men); all danced near the sacred cedar where the Okipa maker now showing the effects of his ordeal prayed. Inside the Lodge the young supplicants continued their torture. Midmorning there appeared staggering into the village a man called "Foolish One." In him were embodied malevolence and buffoonery. His appearance was startling! Catlin remarked:

> The bizarre and frightful character . . . who approached the village from the prairies, and entered the area of the buffalo dancers to the terror of the women and children, had attached, by a small thong encircling his waist, a buffalo's tail behind; and from under a bunch of buffalo hair covering the pelvis, an artificial penis, ingeniously (and naturally) carved in wood, of colossal dimensions, pendulous as he ran, and extending somewhat below his knees. This was, like his body, painted jet-black with the exception of the glans, which was of as glaring a red as vermilion could make it.[41]

The Okipa maker went forth to meet him, "challenging that one's right to come among the people to frighten them and bring misfortune or death at the hands of their enemies by breaking up the dances for the buffaloes."[42] The people fell silent, the singing and dancing ceased abruptly, all eyes intent upon the confrontation between the Foolish One and the Okipa maker who brandished Lone Man's pipe. Foolish One fell back frightened by the pipe; the watchers roared approval and chanted songs of victory. Defeated, Foolish One entertained the crowd. Catlin vividly chronicled the scene:

> . . . He returned to the buffalo dance, . . . he stepped back, and looking at the animal, placed himself for a moment in the attitude of a buffalo bull in the rutting season; and mounting on to one of the dancing buffaloes, elevated his wand, and consequently the penis, which was inserted under the skin of the animal; whilst the man underneath continued to dance, with his body in a horizontal position.
>
> An indescribable excitement was produced by the new position of this strange being, endeavouring to time his steps in the dance in which he was now (apparently) taking part, with the motions of the animal under him. The women and children of the whole tribe, who were lookers-on, were instructed to clap their hands and shout their approbation, as they all wanted buffaloes

[41]Ibid., p. 83.
[42]Bowers, *Social and Ceremonial Life*, p. 145.

to supply them with food during the coming year, and which supply they attributed to this indispensable form.[13]

After several such performances the women rushed at him hurling rocks and clumps of dirt and drove him out of the village. Men followed him to the river where he was bathing and collected part of his clothing. These they tied to a pole in front of the Lodge as an offering to the "Foolish One" who lived in the sun.

The Okipa reached its zenith on the fourth day. Some of the debilitated wounded young men had gone from the lodge the night before, leaving only the Okipa maker and a few fasters to endure more agony as the ceremony climaxed. Four Bulls danced while men impersonating hunters charged them spearing their legs. Bleeding, the Bulls moved to the sacred cedar and stood at the cardinal points each bellowing in imitation of a bull. Bowers described the conclusion:

> After the calling of the buffaloes from the four directions, the remaining portion of the ceremony progressed quickly. The drummers began beating rapidly, and the hunters formed a circle about the sacred cedar, holding to the willow hoops. The four bulls threw off their masks and danced around the circle as rapidly as possible. Each of the remaining fasters was led out of the Okipa lodge by two of his father's clansmen who had the right half of their bodies painted blue and the left side red. They held straps wrapped around the faster's arms. Each faster had one or more buffalo skulls dragging from skewers fastened through the skin; those who had struck an enemy were permitted to wear a skull as a necklace. The father's clansmen led or dragged the young men around the sacred cedar in clockwise direction as fast as they could travel until the victim fell unconscious. When the last faster fell to the ground, the drumming ceased, and the hunters threw their hoops into the air. All the fasters returned to the Okipa lodge where those on the west side moiety rubbed their wounds with buffalo marrow while those of the opposite moiety rubbed theirs with ground yellow corn.[14]

Lone Man threw the knives into the river as an offering to the Grandfather Snake. The Okipa maker distributed all the goods he had collected to the participants, and the holy pageant ended. The welfare of the village was insured, the Mandan renewed, and the young men passing through the Okipa crucible crept back to their homes blessed by the supernaturals. The wounded and agonized Okipa maker returned to his lodge proud of his dedication and courage: He was now a leader, a man respected.

The Mandan drifted to the Missouri River valley probably from southern Minnesota or Iowa. Dates are difficult to ascertain, but likely the movement started in the middle of the thirteenth century. Bowers, interpreting archaeological evidence, suspected that there may have been two

[13]Catlin, *O-KEE-PA*, p. 84.
[14]Bowers, *Social and Ceremonial Life*, pp. 149–150.

streams of Mandan ancestors: one settled near the Heart River, the other downstream in the Grand River region. The southern group ultimately moved north to join the others. Both were gardeners and pottery makers, a trait which often is associated with horticulture.[45] They modified their gardening skills to utilize the fertile river deltas and continued to hunt large animals including bison. Early villages were small; probably the later elaborate ceremonial complex and age-graded societies were not yet highly developed. While it is difficult to prove, it is reasonable to assume that the matriclan and lineage structure were at least incipient. It is doubtful, however, whether the extended summer hunts were yet a regular feature.

In the ensuing years women improved their gardening techniques and crop preservation sufficiently to produce a surplus. These were traded to peoples both east and west of the Mandan. The introduction and acceptance of other ideas and cultural traits attended the trading. Population increased and the villages grew larger. Bruner remarked that: "Mandan culture in 1750 was the result of five hundred years of adaptive response to the Missouri River valley ecology, fusion with other earth lodge cultures of the eastern plains, contact with pre-horse nomads and internal adjustments to the new settlement patterns."[46] The buffalo had certainly become by 1750, and doubtlessly earlier, a major resource. The Buffalo Bull Society, the White Buffalo Cow Society of the women, the ritual use of skulls, all testified to their importance. Observers including Maximilian thought that the Mandan depended upon the bison as much as the nomadic folk. Bowers found that, in the Okipa ritual, "little recognition was given to agriculture in the 'Everything Comes Back Day' of this important ceremony. The Old Woman Who Never Dies was represented together with other Holy Women by two men dressed as women, and those of one moiety rubbed their wounds with cornmeal. Otherwise little recognition was given to agriculture."[47]

The population growth and density fostered by the rich availability of meat and skilled crop production required political and social control and integration. Village councils, age-graded societies, which had both secular and sacred functions, and the strong matriclan system were responses to the demand. The stratification of clans and people also contributed to social order. Doubtlessly the myth of Lone Man held the original charter for the inequality of the clans, but the system was strengthened by individual abilities in war and hunting, and in success in acquiring power. Endogamous class marriages sustained it.

The sacred belief system so intimately bound up in subsistence endeavors, and in success in battle, no doubt developed in part indigeneously.

[45]Ibid., pp. 16–17.
[46]Bruner, "Mandan," p. 204.
[47]Bowers, *Social and Ceremonial Life*, p. 340.

Mandan man praying with bison skull, circa 1875.
Smithsonian Institution National Anthropological
Archives.

The myths of Lone Man, Furred Robe, and others support the assumption. The Okipa ritual, however, was similar to the plains Sundance of such peoples as the Cheyenne, the Teton Sioux, and many others. Where its origin lay is not entirely clear, yet some think it diffused from the plains people to the Mandan who reshaped it and invested it with their mythology. The self-torture of the Okipa maker and others, however, was more extreme than the Teton Sioux for example.

Until decimated by disease the Mandan flourished, living on the northern edge of effective agriculture as semisedentary horticulturalists and hunters. Their culture like that of their closely related Hidatsa relatives was rich and complex. The Missouri Valley provided the raw material for its development. The social intercourse with many other tribes of the plains stimulated its growth by diffusion and culture contact. The rich ceremonial life reflected their dual dependence on crops and bison and reassured the people that both would continue in abundance. The magnificent Okipa celebration symbolized the annual renewal of their world and prepared their young men for glory. In the span of less than 10 years it was finished.

EPILOGUE

In 1868, decimated by disease, 300 surviving Mandan and 1200 Hidatsa and Arikara came under the administration of the military at Fort Berthold, North Dakota. Almost immediately, well intended but insufferably pious and bigoted Indian administrators set out to civilize the Indians. Agents banned ceremonials; one forbid the men to hunt, to curb "wandering" ways. All attempted with little success to teach the men to farm—this was women's work—as white man did. Chicanery by some of their guardians robbed the Indians of their government rations. Between 1865 and 1868 the spectre of starvation was always present. Tuberculosis weakened many.

The Bureau of Indian Affairs took over the reservation in the 1880s. While somewhat more benign than the military, efforts to make the Indians over in the "white man's image" continued, sometimes by force, other times by a benevolent paternalism. A major blow at tribal integrity was struck with the introduction of land allotment. Families were assigned acreage in various sections of the reservation without regard for tribal affiliation. Small communities developed adjacent to family farms. In them lived people of all three tribes. Intermarriage was frequent, with Indians as well as with some whites. Tribal identities were merged. By the 1950s the Mandan were culturally extinct. Bruner could not find one full blood. No doubt some Mandan genes were still present in the gene pool, but no one spoke Mandan nor claimed Mandan identity.[48]

[48]Bruner, "Mandan," pp. 246–261.

Conclusion: Part Two

The Havasupai, the Western Apache, and the Mandan supported themselves by a combined economy of gardening and hunting supplemented by some collecting. Each group, however, exhibited some differences in the way they practiced the dual economy. The differences lay primarily in the time and techniques given over to either farming or hunting, a consequence, in part, of their diverse environments. The Havasupai remained in their canyon village for 5 or 6 months cultivating, irrigating, and harvesting their crops. These tasks completed, they moved to the plateau from October to winter and lived in semipermanent hunting camps, returning to the village in April to begin the cycle again. The Western Apache tended their crops only about 3 months, leaving their farms when the corn was well up to gather wild foods. In September they returned for the harvest. Late fall and winter found them distant from the farms; some local groups camped together and hunted, others banded together to raid. The Mandan had permanent summer villages on the bluffs overlooking the Missouri River. From April until June the women gardened in the fertile river delta. When the crops were established, the villagers moved in one large group to the plains for the long summer buffalo hunt. Laden with dried meat they returned, picked their vegetables, and processed some for winter food. Ultimately, the cold winter winds and blizzards drove them to protected winter settlements in the wooded bottomlands.

Although each might have chosen one subsistence form over the other, they did not. Explanations for their choices, not necessarily conscious, probably lie in a medley of reasons difficult to ferret out. Yet whatever the reasons, their capacity to utilize their ecological niches effectively allowed somewhat more complex cultural systems than we have yet so far seen. All three had a unilineal kinship system which resulted in lineages and clans, phenomena usually associated with a reasonably secure subsistence. The Havasupai lineages and the Mandan lineages and clans were localized; the Apache clans were not. Clan members lived all over Apache land; the diffusion provided support for the Apache, who wandered further afield in their nomadic phase than the other two tribes did. Mandan and Apache clans were matrilineal and matrilocality was preferred. While not dominant over men, women were important in these groups. Additional evidence for their significance can be seen in the presence of prominent female dieties. This is often the situation in groups where farming is an important enterprise and performed largely by women. Havasupai lineages were, on the other hand, patrilineal, and a patrilocal rule of residence was observed. We might speculate that this departure from the trend resulted from men's participation in gardening as well as their importance in hunting.

Farming is also associated with, at minimum, partial village or collective living. These three societies demonstrated this trait, although they varied in the degree to which they lived communally. To live together even part-time requires organization to maintain social order. The three Indian nations, although they differed, developed social structures more complex than the hunters and gatherers. Chiefs of varying power exercised authority through prestige and leadership skills and were obeyed until weakened by age. Among the Mandan and Apache, war leaders exercised considerable power over their followers. The Mandan and to a lesser extent the Apache had a social hierarchy; some lineages or extended families were wealthier and more powerful than others. Wealth in goods and landownership demanded some sort of an inheritance plan. All three had established norms for the passing on of property to their descendants. Hunters and gatherers own little and so have little to bequeath.

The spectre of starvation did not haunt these peoples, yet they had lingering concerns about the reliability of their food sources. Therefore, supernatural beliefs and rituals attended farming and hunting endeavors in the hope of providing bountiful harvests and abundant game. Illness, always a worry, had supernatural beliefs to explain it and rituals to alleviate it. Of the three, the Havasupai had the least well-articulated theology and fewer collective ceremonies. We might suspect that this was a function of their small number, their early origins—still in dispute—and the relative security of their canyon-bottom home. A search for power characterized both the Apache and the Mandan although paths to its acquisition differed.

Both, however, revered significant culture heroes. Elaborate rituals were directed toward them which reflected the worldview and values of the groups. It is likely that the evolution of some of these complex ceremonies accompanied the discovery of cropping as well as the diffusion of ideas from other groups with which they were in contact over hundreds of years.

The links between environment and culture are readily seen among foragers; environmental limitations are usually extreme, particularly in the absence of a sophisticated technology to tame them. New World hunting and gathering societies were structurally simple and egalitarian. Increased cultural and social complexity cannot be readily explained in simple environmental terms. But if an ecological niche permits farming coupled with large game hunting, and the occupants have the requisite knowledge and exploitive techniques, group living usually ensues and the scene is set for more complex social structure and organization and a richer ceremonial life. What specific forms these may take are contingent upon several factors. Some, idiosyncratic, are shrouded in history thus defying elucidation. Others develop in response to perceived needs of the people relative to their subsistence. A conspicuous reason is, however, the intermingling of diverse people and ideas. Environments permitting agriculture also often allow several culturally different peoples to occupy the land. They exchange ideas and these are woven into a cultural fabric compatible with the borrower's original cultural configuration.

AFFLUENT HUNTERS AND FISHERMEN

There were Indian populations who, during the period of their cultural flowering, neither combined farming with hunting nor practiced full-time farming. Traditionally, ethnologists have classified them as hunter-gatherers, yet such peoples differed significantly from the Canadian Eskimo, the Great Basin wanderers, or the Subarctic forest hunters and fishermen. While it is true that they lived by hunting, collecting, and fishing, they did not fit the typical foraging model. Politically, socially, and demographically, they resembled more closely some of the groups with dual economies. On average, their populations were larger, socially and politically they were more sophisticated, and their ritual life was more elaborate.

These peoples lived in areas rich in resources, and they had the requisite knowledge and skill to utilize them effectively. This is not to say that their wild foods were inexhaustible or that they never faced difficult times, for they did. Yet they were sufficient enough to allow cultural elaboration. Among these societies were some of the plains bison hunters and the myriads of people living along the Pacific Coast from Washington to Alaska.

The Great Plains, as we know, teemed with bison as well as other game until they were systematically destroyed. Ancient early Americans hunted the large *bison antiquus* from early times. Other Indian tribes in following years roamed the area dependent in part upon the modern bison.

Eventually horses and white traders entered the environment; horses enabled the plains Indians to travel widely, chasing the herds, and to pack quantities of meat back to camps near water; the arrival of whites involved them in trade which increased their material goods. These related events transformed their cultures, and for a brief period they were monarchs of their world.

From Puget Sound northward along the Pacific coast and on large off-shore islands to the Gulf of Alaska lived numbers of Indians. Called the Northwest Coast tribes, they spoke at least a dozen different languages and varied somewhat in physical appearance. Yet they, like the plains nomads, shared a number of fundamental culture patterns. This generalized culture type thrived because of skilled exploitation of the sea and rivers. Fishing, sealing, and sometimes whaling were the bases of the economy. These people looked to the waters for their livelihood, especially the rivers abounding with salmon. Several species appeared yearly fighting their way upstream by the millions to spawn. Shellfish littered the narrow beaches. Sea mammals swam off shore; land animals were present too. Bountiful though the area was, to exploit it effectively demanded skill and tools. These peoples developed a technology over the centuries adequate to the task.

In the next two chapters we look at a society from each of these very different geographic regions and examine the relationship between their sociophysical environment and their culture. The first tribe to be studied is the Cheyenne—followers of the buffalo on the northern plains—the other, the Nootka, whalers and fishermen of Vancouver Island off the coast of British Columbia.

CHAPTER EIGHT

The Cheyenne of the Great Plains

Between 1800 and 1860 the Algonkian-speaking Cheyenne rode the great plains from the South Dakota Black Hills through Wyoming, north to Montana, and east to North Dakota. A few bands drifted south to Colorado where they remained in the general vicinity of Bent's Trading Post, one of the first in the area. Both the southern and the northern Cheyenne remained a single tribe, however, and families traveled back and forth from Colorado to Wyoming and Montana.

The early history of the Cheyenne—they called themselves Tsistsistas—is not entirely clear. But George Bird Grinnell and other early students believed that 200 or more years ago they lived in wooded lands bordering the Great Lakes.[1] From there groups moved at different times to the Red River, where they settled until the harassing Assiniboin or Chippewa pushed them westward. Early in the eighteenth century—reaching the Missouri River and influenced by the Mandan, Hidatsa, and Arikara—the Cheyenne adopted a life of semisedentary gardening and hunting. In the

---

[1]George Bird Grinnell, *The Cheyenne Indians: Their History and Ways of Life*, vol. 1. (New York: Cooper Square Publishers, 1962), pp. 1–33. Cooper Square Publishers, Inc., of Totowa, NJ, granted permission to quote from Grinnell. This work was originally published in 1923 by Yale University Press.

middle of the eighteenth century an event occurred which was forever to transform Cheyenne life.

From the south, horses stolen from the Spanish by the Commanche, Kiowa, and Apache reached the northern plains. While the Mandan, Hidatsa, and Arikara used them only to expand their summer bison hunts, the mounted Cheyenne were irresistibly drawn to the capacious plains. Gradually they abandoned their communities; probably by 1830 the entire population (3000 or more), living in bands, ranged widely through the land. Their life focused on buffalo, horses, raiding, and great summer ceremonies. About this time—the dates are obscure—they began to barter European goods acquired from the Mandan to the Arapaho, Kiowa, and others for horses and Spanish items from the south.[2] In this decade, too, they were contacted by representatives of the United States government who persuaded them to sign a treaty which, among other conditions, established trading relationships between the two. The Cheyenne offered fur and hides; the white trader, too often, alcohol.[3]

A member of the treaty delegation described the Cheyenne when he met them in these words:

> . . . The genuine children of nature, they have unlike other Indians, all of the virtues that nature can give, without the vices of civilization. These must be the men described by Rousseau, when he gained the medal from the Royal

[2]Ibid., pp. 40–41.

[3]Stan Hoig, *The Peace Chief of the Cheyennes.* (Norman: University of Oklahoma Press, 1980), p. 23.

Academy in France. They are artless, fearless, and live in constant exercise of moral and Christian virtues, though they know it not.[1]

After the Civil War drew to a close whites pushed westward following their "manifest destiny." Not only the Cheyenne but the Sioux, Blackfoot, Crow, and others witnessed the steady stream of intruders; at first only a few, later wagon train after wagon train passing through along wheel ruts cut deep in the earth. Pressured, angered, and betrayed, the Indian Wars began, culminating in the Battle of the Little Big Horn. Despite the annihilation of Custer and his men, it was a pyrrhic victory for the Cheyenne. Within the year those Indians left—after military assaults on a few helpless encampments—traveled a sorrowful trail to the reservation.

The northern Great Plains west of the Missouri River and stretching to the Rocky Mountain foothills was Cheyenne territory. It was an almost endless expanse of short-grassed land lying under a great canopy of sky. Horizons were distant; trees grew only along streams. A dry country watered in the summer by sudden thundering electric storms, violent rains poured down filling buffalo wallows only to evaporate under the summer sun. Biting hot wind swept the lands in summer; in the winter "Northers" whipped baleful blizzards that threatened life. Only in spring was the wind benign. Warming southerly currents melted the last patches of snow urging the grass to green up. Berries, seeds, and roots—each ripened in its own time. Gradually as spring surrendered to early summer the winter-scattered buffalo herds merged, forming the ocean of black backs so vividly described by early witnesses. Then the land was generous and the Cheyenne bands, like the buffalo, gathered to renew themselves and their world.

E. Adamson Hoebel said of Cheyenne country:

The land of the Cheyennes is not a paradise. But when at its benevolent best, it is a challenging land with the beautiful serenity of vast vistas and the "Big Sky"—a bountiful land of millions of bison and antelope easily taken when the season is right; a land of roots, seeds, and berries for those who know where to find them; a land where a man can get a full, satisfied belly on rich meat balanced with a variety of wild vegetables. But it is still a land where starvation is a spectre never far off, and cold death, thirst and maddening heat must be confronted. It is a land where people must hold together, or perish; where people must "know how," or soon be done in; where the Cheyenne have come to rely not only on technical skill but on mystique and compulsive ritual to bolster their sense of security and give them a faith which will engender courage.[5]

[4]Ibid., p. 24. Quoted from Daily National Intelligencer, Washington, D.C., November 4, 1925.

[5]E. Adamson Hoebel, *The Cheyennes: Indians of the Great Plains: Case Studies in Anthropology.* (New York: Holt, Rinehart and Winston, 1960), p. 57, Copyright © 1960 by Holt, Rinehart & Winston, Inc. Reprinted by permission of CBS College Publishing.

Cheyenne camp, circa 1900.
Smithsonian Institution National Anthropological Archives.

Buffalo migrations largely dictated the major form and events of Cheyenne life.[6] Winter in the northern plains forced the bison to wander in small herds seeking food and shelter. With the approach of spring and early summer the small herds gradually coalesced to form enormous herds which fed on the verdant grass. Late summer and fall withered the vegetation compelling the animals to disperse. Because the people depended upon the huge animals for nearly all their wants, they organized themselves in ways most efficient for hunting them. In the fall, winter, and spring, they too lived in small bands—there were ten named groups— scattered over their territory; only small units could successfully procure food for themselves and their horses in these seasons. In early summer the bands slowly came together to engage in impressive communal ceremonies and remained together for the collective summer hunts.

Related kindred formed Cheyenne bands, although often unrelated folk chose to camp with one or another group. The kindred included the head of the family, his wife or wives, their unmarried children, and their married daughters. Matrilocality was the norm, so married sons lived in another kindred. Although the kindred was a matrilocal extended family there were no lineages or clans.

The Cheyenne viewed marriage as a singularly important affair not to be undertaken frivolously. The reputation of the young people as well as family rank were evaluated; marriage between even the most distant of kin was forbidden. Older people watched their young carefully, ready to intervene should a romantic interest develop between two inappropriate people. Moreover, a daughter was closely supervised, for the loss of virtue shamed her and her family. Grinnell remarked:

[6]The Portrayal of Cheyenne Culture derived largely from the work of George Bird Grinnell, *The Cheyenne Indians: Their History and Ways of Life*, vols. 1 and 2. Direct quotations are cited.

> The women of the Cheyenne are famous among all western tribes for their chastity. In olden times it was most unusual for a girl to be seduced, and she who had yielded was disgraced forever. The matter at once became known and she was taunted with it wherever she went. It was never forgotten. No young man would marry her. This seems the more remarkable since the Arapahoes, with whom the Cheyennes had been so long and so closely associated, are notorious for the looseness of their women.[7]

So dedicated were the people to the principle of female purity that young women wore a "chastity belt" made of rope tied around the waist; the ends of the rope were looped around the thighs, and this apparel was always worn at night or when young women were outside the lodge during the day. Any man who dared to ignore the rope faced death at the hands of the girl's outraged relatives. Grinnell reported this story of a middle-aged man who attempted to violate the protection:

> The girl and her mother were the only two of the family left, all their male relatives having died. Not long after the attempt was made the mother and daughter, arming themselves with heavy stones, waylaid the man, took him by surprise, gave him a frightful pounding, and left him for dead. He recovered after a long siege, during which he received sympathy from no one.[8]

Cheyenne courtship was a long arduous affair. It all began when, first attracted by a young woman, a youth waited for her to leave her lodge on some errand. As she drew close he reached out and tugged on her robe to attract her attention; if she stopped to murmur a few words, he was jubilant, if she did not, crestfallen and humiliated, he hurried away. Boys, less courageous, often whistled at girls hoping to solicit a smile which would embolden them to take more positive action. Should a young man, rebuffed, be unwilling to give up, there were supernatural means at his disposal. A few medicine men specialized in affairs of the heart. One perhaps gave spruce gum to the hapless lover. If he or a female relative could persuade the girl to chew it, her thoughts would rest on him alone. Love magic worked on a flute rendered it irresistible. Hearing his trilling in the distance, the girl was drawn outside her lodge to await his arrival.

Before an ardent wooer had won the girl's consent as well as his parents', usually four or five years had passed. Through an emissary, a friend or an elderly relative, he then made his intentions known to her parents. The messenger led horses and carried other valuable presents to the girl's lodge. After staking the horses, he entered the lodge and spoke of casual things; finally he delivered the message and departed, giving the girl's parents time to gather her male kindred to discuss the matter. If they decided against the union the horses and gifts were returned and the matter ended.

[7]Ibid., vol. 1, p. 156.
[8]Ibid., p. 131.

Should the match be approved, the horses and gifts were distributed among the assembled relatives. The following morning they returned bringing gifts and horses equivalent in value. While they loaded the horses with their gifts, the bride's female relatives dressed her in wedding finery and painted her face. Mounting the best horse, she was led by an unrelated woman to her groom's lodge. His male relatives rushed out, lifted her from her mount, placed her in a blanket, and carried her into her new husband's lodge. Her sisters-in-law removed her clothing and dressed her in raiments they had made for the occasion. A feast followed celebrating the nuptial. Until their mothers and relatives erected and furnished their new *tipi* near her mother's lodge, the young couple remained with his family. As Grinnell reported, her protective rope often remained in place until they moved to the new lodge: "The Cheyenne say that this custom had the advantage of enabling the newly married couple to get used to each other, to sleeping together. Men tell me that they used to lie awake all night, talking to their newly married wives."[9]

Aside from adjusting to one another, marriage imposed no major changes in their lives. Each continued the tasks learned as children. He hunted, raided, and took part in the ritual and political affairs of the group. She ran the household, prepared skins, made clothing, and eventually bore children. Living matrilocally, however, did create a situation to which the young husband had to adapt. His mother-in-law was to be avoided at all cost. He never spoke to her nor looked at her; she entered his lodge only when she was sure he was elsewhere. Some men lived with the taboo a lifetime. But among good families—those with integrity and wealth—the restriction could be ritually removed after a few years. A highly principled son-in-law had a good horse delivered to his mother-in-law. She, were she so inclined, accepted it and selected a fine robe to decorate with porcupine quills. The robe finished, she invited the Women's Quilling Society and her son-in-law to a feast in her lodge—the other occupants were temporarily banished. He entered the *tipi* after the ladies were gathered, turned to the right, and sank down on the robe in the rear of the lodge, pulling it over his shoulders. Taking an ember from the fire, his mother-in-law sprinkled sweet grasses on it; the smoke enveloped the young man "giving him a good heart." He rose and without eating or speaking left the lodge and rode off on a gift horse given by her. The Quilling Society remained to consume the food. The two in-laws were then freed from the onerous taboo.

While most marriages were monogamous, some wealthy men as they grew older married additional women—either sisters or cousins of their first wife. To marry a second woman unrelated to the first invited more trouble than a reasonable man could tolerate. Cheyenne expected marriages to endure, but many failed. Incompatibility often culminated in sep-

[9]Ibid., p. 145.

aration. A woman signaled a divorce by suggesting that her husband leave or made the situation even clearer by eloping with another man. Her new husband mollified the abandoned spouse by gifts. This usually ended the matter, but an especially vindictive man might attempt to injure the couple or their horses—in either case a serious action. A dissatisfied husband divorced his wife by taking his property from their home. Some men—not satisfied to divorce in this way—declared their separation by striking a drum at a dance and hurling the stick in the air. Such a public announcement was especially humiliating for wives, and some were not at all gracious about the maneuver:

> Little Eagle from Ashland danced and then walked to the drummers and hit the drum as hard as he could with a stick. He did not give his wife away to any special one, he just divorced her. She was so mad she hit the drum in the same way and said anybody could have her husband's children just to get even.[10]

In the beginning stages of a marriage all food was prepared in the lodge of the bride's parents. When it was ready she carried it to her *tipi* where she and her husband consumed it. How long this continued is not clear, but probably the birth of a baby brought an end to the arrangement. The young couple, however, in the company of other younger members of the kindred, supplied much if not all of the food for the group. During the seasons when the bands camped apart, a young husband, eager to impress his in-laws, spent many hours, often in bitter weather, searching for game, alone or with one or two friends. Because he was expected to bring home meat aplenty he took extra pack horses: "If he failed to kill enough meat, his friends made it a point of honor to see that his horses were loaded."[11] Often as he approached the camp, his wife or some of her friends met him and led the burdened animals to his mother-in-law's lodge.

Women harvested vegetable foods, and the young bride worked at this in the company of her kin long before her marriage. In the spring they gathered roots and edible plants, and in late summer they picked berries. Small groups of related women and girls carrying digging sticks and containers trudged across the plains gradually vanishing from view. Although the work was demanding, the expedition afforded escape from camp, a chance to gossip, and even gamble! As the sun moved toward the west and shadows lengthened, the women started slowly back to camp, often stopping to wager their roots by throwing their digging sticks or by tossing bison metacarpals (Cheyenne version of dice). Losers forfeited their bundle of roots—not an especially serious matter!

An even more titillating event occurred when they gathered *pomme blanche* (a white turnip which the French called white potato). When in sight

---

[10]John Stands in Timber and Margot Liberty, *Cheyenne Memories*. (New Haven: Yale University Press, 1967), p. 283. This account dates from about 1895.

[11]George Bird Grinnell, *The Cheyenne Indians*, vol. 1, p. 145.

of camp, each woman sat down and put her roots on the ground in front of her. Suddenly one shouted the blood-curdling Cheyenne war cry and waved a blanket in imitation of a returning raiding party. Upon hearing the challenge, young men lounging about the camp grabbed imitation shields and mounted the oldest, spavined, cow-hocked horses available. Spurring and kneeing the sway-backed nags they charged toward the waiting women, who had armed themselves with buffalo chips and sticks. Shouting, twisting, they attempted to dodge the flying buffalo manure. Anyone hit by the debris was wounded and out of the fray. Only a man who had been wounded in war or had a horse killed under him could dismount and plunder the roots, provided he had evaded the missiles. The others milled around creating general confusion. The melee concluded when some roots had been snatched and the men rode off to eat them and brag. The women, amidst the cheers of the bystanders, continued to their lodges.

Except for forays into the plains for food or wood, women worked in and around their lodges doing what women had always done: preparing food, caring for children, tanning hides, and fashioning them into clothing or lodges. To prepare a hide, women stretched it by pinning it to the ground. Kneeling or squatting they scraped all blood, flesh, or fat from it, then thinned it with a flesher (an adzelike tool). Finally the hair was removed if it were not to be made into a buffalo robe. To cure it they concocted a compound of brains, liver, soapweed, and grease, and laboriously rubbed it into both sides. This finished, the hide was folded compactly so that the mixture thoroughly permeated the skin. In the morning they unfolded it, laying it in the sun to dry. Boardlike, dried hides had to be softened, which required hours of arduous work pulling the hide back and forth over a taut rope or through a hole in a buffalo scapula. Even the most industrious of women wearied of the chore and put the skin down to finish another day. The Cheyenne, like other nonindustrial people, were seldom driven by time.

Preparing skins sufficient for a new lodge was a major undertaking and no woman worked alone at the job. Cheyenne lodges varied in size depending upon the wealth in horses of the lodge owners. The larger the lodge the more horses the family needed to move it and carry the rest of their belongings. So lodges ranged from one made of eleven skins and eighteen poles to a twenty-one-skin *tipi* supported by twenty-eight poles. Having a large lodge was a dubious advantage, perhaps, since a poorer woman had less work to do in preparing skins.

When a lodge showed signs of wear, its mistress prepared skins for a replacement. Working on and off for days, she scraped and thinned buffalo cowhides, applied the tanning brew, and dried them. The prospect of softening them, however, was so overwhelming that she invited friends and relatives to a feast. After they had eaten, exchanged news, and visited, each departed for home with a hide and a softening rope. Working steadily, they softened the skins in the ensuing days. When the pliable skins were returned they had to be cut, fitted, and sewn together. Once more she hosted a large feast for sewers. A skilled lodge cutter arrived at dawn to mark the hides for cutting and sewing. While she did this, a child scuttled off to notify the sewers that the skins were ready. The accommodating guests assembled, ate a large breakfast, then worked all day, interrupting their labor only for a sumptious afternoon meal. By dark the task was completed; the lodge was erected and ready for occupancy. Lodges not only sheltered families, they symbolized Cheyenne life and beliefs. *Tipis*, therefore, were ritually sanctified before the family moved in. Grinnell watched a lodge dedication:

> On an occasion when I saw this ceremony performed, Little Bear was chosen to count the coup and to dedicate the lodge. After the lodge had been set up and prepared, the women all drew back, and Little Bear and old men with a number of braves advanced toward it. Those accompanying him stopped at a little distance from it, and stood or sat in a wide half circle. Little Bear, holding in his hand a small stick, walked to the door, and struck the lodge on the left hand (south) side of the door, and about halfway between the ground and the door's apex. Then facing toward the spectators, he said: "We started on the trail after Utes. All were mounted—a large party. Poor Bull and Big Bow [Kiowas] were with us. About the middle of the day in the Raton Mountains [in New Mexico] we overtook the enemy. They were in camp—five lodges of them. We charged upon them, and I rushed to the lodge on the left hand. Just before I reached the door, a Ute put his head out, and I stabbed him with my lance. We scalped him. Besides this I took some horses." When he had said this, he turned about and entered the new lodge. The other men then rose and followed him in; first the more important ones, Little Chief, Man Above, Long Neck, Man on The Cloud—all the bravest men. The other less important men went in afterward.[12]

Counting coup ranked among the most courageous male acts. By counting coup on a lodge the bravest of men acknowledged that the women, too, had accomplished a significant and difficult task worthy of recognition.[13] The cooperating women left for home following the ceremony, knowing that their hostess would return the favor when the time came. The lodge cutter accepted a gift—robe, blanket, or moccasins—for her help. Cheyenne women worked diligently but they had their diversions. They were far from drudges. Grinnell commented that Cheyenne women wielded exceptional power in the affairs of the camp.

While it might appear that the men spent an untoward amount of time in the shade smoking and boasting, providing animal food and protecting their families often put them at risk. Buffalo were vital to Cheyenne subsistence; to a lesser degree they relied upon antelope, black bear, elk, and deer. In the early days the antelope hunt resembled closely that of the

[12]Ibid., pp. 231–232.
[13]Ibid., p. 128.

Great Basin people; a medicine man organized it, directed the activities, and practiced complicated ritual to ensure the success of the surround. The summer buffalo hunt was governed by strict regulations enforced by men of one of the military societies—a situation similar to the Mandan communal hunt. Llewellyn and Hoebel described the consequences of a violation of the norms of the hunt:

> The tribe was moving in a body up the Rosebud River toward the Big Horn Mountain country in search of buffalo. The Shield Soldiers . . . had their scouts out looking for the herds, and when the scouts came in with their report, the order was given that no one should leave the camp or attack the buffalo. . . .
> All the hunters went out in a line with the Shield Soldiers in front to hold them back. Just as they were coming up over a long ridge . . . they saw two men down in the valley riding in among the buffalo. A Shield Soldier Chief gave the signal to his men. They paid no attention to the buffalo, but charged in a long line on the two violators of the rules. Little Man shouted out for every one to whip them: "Those who fail or hesitate shall get a good beating themselves."
> The first men to reach the spot shot and killed the horses from under the hunters. As each soldier reached the miscreants he slashed them with his riding whip. Then some seized the guns of the two and smashed them.[14]

After the punishment the chief and the boys' father each delivered a scathing lecture. Shamed and humiliated, they hung their heads. In typical Cheyenne fashion several of the soldiers volunteered to replace the dead horses and their guns. Hoebel remarked that, "in good Cheyenne manner, first the violators were severely punished and then immediately rehabilitated as soon as the soldiers sensed they had learned their lesson."[15] When the animals were dispersed—fall and winter—men hunted them at will. Winter hunting was arduous; the prairies and plains were cold and often deep in snow. The hunters traveled far searching for the elusive creatures, freezing fingers and toes as they huddled around small fires for protection against the punishing temperatures.

The Cheyenne like many plains nomads were recent arrivals in the vast area, and they—along with Crow, Arapaho, Commanche, Pawnee, and Dakotas—fought to hold their place on the plains. Each tribe had allies and each had implacable enemies. The Cheyenne had as friends the Mandan, Hidatsa, and the Arikara. The Sioux and the Arapaho could also be counted on. Hostilities existed between the Cheyenne, the Ute, and Shoshone, but their hated enemies were the Crow and the Pawnee. After 1840 they battled with the Commanche and Kiowa. Existing as they did in a cli-

---

[14]K. N. Llewellyn and E. Adamson Hoebel, *The Cheyenne Way: Conflict and Case Law in Primitive Jurisprudence.* (Norman: University of Oklahoma Press, 1941), pp. 112–113. Copyright © 1941 by the University of Oklahoma Press.

[15]E. Adamson Hoebel, *The Cheyennes*, p. 54.

mate of endemic warfare, daring and military virtue were dominant themes in men's lives. Grinnell said of them:

> The fighting spirit was encouraged. In no way could a young man gain so much credit as by the exhibition of courage. Boys and youths were trained to feel that the most important thing in life was to be brave; that death was not a thing to be avoided; that, in fact, it was better for a man to be killed while in his full vigor rather than to wait until his prime was past, his powers failing. . . . He lost his teeth; he could not enjoy his food; he sat on the cold side of the lodge; life seemed to hold for him nothing good. How much better, therefore, to struggle and fight, to be brave and accomplish great things, to receive the respect and applause of everyone in the camp, and finally to die gloriously at the hands of the enemy![16]

Public adulation rewarded the courageous warrior and he counted coup on many ritual occasions. Hoebel observed: "The fighting patterns of the Cheyenne are embellished with virtuosities that go far beyond the needs of victory. Display in bravery becomes an end in itself. Prestige drives override the more limited requirements for defeat of the enemy."[17] For most of the plains peoples warfare had the characteristics of a very hazardous sport. Counting coup—touching an enemy with hand, weapon, or a special stick—was the method of scoring. All had rules for claiming coup, for example, how many warriors were permitted to touch the same enemy and in what order. One could claim a coup by saving a fallen companion, taking on a group of enemies singlehandedly, or having a horse shot out from under one. Killing and scalping were laudable too, but they did not compare with the daredevil feats. So important was courage that a young man could not court a girl until he had demonstrated his valor. Women had songs to deride cowardice: "If you are afraid when you charge, turn back. The Desert Women will eat you." This meant that the women would gossip about the reluctant warrior so much that it would have been better were he killed. John Stands in Timber wrote of his people: "My grandfather and others used to tell me that hearing the women sing that way made them ready to do anything. It was hard to go into a fight, and they were often afraid, but it was worse to turn back and face the women."[18]

Private, fraternal, and tribal were the three kinds of Cheyenne war parties; the first was the most common. Any qualified man who could enlist followers—and most young men were eager to join him—might undertake a raid. Among these followers were likely to be a few neophytes, boys 14 or 15; more experienced men carefully shepherded them on their first outings. Seldom did they actually fight, but they secured experience and by the

[16]George Bird Grinnell, *The Fighting Cheyenne*. (Norman: University of Oklahoma Press, 1956), p. 12. This volume was published originally by Charles Scribner & Sons in 1915.

[17]E. Adamson Hoebel, *The Cheyennes*, p. 70.

[18]John Stands in Timber and Margo Liberty, *Cheyenne Memories*, p. 63.

time they were 20 they were tested warriors. At 30 they were emboldened to lead other men.

To lead a war party required no vision quest, but the ambitious young man needed ritual approval to undertake the raid.[19] To solicit permission he visited a mature man, offered him a pipe, and detailed his plan. Somberly the advisor considered the proposal, finally advising him to make an offering to the Sacred Arrows. Once again filling his pipe and wearing a buffalo robe hair-side-out, he trudged slowly to the Arrowkeeper's lodge moaning with each step to signal others of his intention. The Arrowkeeper invited him in and accepted his offering, usually eagle tail feathers or a robe, over which he prayed. The young man tied the gift to the Sacred Arrow bundle while entreating the arrows to protect him and his followers and that he might count a first coup. The keeper lighted the pipe and together they smoked in great solemnity. Prepared now to lead a war party he invited a group of like-minded men to feast and advised them of his plans. All those who smoked his pipe as it passed among them indicated a willingness to follow. These men refilled the pipe and walked to the lodge of a medicine man to whom the leader related his plan. By accepting the pipe the medicine man agreed to perform the requisite rituals; singing a war chant; indicating the direction they ought take; and in a sweat lodge, consecrating weapons, shields, and war bonnets. A man who had led prior forays did not seek the approbation of ritual leaders. He assembled men in his lodge, fed them, and spoke: "I desire to go to war; who will join me?" A successful leader encountered only a few who would not smoke the pipe.

Before the departure day the men assembled their equipment, extra moccasins, and food; the night before leaving they strode in a circle chanting wolf songs. Some well wishers gave them gifts of dried meat, tobacco, or arrows. Early the next morning the leader left alone on foot, part of his gear carried by a dog. Throughout the rest of the day others left in pairs with their loaded dogs. Late in the afternoon they rendevouzed and proceeded single file to a concealed camping spot. Through the night the leader and the men supplicated the supernatural with prayer and song.

As they approached enemy territory the leader dispatched two scouts on a reconnaissance. They moved cautiously, slipping through gullies and arroyos, climbing the high ground surreptitiously to scan the land. Faint smoke in the distance or restless animals indicated the presence of people. Seeing these clues the scouts gestured to the waiting party to move ahead. Creeping silently toward the enemy camp they waited until the deep darkness of the plains descended; a moonless night was especially helpful. Private raiding parties like these were either organized to steal horses or to revenge a fallen friend or kinsman. If horses were the object, they sneaked into the camp and cut loose as many as they could manage and each drove

---

[19]The account of Cheyenne warring derives from vol. 2 of George Bird Grinnell's *The Cheyenne Indians*, pp. 7–47.

his animals to a designated meeting place. When all returned they took off, still keeping the horses separate. At dawn after every man had memorized the markings of his booty, the animals were herded together and driven at a furious pace by the now mounted raiders away from the plundered camp. On occasion the victims attempted to pursue their horses. Not often, however, were they able to catch up with the retreating enemy.

If revenge motivated the war party, the men arrayed in war paint attacked the camp at dawn, counting coup and scalping the dead or wounded adversaries. The Cheyenne permitted three men to count coup on an enemy and receive credit; the first shouted "I am the first," the second, "I am the second," the last, "I am the third."

After the adventure was over and the men had returned to their own people, they sat around a fire of buffalo chips and claimed their coups. Occasionally disputes arose over who was the first to touch the foe. To attest to his veracity a Cheyenne rubbed his hand over the ritual pipe and asserted that he had done what he claimed he did. In the face of an unresolved dispute by oath, there were more formal means to get at the truth. A buffalo skull was adorned ritually and four arrows—representing the holy arrows—and a gun were placed against it. A chief called each man forward to make his claim. Touching the objects he said: "Spiritual Powers, listen to me. I touched him. If I tell a lie, I hope I may be shot far off."[20] He then described his actions; because the Cheyenne feared this oath it was doubtful that any men would knowingly deceive the people and the spiritual powers.

Large war parties—a 100 or more participants—were usually organized by military societies or perhaps by the tribal chiefs to avenge the killing of a number of Cheyenne. When such a party returned victorious with no losses—or if a brave had died and he had counted coup before falling—the *berdaches* organized a Scalp Dance. *Berdaches* were men who wore women's clothing and did women's work; often they served as second wife to a powerful married man. Whether they were active homosexuals has not been demonstrated. The *berdaches*, called "half-men–half-women," were skilled curers and often accompanied large war expeditions; they carried the best scalps fixed to poles as the victors returned from the fray.

The Scalp Dance occurred at night in the middle of the camp circle. Urged by the *berdaches* each lodge owner contributed wood for the ceremony. The half-men–half-women constructed a huge conical pile of wood which they ignited after the singers and drummers arrived. All of the people, young and old, assembled to participate. Babies in cradleboards were hung from saplings or placed on the ground near the dancers. The Scalp Dance was no fiery, fervid affair; it was carefully choreographed by the transvestites and comprised five separate dances each with stylized movements and specific songs. The themes of the dances turned around love

[20]Ibid., p. 34.

and courtship. The first was the Sweetheart's Dance, followed by the Matchmaking Dance. In each the *berdaches* paired the participants. The Round Dance followed: Two lines of boys and girls danced up to and away from each other, then joined a partner assigned from the first two dances and moved about in a large circle, arms about each other. The old people stood in the middle shouting and waving their scalps. Children were kept in order by the *berdaches*. Following the Slippery Dance was another mating dance, the Galloping Buffalo Bull Dance. This symbolized the culmination of courtship and mating. Three or four women tied their skirts up above their knees and approached seated young men. Turning around, they bent over and danced with their back to the men. Accepting the challenge three or four young men arose bent down behind them, and like prancing bison bulls followed the women. Finally all the women baited the men and the entire assemblage bounded and pranced like an excited buffalo herd. The *berdaches* shouted to the dancers to form a circle, and they all—drummers, singers, sweethearts, and elders—danced in a closed united group. Often the rays of the sun climbed faintly on the horizon before the dance ended. On the plains, warfare was the path to honor and Cheyenne men performed bravely. Each hunt tempted their enemies; their camps and animals lured marauders; security was seldom theirs. To wed, to be respected, to become a leader, required them to risk their lives repeatedly for glory.

Intraband and kindred aggression was, however, not the Cheyenne way. Like all people they attempted to control behavior through teasing, gossip, or scorn. They were not content, however, to rely only on informal measures and what some scholars call private law—in which aggrieved parties work out solutions to their conflicts with the indirect approval of society. In contrast to the Commanche, the Assinboin, and other plains people, the Cheyenne possessed a powerful central tribal government which cut across kindred and band. Paramount in the structure was the Council of Forty-four, a body composed of peace chiefs who served a term of 10 years. The military societies formed the other arm of tribal government; they acted as police, enforcing the orders of chiefs, and were the organized military force of the tribe and bands.

Cheyenne myths attribute the formation of the Council to the efforts of a woman. Whatever its beginnings, the Council was a self-perpetuating group; members selected their successors after their 10-year tenure ended. Although each chief represented his band and was chosen from kindred headmen, he was a defender of all the people, the protector of widows and orphans:

> . . . A chief must be brave in war, generous in disposition, liberal in temper, deliberate in making up his mind, and of good judgment. A good chief gave his whole heart and his whole mind to the work of helping his people, and strove for their welfare with an earnestness and a devotion rarely equaled by other rulers of men. Such thought for his fellows was not without its influence

on the man himself; after a time the spirit of goodwill which animated him became reflected in his countenance, so that, as he grew old, such a chief came to have a most benevolent and kindly expression. Yet, though simple, honest, generous, tender-hearted, and often merry and jolly, when occasion demanded he could be stern, severe, and inflexible of purpose. Such men, once known, commanded general respect and admiration. They were like the conventional notion of Indians in nothing save in the color of their skin.[21]

Among the forty-four chiefs were five sacred chiefs chosen from ordinary chiefs who had completed a full term of office. The presiding officer was Sweet Medicine Chief, the head priest-chief of the tribe. He had custody of the Sweet Medicine Bundle and was initiated into the ritual of his office by his predecessor. Four other chiefs—representing cosmic spiritual personages and with ritual responsibilities—assisted him. These men sat in traditional places when the council was in session. Two others acted as doormen; the remaining thirty-seven were equal in status. Hoebel said of the ritual and sacred dimensions of the Council:

> The mystic symbolism of the dependence of the Cheyenne on the supernatural world is thus woven into the very nucleus of their governmental structure. At its heart, in their belief, the council is not just a body of their wisest, but a council of men in empathy with the spirit forces that dominate all life— beneficent forces from which come all good things the Cheyenne heart desires, forces that respond to their hopes and needs so long as the compulsive ritual acts are faithfully repeated.[22]

The Council dealt with matters of interest to the tribe. On minor issues— for instance, if the opinion of one chief was supported by another—the Council usually concurred without further discussion. Major decisions, such as moving summer camp if bison were scarce or adjudicating a crime, required long and deliberate debate. Older men did much of the talking. Each speech was followed by a long silence to give time to consider the remarks. No speaker young or old was interrupted; wrangling or heated exchanges were unheard of. Decisions were reached through consensus and announced through the camp by mounted criers. Meetings were not, however, secret; people with nothing else to do often sat outside the lodge and listened to the deliberations. Following the adjournment of a meeting, the chiefs explained the rationale for decisions with the members of their bands and kindred. Should public opinion have been at odds with Council judgments and the chiefs could not sway the people, policy was likely to be modified.

The investiture of a new Council of Forty-four occurred every 10 years and was as sedate and ceremonious as other major tribal rituals. It took place during the tribal summer encampment; the chiefs' lodge was

[21]George Bird Grinnell, *The Cheyenne Indians*, vol. 1, pp. 336–337.

[22]E. Adamson Hoebel, *The Cheyennes*, p. 45.

erected in the center of the camp circle, the Arrowkeeper's and the Buffalo Hat's lodges were nearby. The surviving chiefs of the past decade gathered in the lodge to commence their deliberations. Four days and nights of rites associated with Sweet Medicine and other Cheyenne supernaturals were conducted by the five sacred chiefs; there then followed the nominations of the new men. Each was discussed, his virtues examined, his valor praised; some encumbents were persuaded to accept a second term. The selection completed, each new chief gifted his predecessor generously. People gathered to view the new Council's emergence from the sacred lodge. The encampment rang with celebrations and feasting; the chiefs and probably other affluent men gave presents of horses and robes to their fellows, especially the poor. Largesse was esteemed. The event concluded with the Chief Dance accompanied by more gift-giving.

Cheyenne government was a type of representative democracy. Although women did not hold Council membership (nor were they ever lesser chiefs), their opinions were sought and their influence was considerable.

The military societies—or fraternities as they were sometimes called—had their charter in the mythologic past. Sweet Medicine, the Cheyenne culture hero, imposed the title of warrior on all males over 15. Erudite medicine men whom he instructed organized the warriors into five societies. Through the medicine men he detailed their responsibilities and dictated their governance.[23] The Fox, Shield, Elk, Dog, and Bow-string, were the original five. In the early nineteenth century the Pawnee killed all of the Bow-strings; shortly afterwards Owl Man formed a new one which he called the Wolf. Still later the Crazy Dogs association was constituted. Although the Mandan Warrior societies were graded, the Cheyenne sodalities were not. A young male joined any club he wished. His parents accompanied him to his first society dance; either they or his relatives bestowed horses on the chief or other members. Differing only in dance, dress, and ritual, the structure of all clubs was essentially the same. Each had four officers who were the main tribal war leaders, positions of great danger. Only men willing to die were elected. Two of them were also ritual leaders and sat at the rear of the lodge when the club convened. The other two, the bravest men in the group, sat on either side of the door and were couriers to the Council of Fourty-four. If a military society chief was appointed to the tribal council, he resigned his position for he could not at the same time be both a peace chief and a war chief.

Five of the societies had four chaste daughters of chiefs as members whom the men called sister and with whom marriage was forbidden. The maidens danced with the warriors and sat with the war chiefs when they met in council. As the warriors were the bravest of men, so the girls were

[23]George A. Dorsey, *The Cheyenne*. Chicago, Field Columbian Museum Anthropological Series, vol. IX, 1905, p. 15. (New York: Kraus Reprint Co., 1971).

the epitome of Cheyenne female virtue. Together they symbolized Cheyenne ideals. Had one of these girls "fallen," bad luck would forever dog the men. For this reason two of the societies were unwilling to risk the membership of virgins.

The military societies acted as units only during the tribal summer encampment. One was chosen to police the annual bison hunt; and all were poised to protect the group from attack. On long marches the Council of Forty-four designated the supervising society. Their authority was almost absolute on these occasions. They also maintained strict discipline within their ranks, using harsh measures. A tribal rule stipulated that the men of the society of the Sun Dance Pledger walk on the march to the site of the dance. Llewellyn and Hoebel related the following consequences when the rule was violated.

> When the Crazy Dogs were marching because their comrade Old Wolf was giving a Sun Dance, one of their number rode up on his horse. He had as an excuse his sore knee, which was badly swollen; but they had no pity on him as they pulled him from his mount, destroyed his saddle, and made him walk. If he had stayed away because of his sore knee, Spotted Elk says they would have killed his horses.[24]

In the matter of murder, an act repellant to the people, the soldier societies often seized or were given jurisdiction. Abortion was murder in the Cheyenne view; Calf Woman described the actions they took in one such case:

> Somebody found an aborted fetus in the vicinity of the camp. The discovery was made known to the Council. They believed that the fetus was that of a Cheyenne, but nothing was known about it. The soldier chiefs were consulted, and by them a plan of investigation was produced. The two head chiefs of a soldier society convened their group, while the society announcer was sent out to broadcast the order of the soldiers for all women to assemble in public. When it was seen that all were at hand, the women were ordered to expose their breasts for inspection. The soldier chiefs looked closely at each one to note lactation enlargements of the breasts as a sign of recent pregnancy. One girl showed symptoms, and she was charged with the crime, judged guilty, and banished from the tribe until after the Arrows had been renewed.[25]

Responding to situations for which there were no regulations—or for those in which potential friction was great—the military societies often enacted new social policy.

The Council and the military societies functioned to maintain order and stability in Cheyenne society. From obscure beginnings, the latter became over the years a powerful enforcer of the common good.

[24]K. N. Llewellyn and E. Adamson Hoebel, *The Cheyenne Way*, p. 114.
[25]Ibid., p. 119.

The design of Cheyenne society provided a satisfying if risky life for its members, but no group can deal with the totality of existence without a system of belief and faith in the supernatural, whatever it is conceived to be. Cheyenne beliefs and worldview, permeating nearly all aspects of life, defined the nature of things and pointed the way toward balance and harmony. In their view there were a number of vaguely understood supernaturals who knew how to make the universe function and to produce that which people desired and needed. If humans turned to them and listened, omniscient spirits would share their knowledge. Four beneficent beings dwelled at the four cardinal points. Above the earth *Heammawhio* lived; below it, *Aktunowhio.* When men engaged in ritual pipe smoking, the stem was pointed first to the sky, then to the earth, and then to the east, south, west, and north.

The Cheyenne received their spectacular summer rituals from the supernatural. Sweet Medicine and Erect Horns, culture heroes, made pilgrimages in the long, long ago to the source of all knowledge. There a Holy One (*Maiyun*) taught them the proper conduct of the ceremonies. They, in turn, went back to the Cheyenne and meticulously instructed them. The emphasis on teaching was pervasive in important rituals. A man was painstakingly instructed in the performance of the Sun Dance by the one who had himself performed it. A woman about to quill her first robe sought the ritual knowledge from a woman who possessed it. As Hoebel observed, "Every Cheyenne ritual of consequence has at least a Teacher and a Novice in its personnel."[26]

The Renewal of the Sacred Arrows was the most holy of Cheyenne tribal rites. Sweet Medicine journeyed to the Sacred Mountain in the Black Hills; a door opened, he entered, and there he remained four years. Great Medicine gave him four magic arrows and instructed him in their care and meaning. Two of the arrows had power over men; the other two over buffalo and other animals. If the Keeper of the Arrows pointed the buffalo arrows at the animals, they became weakened and confused and were easily killed. Man-arrows pointed at the enemy bewildered him, and he fell before the Cheyenne warriors. Man-arrow points also killed women if they inadvertently passed before them. As a consequence no women took part in the Arrow ritual nor saw the sacred Arrows. The Arrows symbolized major Cheyenne anxieties—the failure of food resources or annihilation by their foes—and they likewise formed an emotional bulwark against these ever-present hazards. The Sacred Arrows represented the communal soul of the people. "As the Arrows prosper, the tribe prospers; as they are allowed to suffer neglect, the tribe declines in prosperity."[27]

George Dorsey maintained that the Arrow Renewal ceremony took place annually, but others contended that it was held only when an individ-

[26]E. Adamson Hoebel, *The Cheyennes*, p. 82.
[27]Ibid., p. 7.

ual was motivated by stress or fear to make a commitment to the Holy Ones.[28] Such pledges to sponsor the ceremony were voluntary; but in the event of a murder in the tribe, it was unequivocally mandatory for the Arrows to be renewed. Blood from the crime despoiled the Arrows; game vanished and evil fortune descended upon the tribe until the sin was expiated through the renewal rite.

When a man vowed to sponsor the ritual, he informed the Keeper of the Arrows and his assistants, who anointed him with red paint, prayed for him, and gave him a pipe. His kindred supported him by gathering food and gifts for the event. He then wandered across the plains in early spring, searching for the camps of the Cheyenne bands; at each he announced his intention and named the day. The bands broke camp and moved from the far-flung reaches of the territory toward the designated place. Each stopped four times during its trek to pray, to smoke the sacred pipe, and to appeal to spirits. As each band approached the encampment, its members stopped to dress in their finest clothing and to adorn their horses. To the cheers of earlier comers they rode into the camp from the east, chanting and singing around the great circle to their traditional place. Pack animals were unloaded with dispatch; women erected their family *tipis* and started cooking fires. The camp was alive with sounds of visiting, gossiping, and feasting.

On the first of four days, the Arrow pledger's wife erected his lodge in the center of the circle; to it people brought gifts for the *Maiyun*.[29] Assistant medicine men bundled them together and suspended them over the entrance. Following this, the warrior societies congregated to select the place for the great Medicine-Arrows lodge. After the choice, men of spotless reputation left to cut extra-long poles for the lodge. Others called upon the two men who exemplified all that was esteemed in Cheyenne comportment and asked to borrow their *tipi* skins for the sacred-lodge covering. Such men were greatly honored. The Arrowkeeper and his attendants entered the huge lodge and prepared an altar, a hearth, and spread sage on the cleared ground on which the priests would sit.

On the morning of the second day the Arrow pledger—naked, painted, and cloaked in a robe—accompanied by three virtuous men, collected the tributes from the Offering Lodge and carried them to the Sacred Arrow lodge where they were placed before the altar. Emerging from the lodge, they walked slowly to the Arrowkeeper's *tipi* wailing at each step. At the entrance they halted, retreated, and advanced four times before entering. As they sat before him the Arrowkeeper prayed over them. He then placed the Arrow bundles on the left arm of the pledger; the four trod deliberately and ever so slowly toward the Sacred Lodge, halting four times enroute. The head priest received the bundle and laid it behind the altar.

[28]George A. Dorsey, *The Cheyenne*, p. 5.
[29]Ibid., pp. 5–10.

Before the bundle was opened, the warrior societies, armed with clubs and whips, began their patrol of the camp. Neither women nor children were allowed outside their *tipis*; only men having demanding tasks were abroad; even the dogs were strangely mute. Within the lodge the bundle was reverently opened. If the feathers were soiled or damaged, the priests selected a man of impeccable virtue to repair them.

On the morning of the third day, the priests performed a ritual celebrating the unity of the Cheyenne tribe. For each living Cheyenne family a willow stick was cut and laid beside the altar; at times there were hundreds, at others nearly a thousand. Each was held in smoke rising from two small incense-burning fires, thus blessing every family. Then, each medicine man, employing his private ritual, reconsecrated the sacred power of his paraphernalia and incantations.

On the fourth and final day the Arrow pledger, holding a forked pole, entered the Sacred Arrow lodge where the priest fastened the Arrows to it. Leaving the lodge, wailing with each sedate step, he planted the pole and placed the Arrow before it. Priests brought the offerings from the lodge while boys carried additional gifts to the pole. With every woman secluded in her lodge, each male—from the most ancient to infants in their fathers' arms—gathered to view the Arrows and obtain their beneficence. After each had contemplated the great emblem, the warrior societies struck the Medicine Lodge and, adding a third *tipi* to it, raised it over the Sacred Arrows and offerings. The new structure was called Sweet Medicine Lodge. From it the Arrows were returned to the home of the Arrowkeeper. Where the Offering *tipi* stood, the warriors had built a sweat lodge. Now, the fourth night, the ceremony entered its final phase. The Chief of the Council of Forty-four, called Sweet Medicine—the living embodiment of the culture hero—entered the lodge followed by all the medicine men. Inside, while darkness enveloped the camp, they sang the four sacred songs given to Sweet Medicine thousands of years before. After each, they foretold the future in the manner of Sweet Medicine. Just before the rays of the sun brightened the horizon, all moved to the sweat lodge to chant four times as the vapors ritually cleansed them, making them safe to move among the people. With the dawn the women ended their seclusion; the unity of the tribe was reaffirmed; its people blessed; and all of life was renewed.

The Arrow Renewal ritual was, Hoebel noted, unique to the Cheyenne.[30] The Sun Dance, however, was not; it appeared in one form or another among most of the plains people and resembled the Mandan Okipa ceremony. Details differed as did meanings and purposes. For the Cheyenne it was a rite of rebirth and had its sanction in myth. At a time long in the past when famine stalked the land, Erect Horns, hoping to bring back

[30]E. Adamson Hoebel, *The Cheyennes*, p. 11.

plants and animals, traveled to a sacred mountain with a woman, not his wife. There, a Holy One received them and, for four years, taught the pair the conduct of the Sun Dance. It was said that Erect Horns left his companion as payment for the knowledge and returned to his emaciated people, performed the ritual, and so rescued them from starvation.[31] Historical evidence suggests that the Sun Dance was introduced to the Cheyenne by the Suhtai, an Algonkian-speaking tribe whom they encountered on their westward move. In later years the Suhtai merged with the Cheyenne, although they retained their own dialect.

In the performance of the ritual, the pledger, sometimes called the Lodgemaker, played the role of Erect Horns. The chief priest represented the Holy One (Great Medicine); the Lodgemaker's wife or a designate symbolized Erect Horn's female companion. Like the Arrow Renewal ceremony, a man vowed to give the ceremony for personal reasons. However, it benefited the entire tribe because, by the acts of the pledger, the tribe was reborn and multiplied. The Sun Dance required eight days (a variation on the mystical number 4) to complete.[32] A most important preparation was the raising of the Lone Tipi which represented the cave in the Sacred Mountain. In the succeeding four days—while the priests, the pledger, and his wife ritually renewed the earth and consecrated the buffalo by thrusting water grass in its eye sockets and nostrils—the Great Medicine Lodge was constructed.

A brave warrior, one who had entered an enemy camp alone, was chosen to find a proper tree for the center pole. He first selected a spot where the pole would stand and put up some willow boughs. Then he went out on the "war path," creeping up on a grove of trees searching for the strongest and best. Finding it he counted coup on the trunk. Early on the morning of the third day he circled the camp, then drew close to the willows and struck them and recounted the noble deeds which qualified him for the position. Then, shouting and whooping, the warrior societies galloped into the camp circle and counted coup on the willow markers. Women, too, crowded in to count coup on the markers. All the able men then departed to cut the poles for the lodge; the chiefs cut and transported the center pole, for it represented the world. The completed lodge was a large circle of posts around the center pole; for the roof, qualified men donated valuable buffalo robes. Solemnly, priests dedicated the lodge on the night it was completed. After they finished, the chief priest and the pledger's wife, cloaked in a single buffalo robe, walked together over the smoke from burning incense, purifying themselves. Led by the pledger's wife the priests filed slowly from the lodge to the east, stopping just inside the opening of the camp circle. The priest prayed fervently to *Maiyun*, offered pray-

[31]George A. Dorsey, *The Cheyenne*, p. 185.
[32]E. Adamson Hoebel, *The Cheyennes*, p. 13.

ers to the spirits of the four directions, and beseeched the sun and the stars for their blessings on all things.

Leaving the first priest and the pledger's wife alone, the others returned to the lodge. In the night a crier called upon all the world to heed as he proclaimed the right of the chief priest to enact the ritual on behalf of the tribe. The priest and the woman drew the robe about themselves, purified their bodies again, and sang the sacred pipe song. Then in the silent night under the shelter of a robe they had sexual intercourse so that all life may be reborn.

On the fifth day preparations were made for the dancing. Priests built an altar in the great lodge over the sacred buffalo skull, which designated the earth toward which the entire ceremony was directed—an earth replete with buffalo, water, and life. Men who were to dance assembled, each having made a vow to sacrifice himself by torture to solicit pity from the spirits. In so doing, he also received public approval and prestige. Some men promised to hang from the center pole. Others danced outside the lodge. To hang from the center pole a man had the help of a medicine man who, himself, had done so. The medicine man punched holes in the skin above the nipples of the supplicant, or perhaps in the flesh above his cheek bones. Stoically the man bore the pain as skewers were inserted in the slits. Ropes attached to the skewers were fastened to the top of the pole. Through the night the sacrificer danced about the pole until he dropped from exhaustion, tearing loose the skewers. Others dragged heavy buffalo skulls from skewers plunged into their backs, until the skulls, caught in grasses or thorns, ripped the thongs free. The Sun Dance ended as the last wounded man made his way to his lodge and those watching the spectacle dispersed. Only participants benefited by their torment; neither the earth nor the Cheyenne profited from the painful deed.

The Cheyenne stressed keeping an equilibrium in their world and periodically renewed it through great dramatic ceremonies. Individuals, how-

Cheyenne sun dancer with skewers and thongs in his back, circa 1903. Smithsonian Institution National Anthropological Archives.

ever, required more intimate support for their lives. This they achieved by acquiring a Guardian Spirit—a personal *maiyun*. To find it or solicit its favors, men retreated to the hills to suffer and to await a visitation. Some hoped for protection in battle, others for curing skill, or perhaps the gift of prophecy:

> Horn, later named Blind Bull, formerly had this power in high degree. He was born toward the end of the eighteenth century and was the father of Brave Wolf, also known as Box Elder or Maple (died about 1885), and to Brave Wolf the father had taught all that he knew. This knowledge came to Horn, and later to his son, through the wolves, though they did not give him his power; they were only the messengers who brought it. His power came from the maiyun. The wolves with whom these two men communicated told Brave Wolf that he would die of old age; he would not be killed in battle; yet he was much on the war path and often in danger.
>
> His power was such that he always knew what was going to happen. Before starting on one of his early war-paths, he predicted that he would bring back captives, and he returned with four captured Pawnee women.[33]

Despite protection from the *maiyun*, amulets, spells, or prayers, all Cheyenne must die. After death their souls, called *tasoom*, followed the Milky Way and joined Heammawhio. Brave or cowardly, generous or niggardly, good or bad, all lived there as they did on earth, riding free, hunting buffalo, quilling robes, in the company of all who had gone before.

The Cheyenne as well as other plains nomads came to the plains from horticultural-village traditions; the Kiowa, Commanche, and Shoshoni were among the exceptions. The Cheyenne and others adapted their culture and society to their new environment. The question which has plagued scholars is what dimensions of their cultures were a direct response to life on the plains and what dimensions derived from their earlier lives. It has never been an easy problem to solve; anthropologists of the 1930s through the 1950s debated the issue vigorously. A few contended that the new way of life was a simple graft on the old; the horse only made possible the flowering of incipient tendencies.[34] The anthropologist John Ewers to a lesser degree agreed.[35] He observed that the horse caused the preequestrian bison economy to flourish, but added that all the activities attendant upon horses—breeding, training, horse medicine, et al.—were new and developed out of equine ownership. He also suggested that the culture contact with its inevitable exchange of ideas resulted in culture modification.

[33]George Bird Grinnell, *The Cheyenne Indians*, vol. 2, pp. 112–113.

[34]Clark Wissler, "Influence of the Horse in Plains Culture," *American Anthropologist*, vol. 16, 1914, p. 16.

[35]John C. Ewers, "The Horse Complex in Plains Indian History," in *The North American Indians*. Roger C. Owen, James J. F. Deetz, Anthony Fisher, eds. (New York: MacMillan Co., 1967), pp. 501–502.

Cheyenne burial in travois, circa 1900.
Smithsonian Institution National Anthropological Archives.

Typical of the other position were Hoebel's remarks.[36] He thought that while astute scholars might discern cultural traits consonant with a woodland history, Cheyenne culture in its major manifestations was typical plains. Fred Eggan too, pointed out that most of the plains people arrived with different cultural backgrounds including language, yet they all ended up with broad similarities in their kinship systems and in their overall social structure.[37] It was as if a giant watercolorist painted the plains canvas with one great wash. The acquisition of horses was the significant event which resulted in the common plains lifeway.

Mounted, the people were able to built their economy around the buffalo. To exploit the resource to its utmost, their perigrinations had to match those of the animals. Therefore, in fall, winter, and spring the Cheyenne tribe was dispersed in bands. Only the smaller units were mobile enough to hunt effectively the small herds of wintering bison and find sufficient winter fodder for horses. While it would, no doubt, have been possible for a unilineal clan system like that of the Apache to survive on the plains, the bilateral kinship structure and the extension of kin relationships to very distant cousins made it possible for Cheyennes to be related in some way to a goodly number of their tribe, resulting in the formation of local kindreds. Such an organization, more flexible than the clan organized semisedentary Mandan, was well suited to a nomadic life. The kindreds were efficient economic units. In each were sound hunters and in each lived enough women to attend to the meat and hides. Yet kindreds could

[36]K. N. Llewellyn and E. Adamson Hoebel. *The Cheyenne Way*, p. vii.
[37]Fred Eggan, *The American Indian*. (Chicago: Aldine Publishing Co., 1966), p. 72.

not survive in isolation. The bands which they composed afforded protection from enemies and aid in hard times.[38]

Most of the plains tribes had a loose tribal structure; the Cheyenne were the exception. The Council of Forty-four was a strong governing institution and moreover it was an integrating device for the far-flung bands, checking potential centrifugal tendencies. Every summer when the bands came together for the great ritual dramas, the band chiefs sat in council exchanging ideas and debating issues of central importance. Life on the plains, however, confined the convening of the Council to the summer months. Its influence, however, was maintained throughout the year by member chiefs. The Council of Forty-four may have had its source in the village period of Cheyenne history—myth, while not historically precise, seems to indicate ancient roots; yet it certainly climaxed on the plains. The mobility afforded the bands by the horse made it possible and necessary to separate during the long cold months and likewise to come together from vast distances for the summer reunions.

As a political and legal force, the Council seemed to have matured before the military societies. The origin of the societies is unclear. They may have had their beginnings in the village period or may have been borrowed from other groups. In their earliest existence, however, they were largely social and fraternal. With the move to the plains, they gradually took on greater influence, a development, it could be argued, necessary for the exigencies of the new life. Society officers were Cheyenne war chiefs, important personages as the war complex grew among all the plains people. The summer communal hunts required individual control for success. The societies took on this function. They also preserved order on occasions when the entire tribe or a great part of it went on a march. The Sacred Arrow ceremony demanded constrained behavior; the military societies saw to it. The summer congregation of all Cheyenne bands tempted enemies; military societies protected the camp. The societies, of course, functioned as units only during the summer, but members were present in all the bands. They continued their policing, law making, and protecting activities during the months of band dispersal. Regardless of their origin, their power increased as the eighteenth century progressed, becoming a strong arm of government in both private and public affairs.

The Cheyenne kinship structure as well as their governing institution assumed their final form on the plains. They were the Cheyenne response to plains life which was made possible by horses. Although they were indispensable in the food quest, horses took on an even greater significance. They accorded wealth and prestige to their owners; because horses were

[38]Fred Eggan, "The Cheyenne and Arapaho Kinships System," in Fred Eggan, ed. *Social Anthropology of North American Tribes*. (Chicago: University of Chicago Press, Enlarged Edition, 1955), pp. 82–95.

not equally distributed among families, a class structure based primarily upon wealth in horses evolved.[39] It was not rigid—family rank could be altered—but the exchange of horses preceding and ratifying nuptial arrangements tended to link prosperous families, so creating a class organization.

Although horses had both intrinsic and practical value, their great importance lay in the plains trade networks.[40] The Cheyenne bartered horses and robes to the Mandan and Hidatsa for horticultural produce and European goods. They kept part for themselves and traded the balance to tribes farther west for horses. They were, in economic terms, middlemen. Later, after the Bents opened their trading posts (c. 1832), the Cheyenne engaged in heavy trading there. For horses, mules, and buffalo hides, they received tobacco, wool blankets, guns, and metal goods. The Bents shipped the animals and hides east to St. Louis. The demand for horses increased. The Cheyenne as well as the other northern plains tribes could not satisfy the needs through their role as middlemen. Increased raiding for horses was the answer. They went farther and farther south to steal horses from the Commanche and Kiowa so intensifying the hostilities. To be sure, although raiding and warfare were themselves a path to glory and were surrounded by ritual, they developed strong economic motivations. Grinnell described men who went to war for the singular reason of increasing their possessions by stealing horses:[41] ". . . They carried on war as a business—for profit. Some of these—men who possessed high reputation for courage, success, and general well doing—made it their boast that they had never killed a man, and perhaps had never counted a coup."

Life on the plains with all that it involved was harsh and precarious, yet the Cheyenne saw it as good. To keep it so required proper conduct and reverent behavior toward the supernatural. Most of the Cheyenne faith and courage derived from the Four Sacred Arrows given them by a Holy One. The Arrows embodied the collective soul of the tribe and also reflected their shared anxieties: buffalo and foes. The correct performance of the Arrow Renewal rite diminished their emotional burden: The buffalo would thrive, their enemies be vanquished, and the tribe would endure. Confidence in their world was restored. The Sun Dance, although introduced from outside, had its charter in Cheyenne myth. Like the Arrow Renewal ceremony, it symbolized Cheyenne concerns and had regenerative themes. Through the sexual union of the two principals, the growth of the world and of its plant and animal life was promised. Men who participated

---

[39]Bernard Mishkin, *Rank and Warfare Among the Plains Indians.* American Ethnological Society Monograph #3. (Seattle: University of Washington Press, 1940), pp. 57–63.

[40]Joseph Jablow, *The Cheyenne in Plains Indian Trade Relations: 1795–1840.* American Ethnological Society Monograph #19. (Seattle: University of Washington Press, 1950), pp. 79–80.

[41]George Bird Grinnell, *The Cheyenne Indians,* vol. 2, p. 2.

in the harrowing torment sought individual good luck bestowed by pitying supernaturals. Enduring the excruciation stoically also conferred prestige, a prized goal of Cheyenne males.

EPILOGUE

For 30 or more years, the Cheyenne roamed the plains hunting, raiding, and trading; their culture enriched by the horse and nourished by the land and its people. Their rituals symbolized their central focus and sustained them. It was all to come to an inglorious end. Inevitably they were caught up in the ultimate battle with the United States Army for control of the plains. In spite of the victory at the Little Big Horn and other battles less well known, the Cheyenne were overpowered in the end. Wounded spiritually and physically, they were herded to a life of ignominious humiliation—and death from starvation and illness—on an Oklahoma reservation. Driven by despair, Chiefs Dull Knife and Little Wolf led a tattered band of men, women, and children north. Fighting and marching, marching and fighting, they defied 13,000 troops and reached their cherished homeland. Although they laid their arms down, they were returned to Oklahoma. In a desperate attempt to escape the unheated barracks in which they were confined, they broke out; more than 60 were killed by soldiers, others were recaptured, a few escaped. At last responding to their undying wish to life on the northern great plains, a reservation was established in Montana. Here descendants of the proud Cheyenne live, some barely eking out an existence, demoralized by alcohol, poverty, and suicide.

CHAPTER NINE

The Nootka of the Northwest Coast

The Pacific coastline from northern California to southwest Alaska is precipitous; high cliffs tower over occasional windswept beaches. From Puget Sound in the south to the Gulf of Alaska in the north the shoreline is hemmed by formidable mountains rising 3000 or more feet from the edge of the sea. Rugged islands, remnants of a partially submerged mountain range, lie short distances offshore creating inlets and sounds. The same geologic event produced the breathtaking fiords which penetrate the northern coast. To the south and west of these smaller islands are Queen Charlotte and Vancouver Islands. These, too, were formed by the subsidence of a mountain range in the distant past. Although the hills are rounder and softer in Washington, Oregon, and California, they also drop swiftly and are edged by long narrow beaches.

This area hardly seemed hospitable for human habitation yet the entire region was dotted with thriving societies when Captain Cook entered Nootka Sound in 1778. Despite the awesome appearance of a jagged mountain wilderness and narrow surf lashed beaches, the region has a relatively benign climate. The long narrow ribbon of coast from northern California to Juneau, Alaska is similar in temperature and rainfall. The Japanese Current produces the moderate temperature and drenching rain. As the current courses southward, warm vapor banks rise to be driven

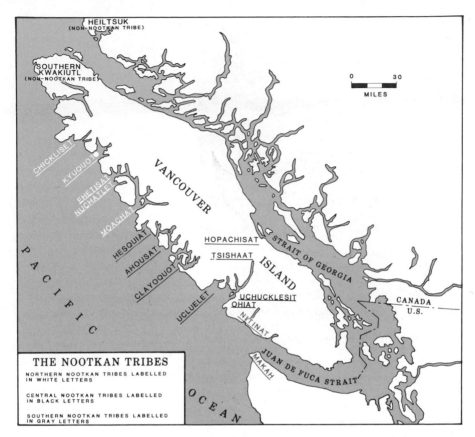

shoreward by prevailing winds, thereby warming the coasts. When the vapor banks meet the coastal range they release their moisture, soaking the land. In the south the same effect is caused by the Cascades and the Sierra Nevadas. Jose Moziño, a botanist and a member of a 1792 Spanish expedition, observed:

> If one can discuss the climate on the basis of robust health which is enjoyed not only by all of us, but by all those we find here after two winters, one can say that it is benign and incomparably better than that of the countries situated at the same parallel on the northeastern coast of America.[1]

John Hoskins, a New Englander and no doubt hardened in the crucible of a colder, dryer environment disagreed with Moziño.[2] He remarked: "The

---

[1]Jose Mariano Moziño, *Noticias de Nutka: An Account of Nootka Sound in 1792,* rev. ed. Translated by Iris Higbie Wilson. The American Ethnological Society Monograph #50. (Seattle: University of Washington Press, 1970), p. 5.

[2]Frederick W. Howay, ed. *Voyages of the "Columbia" to the Northwest Coast, 1787–1790 and 1790–1793.* Massachusetts Historical Society Collections, LXXIX. (Cambridge: Harvard University Press, 1941), p. 280.

Vancouver Island mountain lake, circa 1896.
Smithsonian Institution National Anthropological Archives.

climate of this part of the country (if I may be permitted to judge) is certainly much milder though not so healthy as that on our side of the continent."

The native people not only found the climate beneficial, they found the land and marine resources abundant. Timber for shelter and boats abounded. Acid soil, moderate and even temperatures, and heavy moisture, joined to provide firs and spruces in the north, giant redwoods, hemlock, and cedar, in the south. These brooding forests grew from shoreline to timberline, their floors blanketed with fern and moss. At slightly higher elevations tangled masses of shade-tolerant shrubs flourished, among them: salmon berry, huckleberry, and elderberry. Sharing the land with people in early times were deer who fed on the plentiful browse. The Olympic Penninsula and Vancouver Island supported large bands of elk. Mountain goats leaped gracefully from pinnacle to pinnacle. Grizzly, brown, and black bear roamed the sodden woods and beaches. Otter, beaver, mink, and fish lived in inland streams. Overhead, waterfowl—geese, ducks, and swans—migrated with the seasons. Crow, raven, eagle, and hawk wheeled in the sky searching for food and providing material for aboriginal myth and ceremony.

It was, however, largely, to the swift-flowing rivers and the ocean that the original settlers turned. Five species of salmon congregated by the millions to struggle toward the headwater of numerous rivers and streams to spawn and die. Along the coast great schools of herring, smelt, and candle fish, (olachen) gathered annually to spawn. Off the coast halibut and other coldwater fish lived year-round. Clams and mussels littered the beaches, trout and the migratory steelhead lurked in freshwaters. Like the people, sea mammals prospered on the abundance of fish. Seals, sea lions, and the prized sea otter played offshore. Whales cruised along the coast and entered some of the deeper inlets.

The Northwest coast environment was challenging to its early inhabitants. While its food resources were plentiful, exploiting them was difficult. Game abounded on the land; hunting it, however, was laborious because of the brutal terrain and the almost impenetrable forest undergrowth. Foot travel was slow and arduous. Sea animal hunting brought greater yield on the time and energy invested, but it was hazardous. Success in the venture depended upon appropriate technology and seafaring skill. Water travel and sea hunting were efficient if the boatman was a good navigator, adept in handling racing currents, treacherous reefs, and swirling rip tides, and if his crew were strong paddlers and accurate harpooners. Over the two or three thousand years of life on the coast the dwellers acquired the requisite equipment, skill, and knowledge to adapt to their complex and beneficent environment.

In describing the northwest coast we have noted that the entire region was densely populated by 1700. These Indian groups, often separated by natural barriers of water and impassible terrain, differed considerably in language. Their cultures, however, displayed a number of similar patterns leading scholars to recognize a generalized Northwest Coast civilization. They used the language spoken to identify the numerous populations. The people, however, employed other words to label themselves and their neighbors. Self-designations, loosely translated, meant "the people," "human beings," or dwellers of a certain location. Apellations given to others were often less flattering. Groups who spoke the same language or a variant of it resembled one another very closely in their lifeway and either consisted of local independent societies or were linked into tribes or confederacies. Any semblance of an overall political authority, however, was absent. There were no nations as the term is currently used.

The distribution and history of Northwest Coast populations is complicated, and anthropologists have isolated at least twenty-seven groups, some large, others smaller and less well-known.[3] Here we shall mention only major groups. In the north, the Tlingit consisting of fourteen tribal divisions occupied most of the Alaskan panhandle. Linguists think that Tlingit belongs to the Athabascan language family. The Haida lived on the southern end of Prince of Wales Island and on the Queen Charlotte Islands. Haida, too, is probably an Athabascan language, although Tlingit and Haida were mutually unintelligible. South of the Tlingit people, the Tsimshian speakers inhabited the Canadian coast and some offshore islands. Tsimshian linguistic affiliations are not clear. Kwakiutl resided on the mainland, as well on islands including the east coast of Vancouver Is-

---

[3]For a complete and clear account refer to Philip Drucker, *Cultures of the North Pacific Coast.* (San Francisco: Chandler Publishing Co., 1965), pp. 103–113.

Nootka men at Friendly Cove, Vancouver Island, circa 1873.
Smithsonian Institution National Anthropological Archives.

land.[4] The speakers were divided into three dialect divisions: Haisla, Heiltsuk, and southern Kwakiutl. The language may be a member of the Wakashan family.

On the southwest coast of Vancouver Island and on the tip of the Olympic Penninsula the Nootka lived. They spoke at least two dialects, Nootka proper and Makah. The Nootka, unlike most of the other tribes, specialized in hunting whales from canoes. The Nootka canoe was exceptionally well designed and amazingly sea worthy. Nootka likely belongs to the Wakashan family. Along the coast of Washington were Salish speakers including the Tillamook and the Bella Coola. Further south were enclaves of independent language speakers.

All of these people from Alaska south to northern California exhibited, in varying degrees, the generalized Northwest Coast culture pattern, although they differed in many specific details. The further away the groups lived from the heartland of the region, the more they departed from the major patterns; for example, the people of Washington, Oregon, and California exhibit a cultural pattern that diverges recognizably from the generalized Northwest coast pattern.

This incredible linguistic diversity indicated that the area was settled by various groups who originated in the interior.[5] A succession of migrations and subsequent movement of peoples up and down the coast explains not only the diversity, but the irregular distribution of languages. Local cul-

---

[4]Franz Boas pioneered Kwakiutl studies. For a sensitive novel concerning contemporary Kwakiutl, read Margaret Craven's *I Heard the Owl Call My Name.* (Garden City, NY: Doubleday & Co., 1973).

[5]Drucker, *Cultures of the North Pacific Coast*, p. 108.

tural differences and emphases probably derived from original traditions modified by life in specific ecological nitches.

About 10,000 Nootka peoples were spread along the stormy west coast of Vancouver Island as the eighteenth century drew to its end.[6] A closely related group, the Makah, lived around Cape Flattery.[7] Sharing the island with the Nootka were the Southern Kwakiutl who lived north of Cape Cook and on the east coast. Coastal Salish Indians controlled the lower end of the east coast. Philip Drucker divided the Nootka into the Northern, Central, and Southern tribes (probably not a very good use of the term).[8] The northern groups were welded into tribal confederacies. The central and southern groups functioned independently of even close neighbors, and indeed, often fought with each other to the extent of exterminating one or two villages.

The Vancouver shoreline is among the most varied in the world. Deep narrow fiords empty into the sea, forming inlets and sounds. Small rugged islands, giant rocks, and reefs lie offshore. The beaches and rocky shores are littered with quantities of driftwood twisted into surrealist shapes by water and wind. The sounds and large inlets provided natural settings for the sociopolitical divisions Drucker noted. Outside contacts were limited. Violent storms, high tides, and pounding surf often prevented voyaging around the headlands; travel by land was seldom undertaken. The isolation resulted in the growth of characteristic mannerisms and speech patterns, the differences comparable to those between New England and the deep south.[9]

The west coast is the more vulnerable to nature's whimsy. In early fall the violent season starts. Pitiless western winds whip the coast with driving sheets of rain; surf on outer beaches pounds incessantly. On rare occasions a north wind may blow over the mountain, interrupting the storm to bring a few clear, crisp days. Then the westerlies begin again. There are times when the sea grows calm, almost mirrorlike in late spring and summer. Fog from the Japanese Current rolls in day after day, breaking up only with a rising breeze. Sudden unpredictable squalls mar late summer days. The autumn storms resume in August.

The climate is raw and damp but seldom bitter. Rainfall averages about one hundred inches. The annual temperature is about 47° F; during January the temperature averages 36° F, and the July mean is 57° F. The moderate weather is caused by the Japanese Current and paradoxically it is

[6]Drucker, *Cultures of the North Pacific Coast*, p. 144. The figure is only an estimate, yet it is probably reasonably accurate.

[7]Elizabeth Colson, *The Makah Indians*. (Minneapolis: University of Minnesota Press, 1953), pp. 3–5.

[8]Philip Drucker, *The Northern and Central Nootkan Tribes*. Bureau of American Ethnology, Bulletin 144, 1951, pp. 1935–1936, Smithsonian Institution. Reprinted by permission. We have relied heavily on his research for this work.

[9]Ibid., pp. 6–7.

responsible for the biting cold water so characteristic of the coast. It rolls the deep frigid water off the continental shelf and pushes it toward the coast. Tides are a constant force to be reckoned with: In the spring they rise more than 13 feet; neap tides (those occurring in the first and third quarters of the moon) average about eight feet. Strong currents, some swift as seven knots, flow in the channels and inlets, a consequence of the rise and fall of the tides.

Despite the poor thin soil the rainfall supports dense forests which edge the beaches and shorelines and extend inland for miles. Douglas fir, hemlock, red and white cedar, and yew are the dominant conifers. Some deciduous trees and shrubs grow along water courses. The damp woods form an almost impregnable barrier to the interior. The dank forest creates a dim, moss-covered, dripping world. Monstrous branchless tree trunks jut upward, their crowns forming a great awning through which little light passes. Gnarled little trees attempt to reach light; defeated, they fall to join aged, toppled giants making passage almost impossible. Slippery mosses, concealing crevices and pitfalls, render the footing treacherous.

Above the forests are the mountains, peaks thrust upward, a few 7000 or more feet; minor ranges seem to run in all directions. Among them alpine meadows appear unexpectedly. Here trout thrive in shallow cold lakes, some harboring ice through July. Snow, too, lingers in summer. Frequenting these highlands are deer, elk, black bear, and other game animals. In October the rivers teem with migrating salmon, some containing four or five species. Aboriginal people, however, seldom, if ever, trudged through the forbidding forests to the high-lands. Their life was intimately connected with sea, sound, and rivers. Whale, seal, sea lion, and sea otter were plentiful. Berries and edible roots were easy to harvest. All that the Nootka needed to flourish was to be found in the water, on the beaches, or at the edge of the forest. Here they built their villages.

The Nootka, like some other North Pacific peoples, had both winter and summer villages. They built their winter villages on level ground in the upper end of deep coves; the sites afforded protection from the prevailing winter winds. Houses were located above the high tide mark and looked down over a narrow gravel beach. Fresh water was plentiful; small rivulets coursed around the villages; rain water was trapped in wooden containers. Smaller summer settlements were located on outer branches or at the edge of inlets. Water, more than shelter, was the important factor in selecting sites, and good beaches were necessary.

Nootka winter houses were large wooden gabled structures; a 40- by 100-foot building was not unusual. Center posts, ridge poles, side plates, and side posts were permanent. Planked siding and roofing were moved by canoes to frames standing in the summer villages. They were transported back as summer waned. John Jewitt described a move:

Nootka house interior.
Smithsonian Institution National Anthropological Archives.

On the third of September, the whole tribe quitted Nootka, according to their constant practice, in order to pass the autumn and winter at Tashees and Cooptee, the latter lying about thirty miles up the Sound in a deep bay, the navigation of which is very dangerous from the great number of reefs and rocks with which it abounds. On these occasions everything is taken with them, even the planks of their houses, in order to cover their new dwellings. To an European, such a removal exhibits a scene quite novel and strange; canoes piled with boards and boxes, and filled with men, women, of all ranks and sizes, making the air resound with their cries and songs.[10]

The houses were built of almost imperishable red cedar; constructing one demanded numbers of workers who had to be supported and feasted during the backbreaking feat of building. The heavy beams, poles, and rafters, were lifted and set into place through strength and a knowledge of levers. As a house aged, a rotting post or beam was replaced. Over a long time, perhaps several generations, piece by piece, a house frame may have been renewed. House ridgepoles of especially important men jutted beyond the walls and were elaborately carved. Abstract human figures were also carved on the posts supporting the center beam. Only in a later period (c. 1900) did the Nootka erect carved free-standing totem poles.[11]

Inside the house were food storage and cooking utensils. Bladder and gut containers held oil; wooden boxes and baskets contained food. Fish was boiled in shallow wooden troughs. People ate from wooden trays; clam

[10]John R. Jewitt, *A Narrative of the Adventures and Sufferings of John R. Jewitt, 1815.* The Garland Library of Narratives of North American Indian Captives, Wilcomb E. Washborn, arranger. (New York: Garland Publishing Co., 1976), pp. 102–103. Garland Publishing Co. has granted permission for use of this material.

[11]Drucker, *The Northern and Central Nootkan Tribes*, p. 76.

shells served as dippers and soup spoons. Women wove cedar bark mats for sitting and sleeping. Large wooden boxes storing a miscellany of tools and equipment were stacked about the dirt floor. In general Nootka interiors did not appeal to fastidious ethnocentric European visitors:

> They invariably complain of the disorder of the houses, with bladders of oil and bundles of greasy fish dangling from overhead at just the height to smear one's face as he blinked his smoke-irritated eyes; baskets, boxes, dishes, mats, and tools scattered about the floor; and the floor itself a seething stinking mass of trash, fish guts, shell fish, and other refuse.[12]

Yet there was a kind of order in the Nootka household—order with regard to human spatial arrangements. Who lived in the large house and where, was related to the hereditary class system. The Nootka were intensely conscious of rank, recognizing three strata: royalty, commoners, and slaves. Chiefs and their close descendants made up the nobility, but privileges and power varied. Primogeniture was the basis of ranking. No one was more important than the eldest son of an eldest son. His brothers, although prestigious were slightly lower than he in rank, his paternal cousins even lower. Their descendants, while considered royal, owned few privileges and were the least significant of the "royal" group. Drucker proposed that they made up a "middle class."[13] People whose connections to a noble line were absent or tenuous were commoners. Slaves were outside the pale. The Nootka captured them from other groups and sold or traded them up and down the coast. A captive's relatives tried mightily to liberate him through battle or ransom. It was exceptionally galling to be of noble blood yet be a slave in a foreign household.

Living in the rear righthand corner of the house was the highest ranking chief, his family, and some lower ranking kin, whom he called "those under the arm." Occupying the rear lefthand corner was the next highest chief, a younger brother or perhaps a close male relative. He, too, had a coterie of "under the arm" people about him. Corners to the right and left of the door belonged to other important lineage males. Lesser people and commoners, called tenants, the closest English translation of the Nootka term, lived along the walls between corners. In front of each living area was a hearth; all families ate separately.

Men expected to live with their father's people but the patrilocal rule was loosely followed. Practical matters, usually economic or rank, dictated choices. Chiefs often remained with the group or household in which they owned property. "Under the arm" people chose to live with a particular chief either because of close kin ties or because they liked him. In order to bind them more closely a chief often gave them extra privileges and rights. Tenants moved in and out at will, forming a peripatetic stream of people

---

[12]Ibid., p. 72.
[13]Ibid., p. 245. Members of the middle class were often close kin of "royalty."

carting their belongings from one house to another. Frequent migrations did not please a chief, for what good were his rights and privileges if he could not depend upon his followers? To build or man his fish traps required many helpers. A stranded whale on his beach became his, but if he had no strong backs and arms to dismember and carry it to the house it would lie decomposing where it beached. All of his great hereditary ceremonials required singers and dancers, without them he was unable to demonstrate his ritual prerogatives or give feasts. Recognizing their dependence upon their followers, chiefs tried in all sorts of ways to attract and hold followers. Wise chiefs or smart ones gave generously to people: They named their children; gave them some ceremonial rights; or permitted fishing in certain places otherwise off limits. Industrious families were courted unabashedly; even the shiftless were tolerated in the household for fear that their relatives would move out too.

Power was paramount in the Nootka culture and was unequally distributed. Head chiefs, "real chiefs" people called them, possessed the most; lower chiefs owned less; usually commoners had none. Power came from rights and privileges which men and some women inherited; they owned them until they bestowed some or all upon their children. The concept of property ownership was exceptionally elaborated in Nootka thought. Privileges people owned can be divided into economic and ceremonial. Economic rights included: houses, fishing waters extending for miles offshore, land, beaches, and salvage rights. Ceremonial property—equally as important—comprised rights to give specific rituals, ownership of dances, songs and incantations, names, and house post emblems. High chiefs owned all village land; in fact only remote areas were not owned by someone. From this large body of rights and possessions chiefs could and did allocate minor privileges to relatives or valued followers. Some were allowed to cut blubber from stranded whales; others had access to the second picking of berries. Salmon streams were among the most important asset of chiefs. Regardless of whether they had permitted others to set traps in certain places chiefs claimed the entire first catch in their rivers. After this the men could fish as they pleased but as the season wore on and large quantities of fish had been smoked and dried the chief dispatched an emissary to collect *o'umas* (tribute). No amounts were dictated; each gave what he could spare. The chief used the tax to host a large feast. During the celebration he announced that the *o'umas* were his hereditary right and admonished the people to remember that the hunting and fishing areas as well as the berry patches were his although they could use them after he had officially opened the season; they were to take good care of them, too. While sea hunters owned their catch, people expected them to give a feast for their household members.

The idea of private property permeated every phase of life. Those of low rank depended upon chiefly largess for shelter, food, and all of life's necessities including their relationships with the supernatural. Beliefs and rituals figure in all cultures. Nootka people had developed a rich ceremonial life and seized every opportunity to have a celebration of some sort. But without the chiefs there would have been no spectacular dramas. They owned the ritual privileges which were almost infinite in number. Only they owned names; some they took themselves, others they bestowed upon their relatives and even their relatives' dogs. The carved beams and posts in their houses had names, so did big canoes; great feast dishes also had names. Naming or consenting to the use of a name required a feast.

Potlatching, an institution entrenched among all Northwest coast people featured display privileges: masks, costumes, and dances associated with supernatural beings. Each chief owned his particular ones. During the feasting and gift giving, so much a part of the potlatch, displays, some unbelievably complex took place. Drucker described some belonging to a Kyuquot chief.[14] For displays at potlatches after the Shamans' Dance, he had the following: a *tuta* ("Thunderbird") that was a figure of the thunderbird which rose from the floor and flew across the house while the chief sang its songs; a *winatcict* ("Supernatural Canoe") that moved across the house suspended in the air; a *pitil*, a large mask concealed in a hole in the floor which rose to startle the guests. Two concealed men perpetrated the trick. A monster with the body of a bear and a birdlike head with a huge beak (*huhuqw*) sat on the floor and snatched at little birds that flew about. The chief also had two figures representing loons which came up out of the floor, moved across it, and dove out of sight. A flag board, with a wolf's head carved on either end, about five or six feet long by six inches or so wide (it was telescopic, and expanded to more than twice its original length as the owner sang) amazed the audience. Such intricate devices awed people and impressed them with the chief's ritual privileges.

Just as chiefs enjoyed reserved places in their houses so did they own designated seats at the Potlatch. Seats were ranked and corresponded to the chief's standing. When they arrived at the affair, the highest ranking among them was called, and with great pomp, escorted to his seat. He was followed by the next in the hierarchy, until all were seated. Commoners sat wherever they could find space, men on the right, women on the left.

Some chiefs held rights associated with various life cycle events. A chief at Kyuquot owned "cutting the umbilical chord" privileges. Parents of any child born in the village paid the chief for the cutting. He, however, did not perform the ritual; the midwife or shaman attending the birth did, but the chief collected the fee. Other chiefs might own the pubescent girl's hair ornaments worn at puberty rites. Her parents either borrowed them from him or made them but in either case the chief collected his due. The wealth accumulated through these and similar privileges was redistributed at

[14]Ibid., pp. 259–260. Kyuquot was a northern Nootka village.

feasts. Each chief remembered the amount he had gotten from his ritual ownerships and when he potlatched, he announced to the assembly what portion of the gifts and foods came from these rights.

By controlling the economic and ritual life of his people a chief was assured of his position and authority. Others, members of the middle class (usually the chief's poor relations), owned some rights—fewer and less significant than chiefly ones. Speakers and war chiefs came from this group. A speaker delivered formal speeches for his chief. To become one required an intimate knowledge of family tradition and rights and a stylized elocutionary skill. To inherit the office meant a long training provided by a boy's father who himself had been a speaker. War chiefs led war expeditions, played important ceremonial roles at feasts, and were, in general, among the chief's most loyal retainers. High chiefs appointed their younger brothers or cousins; occasionally a deserving commoner was rewarded with the position; thereafter it descended through his family.

Commoners, of course, had no inherited rights or privileges. They worked for the chief who reciprocated with gifts in kind. Most men and some women were specialists of one kind of another. There were whalers, sealers, canoe makers, carvers, carpenters, midwives, and shamans. Rituals accompanied the performances of the specialities. Fathers taught sons, mothers taught daughters the techniques and rituals which went along with the trades; practitioners guarded their trade secrets jealously.

Marriage maintained and buttressed the Nootkan caste structure. People plotted and planned to marry their children to others of the same or very similar rank—a situation called rank endogamy. To marry beneath one's station frequently had unfortunate repercussions. Should a chief wed a lower rank woman he forever blemished his noble line; his children and theirs of generations to come would always be known as half commoners. In 1935 there was an important chief whose grandfather had married a low-rank woman. A woman informant of Drucker's was distantly related to both the grandparents.

> Through her relationship to the chiefly line she calls the present chief "nephew"; through her kinship to the low rank woman she could address him as "brother." To use the latter term would refer to his partial commoner ancestry, however, so to save his feelings she never uses it. His paternal line traditionally goes back with not a break to the ordering of the world at Creation; it is right royal, if ever a family was. But "it brought them down a little" when the grandfather married the low-rank woman; "it spoiled their good name."[15]

Often without the knowledge or consent of their children parents arranged their marriages. Alliances between families took precedence over individual desires; vigilant chaperones insured female chastity so desired

[15]Ibid., pp. 244–245.

by the Nootka. In general, all first marriage rituals called *tutcha*, were similar; any differences stemmed from the social position of the principals, the value of the gifts, and the elaborateness of the ceremony.

The family of the boy made the first overture; either his parents or their delegates—two or four men—went at night to the girl's home. Entering quietly, they slipped through the dimly lighted great house to her parents' place. One, a skillful speaker murmuring softly and at length detailed the rank of the suitor, his ancestry, and the kin links between the two families. While first or second cousin marriage happened rarely, the union of more remote relatives was desirable. The father of the girl sat imperturbable, listening to the declamation. Several of the men left blankets as the proposal party withdrew. If they were accepted—they seldom were the first time—the alliance was approved. Most often, however, the intermediaries made several trips before a decision was made. If several men sought the same girl, complications and difficulties increased. The situation required a meeting of all her relatives, each of whom offered an opinion on the proposed match. Drucker heard of a case where there were six suitors for the daughter of a chief.[16] That the girl had been married before complicated the situation even further. Strong willed, she refused to sleep with her husband and finally left him. Her parents were anxious to avoid a similar situation as they "had lost too much money over her already." The girl's mother favored one young chief to whom she was related; her husband, however, did not like the family. He had once been married to a member who had left him. One evening one of his brothers came in saying, "I have heard that the Icsaath are coming, the Nuchatlet are coming, and one of the Moachat chiefs is coming, all for your daughter. You had better decide quickly to whom you are going to give her." The problem was too much for the chief. In despair he said, "Whoever gets here first gets her."

After the agreement was made, the bride's father feasted his people, announced the forthcoming nuptials and selected people for the wedding party, many of whom would make contributions to the bride's dowry. The arrival of the groom and his large (men, women, and children) party in wedding canoes began the ceremony. Paddling the large boats toward the water's edge they chanted their chief's marriage songs. After beaching the large boats, the groom and his associates performed hereditary display privileges called *topati*. In the "whaling harpoon" *topati* the groom brandishing his harpoon danced up the beach to the bride's house, sang two songs and embedded the weapon in the door. Following the *topati* performance an orator stood on the beach and for hours praised the groom and his family. Sitting in silence, betraying little emotion, the bride's father and his people listened. As the day wore on the orator concluded his speech by calling out names of members of the bride's party: Two young men carried gifts up the beach to each depositing them on new mats in front of the

[16]Ibid., p. 289.

houses. As dusk fell the recipients loaded them up and transported them all back to the beach. Expecting the rejection the groom and his entourage settled down to a damp night on the beach. The following morning they repeated the performance but enacted a different *topati* more spectacular than the first. Drucker describes such a one:

> The old people paddled the canoes. They had two rafts "fixed up like islands," covered with structures of poles and canvas. . . . Children danced on the rafts, wearing maskettes in the forms of little beaks, and young men, wearing similar maskettes leapt from the canoes to wade about in shallow water, blowing whistles. They represented little shore birds called *kwokwip* that were always to be seen . . . the actors ended the drama by singing four songs.[17]

Once more speeches were made and gifts were brought to the houses only to be returned as the day faded. The performances, speeches, and the transporting of the gifts back and forth, continued until some time on the fourth day when the bride's father's speaker emerged from the house and gestured to the orator to cease, thus signalling the acceptance of the bride price and the marriage.

The bride's party, learning of the decision, swung into action to prepare for the bride's *topati*. She, too, had marriage privileges owned by her father or grandfathers; these were usually contests, games, or trials, which tested the skill of the suitor and his attendants. Men of her house or village assembled the gear for the events. Her father's speakers selected the participants. Some young men attempted to climb up a long well-greased plank; others sat unflinching before a blazing fire while someone poured whale oil on the flames.[18]

The speaker might throw a wooden ball into a crowd of women or men; a "no holds barred" melee ensued; the players often were carried into the cove in their effort to retrieve the object. In each *topati* the winners or those who endured, won substantial prizes. When four privileges were finished her father announced through his speaker that his daughter belonged to the young man. Unless, however, the bride had menstruated, she remained with her parents until she celebrated her puberty ritual.

Before the groom departed, either with or without her, his father-in-law collected blankets from his people (the same ones which they had received much earlier) and handed them and other small gifts to the groom's party. Both groups danced, sang, and ate; the blankets were again collected and presented to the bride's father. Clearly blankets changed hands often in nuptials. There followed then, at the discretion of the bride's father, trips to deliver the dowry. Items in it, such as canoes, blankets, otter skins, food, were donated by those who had shared in the bride wealth. If she

[17]Ibid., p. 295.
[18]Ibid., p. 169.

were of a chiefly family the dowry included various privileges which were transferred to her husband with the condition that the couple remain married and that children were born to the pair.

Second marriages—either by the widowed, divorced, or polygamous chiefs—were seldom as elaborate as the first. Exchanges of gifts and feasting, perhaps a small bride price, sufficed to legalize the match. While marriages usually required some ceremonials, divorce was simple. A disgruntled husband could send his wife home, or she, displeased with the situation, could leave. There was no return of gifts or dowry, but privileges, if they were a part of the ceremony, reverted to the original owners. Marital discord occurred often: Barren marriages, adultery, cruelty, often led to divorce. Sex conflict, or perhaps ignorance, drove many young brides home. The Nootka did not prepare their daughters (who were under constant scrutiny until their weddings) very well for things to come!

After all the celebration and ritual, the groom and his companions in a lavish bridal canoe ceremoniously paddled the bride to her new home. Overcome with anxiety and loneliness, she hesitantly entered. Her new family, frequently strangers to her and aware of her fears, tried to make her welcome. They feasted her, admonished the young husband to be nice to his wife, to speak kindly, and to wait to have intercourse. After sleeping with his brothers or cousins for a time, he tentatively approached his bride. At his touch she often sat up, wept and wailed, until he returned to his friends. If eventually she accepted his advances, the marriage was underway, but should she continue to scratch or strike him, he gave up and sent her home.

With amicable relationships established the young couple settled into the routine of Nootka domesticity. Their economic and subsistence activities were largely dictated by the seasons. She and other women of the household collected and prepared food, wove clothing, mats, and baskets from red and yellow cedar bark. While living in the summer village the women wandered inland to gather wild greens. Later when the berries ripened the chief dispatched parties of women to his berrying grounds; after giving him his part they kept the remainder for their families. As the summer wore on, they dug roots; with proper storage these would last the people through the early winter. The single most critical food source, however, was salmon.

In anticipation of the fall and spring runs men built traps at the mouths of the rivers. Further upstream they constructed sophisticated cylindrical latticework traps and weirs. Great quantities of fish were harvested in early fall, but before the people could utilize them, rituals in their honor were necessary. The first salmon—usually dog salmon—were placed on new mats in the chief's house; regardless of who had built the traps and weirs the chief owned them. He dusted the fish with goose down saying: "We are glad you have come to visit us; we have been saving these (feathers) for you for a long time. We have been waiting a long time for you and hope you will return to visit us soon."[19] Women cut up and cooked the anointed fish, and all feasted except menstruating women. Until the butterball ducks appeared, the bones and viscera were returned to the water else the salmon on reincarnation in the deep ocean home would be deformed and the angered salmon would not return to the streams and rivers in the future. All through the salmon season numbers of taboos were in force and restraints upon menstruating women were especially rigorous. Preparing the salmon for storage required the efforts of everyone. Men and boys carried baskets of fish to waiting women who filleted them with mussel shell knives (to have used other implements would have offended the fish). Fires burned throughout the village, smoke and the odor of fish drifted up and down the beaches. The fillets were hung on drying racks, then broiled, and finally smoked. Several women working together stacked the smoked steaks on a board, covering the pile with another. Two sizable women sat on the top plank to compress the meat. They then baled and stored the flattened pile in large baskets. Salmon roe, carefully saved, was put in boxes or seal bladders and hung close by a smoking fire. After a time it compacted into a mass which, according to some observers, despite its rank smell was delicious. Other fish, halibut, cod, and herring caught in spring were sun dried.

When the salmon season ended people moved back to the protected winter villages to escape the full force of the violent winter storms. Although men fished by hook and line or harpoon when the weather moderated, and women clammed at low tide, most of the time was spent indoors. Men made the intricate wooden containers necessary for cooking and housekeeping; their wives repaired clothing, wove new garments, mats, and baskets. Children played with wooden toys; oldsters enthralled them with the legends and myths which lent meaning to Nootka life. Outside the wind moaned through the storm tossed trees. This, too, was the season for festivals, feasts, potlatches, and most important the Shaman's Dance, a spectacular winter ceremony.[20] Specifics of the ritual varied from place to place, a consequence in part, of isolation and local tradition and a chief's ownership of particular display privileges, songs, and dances. The main plot was, however, invariable; it involved the abduction of children (called novices) by wolf spirits who hid them away from their parents and the villagers until the requisite rituals and dramas were completed. The 8-day performance included everyone in the community.

The sponsor, a high-ranking chief, and three lesser ones met secretly weeks before the festival was scheduled. They made elaborate plans: Novices were identified and their fathers notified; "the wolves" were alerted;

[19]Ibid., p. 175.

[20]Alice Henson Ernest called the affair the Wolf Ritual. *The Wolf Ritual of the Northwest Coast.* (Eugene, OR: University of Oregon Press, 1952), pp. 63–81.

and various clubs of both men and women were advised of the event. Although the plans for the affair were cloaked in mystery and secrecy only the young children were unaware that something was afoot. The principal chief's speakers circulated throughout the village; speaking in euphemisms, they invited the villagers to the sponsor's house for a feast. At dusk, the people entered it. A great fire burned. Ignoring the customary seating arrangements they spread out along the walls, talking excitedly until someone extinguished the fires. The speakers began to sing; onlookers joined them beating sticks; some danced. Bewildered children pressed close to their parents. Then, in the glow of the fading embers, the Chief stood twirling a stick and began to sing his lineage song. As he chanted the final notes, from the darkness outside, whistles were heard, blows fell on the house walls. Abruptly from the rear of the house the "wolves" burst in, men clad in wolf skins or blankets, their skin daubed with back paint. The people, pretending fear, scattered, upsetting boxes, cooking containers, and other utensils. In the middle of the pandemonium a "wolf" snatched a novice and made off with the child. People chanted songs intended to drive the predators away. Parents of the abducted child followed the captors outside shouting and threatening them. Once a child had vanished in the night others turned on its parents, scolding them for allowing their child to be stolen. The hapless parents were mauled and dragged to the beaches and tossed into the frigid water. As the night drew to a close people returned to their own houses or settled down in the chief's house. The following day men, dressed as if for war, went through the houses looking for the missing children, threatening people, tipping over their furnishings, and, if in early morning, pulling people from their beds and dousing them with cold water. In each of the next three nights the same activities took place. The children, as they were captured, were hidden in comfort in the sponsor's house or in a shelter in the forest. The fifth night the "wolves" raced through the village blowing on their supernatural whistles; they struck the walls of the novices' houses with clubs "killing" them. The children's fathers or close relatives returned to the sponsor's house to lay out the "dead" behind a curtain and the "resuscitating" rite began. A group of men, their faces painted black, wearing cedar-bark rings on their heads, marched to the house; each in turn announced the name of a child saying he or she had been killed by the wolves. The sponsor asked household chiefs to bring their people to his dwelling to heal the children. Wearing their dancing ornaments, their faces painted, they moved in a rhythm in the sponsor's house. Each group danced and sang; others gathered there, joined in singing or drumming; the noise was deafening. The parents of each of the initiates had brought a pile of wooden vessels to present to the sponsor. Various chiefs owned rights to some of the articles. After the gifts were distributed the people quieted. Men sat or knelt by drumming planks; the women who were to sing stood behind them. The rest of the people crouched behind the singers. Two men costumed in black blankets belted with cedar bark, their heads festooned with cedar pompoms, appeared and sang their hereditary song. No sounds were heard; the leader sang a phrase, the second, the whole song, then all the people sang; drummers set the rhythm. Four songs were thus sung. The speaker shouted silence; all listened. The only sounds to be heard were the wind and waves. The singing had been in vain, the "wolves" had not heard it. The performance was repeated by a second pair; two dancers who owned the right to dance joined them. The onlookers bellowed loudly, promising them dire consequences if they failed to summon the "wolves." After the four songs whistles were heard; out of the shadows the novices appeared and sang their spirit song taught by the "wolves." Some related how the wolves had killed them, taken them to the locality of their ancestors, and bestowed names upon them. The next three days and nights were given over to dancing, to elaborate masked drama, and many ribald skits. While the ritual officially concluded on the eighth night, the morning of the ninth day everyone gathered again in the sponsor's house to dance and watch the shamans drive away the wolf spirits. The spirits banished, the initiates and all the rest of the people plunged into the cold Pacific waters to be purified. A few days later the sponsoring chief potlatched the villagers.

All the children were seized at least once by the "wolves" when they were old enough to learn their spirit song and simple dances. Often high ranking infants, however, went through the ritual carried in their mother's arms; almost all "royal" people participated in it over and over, each time they received another hereditary crest and name: "The procedure was in no sense a 'tribal initiation.' Rather, it was a method for defining each individual's place in the social order."[21]

Eventually the stormy season abated yielding to spring, the time for hunting the prized sea otter whose luxuriant pelt adorned the clothing of a chief and his spouse. Any man could participate in the hunt, but a chief or his designee always was in charge of the venture. To ensure good fortune the chief carried out an essential ritual. Drucker described one in which "an Ehetisat Chief bathed in salt water for success at sea otter hunting.[22] To a headband of dyed red cedar he attached four pieces of human flesh and a crystal endowed with magical power which an ancestor had obtained. He followed the shoreline swimming, floating, and diving like a sea otter as long as he could stand the cold." Before dawn next morning the hunter, with his crew of one or two went to kelp beds where otters often slept. Silently they paddled the canoe within arrow range. The hunter shot the animal, usually only wounding it; the otter dived underwater but surfaced quickly. Either the hunter released another arrow or harpooned the animal.

[21]Drucker, *Cultures of the North Pacific Coast*, p. 160.
[22]Drucker, *The Northern and Central Nootkan Tribes*, p. 169.

Spring and summer were also the time for whaling. It appears that whaling ritual and skill were the property of certain lineages, therefore, not all Nootka men engaged in it. Moreover, most of the Nootkan groups did not depend upon the large mammals for sustenance. Evidence suggests that whaling was another avenue to prestige. It was not an adventure to be undertaken lightly or spontaneously. Early in November (the Elder Moon according to the Nootka calendar) the harpooner—invariably a chief— began an eight month ritual. Each night of the first born waxing moon he rubbed his body with herbs and nettles to mortify the flesh and bathed in water. Garbed in a bear skin robe, secret marks painted on his face, and wearing a red cedar headband, he trudged heavily to and from his bathing site so that the whales would swim sedately, making easy targets. In the waxing moon of the succeeding four months he swam slowly in a circle four times in the bitterly cold salt water. Submerging, surfacing, and "blowing" four times, he mimicked the whales. He then waded ashore and scoured his body with medicinal plants and prayed. He repeated the act three more times. During these ritual times he did not sleep with his wife. The seven members of his crew were also to bathe and remain continent for brief periods. When the long months of ritual ended and the weather was favorable, the chief assembled his seven man crew. Just before sunset they carefully carried the 30-foot canoe to the water and stowed away the gear—harpoon and lines, paddles, bladders, and lances. Often another party went along captained by a younger relative of the whaler. He, however, retained the right to strike first. The crews paddled through the night to the whaling grounds. Waiting for the first light, they checked the weapons and inflated the bladders which acted as a drag on the injured whale and also marked its course. At the sighting of an animal, both crews paddled swiftly and silently toward it. If they were lucky the large cetacean surfaced to blow close by. Skillfully the canoe was brought to the port side of the whale just behind its line of vision as it submerged, a task demanding timing and patience. As the beast slowly sank the chief thrust the harpoon into it just behind the fluke. After a solid strike the crew swiftly swung the canoe to the left and away from the thrashing giant to let the line play out and, most important, to avoid a crushing blow by the whale's tail. This was a critical moment: The animal could capsize the boat; drag it beneath the water; or a man could be ensnared in the line and dragged to his death. Should one of these have occurred it was thought it was because someone had been careless about the important rites.

Once hit, the whale sounded, the paddlers pursued, hoping against hope that it would not head far out to sea. When it surfaced again the leader of the accompanying crew drove in another harpoon. Hindered by the lines, encumbered by the floats, and losing blood, the whale slowly ceased its struggles. The animal would be badly wounded and exhausted, but not yet dead. The chief's first paddler delivered the coup de grace with a lance. Another leaped into the water to tie the victim's mouth shut to prevent taking on water. Lashing the beast to the canoe they started for home. Towing the behemoth was backbreaking; the crew chanted songs intended to make the task less laborious but without much effect. A crew member told Drucker that "When I looked back at the whale my heart felt sick. Every time a swell went over it, the whale seemed to go backward, I couldn't see how we would ever get to shore with it."[23] It was not unusual to spend several nights at sea while towing the carcass home.

As the whaling party drew close to the village, people collected on the shores to welcome them home with wild enthusiasm. At high tide the canoes were beached and when the water receded the whale was firmly grounded. The chief, with a flourish, cut off a piece of blubber and announced to his village that he had killed a whale. The butchering began in earnest when the first paddler repeating the chief's instructions directed the cutting. The latter stood apart from the proceedings holding his nose with shredded cedar bark so that he might not smell the odor of whale. Portions were given to his crew and to the leader and crews of the second canoe. Anyone who had helped to bring the animal to shore also received pieces. The remainder of the blubber and meat was cut and laid on the beach. The chief through his speaker distributed it among all members of group according to rank.

The arrival of the whaling season, spring and summer fishing, and collecting, completed the young couple's first shared subsistence cycle. Sometime during that first year they realized that a baby was on the way. Her mother and female relatives saw her through the event, warning her against eating leftovers, drinking stored water, or lingering in the doorway of the great house. Had she not observed their advice the baby would have stayed in her womb long past its time for birth. Pregnancy afforded her relief from weaving and basketmaking lest she cause the umbilical cord to twist and choke the baby. In general, the young wife led a quiet and inactive life; her relatives did her chores and made all the necessary mats and cradles for the baby. Both she and her husband avoided watching the death struggles of animals, they never looked at a corpse, nor did they listen to laments for the dead. Because the young father had to curtail his hunting and fishing, others saw that they did not go hungry.

At the first signs that birth was imminent, the wife repaired to a small hut built apart from the center of activities. There, assisted by her mother, a shaman, if the birth were difficult or if she were the daughter of a chief, she delivered the infant. The trial was aided by infusions of magic herb and oil concoctions belonging to her family; had they none they paid another to provide them. Four days following the birth she remained in the hut eating boiled dried dog salmon, black cod broth, and steamed clover roots. The

[23]Ibid., p. 55.

baby lay in its first cradle made of woven mats, its head padded with a head shaper to produce the desired long narrow form. During these four days its father remained in the great house eating nothing but dried fish. At the close of the fourth day the mother emerged and returned to the family space and placed the baby in a large wooden cradle shaped like an eating dish and padded with red cedar bark. Except for those times when the baby was washed or the cedar bark was changed, the infant lay securely laced in the cradle, its head still gently pressured by the head shaper.

The birth of twins imposed special and severe restrictions on the parents. The basis for these lay in the belief that twins were closely connected to the Salmon Spirits and that the abundance of salmon in the future depended upon their care. Following the mother's isolation in the hut for four days, she, her husband, and infants moved to another in the woods. On tall poles in front of the structure were two carved sea gulls. (Sea gulls were associated with twinning.) The pair existed on dried salmon and roots, their relatives supplied them with water, wood, and food. They moved three more times until they were so isolated they could forage for their own food without being seen. From time to time kin visited them bringing dried salmon. At night the couple chanted and sang to bring salmon, herring, and whales to their home waters. When their period of deprivation and isolation ended, relatives brought them home; gradually they were reincorporated into the household. Twins who survived to adulthood were believed to be clairvoyant; frequently they became shamans.

Nootkans were no different than most other Native Americans in their fondness for children. Little ones were indulged; spanking was unheard of; nor were children threatened with supernatural peril. A young miscreant received soft lectures intended to produce shame or guilt. Parents talked to their children, even as infants, stressing good manners and behavior appropriate to their rank. The children of chiefs were constantly admonished with regard to their responsibilities; the traditions and privileges to which they were heir were drilled into them as soon as they could understand. Both parents and grandparents whispered closely guarded family secrets to children—prayers, herbal formulae, and hunting and fishing rituals.

Unlike many other Indian children, a Nootka child was not confronted with a complex kinship system to master. Consistent with the emphasis on generation and birth order, there were a minimal number of kin labels. Parents' brothers and sisters as well as their cousins were all called by the same term. Own siblings and cousins were identified by age; the term for older sibling was extended to include the parents' older sibling's child. A different label indicated younger sibling and parents' younger sibling's child. Parents referred to their child and its cousins by the same term. A word, which loosely translated meant "ancestor," was used for grandparents. To identify a person by sex and in some cases specific age, Nootkans used qualifying words. In a round about way (perhaps not unlike our own) Nootkans could, if pressed, explain any particular person's relationship to them. With such a system as this (technically called Hawaiian) there was no institutionalized behavior such as avoidance or familiarity. One ethnologist theorized that the importance of birth order ranking cut across the usual kinship categories and weakened them as determinants of etiquette.[24]

Until adolescence children played at adult activities—little boys, perhaps, did so more than girls, for the latter went berrying and helped in small ways around the house. Men's work was too strenuous and in some cases too dangerous for boys to tag along, but they tried to spear small fish in tidal pools and threw miniature harpoons at imaginary whales. After puberty—easier to determine in girls than boys—life became more serious. No special celebration marked a boy's maturing but his sister underwent ritual. When her mother learned that the time had come, she summoned a female shaman to rub her daughter's belly; this would help her to have easy childbirth. For the following four days the youngster sat up with her back to the family fire. After all others had gone to bed each night she lay down but was forbidden to turn over. Before anyone in the village arose in the morning she resumed her stiff sitting posture. She was the last to sleep and the first to awake. Looking at people or glancing around the house was forbidden. During these four days she ate only freshly boiled dried cod or old dried salmon. Reminiscent of some of the restrictions placed on a pregnant woman were those requiring her to avoid leftovers and consume only fresh water. On the fifth day her mother and aunts accompanied her to a bathing place, disrobed her, and rubbed her vigorously with bundles of hemlock twigs, praying that she enjoy a long life, bear many children, and acquire wealth. She then entered the water escorted by two small boys; this was intended to ensure male children. Swimming four ceremonial circuits she blew bubbles during each. The bubbles represented a boiling pot and the hope was that she be a good cook!

Upon returning to the house her relatives groomed her and attached hair ornaments. The ornaments varied in elegance consistent with the rank of the girl and her birth order. If her father did not own ornaments, a special chiefly privilege, he paid a chief for their use. Following the attachment of the ornaments, either a feast or a potlatch was given. A chief gave the most grandiose potlatch of all for his oldest daughter, displaying all the privileges her children would someday inherit. From that moment on the girl, now regarded as a young lady, played no more, nor did she wander about the village alone. Like the Cheyenne the Nootka tried to guarantee chastity.

No such ritual celebrated the coming of age of boys. They served an apprenticeship in economic, social, and ceremonial activities. Even after

[24]Elman R. Service, *Profiles in Ethnology.* (New York: Harper and Row, Pub. 1963), p. 214.

their marriage, their fathers and other middle-aged men dominated Nootkan life. Only after their fathers declined in health or died did they assume active roles, particularly in the complex ceremonial life.

Despite the older generations' efforts to mold children's character to conform with the Nootkan value of getting along with others, as they grew up, they did not always comply with the norms. Conflict appeared from time to time: Men disputed property rights; women quarreled too; and of course, adultery provoked contention. On the whole, however, little overt discord occurred. People disapproved of violence and made every attempt to discourage it. Jewitt remarked:

> The Nootkians in their conduct towards each other, are in general pacific and inoffensive, and appear by no means an ill tempered race, for I do not recollect any instance of a violent quarrel between any of the men or the men and their wives while I was with them. . . . But when they are in the least offended, they appear to be in the most violent rage, acting like so many maniacs, foaming at the mouth, kicking and spitting most furiously; but this is rather a fashion with them, than a demonstration of malignity, as in their public speeches, they use the same violence . . .[25]

A ranking system coupled with village life, both characteristic of the Nootka, would suggest the presence of formal machinery for social control. The Cheyenne, without permanent villages and the semi-sedentary Mandan, had developed formal institutions for control. This was, however, not the Nootkan situation; the most common devices for control were informal. Should a quarrel have escalated into fisticuffs or hair pulling—the more common method of attack—bystanders watched for a few minutes then separated the two; the combatants then retreated into an oral battle. Each, at the top of his voice, pointed out his own excellence, superior rank, and exceptional skill, and villified the other with every jibe, insult, and insolence he could summon up, much to the amusement of the onlookers. Eventually the two, hoarse and weary, were pacified by their relatives: "Don't think about him anymore. It's not right to fight. You have a good name; don't bring it down. You would be bringing shame to all of us, if you made more trouble. Don't think about it—just let it go."[26] If the rambunctious person failed to respect the counsel, a ringing public reproach would shame him into conformance. At a feast or some public assembly, usually an elder kinsman would berate the reprobate with a blistering rebuke. Few could withstand such public humiliation.

Like most other Indian groups, the Nootka believed that some of their fellows could work magical harm; they were not, however, riddled with suspicion. The belief, mild as it was, exercized some social restraint. Young people were advised not to offend elderly men or women for al-

[25]John R. Jewitt, *A Narrative of the Adventures and Sufferings of John R. Jewitt*, p. 176.
[26]Drucker, *The Northern and Central Nootkan Tribes*, p. 312.

though they might be physically weak, they could retaliate with inexplicable illness or bad luck.

The Nootka emphasized amicable relationships within their villages and with tribal associates, but they frequently fought groups from other Nootkan tribes or confederacies. Vengeance provided a motive for war but, by far, the most common cause was economic. A group whose fishing territories were limited, or whose population exceeded their resources, and who were unable through marriage or other alliances to share in another group's rights, often embarked on an expedition to eliminate their rival and gain control of their lands and waters.[27]

Whatever the provocation may have been, covetous chiefs made plans for an assault in utmost secrecy. Each gave a long speech denouncing the enemy, speaking of treachery and old grievances. Once the decision was made the ranking chief, his associates, and war chiefs planned the operation down to the finest detail, a practice at variance with typical Indian raiding. In addition to ritual preparation, the leader directed simulated invasions. Men practiced beaching war canoes in stealth, running up slopes, and dodging long club blows. The number of warriors trained depended upon the manpower pool as well as the strength of the intended victims. To leave little to chance, intelligence gathering was an important dimension of the preparations. Scouts went on reconnaissance to discover in which houses the chiefs were currently living and the sleeping arrangements of the occupants; occasionally such information was innocently volunteered by visitors. The attackers were divided into squads and each assigned a specific dwelling; war chiefs were charged with the killing of their counterparts or other important people. With their leaders dead, the defenders were quickly demoralized.

Attacks were usually mounted on moonless nights; the roar of waves and wind muted any noise of the invasion. Every man, knowing his mission, crept to his target to await the signal to attack. Bursting into the darkened houses they went about slaughtering and beheading the helpless occupants; occasionally captives were taken. Houses were looted and canoes burned to prevent a counterattack if there were any survivors. Triumphant, they returned home singing with the booty and heads of the unfortunates. These were displayed for four days then concealed in the forest.

Although the Nootkans were ruthless in executing enemies, a death of their own inspired deep fear. Hastily, the deceased's remains were wrapped unwashed—a chief, in otter skin or a red cedar blanket—and stuffed into a box. Four men carried it off to a cave or tied it to branches high in a tree; often they towed it in a canoe to a secluded burial inlet. While they were gone women hacked their hair off to shoulder length and burned it. After the burial party returned, the bereft males, if the dead

---

[27]The Ahousat war on the Otosat appears to have been a direct consequence of the abuse of salmon streams in their territory. See Drucker, Ibid., pp. 344–353.

were a chief or of an important chiefly line, sang dolorous songs to a slow drum beat. A few days later, the heir gave a "throwing away potlatch" in which the departed's possessions were given away to the guests and his rights and privileges were retired for a time. From this moment until a year lapsed, no one could speak his name or even a syllable of it. Belongings of people of lesser rank were distributed at a small feast; the name taboo was not invoked. Regardless of the rank of the dead, even close kin did not observe a long mourning period and there was no regularized seclusion.

Nootkan notions of afterlife were vague. The northern groups thought that their deads' spirits wandered aimlessly about in this world doing little harm. Central tribes believed that owls were spirits of the dead. The topic was, in general, of little concern to anyone.

Ideas about the nature of the universe corresponded closely to Nootkan daily experience with it. Because the land was forbidding and nearly impenetrable, people seldom ventured very far from the coast; it was an unknown world, and they peopled it with a host of mysterious and malignant supernatural beings. Tall, tangled-hair, red-skinned beings chased people with spears; dwarfs lived in the bowels of the mountains and enticed the unwary to them; a cougar that walked backward killed men with its long lance-like tail. Souls of trees, visible only as shadows, could kill the viewer. The list of malevolent spirits lurking in the vastness of the forest was long.

The sea, the rivers, and streams meant life for the people. Here were few malicious beings. There was an undersea world offshore where the Salmon and the Herring People lived, each occupying one side of a large house; the souls of twins lived there with them. Whales and Hair Seals also dwelled in homes under the sea. To these "people" were accorded proper deference, and appropriate ritual was directed toward them; they were beneficent. Offending them, however, would bring disaster.

Nootkans did not approach the supernaturals with reverence, nor can it be said that they worshipped them as the term is usually understood. Their rituals were primarily aimed at forcing or persuading supernatural powers toward their own ends. Most economic endeavors were accompanied by such rites. Ritual warded off illness; ceremonies cured the sick. Manipulative rites assured the growth of babies, the prowess of war chiefs, and in general provided skill and luck for almost any of life's tasks. Many of the rituals belonged to individual families whose members kept them wrapped in secrecy. The closely monitored details—formulas, herbs, procedures—were inherited from generation to generation.

While the Northwest Coast ritual was largely mechanical and was a technique to exploit supernatural power, the people did have the beginnings of a priesthood. Eleman Service viewed the behavior of a high chief as priestlike when he performed rituals on behalf of his people. A major occasion took place at the beginning of the salmon run. The chief ritually purified himself and carried out a complicated ceremony to insure the arrival of the cherished fish. The practice resembled the "First Fruit" ceremonies common to many horticulture groups and some of the foragers who, like the Washo, relied heavily on a particular wild crop.[28]

EPILOGUE

The Nootkans encountered their first white man, a Spaniard, in 1774. Captain Cook anchored in Nootka Sound four years later and took aboard a few sea otter pelts. He later lost his life in the South Pacific but his introduction of the luxuriant pelts to the China trade started an influx of maritime traders hungering for the "black gold." Coastal tribes rapidly hunted the animals almost to extinction by 1875, trading the pelts for iron, guns, and other European goods. From about 1820 to 1875, as the animals vanished, the seaward side of Vancouver Island was neglected by foreigners; the Nootka followed their traditional ways, modified somewhat by metal, thriving on fish and sea mammals supplemented by roots and berries. They held their great winter ceremonies, potlatched, and feasted without interference.

Late in the nineteenth century seal skins became valuable. Nootkan men signed aboard schooners bound for more distant ports; their wages allowed their families to purchase goods and food from trading posts, such as the Hudson Bay Company. The change to nontraditional foods was necessary because their seafaring providers could no longer harvest the salmon, halibut, and herring. Eventually the Canadian government established reserves for the native peoples. The Nootka, however, were not displaced; their land included their summer and winter villages, salmon streams, and collecting grounds. Catholic missionaries arrived to introduce literacy and to combat "native superstition," but did not tamper with other aspects of Nootkan culture. In the early twentieth century Canadian and American companies established salmon canneries nearby. Logging operations started, but Nootka territory was not seriously threatened. The storm-tossed west coast did not encourage large white settlements or even heavy tourist invasions. The Nootkans live today somewhat isolated still, subsisting largely on wage labor in canneries, or as independent fishermen more at home with gasoline or diesel engines than the canoes of their ancestors. Most are literate; some of their young people have migrated to urban areas. Potlatches are gone, although they love a good feast still. Most of the old rituals exist only as fragmented memories in the minds of the very oldest. A few men and women have tried to replicate the ancient artifacts for collectors or tourists, but the elaborately carved masks, intricately constructed boxes, and woven containers rest in museums.

---

[28]Eleman R. Service, *Profiles in Ethnology*, pp. 222–223.

Conclusion
Part Three

The Cheyenne and the Nootka lived in environments of relative plenty in which each depended heavily on a dominant food source. The plains bison provided for most of Cheyenne needs; fish, especially salmon and herring, sustained the Nootka. The abundance of wild food obviated the need for farming and, without modern knowledge and technology, the rugged climates prevented it.

The Cheyenne year was based on the habits of the buffalo. In the harshest season the animals clustered in small herds in protected areas. At this time the Cheyenne, too, lived in small bands surviving on dried meats. Occasionally if the weather moderated, men searched for fresh game. With the advent of spring—late in Cheyenne land—the buffalo congregated in vast herds on the open plains; the bands also gathered together, setting up their hide *tipis* at a designated place in the great tribal circle. The Council of Forty-four assembled for deliberations; spectacular summer ceremonies involved the entire populace. Military societies patrolled the encampment and policed the traditional summer bison hunt.

In a similar fashion, the Nootkan annual cycle corresponded to the periodic fish spawns and migrations. During the spring, summer, and fall, people lived in small summer villages to fish and preserve the catch for the long tumultuous winter. High-ranking chiefs who owned the rights to streams, rivers, and beaches guided their pursuits. Chiefs initiated the beginning of fishing and collecting by performing their esoteric ritual. When winter threatened, Nootkans moved back to large permanent winter villages. Lineage-like groups occupied huge wooden long houses. The towering trees of Vancouver Island provided timber, wood, and bark for most of their needs. In one or another of the large structures, chiefs potlatched villages and visitors from neighboring groups. The dramatic Shaman Dance also lessened winter boredom.

Both the Cheyenne and the Nootka exhibited a class structure. The Nootkan, however, was much more rigid, emphasizing primogeniture and strict inheritance rights in chiefly lines. A younger son could rarely hope to become a ranking chief. The Cheyenne system was more fluid; class boundaries were somewhat permeable. Through skill, courage, and determination, a young Cheyenne male might achieve wealth and high status. People in both groups attempted to maintain class positions by arranging their children's marriages with those of similar status. It is interesting to note that both insisted on female chastity, especially in important families; we suspect that this value was associated with the phenomenon of social hierarchy.

To control interpersonal relationships the Cheyenne developed a formal legal apparatus. The tribal council or the military societies heard cases, formulated laws, and acted upon precedence. The village-dwelling Nootkans produced no formal devices for social control, depending upon social pressure exerted upon one another to maintain order. Chiefly management of major resources also constrained people, but chiefs themselves had no power to punish.

It is likely that the Cheyenne may have brought an incipient governmental structure with them from their woodland home, but life on the plains encouraged it to become more elaborate. Effective mass buffalo hunting on horseback demanded organization, cooperation, and direction. The summer assembly certainly benefited from the order and protection afforded by the men's organizations. The absence of formal political power among the Nootkans is not so readily explained, but of course massive fish movements did not depend upon human husbandry. There was little need to organize the behavior of fishermen to protect the fish either from interrupting their upstream journeys or from overfishing. In general, extracting a living from ocean and rivers did not depend upon group control. Nootkans did not wander freely through their land, thus tribal integrative devices to bring them together for ritual and annual reunions were not necessary.

The origin of the Northwest Coast ranking systems is lost in the distant past, yet it functioned to see that all had access to resources, one way or another. The lavish potlatches and frequent feasting associated with rank acted as a redistributive economic system; people contributed to important chiefs and, in turn, received from them. Some scholars have argued that the potlatches were a response to periods of scarcity. There were lean times of course, but there is little evidence to show that the Nootkans were threatened with extreme privation or starvation. If specific territories ceased to yield sufficient bounty their people seized other group's areas through well-organized tactical warfare. Motives of Cheyenne raids were only partially economic. To be sure, successful attacks increased horse herds, but equally important to participants, horses were avenues to prestige. Perhaps because goals and targets differed, Cheyenne warfare never equaled the complex tactics and strategies of the Nootkans.

Like so many other North American Indians, Cheyenne and Nootkan belief systems and cosmologies centered on life's most dicey or perplexing problems. In their view, spirits, both beneficent and hostile, populated their worlds. With appropriate manipulation—details varied—their aid could be enlisted or their malignancies turned away. And important rituals assured both Cheyenne and Nootka of the continued existence of their primary food sources. Each, through medicine men or shamans, attempted to combat sickness. Data suggest that the Cheyenne were somewhat more beseeching in some of their postures toward the supernatural than were the Nootka.

These populations inhabited generous although taxing environments. The relative security they provided encouraged the development of fairly complex cultures for both. Only the Mandan, because of their dual economy, equaled or surpassed them in cultural sophistication. This is not to contend in a narrow way that the environments determined or caused the cultural specifics, but they fostered them and certain emphases were environmental consequences. We must not overlook either the importance of the diffusion of ideas and technology to each society. Both the Cheyenne and the Nootka were in intermittent or close contact with other peoples in their region. Some ethnohistorians have speculated that aspects of the general Northwest Coast cultural patterns looked as if they might have been derived from a Polynesian influence! Both groups incorporated useful items from white culture at different times in their histories. Regardless, however, of what was indigenous or borrowed, both societies flourished in their time in symbiotic accord with their environments.

PART FOUR

INTENSIVE FARMERS

In this final section we will examine two farming groups: the southeastern Cherokee and a New Mexican Rio Grande pueblo. Both relied more heavily on cultivation than they did on hunting and collecting wild edibles. Frequently the term "full-time" agriculturalists has been applied to such people. Full-time is, however, misleading, for most Native North American farmers hunted, fished, and gathered wild vegetables to supplement their diets. The Cherokee, for example, hunted more actively than did the Pueblo people.

Anthropologists and historians have associated the appearance of permanent villages and more complex social and political organization with the rise of agriculture. The relationship is, however, not a simple one; there are many intervening variables between the two. Of course the combination of fertile soil, sufficient water, and gardening knowledge may encourage sedentary life, but much depends upon population densities and the way in which the resources were used. Resource use correlates with environmental factors. Irrigation farming typical of arid areas tended to be labor intensive; ditches had to be maintained and fields nourished because they were sown over and over. Dry land farming in aboriginal times required less consistent energy expenditure. Although these people lived in settled communities, they did not necessarily have permanent fields. Depending upon the extent of arable land and the population pressures on it, they were frequently able to fallow garden plots for five or more years while they cleared and cultivated new ones. This difference in farming methods was reflected in many dimensions of their cultures. In many farming societies the individual household supplied almost all the necessary labor. In others, extended families or even lineages worked the land. Land ownership and crop distribution were often a consequence of the organization of the workforce. Social organization was closely connected to land management and method. Agriculture encouraged village life and village dwellers required some form of governance.[1] Political organization differed among the agriculturalists but each tribe had some type of governmental structure. We might speculate that the forms they assumed were, at least remotely, a function of land use and ownership. It can be argued, too, that the nature of ideologies and attendant rituals were an outgrowth of social and political organization and the nature of the environment.

The Cherokee were dry land farmers and, until they were constrained by advancing white settlers, tillable land was abundant in their region. They cleared new garden lands as they needed them. The fields of the Rio Grande pueblo were irrigated with water diverted from the river by means of ditches. Only rarely did they prepare additional land for irrigation. The two differed from one another in some significant ways, a function of a number of factors including their environments. Yet they had commonalities. These similarities as well as the differences, both typical of agriculturalists, set them apart from foragers and most of the part-time farmers.

---

[1]Scattered homesteads on widely separated farms are much more typical of the United States than they are of other parts of the world.

CHAPTER TEN

The
Cherokee
of the
Great Smoky Mountains

Beginning in the Gaspé Peninsula, the ancient Appalachian Mountain chain stretches in a southwest direction terminating in northern Georgia and Alabama. Different names have been given to its major ranges and peaks. Mt. Washington juts upward in the rugged White Mountains. The Green Mountains, which become the Berkshires in southern New England, are gentler ranges. South of Rip Van Winkle's Catskills are the Kittatiny Mountains of New Jersey and the Pennsylvania Poconos. The Alleghenies and the Blue Ridge Mountains are separated by miles of smaller hills, plateaus, and valleys. Further west lie the jagged Cumberlands. Many northeastern peaks thrust above the tree line. Mt. Mitchell in North Carolina is the highest in the Appalachians; it has no timber line. Mysterious grassy or heath areas crown saddles connecting the higher peaks in the Blacks and the Great Smokies.

Except for elevations above the timber line and the bald areas, the Appalachians are heavily forested; conifers are dominant in some areas or elevations; in others, mixed hardwoods flourish. Unlike the grim splendor of the towering western mountains, the southern Appalachians inspire a sense of tranquility. Like dark green waves the more southerly ranges cover miles in an undulating panorama. Smaller crossridges separated by valleys connect them. From their flanks the French Broad, the Nolichucky,

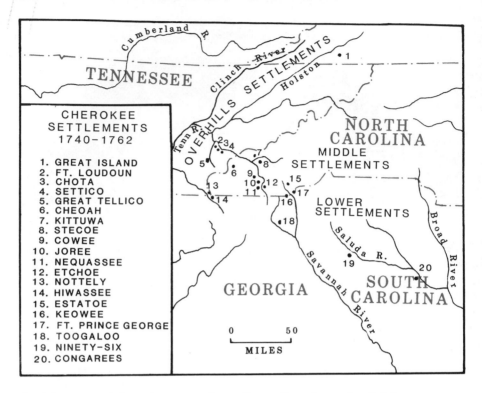

CHEROKEE
SETTLEMENTS
1740–1762

1. GREAT ISLAND
2. FT. LOUDOUN
3. CHOTA
4. SETTICO
5. GREAT TELLICO
6. CHEOAH
7. KITTUWA
8. STECOE
9. COWEE
10. JOREE
11. NEQUASSEE
12. ETCHOE
13. NOTTELY
14. HIWASSEE
15. ESTATOE
16. KEOWEE
17. FT. PRINCE GEORGE
18. TOOGALOO
19. NINETY–SIX
20. CONGAREES

the Pigeon, and the Hiawassee rivers flow, often through wild deep gorges, ultimately entering the Tennessee river. Branches and tributaries, whose beginnings are in cascading falls in the connecting ridges, course through the valleys. Secluded smaller valleys, called coves, nestle in the foothills, each with its own creek or fork. The valued bottomland is made up of these valleys and coves.

The mountains still shelter an amazing number of animals. True, the bison vanished in the nineteenth century. Wolves, and mountain lions, too, may have disappeared. Occasionally reports of one or the other are circulated. Bear and white-tailed deer still feed on berries and browse. Small ground-dwelling mammals scamper on the moist forest floor in a constant quest for food. Some fall prey to bobcats, rattlesnakes, owl, and hawk. Once plentiful, golden and bald eagles still wheel in the skies; the cry of the peregrine falcon can once more be heard.

The Great Smoky Mountains tumble over both sides of the high boundary shared by Tennessee and North Carolina and dwindle to low hills in Georgia and Alabama. The Cherokee country was situated across the range almost at right angles. At their most powerful, the Cherokee held the entire Allegheny region from the headwaters of the Kanawha and the Tennessee rivers almost to Atlanta, and from the Blue Ridge to the Cumberlands in the west. This territory of about 40,000 square miles with no

The Smoky Mountains, Oconaluflee River, circa 1888.
Smithsonian Institution National Anthropological Archives.

fixed boundaries prompted rival groups to challenge Cherokee claims. The
Virginia Powhatan and Monacan tested them in the north. In the east the
Catawba and Tuscarora were constantly at war with them. The Creek con-
tested Cherokee claims to Georgia land; they fought with the Chickasaw
and Shawano over the fertile valleys of the lower Tennessee and the Cumberlands.[1]

This land of mist-shrouded peaks, cold crystal clear water, and verdant cover provided an abundant habitat for game. Until they were extir-
pated in the middle of the nineteenth century, bison and elk roamed the
area. Wolf and Indian fed on white-tailed deer. Gray and red fox dined on
mice, grouse, and quail. Bobcat and cougar screams punctuated the silence
of mountain nights. Black bear and raccoon sauntered through the woods
and fished for trout, perch, and other fish in shallow rivers. Wild turkeys
strutted beneath the forest canopy. Other animals and birds, too, shared
the land. Whippoorwills and chuck will's widows cried out at dusk and
dawn. Barred, great horned, and screech owls flew silently through the
darkness, their haunting calls echoing through cove and valley.

The Appalachian woods provided more than just animals for the
Cherokee. An abundance of flora—herbs, lichens, mosses, ferns, and delicately flowering plants—thrived along stream banks and bottoms, in rhododendron and laurel slicks, and on mountain slopes and ridges. In the
Cherokee view, plants were beneficial but animals were hostile.[2] They gathered some plants for food, but plants' great importance lay in their contribution to the Cherokee *materia medica*. The bark of some of more than 130
species of trees also contributed to the pharmacopoeia.

The southern Appalachians are moody mountains. On sunny winter

[1]James Mooney, *Myths of the Cherokee*. From Nineteenth Annual Report of the Bureau
of American Ethnology to the Secretary of the Smithsonian Institution, 1897–1898, by J. W.
Powell, Director, Part 1, p. 12, Smithsonian Institution, Washington, D.C., 1900. By permission of Smithsonian Institution Press.
[2]Ibid., p. 240.

days the temperature may rise to 50 or 60 degrees Fahrenheit and at night drop to 15 or 20. Denuded trees cover the stark and gray slopes. On cold winter mornings cloud vapors freeze coating the higher peaks with rime. Sunshine suddenly yields to dark clouds and wind, and snow falls, sometimes gently, other times furiously. Cold rain pelts down often to freeze on the skeleton-like trees. With the return of the sun, the glistening branches shower crystal daggers. Winter precipitation may average 30 or more inches. Appalachian spring comes reluctantly in late March and April, reaching the lowlands first, then hesitantly creeping up the ridges as shades of green blend into each other. Trees are just budding on the high peaks when lower regions are a sweep of green. Rhododendron and flame azalea bloom there long after they have gone from the bottoms. With summer comes warm days. Often hot afternoons, 90° or above, portend a violent thunder storm. Jagged lightning streaks across the sky and through the cove; thunder rumbles from ridge to ridge. Water rushes down the shallow fork beds overflowing banks and eradicating the footpaths and trails that wind around them. Summer gives way to fall; grasses turn brown; wild flowers fade. The valleys, ridges, and distant mountains blaze with red and gold. The dark greens of the conifers relieve the endless quilt of brilliant color. Often in the distance a haze hangs over the peaks. Small animals rush from hickory, walnut, and buckeye trees, storing up food for the coming lean days. Rodents gather seeds. With cheeks full they disappear into their burrows. Rattlesnakes and copperheads move lethargically to rock shelters to den, often together, for the winter. Bears, fat from summer and fall foraging, search for a hidden sanctuary to dream away the winter. Only the deer and the predators remain active, each striving to survive the season.

De Soto met the people first in 1540 as he pushed up the Savannah river. In an insatiable thirst for gold, other smaller Spanish expeditions a few years later continued the search. What effects they may have had on the Cherokee is conjectural. One hundred or more years later the Cherokee encountered the British: By 1700 they had acquired guns and other trade goods from them.

Between ten and twenty thousand Cherokee lived in these hills in the late seventeenth and early eighteenth centuries. Cherokee was not the name they used for themselves. Although it appeared in travelers' journals as early as 1708, the Cherokee were, in their language (a variant of Iroquoian) Ani-Yunwiya, the Real People or Principal People.[3] They built their settlements beside streams and rivers wherever there was sufficient fertile bottomland. These communities varied from a few households to populations of 400 or more, each partially isolated from the other by the craggy highlands. The Lower settlements were strung along eastern slopes bordering the Savannah river. On the western side of the mountains, about

[3]Ibid., p. 15.

100 miles distant in a deep valley gouged out by the Tennessee river and its tributaries, lay the Overhill settlements. Between them, the Middle and Valley settlements were hidden in narrow mountain coves watered by streams of the Hiwassee and Tennessee rivers. Numerous trails snaked through Cherokee territory connecting the settlements and leading to domains of other Indian groups. The distances between the settlements encouraged the formation of three dialects. People of the Lower settlements spoke Elati, now extinct. Atali spoken in the Overhill and Valley settlements is now the dialect of the modern day Oklahoma Cherokee. The Middle settlements spoke Kituwha; it is still spoken on the North Carolina reservation.[4]

Every Cherokee belonged to one of seven named matrilineal clans. Because of marriage patterns, all villages usually included some members of each. Although the communities were autonomous, each with its own politico-religious structure, the intervillage kinship web linked them together in peaceful coexistence. A council of older men governed the communities. While early observers spoke of seven mother towns, a later scholar, Fred Gearing, thought they were probably intellectual centers where priests attempted to systematize traditional beliefs.[5] Their influence, perhaps, affected priests throughout the settlements.

Any male over fifty was called a "beloved old man"; all "beloved old men" sat on the council. A priest chief, three lesser priests, and a lay leader guided deliberations. From the main body, seven "beloved old men," one from each clan, made up an inner council which advised the chief priest and spoke for their clans. To announce a council meeting a white flag was raised over the seven-sided council house; as many as 400 men, women, and children might crowd in. Each clan sat together along the sides; "beloved old men" sat on front benches; younger men and women sat behind them. The priest chief, his aides, and the seven-man inner council (the whole organization), rested on special benches toward the center. To come to a decision the council had to arrive at a consensus. Because any man could speak at length on an issue, meetings continued for days, even weeks, as the people listened to long, softly spoken speeches.

By the early 1700s the Cherokee lived in squarepole or log houses. Some contained two or three rooms and some were two stories high. Inside and outside walls were plastered with clay tempered with dry grasses. Through a hole in the chestnut bark roof smoke from constantly burning fires escaped. There were a few openings for light but the interiors were dark and the air often pungent with the aroma of smoke. Furnishings were few. Boards covered with bear skins served as beds; basket and clay con-

[4]William H. Gilbert, Jr., *The Eastern Cherokees*. Bureau of American Ethnology, Bulletin 133, Anthropological Papers Number 23, 1943, p. 199, Smithsonian Institution. By permission of Smithsonian Institution Press.

[5]Fred Gearing, *Priests and Warriors: Social Structure for Cherokee Politics in the 18th Century*. American Anthropological Association, vol. 64, Memoir 93, 1962, p. 80.

tainers were scattered about on the earthen floors. On the walls hung blow guns, bows, and ceremonial objects. Opposite the door in the yard stood a low sweat house. The fire within glowed constantly. Sick people retreated to it to purify themselves.

Although men built the houses, women dominated them. An elderly couple, their unmarried children, and their married daughters lived together. The Cherokee preferred matrilocal residence, although adhering to the rule was not always possible, a result of the vagaries of births, deaths, or disputes. The household was the important economic group among the people, and its activities corresponded to the rhythms of the seasons.

The Cherokee, however, recognized only two seasons: winter and summer. The lunar cycle marked the seasons. The first new moon in October signaled the start of winter. Seven new moons later, usually in April, summer began. It ended seven moons later in October: "Thus the two important new moons were in each case seventh in a continuous series reckoning from the other. Each ended and each began a new season as the boundary points of the chief periods of the year, winter and summer."[6] The Cherokee new year began with the October moon, and they celebrated its arrival with three major ceremonies.

At noon on a day in September when the corn was ripe, the village men, carrying evergreen boughs, filed sedately before the priest chief and his attendants to initiate the Green Corn Feast. Later in the afternoon they danced in the town center, accompanied by solemn drumming. Women, forbidden to observe, remained secluded in their houses. At dark they joined the men for social dances, many of which were based on myths. Flickering flames from a large fire cast shadows around the dance ground. To the rhythm of a hollow drum, men and women promenaded toward each other, then away, in the pheasant dance, the stamping of their feet imitating the bird's drumming. It was said by the old people that

> a pheasant once saw a women beating corn on a wooden mortar in front of the house. "I can do that, too," he said but the woman would not believe it. So the pheasant went into the woods and got upon a hollow log and "drummed" with his wings as a pheasant does until the people in the house heard him and thought that he was really beating corn.[7]

While the people recovered from the four-day Green Corn ritual, the priests calculated the date for the Great New Moon feast which celebrated the start of the new year. Seven days before it, men left to hunt. Seven men were selected to organize the feast and seven honorable women to prepare it. At dawn on the appointed day all the people assembled, entered the council house in single file, and gave offerings—seven ears of corn, dried squash, and bits of every other crop—to the perpetual fire. Following the

[6]Gilbert, *The Eastern Cherokees*, p. 325.
[7]Mooney, *Myths of the Cherokee*, p. 290.

Cherokee cabin, woman grinding corn, circa 1888.
Smithsonian Institution National Anthropological Archives.

women's sacred dance, the priest chief led the villagers to the river, where fallen leaves swirling in its eddys released their medicinal properties. All bathed seven times. Purified and restored, they returned to the village to participate in the communal banquet.

A few days later the priest chief and his inner council entered the council house to decide upon the time for the most important ceremony of the three, a ritual designed to eradicate bad feelings among the people. Seven days prior to its beginning, seven men were sent out to hunt. The priests appointed seven women to dance and selected a fire maker and six assistants. Finally they chose seven men to clean the council house. Except for the hunters, all the officials fasted seven days. On the sixth evening the women danced until the autumn night chilled their audience. The next morning the cleaners extinguished the sacred fire and each household smothered its fire. The perpetual sacred fire was rekindled; a woman of each house carried a burning faggot to light anew the family fire. A singer rattled his gourd and chanted seven verses. The people followed the priest to the river and plunged in seven times; they then stripped and let the current carry their old clothes downstream. Wearing new clothes they danced and feasted until the moon rose on the fourth evening. Village unity was once more ritually renewed and anger among the town people dissipated.

While the three great rituals celebrated the coming of the new year, they also provided the backdrop for important council decisions. Interspersed between the rituals the white banner hung over the council house. The "beloved old men" took their places and the entire populace followed to listen. The most important question they addressed was: Shall there be war or peace this winter? Older men spoke at length, some favoring war with the Shawnee to avenge a fallen clan brother. Others, for the same reason, wanted to attack the Iroquois. Some advocated peace. Younger men listened and murmured among themselves; some commented softly on the plans. Because the priest and the council lacked coercive power, the conflicting interests had to be reconciled, a process often requiring days of quiet debate. Until a clear sentiment emerged and overt disagreement quieted, the council could make no decisions.

The three fall rituals interposed between council meetings do not appear to have been coincidental. Gearing suggested that the first created a favorable atmosphere for the forthcoming deliberations.[8] The second, interrupting political activities, perhaps quelled tensions. The third explicitly set out to eliminate any unspoken resentments and to promote the village unity necessary to execute the council decisions.

After the emotionally charged ritual and political season ended, people turned to the mundane matters of daily life. Each household made its individual plans for the day or week. Because of the time spent in ceremonies and meetings, families were short of fresh meat. The young men of the household, perhaps joined by a physically able "beloved old man," sat by the fire to prepare for an extended hunt. While they discussed the probable location of game, they repaired weapons and filled pouches with parched corn. They stared into the fire looking for a sign of the whereabouts of deer. Before they left, a lesser priest conjured for their success. Leaving the village in the morning, they carried consecrated velvet from the antlers of young deer to attract the animals.[9] During their long absence their wives and sisters fed villagers who remained home, wove baskets, dressed skins, and sometimes made clothing from trade calico. Women's household tasks varied little from season to season. When the day ended and the deep mountains brooded over the town, old men sat in the shadows of the firelit room and told children the ancient legends, for example, saying: "This is what the old men told me when I was a boy about why the mink smells."

> The Mink was such a great thief that at last the animals held a council about the matter. It was decided to burn him, so they caught the Mink, built a great fire, and threw him into it. As the blaze went up and they smelt the roasted flesh, they began to think he was punished enough and would probably do better in the future, so they took him out of the fire. But the Mink was already burned black and is black ever since, and whenever he is attacked or excited he smells again like roasted meat. The lessons did no good, however, and he is still as great a thief as ever.[10]

About 10 days later the weary men returned laden with game. Each time one of them dressed a deer, he threw a small piece of liver into the fire in gratitude for its help in locating animals. Deer entrails were carefully burned. To have ignored this action would have courted trouble. An angry deer ghost could inflict disease on its killer. If the offal of small game—rabbits, squirrel, and turkey—were not carefully hidden in a secluded spot,

[8]Gearing, *Priests and Warriors*, p. 5.
[9]Mooney, *Myths of the Cherokee*, p. 264.
[10]Ibid., p. 277.

the animals would visit rheumatism on the careless man. The Cherokee, like so many other Native Americans, viewed the bear with special reverence. Whenever a hunter killed one, he humbly asked forgiveness.[11]

In addition to hunting, Cherokee men also warred in fall and winter. Among the southeastern Indians, however, it was as much a danger-filled game as serious business. They seldom fought to gain territory and resources although their boundary claims did shift with their success or failure over a long time.[12] If the council opted for war a red standard hung over the council house and the red (war) organization began its elaborate preparations. Like the white (peace) political body, there were eight war officials: four "beloved old men" possessing the arcane ritual needed for war; a war chief; a war priest; a speaker for war; and a surgeon. These officials appointed eight leaders from among the young men. In addition, one eminent warrior of each of the seven clans formed a war council. Unless there was to be a major campaign, not all the village males participated in every expedition. A typical war party might involve twenty to forty men. On occasion a few militant women joined them.

The warriors convened at the council house 24 hours before the foray was to begin. The four "beloved old men" purified them through prayer, led them to the water to bathe seven times, and supported them while they fasted. That evening after the shadows intensified and the cold crept into the houses, the sound of drums echoed through the hills as the warriors danced. Shortly before dawn they rushed to the river and immersed themselves seven times. At sunrise the war priest sought counsel from the supernatural by divination. The war party crowded around while he threw a deer tongue on a fire kindled from the sacred flames. It augured well for the expedition if the fire consumed the tongue; if the flames died down it portended defeat. Then, turning toward the heavens, the war priest raised his arms and prayed. Between the thumb and forefinger of each hand he held divining beads. Were they to conquer, the righthand bead would dance and sparkle. Failure was probable if the lefthand bead shimmered. Regardless of the omens, plans continued, although if the death of an individual was predicted, he could withdraw without shame. After the women brought provisions (parched corn and corn bread) and equipment was readied, the war speaker exhorted the warriors to fight valiantly and to vanquish their fear.

During the trek toward the enemy the warriors bathed seven times night and morning and refrained from any trivial talk. Scouts preceded them each morning going in different directions. Slipping silently along the wooded trails, one would give the cry of a raven, another, the sonorous

---

[11]James Mooney, *The Swimmer Manuscript: Cherokee Sacred Formulas and Medicinal Prescriptions*. Revised, completed, and edited by Franz M. Olbrect. Bureau of American Ethnology Bulletin 99, 1932, p 38, Smithsonian Institution. Permission by Smithsonian Institution Press. Mooney collected the original information from "He is swimming," in 1888.

[12]Gearing, *Priests and Warriors*, p. 54.

hoot of an owl, yet a third, the mournful howl of a wolf if an enemy were sighted. When the target was reached, with piercing, fearful whoops the party descended upon its unsuspecting victims, killing and capturing a pre-agreed upon number and pillaging the town. Whether victorious or defeated, the war chief dispatched a messenger home to advise the people of their return. Two men and the village women met them chanting songs praising their valor. Spoils, including prisoners, were turned over to wives or sisters. Because killing or contact with blood was defiling, the men entered the council house for purification. The four "beloved old men" conducted rites and prayers to remove the pollution. For the four purifying days, the warriors avoided sexual contact with their wives. Each night the women danced the scalp dance, following it with the snake dance. Men joined in holding staffs bedecked with scalps. Valley and cove resounded with the sound of drums and the chants of war songs. The prisoners wondered whether they were to be adopted or tortured to death. When it all ended, the warriors became civilians again and the red organization disbanded.[13]

As the snow slowly left the bottomlands, green tinged the grasses and hardwood buds swelled—maples first. In spite of late storms, winter gradually surrendered to spring. Women gathered creesys (a small edible plant growing in meadows, something like watercress) which appeared in damp earth along low-lying creeks. Men cleared the garden of fall's dead growth. Soon the quavering call of whippoorwills sounded in the advancing darkness. People looked at one another apprehensively. It was a bad omen. Somewhere a ghost or a witch was abroad. If by chance the bird landed close by a house, its occupants tried to kill it. In 1959, a Cherokee woman, Lucy, spoke of her efforts:

> One time one came and sat right on the roof about four o'clock. I got a stick and hit it. I said another one is coming, and sure enough the next night another one came and I killed it, too. You are supposed to ask who they are. A person in Birdtown died and one in Soco; they could have been them.[14]

When the variegated colors of green started their climb up the mountain flanks to the ridges, the laurel and rhododendron budded in the ravines, the Cherokee prepared for the first-new-moon-of-spring ritual. When the pale crescent rose they congregated around the council house, carrying quantities of food. The next morning, as the first shafts of light appeared, they went to the stream, faced the east, and, defying the bone-chilling water, bathed seven times. Purified although shivering, they shared a communal feast. The third day demanded a fast by all but the very

[13]Gilbert, *The Eastern Cherokees*, pp. 348–356.

[14]Harriet J. Kupferer, *The "Principal People" 1960: A Study of the Cultural and Social Groups of the Eastern Cherokee*. Bulletin of the Bureau of American Ethnology, Bulletin 196, Anthropological Papers Number 78, 1966, p. 297, Smithsonian Institution. By permission of the Smithsonian Institution Press. The tale was recorded in 1959.

youngest. A "beloved old man" dropped tobacco and the tongue of a buck in the sacred fire to determine the propitious time for planting. When the light faded, a great fire was kindled and friendship dances started which would last through the night.

Women wearing tortoise shell leg-rattles joined the men in a circle. The leader began the dance with a chant to which the partners moved in a shuffling trot. With each verse the words became more bawdy. Speck and Broom recorded such a verse which they loosely translated: "I am called an old man (poor and ugly) but I am not this. I am going to take this young woman home with me, as I did not know there was such a good shaker, none like her. I'll take her home to my settlement."[15] In the course of the evening the songs grew increasingly Rabelaisian; the leader reached the height of his wit when he sang: *di: tâ san hè hi*: "We are going to touch each other's privates."[16] The dancers, to the noisy amusement of their audience, enthusiastically followed the directions. When the last star dimmed the revelers wandered off carrying sleeping babies; weary toddlers tottered after.

In succeeding days the soil was prepared for planting. When the ordained time arrived, men and women of each household sowed seed saved from last year's crops of corn, beans, pumpkins, and squash. Until harvest, men and women turned to separate activities. Men occasionally hunted, more often fished, and repaired village buildings. Later in the summer they played ball—a game similar in many ways to lacrosse. Men of one settlement challenged men from another. Some information suggests that intertribal games were also played.[17] For seven days prior to the game, played usually when the moon was full, conjurers (priests) led the prayers through lengthy rituals. They murmured ceremonial prayers for the contestants and scratched them—often deeply—with a tool made of seven splinters of turkey bones; a few elected to use rattlesnake fang scratchers. After herbal emollients were rubbed into the wounds, the players plunged into the cold mountain streams. Specific foods were denied them: They could not eat immature animals because their bones were brittle and this might cause one to break a limb; rabbits, timid creatures who panic easily, were also avoided. Additional taboos prohibited sexual intercourse for seven days. Women were restrained from walking on the paths used by the players during the ritual of "going to the water."[18]

Village women spent the summer days weeding gardens, cooking, or making clothes. Under the shade of a tree they often sat together talking

[15]Frank G. Speck and Leonard Broom in collaboration with Will West Long, *Cherokee Dance and Drama.* (Berkeley: University of California Press, 1951) p. 67. The collection was begun in 1913 by Speck. Broom joined him in 1935. Will West Long, one of the remaining Cherokee sages, died in 1946. He was 77.

[16]Ibid., p. 67.

[17]Raymond D. Fogelson, *The Cherokee Ball Game: A Study in Southeastern Ethnology.* PhD. Dissertation, University of Pennsylvania, 1962. University Microfilms, Ann Arbor, p. 48.

[18]Ibid., pp. 57–60.

Cherokee ball players, circa 1900.
Smithsonian Institution National Anthropological Archives.

softly as they wove intricate cane or split baskets. Naked "knee babies" played about their feet. "Lap babies" sat astride their mother's backs or were propped against a tree in cradle boards—wide-eyed witnesses to the activities about them. Neighbors stopped to gossip on their way to gather wood or water.

Courtship and prospects of marriages dominated many a conversation. It was even cautiously whispered that a would-be suitor had enlisted the services of a conjurer to utter love magic incantations, perhaps to destroy a rival or to cause a girl to favor him.[19] A young man in love dispatched his mother or a female relative to visit his intended's mother. After a long and somewhat oblique conversation, the messenger departed to await the decision, knowing that weeks would pass before an answer could be expected. Although it was not necessary, the girl's mother often consulted her brother or even her oldest son about the matter. Clan members, of course, could not wed, nor could young Cherokee marry into their father's clan. Because people preferred their son to marry a girl from his father's father's or mother's father's clan, genealogical facts had to be examined. Moreover, even if the clan connections were right, people were loath to marry their daughter to a man whose family or lineage reputation was sullied. After all the details were ironed out and the girl agreed, the village priest examined omens. If they were auspicious the marriage was approved; the groom brought gifts to the girl's parents and moved in with his bride. There he faced a group of people—his in-laws—who expected him to conform to the Cherokee notion of proper behavior.

His wife's parents required his utmost respect; when speaking to them, he lowered his eyes. Any requests he might make of them or they of him were always indirect. Other males in the household were his wife's

[19]Mooney, *The Swimmer Manuscript*, pp. 154–155.

unmarried brothers or her sisters' husbands. Together they hunted and worked on male domestic chores. Unless one of them had reached the status of "beloved old men" they were all viewed as age mates. They teased and lampooned one another with spicy banter and devised numerous practical jokes. His wife's sisters were reciprocal joking partners too; exchanges among them were openly sexual. To comment ribaldly on the other's prowess in such affairs or to make droll observations on genitals afforded endless amusement. His wife—for she, too, was a sister—accepted the byplay. Lewd comments were customary and seldom threatened affectionate relationships between spouses. Should a young man have ignored these expectations, especially those governing his behavior toward his wife's parents and his contribution to the economic welfare of the household, village gossip and his sisters' reproaches would have forced all but the most unrepentant into line.

As the first days of marriage passed, the young couple settled down in her extended family. Except for farming, most of the household chores were assigned by sex. She spent the days in the company of women and he with the men. When she menstruated she withdrew to a small hut; others fed her husband. Had she cooked for him she would have caused him to weaken. Both the fish in the river and the crops in the garden would have been jeopardized by her presence, too. Finally a month came when she did not go into seclusion. After she was sure that "she carried it," she confided in her husband, mother, and sisters. The news spread through the village when she and her husband began six or seven months of taboos and injunctions. One which every woman fulfilled was going to the river with her husband and a priest at each new moon. There the priest recited prayers for the "little human being" and, if requested, manipulated white and red beads to determine the sex of the infant and the time of birth. On each occasion before leaving for the river the mother drank a concoction of red or slippery elm bark, stems of spotted touch-me-nots, roots of speedwell, and Table Mountain pine. Each of the ingredients had a beneficial effect on the infant. The bark with its viscid properties made the "inside of the girl slippery"; the second was believed to scare the child and make it "jump down" quickly. The last two are evergreens and people thought that they would ensure longevity and good health. Before she entered the water to bathe ritually, she vomited up the elixir to purify herself.

With their welfare and that of the baby in mind, women observed a number of food taboos. They never ate squirrels: The animals, when frightened, dashed up trees; the baby, therefore, might retreat up the birth canal. A squirrel also sat in a hunched position; this would make for a difficult delivery. Rabbits were avoided, too: Their meat would cause the baby to sleep with its eyes open. In order to prevent their babies from developing spots on their faces, mothers avoided eating speckled trout. When entering or leaving the house, an expectant mother did not linger on the door sill; this, too, delayed the birth. The father did not loiter on his way in or out either. Neither of them looked at a corpse, for the child would be stillborn, and neither wore belts, which could cause the umbilical to wrap around the baby's neck.[20]

When the birth was imminent, the father selected four women to attend his wife; at least one was an experienced midwife. She had the primary responsibility and knew the proper incantations and herbal prescriptions necessary for complications. The four arrived at first signs and administered a warm "tea" of wild cherry bark to the expectant mother.[21] All then moved to the menstrual lodge for the birth. A medicine man, less often a woman, visited the hut to inspect the preparations. When things were to his satisfaction he walked ceremonially to the east corner of the hut and recited a prayer to the unborn: "Thou little boy jump down." From there he moved slowly to the northside where he said: "Thou little girl jump down." He called the boy again at the west corner, and on the south, the little girl. To prevent unwelcome intrusion of witches who preyed upon the weak, he circled the lodge again and lingered in the vicinity to provide special attention if the need arose.

Inside the hut, warmed and lighted by glowing coals, the attendants waited for the delivery. When the gasps of the mother indicated the moment was near, two of them reached under her arms and pulled her to a semireclining posture. The midwife knelt in front to catch the baby. The fourth woman crouched at her side ready to cut the cord. After the baby was delivered it was washed and the midwife put a puff ball on the navel where it would remain until the stub dried and fell off.

In the event of a difficult delivery the waiting medicine man entered the case. He administered an infusion of slippery elm bark and touch-me-not stems; the latter was thought to "scare" the baby. To frighten it further, in a soft measured voice he recited:

> Now then! Thou little man, ha, now! Get up right away. Yonder the old grannie is coming. She is approaching, behaving frightfully as she comes. Now then! Let us both run off forthwith. Take thy mattress over yonder. Sharp now!
>
> Now then! Thou little woman, ha! Now get up right away. Yonder thy (old) maternal grandfather is coming.[22]

To expel the afterbirth, a helper warmed her hands over the coals and with her right hand rubbed the mother's abdomen while the father waited outside. As soon as he received it he set off up the mountain. After he crossed two ridges he stopped, dug a hole, and placed the placenta in it

---

[20]Ibid., pp. 118–122.

[21]Wild cherry bark tea was still used by traditional Cherokee for menstrual cramps in 1959–1960.

[22]Mooney, *The Swimmer Manuscript*, p. 274. This is a free translation of the prayer uttered in somewhat archaic language.

whispering: "Now then! Two years from now again I will see it my child."[23] By crossing only two ridges he hoped to have another child in two years; had he crossed three, the couple would look for another baby three years later. He made his journey in secrecy to prevent an evil doer from reburying the afterbirth deeper and placing four or seven rocks on it with the result that no more children would be born to the parents. On the fourth or seventh day after birth the infant Cherokee received its first name—usually from its father's sister. To all members of the household it was a welcome arrival; they—especially the women—could be depended upon to assist the new mother with its care. In a few weeks the mother or grandmother carried it about the town securely swaddled on her back. In fact the Cherokee term for grandmother is *gilisi* which also means "She bears me on her back."[24] Until the baby started to walk it was always on someone's back or lap.[25]

Mothers kept a close eye on their toddlers else some mischievous person might scratch it with some part of an animal. To be scratched with a bear claw, for example, could make it mean. A mother, of course, might scratch the child herself.

> If you scratch them over the eye with a lizard they'll go to sleep wherever they are, but it makes them bad to climb . . . Sometimes I think some of the people catch the little ones and scratch them with something so they will grow up like they think they should, and the parents don't know anything about it.[26]

When Cherokee children grew older they realized that their social universe extended much further than their household. All the people, they learned, belonged to one of seven matrilineal clans: Wolf, Deer, Bird, Red Paint, Blue, Twisters, and Wild Potato. Close relatives formed lineages within these larger units. To these kin they learned to apply proper terms and to behave toward them in predictable ways. Like the Mandan, the Cherokee kinship system was of the "Crow Type." Although mother's lineage was the most important, three factors—father's lineage, mother's father's lineage, and father's father's lineage—were also significant. Every Cherokee recognized that to a specific class of relatives a particular conduct was indicated. Parents supported and helped their children to acquire adult skills, yet the relationship between them was constrained by a high degree of respect. Only the mildest of familiarity occasionally occurred. The same circumstance prevailed with their parent's siblings; mother's brother was especially respected. He disciplined them and could be counted on to come to their aid when they were in trouble. They thought of their father's sister as a "female father" and deferred to her in much the same manner that they did their father.

---

[23]Ibid., p. 126.

[24]Gilbert, *The Eastern Cherokee*, p. 254.

[25]Whether it was traditional, in 1959–1960 Conservative Cherokee babies were seldom allowed to crawl.

[26]Kupferer, *The Principal People*, p. 296.

Brothers and sisters formed a strong bond of solidarity. Older brothers protected their sisters and younger brothers. They all teased and censored one another for inappropriate conduct. To the Cherokee children, however, grandparents were the people who gave them the greatest pleasure and affection. They played with them, told them countless stories, and joked endlessly with them. Grandchildren freely returned the joking and teasing to the great amusement of the old folk.

Cherokee extended all the kinship terms used for people in the four matrilineages to everyone in the four clans. As a consequence all the members of a person's mother's clan—other than aunts, uncles, and grandparents—were "brothers and sisters." In father's clan, with a few exceptions, all the people of an individual's generation or younger were also "brothers and sisters." None of these "brothers and sisters" were eligible mates. Regardless of age everyone in the two grandparent clans was called "grandfather or grandmother." From them a person chose a marriage partner. Cherokee married their grandparents!

In the course of learning to be a responsible Cherokee, youngsters absorbed, in subtle ways, the cardinal Cherokee value: the "Harmony Ethic."[27] It was woven into the cultural fabric governing both the behavior of Cherokee to one another and to nature. The fundamental tenet was that a good person avoided giving offense by not expressing anger nor causing it in others. Guided by the ethic, people went to great lengths to eliminate face-to-face conflict. A proper man was circumspect; he tread carefully, "feeling out" others lest his unspoken wishes conflict with the desires of others. One method people used to avoid an open clash of interests was to enlist a neutral third person in circumstances they conceived to be threatening to amicable relationships.[28]

In the 1950s and early 1960s the practice was still evident. School children, including high school students of traditionally oriented parents, sent others to ask the teacher for permission to leave their desks. When people applied for work they took another along. One young woman told this writer, "I'd go to see the manager if I could get someone to go with me." The writer went along and made the first overture to him. Go-betweens were used in court, too. Defendants, even those conversant in English, brought an intermediary through whom they addressed the court.

The conduct was not restricted to contact with whites or nonkin. For example, a family lived rent-free in a house owned by the wife's aunt. Although the owner wanted the occupants to move, she said nothing to them. Eventually she remarked to another, "When I said they could live there, I didn't mean forever." The neutral advised the unwelcome tenants that

[27]Robert K. Thomas, "Cherokee Values and World View," Manuscript. Cross Cultural Laboratory, Chapel Hill, NC, 1958.

[28]Although the examples used to illustrate the point were collected in 1959–1960, Kupferer, *The Principal People*, p. 290, Gearing argues that there is evidence the same value guided behavior in the 1700s. See *Priest and Warriors*, pp. 32–36.

their aunt wanted them to leave. A similar example in the use of the indirect method to avoid face-to-face disagreement was apparent in the situation of an elderly woman whose son owned a taxi and charged his mother for trips. "He shouldn't do me that way," she said. "I told some of my friends about it down in Cherokee. They must have jumped on that boy because for a long time he quit charging me."

When opposing interests became evident, good persons went their own way, minded their own business, and kept their own counsel. They continued, of course, to follow their own interests, but carefully avoided any confrontation. A case in point can be seen when a Cherokee woman, Lizzie, went to visit a friend who had promised her some flower cuttings. Getting the flowers was the expressed purpose for the visit. After a long stay during which neither woman mentioned the cuttings, Lizzie departed empty handed. On our way home she mentioned several times how much she wanted those flowers.

When direct conflict seemed inevitable, a good Cherokee withdrew from it, either physically or emotionally. Aggression of any kind, overtly hostile or assertive, was "giving offense." For example, a young women felt that her employer made too many demands upon her at work. She, however, did not speak of her dissatisfaction to him. She quit. When asked what she had told the boss, she said, "I didn't tell him nothing; I just didn't go back to work the next day." The assertive behavior of her boss coupled with the value of personal autonomy was responsible for the manner in which she left her job.

Generosity was an additional feature of the Harmony ethic; good Cherokees gave of themselves and their possessions. People gossiped about a niggardly person. If this did not cause a change, they withdrew from the culprit and eventually isolated him. Robert K. Thomas pointed out that this generosity was particularly apparent in dealing with food.[29] Food sharing had a great symbolic value in Cherokee society; there was a special Cherokee word meaning stingy with food, distinct from another term which meant stingy in other matters.

Ideally children in all societies, in a variety of ways, learn not only the tasks appropriate to their gender but also to their peoples' cherished values. Cherokee socialization was itself a reflection of the Harmony ethic. Apart from keeping them from danger, parents allowed their children a great deal of autonomy. When admonishing measures were necessary, they corrected their children quietly and in an indirect fashion. To strike a child was completely out of character. When autonomy led to fractiousness no longer tolerable, adults warned the youngsters that a *tskili* (horned owl or witch), a booger (a character in masked dances), or a *Unega* (white person) would get them. Such dire threats almost always sufficed; if they did not, an exasperated mother surprised the rambunctious one by swiftly dashing

[29]Thomas, "Cherokee Values and World View," p. 7.

cold water on it. In invoking the assistance of menacing external figures to control children, adults were not themselves assertive. While throwing cold water was active interference, it was not preceded by a series of threats or promises to punish. The quickness of the act served to minimize the authoritarian role of parents.

The Harmony ethic, like all values systems, set the norms for proper comportment; when people followed its implicit dictates, discord and friction did not occur. But some breached the principle: They did not always defer to age; they loudly upbraided others; a few were miserly. Such unruly people were not directly censored, for that, too, would have violated the ethic. Social control was attempted by more devious means. Offended people gossiped about them. Others more affronted by such unseemly behavior might enlist the services of a conjurer. Carrying a buckskin or a piece of cloth and a black bead for the fee, such a person would explain his intent to the medicine man who replied saying he would try to help him. On a night in the dark of the moon he went to a tree struck by lightning near a stream, taking some of the victim's saliva, as well as other objects with magical properties. As he buried these at the base of the tree he uttered:

> Listen [Ske]! Now I have come to step over your soul. You are of the _____ clan. Your name is _____. Your spittle I have put at rest under the earth. I have come to cover you over with the black rock. I have come to cover you over with the black cloth. I have come to cover you over with black slabs, never to reappear. Toward the black coffin of the upland in the Darkening Land your paths shall stretch out. So shall it be for you(?). Instantly the black clay has lodged there where it is at rest at the black houses in the Darkening Land. With the black coffin and with the black slabs I have come to cover you. Now your soul has faded away. It has become blue. When darkness comes your spirit shall grow less and dwindle away, never to reappear. Listen![30]

If conducted properly the victim was expected to become seriously ill and eventually die.

Murder, which did take place, required more direct attention. It fell to the clan to avenge the death of one of its members. Local clan members formed a group and killed the guilty person or one of his clansmen; guilt was corporately assigned just as vengeance was a group affair. If the death were unintentional, the two clans met in the house of the village priest chief where he mediated settlement.

Beyond the implicit canons of the Harmony ethic were a number of shared beliefs which shaped Cherokee behavior, helped them make sense of the world and its inhabitants, and bestow order on it. They furnished the

---

[30]James Mooney, "*Sacred Formulas of the Cherokee.*" By permission of Smithsonian Institution Press from Seventh Annual Report of the Bureau of Ethnology, to the Secretary of the Smithsonian Institution 1885–1886, p. 391, by J. W. Powell, Director. Smithsonian Institution, Washington, D.C., 1891.

explanations, ceremonies, and ritual techniques necessary to adapt to a capricious universe. None of these, however, existed apart from daily life. They were woven into the cultural tapestry. Cherokee did not distinguish between the sacred and the secular.

Important in Cherokee belief was *gitum,* power or energy. It was inherent in lightning and running water. Spirit beings—deities, animals, ghosts, and witches—possessed it. Human beings could acquire it, too.[31] Power of this kind could either benefit or harm people. A second type of power was automatic. When a thoughtless person broke a taboo, trouble automatically followed.

Although there was no single supreme supernatural, there were several supernatural powers which were prominent in Cherokee belief, ritual, and myth. The sun, a female, was one. She and fire (believed to be the same) rarely harmed human beings; her help was solicited by priests and medicine men before any crucial undertaking. The moon was the sun's brother; in his different phases, he bore witness to important rituals. Each month on the first night of his appearance, people addressed him as a grandfather in a ritual prayer and sought his protection from illness or accident in the following days until he vanished from the night sky.

No natural phenomenon was of more spiritual importance for the people than the river. "Going to the water" was paramount in almost all Cherokee ritual. They called the river *Yun wi Gunahi ta,* Long Man. He lay with his head resting on the mountain and his feet stretching down to the lowlands. Sometimes softly, other times roaring, he spoke constantly to those who could understand his message. Long Man provided bountiful protection for life's critical crises. The dangers of pregnancy and birth were lessened by going to the water; longevity was assured. He purified returning warriors, hunters, and ball players, and cured illness by carrying away the vomit of sick persons. Angered by people urinating or discarding rubbish in his flow he retaliated by sending disease.[32]

The violent crash of thunder was the voice of Red Man reverberating from the mountain peak to ridge. His sons, Little Redmen, spoke in less ominous distant rumbles. Cherokee relied on their help to expel disease. More important to them, however, was Redman's implacable hatred of Blackman or anything else which lived in the Dark of Nightland, the abode of death. Redman or Little Redmen were implored, in curing formulas, to take disease spirits (especially if related to snakes) to the Nightland in the West and put them away in the black boxes or coffins.[33]

Living together in settlements among distant rocks, on the mountain, or in the forests, were Little People. Like the Cherokee, they had clans and a council house. Solitary wanderers often heard their music in the dark

[31]Fogelson, *The Cherokee Ball Game,* pp. 222–225.
[32]Mooney, *Myths of the Cherokee,* p. 547.
[33]Mooney, *The Swimmer Manuscript,* p. 177.

woods. They rarely endangered humans and even helped lost and weary travelers. Yet Little People could cause illness. It was thought that they were responsible for many childhood sicknesses and accidents.[34] In 1959 a woman spoke of Little People whom she called brownies: "They stay out in the woods, mostly around the rhododendron slicks."

> There was a woman once who was in the woods and put her little girl down, and when she came back she couldn't find her. She looked and then she saw her with a brownie. That brownie was feeding her crawfish. When he held it in his hand it turned red just like it had been cooked. The brownie told the little girl her mamma was looking for her. That woman told about it . . . and soon she and the little girl died. . . . They didn't last long; that's what happened when they told about it.[35]

By far the most numerous and malevolent supernaturals were animal spirits. Acting in self-defense or out of a desire for revenge they plagued humans with all manner of disease for the injuries and unremitting assaults upon them by mankind. The origin of the animals' antipathy toward humans was explained in a long myth:

> In the old days the beasts, birds, fishes, insects, and plants could all talk, and they and the people lived together in peace and friendship. But as time went on the people increased so rapidly that their settlements spread over the whole earth, and the poor animals found themselves beginning to be cramped for room. This was bad enough, but to make it worse Man invented bows, knives, blowguns, spears, and hooks, and began to slaughter the larger animals, birds, and fishes for their flesh or their skins, while the smaller creatures, such as the frogs and worms, were crushed and trodden upon without thought, out of pure carelessness or contempt. So the animals resolved to consult upon measures for their common safety.

The tale continued with each species of animal meeting in council to decide upon the measures to be taken to protect themselves. The last to convene were the birds, insects, and smaller animals. They listed their grievances, then:

> They began then to devise and name so many new diseases, one after another, that had not their invention failed them, no one of the human race would have been able to survive. . . . When the Plants who were friendly to Man, heard what had been done by the animals they decided to defeat the latter's evil designs. Each Tree, Shrub, and Herb, down even to the Grasses and Mosses, agreed to furnish a cure for some one of the diseases named, and each said: "I shall appear to help Man when he calls upon me in his need." Thus came medicine; and the plants, every one of which has its use if we only know it, furnish the remedy to counteract the evil wrought by the revengeful animals . . .[36]

[34]Ibid., p. 25.
[35]Kupferer, *The Principal People*, p. 297.
[36]Mooney, *Myths of the Cherokee*, pp. 250–252.

Fellow Cherokee turned against one another, too. People, of course, knew that had they offended someone the aggrieved would very likely conjure against them or employ another to redress the offense. This was understandable and they knew that they had only themselves to blame. Witches, however, were another matter: *Tskili* were the most baleful of all humans. They attacked randomly out of pure malevolence. While any man or woman could become a witch by drinking an infusion concocted from the roots of a rare plant and fasting for four or seven days, most witches were twins whose parents raised them for the profession. Witches lurked near the sick or enfeebled to steal their breath, so adding to their own power. Relatives and friends of an invalid watched through the night to protect the stricken patient. While some slept the others dropped bits of old tobacco on glowing ashes. Any particle catching fire to the right or left of the center indicated the direction from which the witch would arrive. Had the tobacco burst into flame in the center, the witch was already present but the sudden flash would cause its death in four or seven days. Despite their enormous power, witches tended to assail the decrepit because they were far more vulnerable than hale, hearty folk. Yet they never missed an opportunity to afflict any unsuspecting person with a dread disease.[37]

Through the prowess and esoteric knowledge of priests and medicine men, the power invested in many of the supernaturals could be harnessed for human benefit. The cyclical rituals beseeched or commanded the power of the sun, moon and river. The forces of plants were tapped through ancient formulas and concoctions to cure. Even the potency of some animals could be used against others. If, for example, worms caused a disease, various worm eating birds were called upon to dispel it. Beavers, rats, and other tenacious animals, were directed to tug away at a stubborn illness.

Ultimately, when no power was strong enough to cure or safeguard, people died. In a grave on a mountain slope the deceased was laid, its head toward the west. Its soul became a ghost, and in the ensuing seven days traveled west to ghost country in the Nightland. There it joined ghostly clansmen who lived in settlements as they always had, doing what they had always done.

After the burial the mourners "went to the Water." Then the immediate survivors went to their house, to scatter the ashes from the old fire. A new one was kindled from the sacred fire. For the next four or seven days they left the house only for the most pressing needs. It was thought that whatever people did during this interval they would do the rest of their lives. A daughter remarked about her mother: "She never stays home. The old people used to say if you didn't stay home seven days . . . after someone died, you'd never stay home again, and she didn't stay home after Daddy

[37]Mooney, *The Swimmer Manuscript*, pp. 29–32.

died. I believe what the old people say. . . . She's never stayed home since."[38]

The southern Appalachians furnished an abundance for the Principal People. Garden crops watered by spring and summer rains flourished in the fertile soil of cove and bottom. Wooded mountains sheltered a great variety of animals which men hunted for meat and skins. Thriving at all elevations, plants contributed to the Cherokee pharmacopeia. That the people could live in permanent settlements was, in great measure, due to the generous natural resources.

Village life is usually associated with some form of political structure. The Cherokee formal organization lay in the village council composed of "beloved old men" and "chaired" by the priest chief and his advisors. Issues with regard to relationships with other tribes and, eventually, alliances with colonists, were discussed at length. Because coercion was foreign to the Cherokee, meetings continued until there was general accord. Council attitudes and behavior reflected the emphasis on harmony and equilibrium.

Clans, especially matrilineal clans, were often found in agricultural societies. Cherokee matri-clans, present in each town, allocated land to constituent extended families, regulated marriage, and avenged fallen members. Travelers to other Cherokee towns enjoyed the hospitality of clansmen, a situation similar in a general way to the Apache.

Other situations requiring social control fell to individuals. Cherokee, like so many other Native American groups, affected behavior through gossip, teasing, and sorcery but the most pervasive shaper of comportment was the Harmony ethic. To attribute it to environment, however, would be stretching ecological theory. Its origins are obscure, but with the exception of the ebullient people of the Northwest Coast, the behavior of many Indian groups showed some affinities with it. To argue that some variation of it was almost a pan-Indian personality characteristic, and thus very ancient, is tempting, yet the evidence is not there. In any case, the Harmony ethic was one way of keeping overt conflict to a minimum.

The land and its resources on which Cherokee depended also had mysterious qualities. The brooding mountains, the dark rhododendron slicks, eerie night birds, and the clear, swift rivers and branches all encouraged "old people" to see explanations in them for the otherwise unfathomable. They saw, too, ways of using them to combat the eternal vicissitudes. The sun and fire yielded to supplications; the river purified; plant infusions healed. Even animals, enraged by human callousness, could be compelled to relieve suffering. Almost all of nature was incorporated some way in their myths and legends.

Living in the southeast were other agricultural tribes with whom the Cherokee fought or traded. Regardless of the relationship, each affected the other's culture. Charles Hudson saw so much similarity among them

[38]Kupferer, *The Principal People*, p. 296.

that he claimed they were socially diverse but culturally similar, a position not all would support.[39] Resemblances were at a general level, they would argue.

By 1700 the Cherokee and the British were in close contact. Yet, despite the eagerness of the Indians to trade deer skins for cloth, guns, and metal, their culture remained fairly stable and allowed the Cherokee to follow their traditional life in their beloved highlands.

EPILOGUE

As the years passed, whites intruded further into Cherokee country, provoking frequent raids on colonists. Because the British viewed the Cherokee as a single political entity rather than a collection of independent towns, all Cherokee were held responsible for attacks. To avoid reprisals on innocent communities, a priest state gradually evolved with the aim of restraining young warriors.[40] In this, the tribe officers were unsuccessful and relationships between the Cherokee and the colonists vacillated between peace, hostilities, and broken treaties. Ultimately embittered by their experience with the colonists, the Cherokee joined with the British in the American Revolution, a decision that led ultimately to the loss of much of their original territory. With the end of the war, the people rebuilt their farming communities in the areas left to them and established a new way of life, combining selected white customs with their own ways.

In 1820 they founded the Cherokee Nation, modeled on the United States government; New Echota, Georgia, was the capital. It was a period of peace and relative prosperity. The population was over 13,000 and included more than 200 marriages between Cherokee and white. Many of the prosperous farmers owned slaves. During this peaceful interval Sequoyah (George Gist) devised the Cherokee syllabary, a system in which symbols represented the syllables in the Cherokee language. Soon after it was adopted, thousands of Cherokee were literate in their own language From the capital, a newspaper, the *Cherokee Phoenix*, was disseminated. That time was to be transitory. The rich farmland was coveted by whites; the discovery of gold in northern Georgia fueled their greed.

White avarice coupled with the Federal policy of moving all Indians east of the Mississippi to land west of it doomed the young Cherokee nation. In 1838 troops rounded up the Cherokee and herded them west to the Indian territory. Hundreds perished of cold, hunger, and disease on the "Trail of Tears." Eight or nine hundred of the most isolated folk escaped the removal by fleeing to the mountains. Their descendants and the

[39]Charles Hudson, *The Southeastern Indians.* (Knoxville: University of Tennessee Press, 1976), p. 5.

[40]See Gearing, *Priests and Warriors*, for a brilliant analysis of the process.

few who came back composed the Eastern Cherokee who now occupy a reservation in the Great Smokies. Qualla Boundary, as it is called, is over 40,000 acres. Separated by private land are smaller tracts that are also part of the reservation.

Cherokee family income does not equal the average of white North Carolinians but the tribe is appreciably better situated than many of the reservation tribes in the west. Cradled in the mountains, adjacent to the Smoky Mountain National Park, they benefit from streams of tourists who attend the Cherokee Drama, "Unto These Hills," buy crafts, and patronize tribal and individual businesses. Small industries, both on the reservation and in nearby communities, add to the economic opportunities. Areas once reached by bouncing and grinding over narrow, washed-out dirt roads are now reached on paved roads. Education, especially that provided for the youngest children, is striving to encourage the appreciation of Cherokee heritage while preparing children to succeed in the upper grades. The picture is not, however, without its defects. There are problems with alcohol, diabetes is almost endemic, and unrelieved poverty grips some families. But there is reason to hope.

Those who survived the wretched journey to the Indian Territory did not find a trouble-free life. In a very short time three dissenting factions emerged, hampering badly needed tribal cooperation. But by 1857 the western Cherokee had overcome their initial difficulties. The Nation published a newspaper, operated a school system, and farmed and raised cattle on more than 100,000 acres. The Civil War was to bring an end to their achievements.

Although they had hoped to remain unallied, they were pressured by other Indian groups and whites to support one or the other side; they chose the Confederacy! The cost of their ill-fated decision was enormous. Thousands of young men died in battle; farmland and cattle suffered from neglect. The Reconstruction Act punished them harshly. In 1887 the infamous Dawes Act demanded that the tribally owned land be allotted to individual Indians. The rest of the territory was opened to white homesteaders. Tribal courts and laws were later abolished. A final blow came when the United States government dissolved the Cherokee Nation government. Each family was forced into a white pattern of land ownership; many were poorly prepared for the event. Although white cupidity and arrogance destroyed their culture, the western Cherokee survived and increased. About 50,000 Cherokee, many of them with some white ancestry, now live in Oklahoma. Some are affluent, others impoverished. In counties with large Cherokee populations, efforts to preserve cherished traditions and Indian identity continue.

CHAPTER ELEVEN

The Santo Domingo Pueblo of the Rio Grande

The San Juan mountains rise more than 4000 feet above the northern part of the Colorado Plateau. Ribbons of water converge on the slopes to give birth to the Rio Grande River. Gradually widening, it courses eastward through the Alamosa valley of Colorado to the town of Alamosa. Here it bends to the south continuing its way through the wild, starkly beautiful country into New Mexico. Flowing ever southward it enters the southeastern New Mexican plains and desert on its journey to the border.

From the river, the vast plateau, gouged by washes and arroyos, rolls in all directions. Widely separated mountains in the east reach up more than 10,000 feet. Geologically eroded canyons knife through it; mesas and buttes carved by wind and sand break the vista. Often the sky is an empty intense blue; at other times, clouds, like heaped banks of white wool, create stupendous effects. The night sky is filled with brilliant stars that seem to be almost within reach.

The plateau is rich in southwestern prehistory; magnificent ruins—Mesa Verde, Canyon de Chelly, Chaco Canyon, and many others—were the work of the Anasazi, the "Ancient Ones." There they lived and farmed until drought and perhaps the arrival of the nomadic Athabascans forced them to abandon their cities. By 1300 AD the people lived in pueblos in the oasis formed by the Rio Grande and its tributaries or in villages to the west

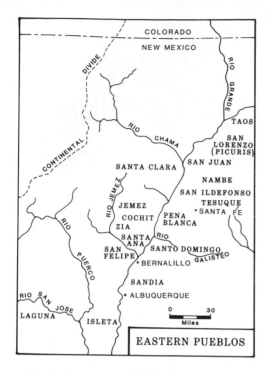

of it. Following the ways of their ancestors, for the next 300 or more years they dwelled in towns which blended with the sands of the tawny plateau.

In 1540, lured by stories of untold riches in gold, Coronado pushed north to appropriate the wealth. Reaching the Zuni first he found a peaceful farming community but no treasure. Disappointed, but determined to continue the search, he ransacked the town for food and led his men east to investigate the Rio Grande valley. The exploration convinced the conquistadores that their quest was fruitless; they left the region empty handed and returned to New Spain (Mexico). At the time of their departure there were about ninety inhabited villages. Although the rumors of fabulous wealth for the taking were false, Spain was determined to extend her holdings in the new world.

Juan de Oñate entered the Pueblo world in 1598 claiming the land for Spain. The Acoma pueblo, on its mile-high mesa, resisted his ruthless oppression but soon fell before the intruders' guns. The other towns offered no resistance, thus providing the way for the enthusiastic Franciscan friars to convert the heathens, more by floggings and executions than by gentle persuasion. Although the zealous Franciscans built churches in the ninety villages and boasted of thousands of new Christians, the converts continued their ancient rituals out of sight of their pastors. In the following decades the oppression and exploitation finally became so intolerable that the Pueblos in 1680 united to defeat their despised rulers. The victory was short lived. Fourteen years later Diego de Vargas subjugated the Indians again and restored the church, but it was much weakened by the death of many friars in the rebellion. As a consequence of conflict with the Spanish and drought, only thirty of the original towns remained; they are there today.

Hopi, Acoma, Zuni, and Laguna are the "western" pueblos located on the mesas or in the desert miles away from the Rio Grande. Situated along the usually placid river and its tributaries and drawing upon the water for their fields are the "eastern" pueblos. Among them are a number of superficial similarities, but close examination reveals significant differences. One of the most striking is the babel of tongues present. The people speak four mutually unintelligible languages. Tiwa spoken by Taos, Picuris, Sandia, and Isleta, is a member of the Tanoan family. Pojoaque, San Ildefonso, Nambe, San Juan, Santa Clara, and Tesuque spoke Tewa— also a Tanoan language. Towa, belonging to the Tanoan family, was spoken at Jemez. The people of Zia, Cochiti, Santo Domingo, Santa Ana, and San Felipe were speakers of Keres, a language that has not yet been classified. Although nine of the eastern pueblos are known by Spanish names, each has a native name. The names of the others are English corruptions of the original Indian ones.

The Pueblos had a common worldview that provided a structure of reality, ordering, defining, and classifying phenomena in the universe, in their world, and in their society.[1] Ortiz, in outlining it, reported that they all established boundaries to their world. While the boundaries were not the same, the principles they used were: To set the four cardinal directions, all used natural phenomena—mountains or waters, often both. They all viewed the universe as composed of three cosmic levels: an underworld, the earth, and the sky—or below, middle, and above.[2] Human existence occurred on earth; most of spiritual existence was attributed to below; the above was thought to be like the middle although there was little interest in it.[3]

They had a clear conception of the middle of the cosmos, which they represented by a *sipapu*, an earth navel. In the *kivas*—the sacred pueblo structure—was a hole in the earth, the *sipapu*. The importance of a sacred center was illustrated in the centripetal spatial orientation; all things were defined and represented by reference to a center. The Navajo, on the other hand, had a centrifugal orientation. The contrast was evident in dry painting, a sacred act in both societies. A Pueblo priest outlined boundaries and

[1] Alfonso Ortiz, "Ritual Drama and the Pueblo World View," in *New Perspectives on the Pueblos*, Alfonso Ortiz, ed. (Albuquerque: University of New Mexico Press, 1972), p. 136. To a varying extent this worldview still shapes Pueblo religious thought and behavior.

[2] Ibid., pp. 142–145.

[3] Alfonso Ortiz, *The Tewa World: Space, Time, Being, and Becoming in a Pueblo Society.* (Chicago: The University of Chicago Press, 1969) p. 23.

from them worked inward to the center. A Navajo chanter began in the center and worked outward.

Accompanying the Pueblo attention to boundaries, center, detail, and order was the idea that everything—animate and inanimate—was significant and had its place in the universe. All phenomena, too, had two aspects—essence and matter—and they were knowable and controllable. Because to control required close attention to detail, ritual was precise and repetitive.

The dualities in the worldview also served to unify space and time. The sun was everywhere; it was the father and primary fertilizing agent; the earth was the mother. Because the Pueblos separated them long ago in their myth, they attempted to bring them together through countless myth cycles and ritual. The duality of winter and summer provided the structure for the ritual calendar. The transition between the two was marked by the solstices or the equinoxes. The duality continued in the nature of ritual. Winter rites concerned medicine, fecundity, and war; summer ceremonies emphasized rain and crop fertility.

In human society good and bad were represented by the polarity of priest and witch. All outsiders caused anxiety; at best they aroused suspicion, at the worst they were feared as possible witches. The Pueblos viewed their own uninitiated young as not yet fully human, labeling them "raw" or "uncooked" to account for un-Pueblo behavior.

These implicit assumptions about the nature of man, the nature of nature, and the structure of reality unconsciously motivated Pueblo thought and behavior. Most particularly was this true in ritual and religious life. Although specific details may have differed, especially between different language speakers, Pueblo cultures were variations on a theme.

About 20 miles south of Santa Fe on the east side of the Rio Grande near the confluence of Galisteo creek and the Rio Grande is Santo Domingo. Now as in the past, it is the largest of the Keres pueblos. Its location, almost in the center of the Keresan area, its size, and its adherence to the "old" ways prompted Leslie White to say that it was the most important of the Keres pueblos.[4] Despite the imposition of Catholicism and secular government, some new crops, metal tools, horses, and other animals,the Santo Domingans remained in 1928 little changed in core culture. Edward Spicer, too, concluded that with little exception, Pueblo communities continued their farming economy and especially the Keresans remained staunchly faithful to their sacred traditions and guarded them from outside threat.[5]

[4]Leslie A. White, "The Pueblo of Santo Domingo." Reprinted by permission of the American Anthropological Association from *Memoirs of the American Anthropological Association*, #43, 1935. (Kraus Reprint Co., 1974), p. 21. White collected his data in 1928. This account relies largely upon his work.

[5]Edward Dozier, "Rio Grande Pueblos," in *Perspectives in American Indian Culture Change*, Edward H. Spicer, ed. (Chicago: University of Chicago Press, 1961) pp. 165–171. In 1961 the Santo Domingans revealed very little of the esoteric in their culture.

The land of the Kiwa, the Keresan name of Santo Domingo, lies over 5000 feet above sea level. Without water from the river, farming it would be difficult. Rain fall averages less than 10 inches annually and occurs between April and September, often accompanied by wild thunderstorms. The river, too, can be treacherous. The Rio Grande, about a half-mile to a mile wide at the village, is low during the greater part of the year. Should there be a winter with little snow it remains shallow; but heavy snow melts in May and June can cause it and the Galisteo creek to overflow their banks and inundate low-lying fields. Henry Poore reported in 1890 that a church standing some distance from the river 10 years earlier had fallen into it and many houses had been washed away. A large plaza, too, fell victim to high waters.[6]

Stinging snow may harass the village from mid-December through February, depths varying from a few inches to, much less frequent, a foot or more. Accumulations are usually much greater in the mountains. Winter temperatures are unpredictable: They may plunge to zero or below and then slowly rise to 60° or more. In early spring pitiless winds often whip up choking sand or dust storms. By mid-April the threat of a killing frost has ended and the days become warmer. A few days in July and August may be searingly hot, then ominous clouds build up; lightning razors through the heavens; thunder crashes and echoes from mesa and mountain. Deluging rain freshens the parched land. Abruptly it ends, leaving a rainbow and swollen arroyos in its wake.

About 15 miles north of the pueblo the Jemez mountains rise 11,000 feet above the plateau. To the south stands the Sandia range. By some strange refraction of light they may appear at one time an iridescent pink, at another, purple. Juniper and pinyon thrive in the foothills; at higher elevations they give way to pine, spruce, and fir. Mountain lion, bear, and deer wander the mountain wilderness. Below on the plateau, yucca, cacti, and a variety of tough grasses grow sporadically. Jack rabbits, cotton tails, and other small mammals scurry through the scarce vegetation: Rattlers and a number of nonvenomous snakes lie in wait for them. Overhead hawk and eagle glide on air currents searching for rabbit and reptile. Pronghorn herds forage the open land. Wolves, coyote, fox, and bobcat contend for all the nonpredators; vultures feed on the carrion.

Here in this starkly beautiful land, nature's undulating rhythms governed human existence from the timing and order of sacred pageants to the planning of subsistence activities. Its mystifying remoteness and splendor inspired and nurtured the Pueblo worldview.

Kiwan sacred belief, myth, and ritual, social structure, and economic activities were inextricably interwoven: They formed a cultural web which

[6]Henry R. Poore, "Condition of Sixteen New Mexican Indian Pueblos, 1890," Eleventh Census Report of 1890, Washington, D.C. 1894. Quoted in White, *The Pueblo of Santo Domingo*, pp. 20–21.

included all the people in its threads and directed their activities. The pueblo itself was the focus; individuals were submerged. Here were no individual rites of passage, no vision quests, and no puberty celebrations.

Domingans understood that their social organization and ritual lay in their view of Indian origins. It was told that a long time ago in the beginning, the Indians lived inside the earth with their mother Iatik. Some were priests, officers, medicine men, and even witches. Insects, birds, and animals dwelled there, too. A time came for them to leave. Helped by the birds, animals, and insects, they climbed through four lower worlds on spruce and fir trees, emerging at Shipap (*sipapu*). Before they left, Iatik gave them corn to take her place. "This corn is my heart," she said. "It shall be to my people as milk from my breasts."[7] At this time she ordained that a priest called *Kasik* (*Cacique*) was to care for the people in her place. She told them, too, that when they died they were to return to her in the underworld.

With the people were two sisters who contended with one another to see who was the stronger. Finally they parted: One went toward the east and became the mother of white people; the other became the mother of the Indians.

Because Shipap was too sacred a place to live, the people wandered south to White House where they stayed for a long time. In those days many gods stayed with them: The *Katsina* (Keres people called them *Shiwana*) came to dance from their homes in the east; the *Koshare* and *Kwiraina* came too. The twin war gods, Masewi and Oyoyewi, sons of the sun, were also present. From them and the others the people learned about the world, how to treat the gods and to perform sacred rituals with the necessary paraphernalia. All their customs as well as farming techniques were taught to them at White House. This came to an end when the gods returned to their homes. Before their departure, they appointed priests and organized societies to replace them. Each god taught the Indians the important ceremonies so necessary to their welfare.

From the Katsina they learned how to dress like them and to dance for rain. From the Koshare and Kwiraina they learned to form societies to take over their work; to dance for crops; and help the Katsina bring rain. When Masewi and Oyoyewi returned to their home in the Sandia mountains, the Santo Domingans chose two of their men to replace them. They were the war chiefs and headed the warrior society. The four major curing societies were also formed at White House. Because witches caused illness, it was the curing societies' job to catch them and cure the people of the sicknesses they brought on.

Hunting required power; the *Caiyak* who had such power started the

[7]M. C. Stevenson, *The Sia*. Bureau of American Ethnology, Eleventh Annual Report, 1894, p. 39. Quoted in Leslie White, *The Pueblo of Santa Ana*, New Mexico Memoirs of the American Anthropological Association No. 60, 1942. (Kraus Reprint Co., 1969), p. 87.

hunters' society. In Domingo the society had charge of communal rabbit hunts and performed the Buffalo and Deer Dances.

Other supernaturals went to live in the six directions: the cardinal points (north, south, east, west), the zenith, and the nadir. They sent rain and snow. Supernatural animals lived in the six directions, too: the mountain lion in the north, badger in the south, bear in the west, and, in the east, the wolf. The eagle lived at the zenith and the shrew dwelled in the nadir.[8]

After all this the people left White House, separated, and built their villages. As in the other Keresan pueblos, Domingan culture was created in the distant past, and sacred officials were human replicas of the supernaturals. Every dramatic ritual with its sacred paraphernalia, dance, and song was given by the gods. Kiwa societies, crops, and clans were of sacred origin. The people lived according to divine formulas. Their devotion to them was less a matter of faith or belief than it was a certainty that their affairs were completely integrated with cosmic forces. No crop prospered, no enemy was vanquished, no animal was caught without the help of the forces of the cosmos: "And the whole cosmos so moves that the Domingan people may live. The pueblo is the stage, gods and men the players, the drama cosmic."[9]

To enlist the help of the gods and the cosmic forces, each phase of the Domingan year was celebrated with ritual. Scarcely a month passed without a major dramatic ritual. Conducting these great communal ceremonies required a number of officials. Each of them represented a god who dwelled with the Indians in White House. Societies, too, were necessary for their proper performance. These also had their charter in the mythic past.

The most important and revered official was the *Cacique (kasik)*. It was he who fasted, prayed, and "worked" for his people. In his special house (the *hotcanitsa*) he kept a basket full of tiny clay figures which represented the *hano sicti* (people of Santo Domingo). By taking care of the images, he symbolically cared for his people. To them, he was both father and mother. In 1962 the *Cacique* was elderly and frail. He remarked: "I should retire. . . . I've worked for the people for a long time."[10]

While the *Cacique* cared for his people spiritually, they took care of him in material ways. They planted, tilled, and harvested his fields. A man remarked to Leslie White:

> When the time comes the people go out and plow his fields. One old man smokes; others cook meat and eat it [in the fields]. Masewi and Oyoyewi and Cacique take three praysticks and go out into the [Cacique's] fields and bury them. They [i.e., the people] take care of the Cacique's fields in the summer.

[8]This account of Kiwa origins derives from material from White in both *The Pueblo of Santa Ana*, pp. 87–88, and *The Pueblo of Santo Domingo*, pp. 29–32.

[9]White, *The Pueblo of Santo Domingo*, p. 33.

[10]Harriet J. Kupferer, field notes, 1962. In White's time and before, the *Cacique* served for life.

> In the fall, Masewi tells them when it is time to gather the crops. They harvest
> Cacique's fields before they harvest their own. They take his [Cacique's crops]
> to his house and store it away.[11]

The *Cacique* initiated or approved of all of the important rituals and presided over them. It was his responsibility to appoint the war priests, Masewei and Oyoyewi, and their assistants. At his death, they selected his successor, always a chief priest of the Flint Medicine society.

Although the *Cacique* was powerful and important, he was in no way an absolute ruler. He had the most sacred duties and obligations, but should he have been derelict in their performance, the war priests had the power to discipline him. If such a rare situation occurred, they remonstrated with him if the offense was minor; in the event of a more serious lapse, they could inflict physical punishment.

Because the *Cacique* had much to do he had a helper called *teraikatsi* who did a woman's work in the *hotcanitsa*. He built fires, swept, and stored rabbits from communal rabbit hunts. Upon instructions from the *Cacique* he announced the time to harvest crops. Had there been much illness in the village, he advised the Masewei that a general curing ritual was in order.

The war priests, Masewei and Oyoyewi, sometimes called *tsiakiya* and *tsiakaiy teniente* (lieutenant), were appointed by the *Cacique* for a term of one year. One year Maswei came from one *kiva* and Oyoyewi the other. The *kivas* alternated yearly. Powerful administrative officers, they were in charge of almost all of the major ceremonies: supervising masked dances and initiation rites for the *Katsina* cult, and guarding medicine men during their retreats and curing rites.

To help the war priests, the *Cacique* appointed ten assistants called *Gowatcanyi*. Each carried a small wooden staff as his badge of office. It was they who most often did the actual guarding. A special duty was herding horses in one large band to graze on land away from the village. All houses in the pueblo were grouped into five sections according to the four cardinal points and the "middle." The ten *Gowatcanyi* were divided into pairs and were similarly designated. When the pair from the north were in charge of the activity, boys and young men from the north section assisted them. When their week was over they rounded up the horses and drove them to the pueblo to be counted and examined. The animals were then driven back to the hills by the *Gowatcanyi* from the west and so it continued for five weeks.

As the Spaniards were unwilling to tolerate Pueblo religion so were they unable to deal with Pueblo sacred officialdom. Therefore in the 1600s, the King of Spain mandated that on the first of January, the Pueblos annually elect a governor, *alcaldes, fiscales*, and other officers through which the Spanish could govern. These secular officers as well as Catholicism were

---

[11]White, *The Pueblo of Santo Domingo*, p. 35.

imposed on the Santo Domingans, but they modified both to blend with their cultural system.

Rather than elect a governor (called *Dapop*) the head of the Cikame Medicine society appointed one annually. The governor transacted business with non-Indians, officiated at rooster pulls, and remained on the alert for intruders during sacred secret ritual. He could, if he thought it necessary, intervene in serious quarrels between villagers. Regardless of what his responsibilities were, they had nothing to do with the sacred. To assist the governor the Cikame society appointed a *Dapop teniente* and six *capitani*. These ran errands, delivered messages, and searched for unwelcome people in the pueblo. In 1962 a Santo Domingan friend described his duties as a *capitani* (although he referred to the position as an officer):

> You see there are officers and each two officers got a road and they have to deliver the mail. Like at night the mail all comes in a bunch and in the council house we meet and they call out the mail and you got to know who your people are and take their mail to deliver it. Then if there's a big council meeting and you have to know who the council mens (sic) are on your street and go and get them and make sure they get to the meetings, or if there is something to go on (sic) at night or in the next few days you got to notify everybody by talking to them . . . like now after the feast we got to clean the ditches, every man and boy got to work on the ditches, and that big ditch starts all the way over by Cochiti. Now you got to know who is able to work on the ditches and make a list, then that night you call them and make them work from five until maybe it gets dark, course old men or sick men don't have to, but it's a community thing and everybody got to work.[12]

Although White stated that the head of the Cikame society appointed the capitani, my friend said, "The guy going out appoints you . . . you got to do it, now you know what it's like down there."[13]

The remainder of the Spanish-introduced officers were the *Bickari*, a term derived from the Spanish *fiscales*. The Cikame society head appointed seven annually: *Bicari major*, *Bickari teniente*, and five assistants. When the priest visited the Pueblo for the monthly mass, the, *Bickari* served his needs; they saw to it that the church was plastered; and finally they buried the dead.

The "ditch chief" called *Kokatc* ("looking at it") was the last of the important officers.[14] He maintained the ditches, opening them in the spring, keeping them free of weeds all summer, and ordering their closing in the fall.

In addition to the elaborate system of sacred and secular officials, the Santo Domingan social structure also included two *kiva* organizations and twelve secret societies. *Kivas* were (and still are) very large round semisub-

---

[12]Kupferer, field notes, 1962.
[13]Ibid.
[14]White, *The Pueblo of Santo Domingo*, p. 45.

terranean structures. A staircase led to the flat roof; by ladder through a large hole in the roof people descended into the chamber. Adolph Bandelier, an early visitor to the pueblo, peered down into one and commented that it appeared to be clean. He was able to see dimly a large fire hearth shaped somewhat like an armchair, a drum, and large block of wood or stone.[15] Evidently from his vantage point he could not see the altar and the *sipapu*. Each *kiva* had a ceremonial house called the *sicti* house. Here, officials held important meetings and initiations; the *Katsina* masks were also hidden in the *sicti* house.

Every person in the Pueblo belonged to either the Turquoise *kiva* or the Squash *kiva* (called Pumpkin *kiva* in 1962). Children belonged to their father's *kiva*; women, when they married, joined the *kiva* of their husband. Although this was the ideal convention, there is some reason to believe that the change in *kiva* affiliation was not always welcomed by the girl's family. A conversation with a Domingan friend in 1962 revealed some discord:

> He belongs to the Pumpkin *kiva* and we are Turquoise and Daddy doesn't want me to marry a Pumpkin because I'll have to join their *kiva*. A long time ago the Pumpkin and the Turquoise *kiva* had a quarrel. . . . The Pumpkin were stingy with their women [meaning that they did not want them to marry the Turquoise men].

I asked: "Do wives always have to go with their husband's *kiva*?" She replied, "Yes." I asked: "Then will all your children belong to the Pumpkin *kiva*?"

> Yes, Daddy and Momma were both Turquoise *kiva*. The Pumpkin would love to have me because I dance the Buffalo dance.[16]

Kiva organization required a number of officers or *principales*, as they were sometimes called. At the head was the *sicti hotcanyi* (chief of the people). His major responsibility was managing the masked *Katsina* dances; he rehearsed the dancers and supervised the preparation of the masks and costumes. To help him in his many duties were a number of assistants, both men and women. Boys, called *sicti croyati* and girls—*sicti masitcra*—were "put in" by their father's father. Both underwent a ritual which concluded with a dance for the new helpers. Boys did a number of chores upon request of the *sicti hotcanyi*; women cared for the *sicti* house, sweeping it, removing ashes, and carrying water.

Every adult male belonged to one of the two *kiva*-linked *Katsina* cults. Fathers put their sons in when the boys reached 12 or older. Turquoise men nominated their boys for membership in the Turquoise group;

---

[15]Adolph F. Bandelier, *The Southwestern Journals, 1880–1882*. Charles H. Lange and Carroll L. Riley, eds. (Albuquerque: The University of New Mexico Press, 1966), pp. 117–118.

[16]Kupferer, field notes, 1962.

Squash fathers nominated theirs for the Squash *Katsinas*. When the time arrived, a father prepared *ckwrina*, a sacred bundle of corn meal and crushed turquoise wrapped in corn husks, and gave it to a friend asking him to be his son's "ceremonial father" and to see that nothing happened to him. On the first night of the initiation the friend accompanied the nervous boy to the *kiva sicti* house. There he joined other novices in a darkened room. Shortly, mysterious voices spoke to them out of the darkness: "Do you believe in the *Shiwana*? Will you do your best? Will you guard the secrets?" In the Turquoise *kiva* the Flint Medicine society sat in the gloom listening. The Cikame were present in the Squash *kiva*. Other *kiva* members squatted along the sides bearing witness. When the voices ceased, the novices led by their "fathers" followed a path of corn meal into a lighted room; here Katsina waited to sing *Shiwana* songs. At the conclusion all left the house for home.

The following morning under the direction of their "fathers" the boys vomited to purify themselves. They then were taken to a secret room to view the sacred Katsina masks. After four days had passed, during which the boys vomited and sang in the mask chamber, the time for the dramatic concluding ritual arrived. On the evening of the fourth night, escorted by their "fathers," they once again followed the cornmeal path into the room. There they saw an elaborate dry painting and the medicine men seated behind their *iariko* (sacred corn fetishes). Gathered about the wall were the initiated men. The medicine priests chanted; the wide-eyed boys watched as a man placed a large turtle shell on the meal path in front of the painting; on top of it he laid deer antlers upside down. While the medicine men sang, the door to the mask room burst open and a masked figure entered carrying two long whips and stood behind the deer horns. Nudged by his "father" the first boy in line approached apprehensively and knelt, grasping the antlers. The masked priest whipped him four times across his back; to have cried out or whimpered would have disgraced the boy. After all were whipped, the ceremonial fathers, the watching *Shiwana*, the medicine men, and the head of the *kiva* were each lashed in turn. The masked figure disappeared and removed his mask while another priest took the shell and antlers away. To the singing of the medicine men, both the new and old *Shiwana* danced. Later medicine priests dashed medicine water over all the participants. They slept in the *sicti* house that night.

The next morning the *Shiwana* dressed for a masked dance; medicine men sprinkled them and their masks. Proceeding to the plaza they danced before the people. When they finished women and children were banished to their houses so that they would not see the dancers go to the river to unmask and wash off their paint. Women and children were not to know that the *Shiwana* were fellow villagers impersonating the spirits. The dancers returned their masks to the chambers, the *sicti hotcanyi* plastered the door shut. *Katsina* initiations occurred once in every eight years.

Although the *sicti hotcanyi* was responsible for the masked dances, he remained in the *kiva* while they were performed in the plaza. To lead the dance and signal changes in choreography and song was a *Maicdo*. He, too, was a *Katsina* and an excellent singer. Each *kiva* alternated in giving an important spring ritual, the *Kaiyakayet*, for the crops. Because it was so elaborate, a special *kiva* officer, the *Gait*, was in charge of it.

Equally significant in Domingan life were the secret societies. The Koshare and Kwiraina were two of the most important. Each was affiliated with a *kiva*. The Koshare were members of the Turquoise *kiva*, the Kwiraina belonged to the Squash. Both appeared when the *Katsinas* danced. They, too, reflected the dual organization typical of pueblo organization. Koshare were winter people; Kwiraina were summer people. The division was related to the agricultural cycle.

The ceremonial arrival of either the Koshare or the Kwiraina was startling to behold. Koshare appeared covered from head to toe with white clay paint, black horizontal stripes painted around their bodies, and black paint encircling their mouths and eyes. They daubed white clay in their hair and twisted it around two "horns" made of cornhusks. Although they wore no masks they were unrecognizable as the following remarks indicate: "Did you see Felipe at the dance yesterday?" a friend asked me. "No, I didn't." "Yes, you did, he was a Koshare."[17] The Kwiraina divided their bodies in half by painting the right side orange and the left, white. Vertical orange and black stripes decorated their faces. Their hair was bunched up on top of their heads. Like the Koshare, an old, torn breech cloth, hung from their waists.

Women might belong to either of the groups although they were not privy to all the secrets; they lacked the "power" that men had and did not participate in ritual. They functioned as assistants: cooking food, bringing water for medicine bowls, and helping in the preparations for ceremonies. The duties were arduous as a comment from a Koshare's wife indicated: "I was so tired that week before the feast," she said. "Felipe had to feed all the people in the *kiva* and I had to keep cooking."[18]

Among the other secret societies were four important medicine societies: Flint, Cikame, Boyaka, and Giant. All had major ritual responsibilities. They fought witches and treated illness caused by them, went into retreats before rain ceremonials, and performed rites for the dead. Each had esoteric paraphernalia: a slat altar, an *iariko* representing Iatik, and meal paintings, sometimes referred to as dry painting. Each society had its own house where it retreated and initiated new members. The Flint and Cikame were closely linked with the Koshare and Kwiraina and the *kivas* to which they belonged. White noted that all members of the Flint society were

[17]Ibid.

[18]Ibid. It may have been that Felipe was the Koshare leader as his wife said he had to feed all the *kiva* people. Probably other women helped her.

Santo Domingo Koshare dancers, circa 1899.
Smithsonian Institution National Anthropological Archives.

Koshare but all Koshare, of course, did not belong to the Flint society.[19] The same situation obtained with the Cikame and the Kwiraina. It may have been that the Flint society was the more eminent of the two; the *Cacique* was always the head of the Flint society, which appointed the major religious officers, while the Cikame elected the secular hierarchy.

The Boyaka and the Giant societies were without the alignments of the Flint and Cikame. Their members, however, cured and participated in ritual retreats. The Kapina, Toad (Beraka), Ant, and Snake societies were minor medicine groups.

Kapina treated sore eyes by using dry herbal medicine. Members of the Toad group attended to ear trouble as well as holding a toad ceremony in the spring and summer to rid the village of toads. It was said that the urine of toads poisoned people if they contacted it: "If any one sees a toad in the pueblo he does not kill it. Instead he tells one of the Beraka, who catches the toad and takes it outside the pueblo."[20] Members of the Ant society appeared to be somewhat like "general practitioners" treating illnesses which were not caused by witches. The Snake society, as its name implies, treated victims of snake bite. The society had a leader whose house was its headquarters and where treatment was undertaken. After being bitten by a snake, the patient and the offending reptile were put in the Snake house for four days. Members caught more snakes and put them in the room too: "They put the snakes in there with him so they will get acquainted with him and won't bite him."[21] The Snake leader remained in the house with them all four days. On the final night he made a meal painting and other priests gathered up the snakes and released them outside of the village.

[19]White, *The Pueblo of Santo Domingo*, p. 54.
[20]Ibid., p. 67.
[21]Ibid., p. 68.

The final two societies were the Opi and the Hunter's society (Caiyak). Opi was the Warrior's society. Membership was gained by killing an enemy and scalping him in the appropriate ritual manner. Society members guarded and "fed" the scalps. Hunter's society members were thought to have power over all creatures. It came from animals such as the mountain lion, wolves, eagles, and other beasts of prey. The society was active in communal rabbit hunts and participated in the Buffalo and Deer Dances. A deer hunter hoping for luck might ask the head of the society for "medicine" to ensure success.

Initiation into any of the major societies was long and demanding. Koshare members, for example, may have been "put in" as young children by their fathers or their father's fathers, but their formal initiation was put off until they were adults. Some, perhaps, were motivated to join during a serious illness; others often joined who had dreamed consistently of the Koshare. After a young man made the decision he told his parents; they summoned his relatives to discuss the matter. While few would discourage the candidate, it would cost his kin a great amount in food and other provisions. After they had agreed, his parents informed the Masewi, who with the parents and one or two of his *principales*, visited the *Cacique* inviting him to come to the boy's house. After the *Cacique* arrived, the candidate's father gave him a *ckwrina* and told him of his son's wish. He nodded, spoke softly, and departed with the sacred meal. Later he called the Koshare together including the *Goyawi* (women members) to tell them that a certain person wished to become one of them. Each with some of the cornmeal prayed to important supernaturals. They then decided whether to initiate the supplicant. Often he had to wait three or four years before being taken in. During that period he was taught Koshare songs, dances, rituals, and duties. The formal initiation took place in February. At the appointed time some Koshare went for the young man and placed him in the society house. Here he stayed secluded for eight days and fasted. During the final four days the society members retired to the house to pray and fast. On the final evening members erected their altar and put down a meal painting; the final initiation had begun. Details regarding it have not been revealed; there is, however, a hint that the candidate sang Koshare songs and danced and that he was whipped.[22] At the conclusion of this phase, his family brought a great quantity of food to provide a feast for the Koshare and any others allowed to attend.

The following morning the society went in a body to the Turquoise *kiva*, erected their altar, and once more created a meal painting. They then emerged from the sacred chamber and danced in the plaza. The *sicti* (people) aware of the events of the preceding eight days had gathered to watch, many from the flat tops of houses. From there they threw food, clothing, and other gifts to the dancers below. The decision to join the society was an

---

[22]Frances Densmore, *Music of Santo Domingo Pueblo, New Mexico*. Southwest Museum Papers #12, 1938, p. 142.

individual one, but because the society was instrumental in promoting Pueblo welfare, villagers, therefore, participated enthusiastically in the last phase of the initiation.[23]

Initiations of the four major medicine societies and the Hunter's society were broadly similar, each varying in specific details. In addition to voluntary membership, these groups "trapped" members. In the course of a retreat or an initiation, society members drew a barely visible line of corn meal in front of the society house. Should an unwary person cross it, the medicine men caught him and began his initiation.

Secure in the knowledge that their ceremonial officers and organizations were ever alert to their needs, Domingans moved confidently through life. Farming, as it had for years, formed the basis of their economy. As a consequence, work and ritual corresponded with the cycle of the seasons. Away from the village in irrigated fields near the river they grew corn, beans, squash, and cotton, as well as melons. Wheat and alfalfa were introduced by the Europeans. Each family owned and tended its land; on the sparsely grassed range cattle, horses, and sheep were pastured.

Although rain came in late spring and summer, water from the Rio Grande was essential to farming. A large ditch led from the river; from it smaller ones crisscrossed the fields. Only during the growing season did water flow in them; at others gates prevented water from entering the main ditch. Like every activity necessary for communal welfare, opening the ditches in the spring required a ritual.

On a day in late March or early April, Masewi informed the *Cacique* and *Dapop* that the time had come to open the ditches. *Dapop* dispatched his officers to notify men and boys to prepare for the job; only the infirm and the heads of the four medicine societies were exempt. Early in the chill morning of the appointed day, the workers in wagons or on horseback traveled to the head of the ditch about 15 miles away. Before they started the task, Masewi and the ditch chief placed prayer sticks made by the *Cacique* in the ditch. Working in pairs, the men cleared the weeds and removed the silt from the trenches. When the sun began its descent toward the horizon, the weary and muddy workers returned to the village. The next morning they returned to pick up where they had stopped the night before; so they worked daily for a week or more. When the toilers were near the village, women brought them lunch. On the final day the *Shiwana* appeared to supervise the labor. After the last weed was pulled but before the water entered the head ditch four officers placed *wabani* (prayer feather bunches) in it. A Flint priest sang:

> The Ditch is ready for the water to come
> You, water, come here to me,

---

[23]White, *The Pueblo of Santo Domingo*, pp. 55–57. The same procedures were followed in Kwiraina initiations. The event, however was held in September and the final stage took place in the Squash *kiva*.

Santo Domingo men before opening the ditches.
Smithsonian Institution National Anthropological Archives.

I am set to meet you and talk over things.
My people are waiting for you, they are wishing for you,
Now, as spring time is here.

Mother Earth, I am glad that the crop has been planted,
Who comes first? Mother Wheat.
The second mother is the Corn.
You have heard about her.

You know the colors, they are red, blue, yellow, pure white, and many other colors.

(The plants speak, under the earth:) We are now beginning to move under Mother Earth,
We are thinking of you, a spirit on the way to give us drink
So it will help us to grow,
When we drink from you, a spirit, we want you all summer
In order to show ourselves strong, healthy crops.

After we began to grow stronger and better, we have responsibility toward our father and mother who put us in the earth,
So we come to meet our people.
Not only for our people but for the welfare of the community.[24]

As the notes faded, the *Shiwana* vanished and *Dapop* and Masewi dismissed the workers who, with the women, returned to the village singing.

Men and boys of the family prepared the fields for corn planting. All the men planted each field with seed blessed by the Flint society; singing and throwing water on one another they moved up and down the furrows bending to plant the kernels. The plaintive notes of a flute drifted across

[24]The Southwest Museum granted permission to quote from Densmore, *Music of Santo Domingo Pueblo, New Mexico*, p. 71. There are three more verses not included here.

the land. Flute music, it was said, made things grow better. Men went almost daily to their corn fields to check growth and chop weeds. Little boys tagged along listening to their fathers sing to the young maize.

When men were not farming, many worked in turquoise in their free time. From pre-Hispanic times to the present (1928) Domingans dug the semiprecious stones in mines near Cerrillos, New Mexico. In 1880 an acquaintance told Bandelier that he had met two Indians cutting turquoise with hatchets from veins in a shaft at Cerrillos.[25] Turquoise had both ritual and ornamental value; fetishes were adorned with it and turquoise appeared on altars. People, from toddlers to adults, were seldom seen without beads, pendants, and earrings.

Sitting in his cool adobe house the craftsman meticulously shaped and polished the stones, often spending days at the task. To bore the stones for beads he used a small bow drill; frequently each turquoise bead was separated from the next by a piece of shell acquired by trade. While he worked, his boys watched. To a responsible one he entrusted some of the easier work. They spoke quietly, the father gently correcting the young apprentice. Jewelry not kept was traded to Hopi or Zuni in exchange for woven ceremonial sashes or traditional dresses for his wife and daughters. Domingan men abandoned weaving after Spanish exploitation diminished.

Men farmed, hunted, made jewelry, and moccasins; women tended babies, prepared food, and baked bread in the outdoor dome-shaped ovens, a legacy from the Spaniards. Always there was corn to grind. Bandelier reported that the girls always sang as they ground the maize.[26]

In addition to the daily routines, women made clay pots, some for general use, others for ceremonial purposes. Clay was dug from hills a mile or more from the pueblo. Using a *mano* and *metate* they pulverized it and added water to produce the proper consistency. Ropes of clay were twined around and around building up the pot. Using their hands and small scrapers they shaped and smoothed the receptacles. Outside a hot fire burned. When the pots were ready for firing, the coals were spread out and the vessels were set on flat stones and covered with dung. After they had cooled the women painted typical Domingan designs on them. The Rocky Mountain bee plant provided black pigment. Once more they fired the pots.

In late April families prepared for weeks of ritual performed by the *kiva* groups and the medicine societies. The Flint society started the great ritual dramas by going into a retreat. Before it, the members vomited each morning for four mornings. Masewi joined them. On the third day of purging Masewi's assistants hunted rabbits which they gave to the women society members to prepare. The fourth morning the medicine priests erected their altar and made a dry painting in their society house. Six

[25]Bandelier, *The Southwestern Journals, 1880–1882*, p. 86.
[26]Ibid., p. 104.

prayer sticks were buried in a cornfield. After eating the rabbits they bathed in the river and, together with the women, they danced "like *Shiwana*." At midnight the women went home and the priests retired to their chamber, now referred to as Shipap. For the next three nights the sounds of muffled drums and faint chants filled the night. While the Flint society was in retreat, the Turquoise *kiva* group prepared for the masked dance to follow it. The *sicti hotcanyi* sent an officer to notify the Koshare and the men who were to dance to get ready. They, too, vomited for four mornings, then practiced their songs and dances in the *sicti* house. At night the retreating medicine men walked silently through the blackened streets to visit them. They sprinkled the masks, danced, and sang.

The morning of the fifth day while the dancers were painting their bodies and putting on their costumes, Masewi and a medicine man reported to the *Cacique* that the *Shiwana* had come, asking if he wanted them to dance. He, of course, always agreed.

The masked dancers followed Masewi over a trail of corn meal to the plaza. People thronged the area to watch. In the morning they danced six dances while the Koshare cavorted around the dancers and among the spectators. At noon all women and children were sent away while the dancers ate. In the afternoon they appeared to dance and sing six more times. All of the songs made reference to clouds, rain, and crops. At the close of the last dance, a priest announced that the *Shiwana* were leaving for their home in the east. The dancers disappeared into their house to await night when they went to the river to wash off their paint. One by one they walked in the darkness to their homes.

In the weeks following the other three medicine societies retreated; after each, the *Shiwana* danced. These retreats were the most sacred and significant rituals of the year. At these times the entire cosmos was entreated to water Domingo fields so that the people might live.[27]

With the conclusion of the dramatic communal ceremonies, Domingan daily life resumed: Young couples married, babies were born, and there were deaths.

Domingans violently resisted marriage outside the pueblo but there were always some determined enough to defy public opinion. Few, however, married non-Indians, as this was especially abhorrent. Because they did not have *Katsinas* and had been former enemies, Apache and Navajo mates were condemned almost as much. Marriage with someone of the Tanoan villages was reluctantly tolerated; mates from the other Keres pueblos were accepted although not enthusiastically. As recently as 1962 prohibitions were equally as strong. A Domingan friend of the writer remarked "some Domingos have married whites . . . and one man married a Negro. They none of them can come back to the Pueblo anymore, ever."[28]

[27]This much abbreviated account comes from White, *The Pueblo of Santo Domingo*, pp. 89–98.

[28]Kupferer, field notes, 1962.

Her son was having difficulties too. He wanted to marry a young woman from San Ildefonso pueblo who was pregnant with his child. Anna his sister said:

> He had decided to get married in Chicago (where he was working at the time) when Elizabeth goes there, after the baby is born, sometime in August, but the people don't want him to do that and Mother and I want him to get married in the right way so that people will know he is married. Elizabeth is part white and Santo Domingos aren't suppose to marry Anglos. "But" I said, "She isn't much Anglo." No, not more than an eighth and she has lived with her grandmother most of her life. Anyhow at first he notified the councilmens (sic) that he wanted to marry her. They were supposed to send some officers up (to San Ildefonso) to investigate her past to see if she is all right. If you marry outside the Pueblo the councilmen investigate but they didn't come (sic) up here yet so now he wants to get married in Chicago.[29]

A few weeks later the council approved the marriage and the date was set for Christmas.

Young people experimented with sex and Pueblo adolescents received explicit sexual instructions from certain elders.[30] No stigma was attached to babies born to single women. To marry, however, required familial permission, and, on occasion, a parent coerced a child into marriage. "My mother's mother," a young woman recounted, "made my mother marry my daddy; she didn't want to marry him but grandmother said she had to marry him. My daddy wanted to marry my mother though."[31] After the parents of each had agreed to the union they called their respective matrilineal clan members together to see whether anyone had objections. If there were none, the pair became engaged. This situation still obtained 25 years ago. A friend of mine who had, after a long period of her father's recalcitrance, finally received his permission to marry, said: "In October or November Daddy has to get all my relatives together to see if anyone objects, and his daddy has to do the same thing. I don't think anybody will; several of the people have already told me that they are on my side."[32]

With the betrothal announced, the groom set about collecting the ceremonial clothing for his bride: a new *manta* (a black dress woven at Hopi or Zuni), knee-high white moccasin boots made by someone in the pueblo, and a variety of sashes and scarves. When all was ready, each family gave a large feast to which almost all the villagers came, going first to the bride's house and then to the boy's. When the guests had eaten, respected folk delivered long didactic speeches advising the newlyweds on proper behavior and other pertinent matters. Until Catholicism was incorporated into the original tradition, these feasts legalized the marriage. In later years the

[29]Ibid.
[30]Bertha P. Dutton, *The Pueblos*. (Englewood Cliffs, NJ: Prentice-Hall, Inc., 1976) p. 5.
[31]Kupferer, 1962. This marriage took place in about 1935.
[32]Ibid.

couple would not consider themselves married unless the sacristan passed a scarf behind the shoulders of the couple to be tied in front of them.[33]

Clans were matrilineal but there is little evidence to suggest that a matrilocal rule of residence existed. Circumstances appeared to dictate the location of the new home. If the bride had inherited land her husband cultivated it as well as his own, if he had any. A landless couple appealed to the governor to allot idle land, or they bought plots from others willing to sell.

A baby might be born at any time during the first year of marriage, for often the bride was pregnant. On occasion they might have had a child before the ceremony.

As the time of delivery grew near, the woman's mother or sister hovered about, prepared to send for a midwife when labor began. In the event of a prolonged difficult delivery, she sent corn meal to a medicine priest to summon him to assist. After murmuring prayers he placed a medicine bowl filled with smoking pinyon nut shells under the blanket covering the straining woman. White thought that perhaps this was related to the belief that eating pinyon nuts while pregnant caused birth complications.[34] The midwife grasped the emerging infant, cut the umbilical cord and handed the cord to the waiting father. If the baby were a boy he hurried off to bury the cord in his cornfield. If it were a girl, he placed the cord in the earthen floor close to the grinding bins. After soothing the squalling infant with a warm bath the midwife placed a boy's feet in a black pottery bowl to give him a heavy voice; a girl was held for a moment or two in the grinding bin. The disposal of the umbilical cord and the placement of the baby symbolized the division of labor by gender. A girl of the family tossed the afterbirth into the river.

For three days and nights mother and child lay quietly together, she suckling it at the first whimper. Before dawn on the fourth day a woman chosen by the mother arrived. She picked the baby up and together with the mother stepped outside to greet the rising sun. As the sun appeared the "godmother" raised the child four times and gave it its Indian name. The three returned to the waiting family, announced its name, and shared a meal. The baby was laced into its cradle board and a perfect ear of corn was hung near by. Often the cradle board had been made a generation or two before its current occupant was born. A Domingan man, Joe, in 1962, said of his son's board, "My daddy made that, I slept there, and all of my children did too."[35]

A month or two later, parents often elected to have their baby baptized in the Catholic tradition. They chose godparents to sponsor the child

[33]Father N. Dumarest, *Notes on Cochiti, New Mexico.* E. C. Parsons, ed. Memoirs of the American Anthropological Association #6. Part E, 1920, p. 148. Quoted in White, *The Pueblo of Santo Domingo,* f.n., p. 83.

[34]White, *The Pueblo of Santo Domingo,* p. 80.

[35]Kupferer, field notes.

and give it its Spanish name, invariably the name of a Catholic saint. To all but other Domingans, people were known by their Saint's name. Only rarely did a Domingo reveal his Indian name. Speaking of the naming ritual, an acquaintance of the writer's pointed out a woman saying, "She is like a mother to me, she gave me my Indian name."[36] She did not, however, disclose it.

Like all other Native Americans, Santo Domingans welcomed children; to be childless was a misfortune. Although children were indulged and some mischief was tolerated, disobedience was rare. Jose said: "When we hoe, I say you take that row, you take that row, and you take that [referring to himself and his three boys; the oldest was eleven]. Little Sebastiano is always behind. If the mosquitoes come he stop and stamp his feet and hit his head. . . . In his row the weeds all come up again."[37] Little girls learned to grind corn as soon as they were tall enough to reach the grinding bins; they watched their mothers clean wheat, separating the chaff from the grain by tossing it in a large Apache basket. Life was not all drudgery for the children; boys and girls played together, swam in irrigation ditches, and listened to the old people recount the ageless myths and legends. Through them, they absorbed Pueblo virtues: respect for elders, kindness, industry, and fealty to tradition.

Instruction was not always so indirect. "Our ways are different," the writer was told. "All the younger children are supposed to obey the oldest one. Momma and Daddy say to the others, 'you listen to your sister.' "[38] Seldom did young ones not follow an older sibling's orders.

By listening to greetings and conversations among adults, young children discovered who their kinfolk were and how they were related. Children belonged to their mother's clan and all members were viewed as kin regardless of how distant. People of their father's clan were kin, too; marriage was forbidden with people of either group. Data on Santo Domingo clans are sparse. White found twenty-one clans in 1933 and reported that Bourke had counted eighteen.[39] Domingo clans had no ceremonial activities, held no land in common, nor were they instrumental in controlling sacred or secular offices. No person of either sex headed a clan. Their sole function seems to have been regulating marriage.

Kinship terminology and behavior have not been adequately described either.[40] In a typical matrilineal system, however, mother's mother or mother's brother would have authority over the matrilineage or the matri-extended family. There were hints that this was the case at Santo

[36]Ibid.

[37]Ibid.

[38]Ibid.

[39]White, *The Santo Domingo Indians of New Mexico*, p. 71.

[40]Rubin Fox, "Some Unsolved Problems of Pueblo Social Organization," in *New Perspectives on the Pueblos*, attempted to explain the Keres kinship system based on inferences from Cochiti and Santa Ana data. See pp. 71–85.

Domingo. "See that old lady over there?" a friend asked the author. "She is my mother's mother; I can't stand that old lady. Of course she is the boss of all of us, but I don't like her. She's a funny person. I don't like her son either. . . . My grandmother comes over and asks a lot of questions and bosses everyone around."[41] To be sure, probably not all maternal grandmothers were as irritating, but they could exercise power over their daughters and their children.

In addition to Catholic ritual godparents and the "mother" who bestowed the Indian name, people acquired other fictive relatives. Officers who patrolled the same block called each other brother. When a person was treated by a medicine man or woman, the patient was considered a child of the curers as the following anecdote illustrates:

> That woman is like a daughter to me (the woman was older than the person relating the incident). Francisco made the medicine for her when she was sick so now he is a father to her. One night I was home and Francisco came over and got me so I got up and put my moccasins on and went to Francisco's house. Then some people came and got us and we went to her house. Now I am a mother to her and I have to help her if she wants.[42]

White described two types of curing rites, one involved only one or two curers, the other was carried out by all members of the society and required a vast amount of ritual and sacred objects.[43] Nowhere in his account, however, was an indication that a kin relationship was created between the patient and the curers. Most of the fictive kin relationships carried reciprocal obligations of one sort or another. They served to enlarge a person's network of relatives and bind him or her even more tightly into the Pueblo social organization.

There were times when the patient did not recover despite the best ministrations of the curers. As death approached a relative took a corn husk package of cornmeal and pulverized turquoise to the head of one of the four major medicine societies, asking them through prayer to attend the passing. He with his associates walked solemnly to the house; there they watched and waited for the end. After the priests pronounced the victim dead, grieving householders gathered the deceased clothing for the priests to "kill" by tearing each garment. The body and the torn articles were wrapped in a new blanket and tied with a woman's belt. After washing their faces and hands, the medicine men spoke of the dead person traveling to Shipap to join the corn mother and the *Katsinas*.

Burial took place in the churchyard; men on the northside, women on the south. *Bickari* major and his *Bickari* officiated at the predominantly Spanish Catholic service. Family and friends attended the interment.

[41]Kupferer, field notes, 1962.
[42]Ibid.
[43]White, *The Santo Domingo Indians of New Mexico*, p. 158.

Four days later family, close friends, and the medicine society assembled in the deceased's house to conduct the final rites. The medicine men set up their altar, placing ritual objects such as bear claws, a corn fetish, and a medicine bowl close by. Painstakingly, they made a meal painting before the altar. A trail of meal led from it to the door. Singing and praying the doctors placed an ear of corn, symbolic of the dead's heart, and a wooden poker to defend it, on the bear paws. Women put food along the meal trail to be offered to the deceased. Shortly afterward, the priests bundled up the departed's ritual clothing; one of them left to bury the package in an arroyo. In his absence the remaining priests sang and prayed. He returned and joined in the singing. The parents, real or fictive, if the natural parents were dead, received a corn fetish which they held to their breast. Dipping eagle feathers into a medicine bowl the priests sprinkled the altar, the sacred objects, and the people. After a final set of chants, women served food. The medicine society ate and departed; the deceased began its journey to Shipap.

Scarcely a month passed without an annual ritual or an impromptu one interrupting the tenor of daily life. Had a prolonged dry spell scorched the fields Masewi called for a corn dance. Putting aside their work, designated men and women of the *kivas* danced in the heat and the dust, often in a hot wind. In late June, San Juan's day and San Pedro's day were celebrated by foot races and a "rooster pull." The *Cacique* and the rest of the *principales* gathered in front of the church to the ringing of the bell; at the side of the church was a band of forty or fifty mounted men. A *Bickari* rode toward them dressed in ritual clothing; the riders clustered about him. He handed one of them an object resembling a copper gourd; wheeling they rode furiously out of sight only to return in about five minutes. A *principale* blew a few notes on an old bugle, the church bell rang, and another officer beat a snare drum. The *Bickari* approached the riders holding a white rooster; he plucked a few feathers from it; the bird squawked in protest as it was handed to a rider. He dashed out of the church yard flogging his horse with the hapless fowl and galloped through the pueblo streets with the others in noisy pursuit, attempting to snatch the rooster from him. After several passes, a rider seized part of it, the pair tugged on the rooster until one emerged victorious with the bleeding, dying bird. The scene was repeated until there were no more chickens. The chase started again when the *Bickari* handed a roll of cloth to a rider who rode off on his sweating horse towards the hills followed by the others snatching at the calico. The chases continued through the afternoon until as one bystander observed there was nothing left to hand out. At times during the melee the bugle and drum sounded. To end the affair the participants gathered at the church; Masewi delivered a lengthy talk in which he told the men that they had done well and they should take care of their horses. The contestants rode slowly to the corral, while the rest of the crowd drifted off in the dust.

The rooster pull represented a fusion of Spanish ritual with Pueblo ideology. White was told that the racing is to help the clouds come out and bring rain; the blood of the roosters blessed the land; the sweat of man and horse is a prayer for rain.[44]

People in the pueblo named after saints, as most were, celebrated their saint's day with a feast. It was not unusual to have more than one feast on the same day, especially on St. Juan's day. Days before the date, the family began preparations: The adobe house had to be plastered and calcimined. Dozens of loaves of bread went in and out of the oven the day before. At least one sheep was slaughtered and gallons of hot chile stirred and cooked. Close kin pitched in to help with the heaviest labor. On the appointed day a statue of the saint stood on a box or a table, a candle burning in front of it. Religious cards and turquoise beads dangled from its neck. Indian ritual clothing and objects hung on the walls and from the *viga* (rafters). Friends, both Indian and non-Indian, streamed into the small house to eat, visit, and gossip. Most brought a gift for the honoree. At the end of the affair surplus foods were distributed to lingering kin and friends.

Like its people, each pueblo had a patron saint whose "day" was celebrated with a "corn dance." Santo Domingans honored their saint on the fourth of August. In the week preceding the event everyone was occupied preparing for the affair: Village streets were swept; householders plastered their houses and collected quantities of food; every house was opened to visitors to eat, drink, and rest. Dancers and singers practiced nightly and vomited in the society houses. There was never a night without the sound of drums. An important task which fell to women and girls was plastering the church. Only the infirm were excused; the chore required four or five days of strenuous labor. Under the watchful eyes of pueblo officers women swarmed around the structure dipping cloth pads into the viscous mixture and smearing it on the adobe walls. Younger ones climbed tall ladders to reach inaccessible places; little girls carried pails back and forth to be refilled. At the end of each day the weary workers smeared with whitewash trudged home.

On the evening of August 3, men placed small cottonwood saplings in the earth along all the village streets and erected a cottonwood bower on the east side of the plaza. In every house on the morning of the fourth people bustled around. Women laid out the food shouting instructions to anyone within earshot; others dressed in their finest to attend mass; excited children got in everyone's way. Men and boys slipped away in an attempt to escape female exhortations. Dancers put on their elaborate ceremonial garb, women at home, men in the *kiva*.

At the end of the mass the church emptied in a procession led by two

---

[44]The accounts of the rooster pull, individual feast days, and Santo Domingo Day came from Kupferer. A comparison with White and earlier accounts revealed little change through the years.

Santo Domingo Corn Dance, circa 1899.
Smithsonian Institution National Anthropological Archives.

Bickari holding long, decorated staffs aloft. Another followed bearing a crucifix; the priest came after him. Four men emerged carrying a bier on which Saint Domingo rode. Behind it marched a group of male singers. Accompanying the procession were a drummer and bugler. They paraded up and down the pueblo streets to the bower in which the saint was gently placed. Fine Navajo rugs hung from the shelter frame, incense burned inside; the *Cacique* and other *principales* sat on benches along the wall.

The Koshare appeared from the Turquoise *kiva* capering and joking; they romped through the town warning the dancers to go to the *kiva*. Bandelier in 1882 was incensed by their obscene behavior:

> Drinking urine out of bowls . . . eating excrements and dirt, ashes and clay, washing each others faces with urine and with every imaginable dirt, imitating cohabitation and sodomy, were the principal jokes of the abominable leaders of the Koshare.[45]

Although vulgarities, some amusing, continued after his time, overt sexual acts had all but vanished by 1962, at least in dances that outsiders were permitted to attend. Hollow drum beats reverberated from the *kivas* while the men dressed and the women entered to get their wooden *tabilita* head pieces and spruce branches.

Soon 215 Turquoise *kiva* dancers appeared on the flat roof and descended the steps; sixty-five singers and a drummer tread closely behind. Male dancers wore white breech cloths with fox furs dangling from a belt of bells. Strings of shell beads hung diagonally across their painted chests. Garters of bells circled their legs below their knees. Their moccasins were trimmed with skunk fur. Hair, ritually washed in yucca suds, fell loosely over their shoulders. Bunches of parrot feathers adorned the crowns of

[45]Bandelier, *The Southwestern Journals*, p. 367.

their heads. In the right hand they carried a rattle, a spruce sprig in the left. Black sleeveless mantas covered the women; left shoulders were bare. Around their waists were wide woven Hopi belts. Wound tightly on their left wrists was a string of black oblong beads. Their hair, also ritually washed, flowed down their backs. In each hand they held spruce twigs. In spite of the scorching sand they danced barefooted.

Beneath the hot sun the long line filed to the church to dance. As the Turquoise people returned to the plaza, Squash dancers and singers streamed out of their *kiva* and moved toward the church. Spectators ringed the plaza; many men and boys stood or sat on roof tops.

The returning dancers congregated in the vicinity of their *kivas*. At a gesture from the dance leader the Turquoise people formed two long lines, each male dancer separated by two women dancers. The drummer set the rhythm; the singers—elderly men clad in loose white cotton trousers and a shapeless shirt cinched in by silver concho belts—picked up the beat with song. Dancers moved up and down the plaza; men stamped more vigorously than the women. A searing west wind blew, suffocating dust obscuring the lines from time to time. Babies wailed, spectators wandered back and forth from the houses to rest and eat. Braving the dust and heat, very young children as well as elderly folk danced. After about 45 minutes the dancers withdrew and the Squash people took their place, each man separated by one woman.

The groups continued through the day alternating with one another. Koshare grotesquely imitated the dancers and jibed spectators. When each Kiva had performed for the final time, the dancers lined up at the shrine and entered it in pairs while an old man played a snare drum and another blew toneless blasts on a battered bugle. *Bickari* carried the saint back to the church. The dancers vanished, visitors left, and the dust settled. Domingans returned to their houses contented, for their saint was honored, and confident that the *Shiwana* would send clouds and the crops would ripen.[46]

Chill in early morning portended the end of summer. Farmers harvested corn and wheat; families gathered squash, beans, and melons. Hot chili peppers were strung and hung to dry. *Kokatc*, the ditch boss, ordered the ditches closed. Masked *Katsina* danced; Koshare policed communal rabbit hunts.

In November the ritual cycle intensified. On the first day of the month the return of the dead was marked by the *Ki'botni* ceremony. *Shiwana* danced in the *kiva*, women cooked rabbits provided by early morning hunters. After the feast men made "lunches" for the dead, wrapping bits of food and *wabani* (prayer feathers) in cloth bundles. Anyone who wished to pray and feed the "grandfathers" dug a hole and poured the

    [46]Adolph F. Bandelier and Edgar L. Hewett. *Indians of the Rio Grande Valley*. (New York: Cooper Square Publishers, Inc., 1973), p. 55.

bundle contents into it. After dark a huge bonfire burned in the church yard and the bells rang through out the night.

At the winter solstice the sun rises at its most southern point on the eastern horizon. It was then that people of the pueblo united in the *Haniko* ritual to assist the sun to return to the north. Members of the four medicine societies retreated to their houses to vomit and lay down meal paintings. Ordinary people vomited too, adding their ritual strength in the effort to pull the sun back. Throughout the elaborate ceremonies, cooked (initiated members of the various societies), *crutsi* (uncooked), *sicti* (common people), and children worked together to help the sun on its journey from the south. *Crutsi* (uncooked men) danced in the *kivas* and young boys were encouraged to impersonate medicine men. Moieties dueled with one another in song. Society heads talked long about how they "wanted the sun to come back." Participation of everyone in the ceremony testified to the importance of the sun as well as water to Pueblo existence.

On ensuing days in December the Warrior society danced Comanche or Scalp Dances. Selected *kiva* members performed the Buffalo Dance to symbolize the relationship between the people and the animals that furnished winter food.[47] Days grew longer as the sun rose higher in the sky, and the pueblo rejoiced in his return with the *Hanikikya* ceremony which differed little from *Haniko*. The medicine societies undertook general curing ceremonies for the village. Praying, singing, laying down meal paintings, and preparing herbal concoctions for all to drink, they rid the village of illness and witches.

As the vernal equinox approached, the Koshare danced; farmers examined their seed and walked from the village to their fields, planning for the start of another growing season. Then the day came when the order came to clean and open the ditches.

Tight ritual and social organization controlled most Domingans' behavior, especially as it affected the integrity of the pueblo. Sacred and secular *principales* were powerful enforcers of discipline. Early chroniclers of Domingan society alluded to a practice of forcing a miscreant to stand nude in a circle until he fainted. Edward Dozier observed that if there were repeated violations of behavior which threatened the ceremonial and social life, the officers, "Pueblo gestapo," as he called them, dealt promptly and severely with the offender.[48] A Zuni couple visiting Santo Domingo watched the governor and an officer whip a *teniente* through the streets because he was an habitual drinker.[49]

Conduct that in one way or another annoyed villagers was condemned by gossip, often malicious. This author was told: "That Anna has a

[47]White, *The Santo Domingo Indians of New Mexico*, p. 23.

[48]Edward P. Dozier, "Rio Grande Pueblos," in *Perspectives in American Indian Culture Change*. Edward N. Spicer, ed. (Chicago: University of Chicago Press, 1961), p. 171.

[49]Personal communication from Dennis Tedlock, 1965.

terrible reputation. Everybody in the pueblo hates her; she ran around with everybody, even 16-year-old boys. She is separated from her husband and that last baby, when it was born, the council made them get back together again."[50] Especially nettlesome people were believed to be witches. "One time when my father was a boy," a young woman said, "he and another boy went swimming. When they came out of the water they saw an old man there. The boy ran away but my Daddy didn't. He know who that witch was, it was his uncle!"[51] Domingans believed, too, that strange afflictions beset people who violated pueblo norms: They grew wrinkled and old before their time; their crops failed; or they died suddenly. Such informal methods of social control were present in all Native American peoples.

In some these methods were the sole means of affecting behavior; in others like the Santo Domingans, they existed in consort with societally approved methods.

The Colorado Plateau hardly seemed to be an area conducive to agriculture; yet the Anasazi, ancestors of historic Pueblo Indians, persisted. From their earliest beginnings, the period labeled Basketmakers by archaeologists, people experimented with cultivation. Long winters produced moist soil, benefitting grain-type crops. Slowly, gathering was supplanted by gardening and nomadic life yielded to permanent villages. Climatic changes in the eighth century AD—shorter milder winters and tumultuous summer rain—produced problems. Water was insufficient to germinate seeds in the spring and so abundant in the summer as to threaten crops. The situation spurred innovation. Men planted drought-resistant corn diffused from Mexico in small, protected plots in valleys. Later they learned to terrace fields, construct dams, and build ditches to control water. Despite the adversities, they remained devoted to village life. By the 1300s, some towns sheltered 1200 or more people. At the close of the thirteenth century the plateau suffered an extended drought and a return to longer winters which caused the folk to abandon northern towns such as Mesa Verde and to establish communities in the more hospitable Rio Grande valley.[52]

Through the centuries the Pueblos borrowed and invented techniques to cope with the challenges of their environment. They abandoned some areas and rebuilt in others, always sustained by their beliefs. Origins of Pueblo ideology are lost in the mists of the long ago, but surely the vastness of the land and sky, the beauty of mountain and mesa, and the life-sustaining crops shaped primitive philosophers' cosmology. Domingan supernaturals and ritual centered on corn, water, and health. All ceremonial

[50]Kupferer, field notes, 1962. The story may be accurate, but the woman was certainly not the only person who engaged in such behavior.

[51]Ibid. It is possible that the uncle in question was the mother's brother.

[52]This abbreviated account of Pueblo cultural evolution comes from Alice B. Kehoe, *North American Indians*. (Englewood Cliffs, NJ: Prentice-Hall, 1981), pp. 113–116.

drama, even that introduced by the Spanish, was in some way related to these fundamental concerns. To live in villages supported by agriculture required some form of political control. The gods provided the template for social and political life, too. Through a long, complicated harmonizing of technology, social organization, sacred belief, and environment, Domingan culture took shape as an effective, adaptive strategy.

EPILOGUE

Until the post-World War II years, Santo Domingo was little changed from the post-Spanish era. After the war, pickup trucks and cars slowly replaced horse and wagon. Money became much more important to the welfare of people. Younger men and some women traveled to Santa Fe or Albuquerque to work. Their earnings were fed back into the village in order to support their parents and younger brothers and sisters. Silversmiths improved their skills, and their wives helped, drilling shell and turquoise. Sisters or wives sold the jewelry on the Governor's porch in Santa Fe. Younger people substituted Anglo clothing for traditional styles, reserving the traditional wear for ritual. Electricity and water lines appeared in the pueblo.[53] Yet the soul of the pueblo persists. Officers zealously protect the traditional beliefs from outsiders, a development prompted by Spanish efforts to root out "pagan" religion. Masked dances continue. In the black pueblo night drums throb, evoking vague apprehension in the Anglo listener. What future years may bring is difficult to predict, but for the present, Santo Domingans endure.

[53]Harriet J. Kupferer, "Material Change in a Conservative Pueblo," *El Palacio* 69, 1962:248–251.

Conclusion:
Part Four

Despite living in vastly different environments, both the Cherokee and the Keres Pueblos based their traditional economy on agriculture. Both cultivated crops domesticated in Mexico and, through the centuries, improved upon them. Mountain-dwelling Cherokee planted in fertile bottomlands; when the need arose additional land was available for clearing. Rain was sufficient for growing. Santo Domingans living in the arid southwest relied upon irrigation from the nearby Rio Grande. Rain was important too; it watered fields; but more significantly it kept the river alive. Both peoples hunted to supplement their diets. Game was plentiful and nearer at hand in the Cherokee region. Only rabbits were readily hunted near the pueblo. To capture large animals demanded long treks to distant mountains and desert. Sheep introduced by the Spanish in the 1600s lessened the need to wander afar in search of meat. Like hunting peoples, Cherokee and Santo Domingans sought success in the game quest through appropriate ritual. But it was the welfare of their crops—corn in particular—that evoked the most fervent calendrical ceremonials. Their disparate views of the universe were in great measure responsible for the differences in form and content of their rituals.

Both were town dwellers. Cherokee villages were scattered throughout the Smoky Mountains. Trails connected them, and traveling Indians found relatives in almost all of them. Santo Domingo was one of five compact Keres-speaking towns. The situation in some ways resembled the Cherokee circumstance in that the Pueblo cultures were very similar. Each had the same clans but there was very little to suggest that members considered themselves kin. Keresan towns were far more ethnocentric than were Cherokee hamlets. Both the pueblos and Cherokee towns were politically autonomous. Governments were, however, quite different.

Every Cherokee male after 50 was automatically a member of the council. Decisions depended upon the consensus and "consent of the governed." Ideally, coercion and dominating postures did not occur. Matriclans and lineages rebuked their members, avenged their deaths, and allotted land. Individual Cherokee behavior was guided by the tenets of the Harmony ethic.

Domingan town affairs were rigidly controlled by two sets of officials, one traditional, the other forced upon them. Although separate and appointed by different societies, they worked together to monitor behavior. Here consensus was not the norm. Decision-making powers were inherent in the positions. Unlike the Cherokee, except for the benevolent *Cacique*, all officers were replaced yearly. The rotation mitigated against power becoming entrenched in a few. Cherokee government was in effect, a self-perpetuating gerontocracy, but the Harmony ethic prevented capricious exercise of power by the "beloved old men." It is tempting to account for the contrasting political systems by turning to an ecological explanation.

Town life is made possible by a steady and reasonably predictable food supply. While both the Cherokee and the Santo Domingans could have maintained themselves as wandering foragers, they elected to expend the energy necessary for cultivation. Town life usually presumes some sort of political system, but the form depends upon other variables. Two important ones are the nature of the major food supply and the method employed to produce it.

Cherokee and Domingans farmed, but Cherokee farm land was plentiful in relationship to population. The tribe controlled a vast territory; numbers of swift-flowing rivers and creeks created rich bottomlands. Potential town sites were almost unlimited. Rain and snow kept the cove soils moist. Individual movement from one settlement to another was easy. Fallowing land and clearing new was always possible. To farm required no concerted communal effort. Each extended family tended its own fields and it "rained on the just and the unjust alike." The environment and the technology used to exploit it produced no compelling reason for strong centralized government. The Harmony ethic, perhaps present in the people before the growth of sedentary life and so much a part of Cherokee personality, kept interpersonal friction at a minimum.

Santo Domingans faced an entirely different set of environmental challenges to farming. Fertile land lay close to the river but the region was arid. Rain, when it came, was often torrential and brief, not of great benefit to tender plants. Wheat could survive but other crops depended upon irrigation. The large canal carrying water to Santo Domingo started almost 15 miles away from the village. The main ditch and secondary ditches leading to individual fields had to be cleaned in the spring, one or more times in August, usually right after the Feast day, and closed in the fall. Ditch maintenance without modern machinery required organized labor of many men. A leader with authority was necessary to coordinate the efforts— authority to assign tasks and to see that none escaped them.

For a few discontented people to leave and establish a new village was almost impossible. Could they have found river land not already owned by neighboring pueblos, the labor necessary to construct an adequate water system would have been beyond their abilities. Neither could individuals leave one pueblo to live in another with impunity. The inflexible circumstances seem to have compelled the Santo Domingans to remain in their densely populated town living "cheek by jowl." Ditch irrigation laid the ground work for centralized authority and the compact town life that fostered it.

While specific histories are always important factors in shaping cultures, the importance of ecological factors should not be ignored. One hypothesis, that differences between Cherokee and Santo Domingo habitats explain, at least in part, the contrast in their sociopolitical organization, is appealing.

CHAPTER TWELVE

Native North American Adaptations

In this work Native North American populations (or tribes) have been grouped according to their primary modes of subsistence rather than by culture areas. Underlying this organization was an ecological perspective which argues that culture, in general, is an adaptive system: a collection of strategies and patterns people devise to obtain and use resources in their environments. Note, however, that their choices may not have been the only options, nor necessarily, the best ones. Obtaining resources depends upon available technology, human organization and creativity, and beliefs about the universe. Cultural ecology assumes, too, a functional relationship between environment, technology, social organization, and beliefs and values. A few would claim that technology was the most important variable but as Bennett commented, from illusions or perceptions of nature, human institutions are constructed.[1]

Efforts to apply modern rigorous cultural ecological methods to Native North American societies are few and they often focus on a single institution or behavior pattern. We will review some.

In great detail, Bruce Winterhalder scrutinized the ecology of the Ontario Boreal zone as a foundation for his research on the foraging be-

---

[1]John W. Bennett, *The Ecological Transition: Cultural Anthropology and Human Adaptation.* (New York: Pergamon Press, 1976) p. 253.

havior of a small Cree community in northern Ontario. In addition to isolating the small-scale spatial heterogeneity of the boreal forest, called *patches* or *grain*, which challenge human adaptations, he pointed out the limitations of normative environmental analysis as an explanatory device for specific foraging behavior and its consequences. People hunt animals, not averages; daily snowfall and temperatures, rather than yearly mean amounts, affect hunting.[2] In a related research on foraging strategies, Winterhalder painstakingly calculated time and energy costs in maintaining a hare snare line and in moose hunting. With even more specificity he chronicled the activities in time spent—from minutes to hours—of a beaver-trapping trip.[3] His methods and the data collected contribute in no small measure to a methodology of ecological anthropology.

Harvey A. Feit was interested in the extent to which Cree hunters conserved and managed the animal populations on which they depended. Feit noted the Cree ideology with respect to animals and nature: "Animals give themselves so people can live," therefore animals must be accorded respect and must not be killed for sport. Feit theorized that this principle ideally fostered a balance between humans and animals. But to discover whether, in fact, such a balance existed he calculated the calories expended to hunt moose, beaver, and in fishing, and the calories they provided the hunter and his dependents. Moose hunting followed by beaver was the most efficient with respect to calories expended and the daily human caloric requirements. If these animals decreased in number, energy to hunt them increased and the catch dropped below daily adult caloric needs. People then turned to fish, small game, and commercial food to meet their needs and curtailed the hunt for moose and beaver. Feit concluded that the Waswanipi hunters did manage their harvests of moose and beaver and the distribution and reproduction of the harvested populations either by rotational use of territories, or by an increased use of alternate resources.[4]

Searches for the relationship between environment and selected cultural behavior among the boreal forest people were carried on by others. In them, often the descriptive accounts of the environment were very general. Typical of these was Roger's explanation of dissimilarities between the Cree and the Ojibwa social organization. Both lived in the Canadian boreal forest. Within it, Rogers identified two major subregional environments. The Cree lived in the Laurentian Upland of Quebec and the Hudson Bay Lowland. Inhabiting the Laurentian Upland of Ontario, an area richer in resources, were the Ojibwa.

[2]Bruce Winterhalder, "History and Ecology of the Boreal Zone in Ontario," in *Boreal Adaptations.* A. T. Steegman, Jr., ed. (New York: Plenum Press, 1983) pp. 9–54.

[3]Bruce Winterhalder, "Boreal Foraging Strategies," in *Boreal Forest Adaptations,* pp. 201–241.

[4]Harvey A. Feit, "The Ethno-ecology of Wasanipi Cree; or How Hunters Can Manage Their Resources," in *Cultural Ecology,* B. Cox, ed. (Toronto: Steward and McClelland, Ltd., 1973), pp. 115–125.

Both peoples utilized similar adaptive technologies and in both, the hunting group composed of several nuclear families, was the significant economic unit. Band members congregated only in the summer. Cree and Ojibwa bands were about the same size but population densities (number of square miles per person) were not. In the Ojibwa territory, population density was greater although the size of the hunting groups and bands did not increase. Moreover, during the summer assemblies, Ojibwa houses were often a mile apart while the Cree dwellings were close together. Finding no plausible environmental factor to explain the situation, Rogers speculated that another was at work. He found it in attitudes about witchcraft. The Ojibwa were driven by the fear of witchcraft; the Cree were not as preoccupied with it. The Ojibwa, therefore, distrusting their fellows, kept their hunting groups and bands small, although their environment would have allowed larger aggregates. Summer settlements were dispersed for the same reason.[5]

The articulation of Eskimo life with the environment has also received its share of attention. Eskimo were distributed in "tribes" from Alaska to Greenland. Although the vast territory is labeled the arctic, there are extensive environmental variations within it. Major sociocultural differences occurred among its residents too. Typical of certain Alaskan and Greenland Eskimo were large permanent or semipermanent villages of houses of wood, stone, and sod. Interior Canadian peoples were fragmented and mobile, living in snow houses in winter and caribou hide tents in spring and summer. These and other differences were with confidence attributed to the variations in environment and especially in food resources.

Variant cultural and social behavior as well as similarities were also present among Central Canadian groups. David Damas undertook to locate reasons, observing that the variations between the Copper, Netsilik, and Iglulik were not of great magnitude and character but were sufficiently important to require explanation.[6] Although the general features of their environment were alike, he posited two subenvironmental or exploitative zones as he called them. The Iglulik roamed one: Although living at a distance from one another, the Copper and Netsilik people occupied the other.

Whether there were differences in magico-religious beliefs, Damas did not say: He concentrated on parallels and disparities in social organization. All three groups congregated in large winter settlements—50 to 150 people—to hunt seal at breathing holes. Because it could never be predicted at which hole a seal might appear, manning a number of them was

[5]Edward S. Rogers, "Natural Environment-Social Organization-Witchcraft: Cree vs Ojibway—a Test Case." National Museum of Canada, Bulletin No. 230, 1969, pp. 24–39.

[6]David Damas, "The Diversity of Eskimo Societies" in *Man the Hunter*, Richard B. Lee, Irven Devore, eds. (Chicago: Aldine Publishing Co., 1968), p. 115.

mandatory. Less than ten hunters would have been inadequate to the task. Large winter camps, therefore, were a function of the winter habits of seal. During the rest of the year the peoples split into smaller groups for economic pursuits. The fragmentation was related to the habits of game and fish and the modes of procurement.

Damas also sought ecological explanations for differences between the Iglulik and the other two. Marriage preferences differed. To wed kin was favored by the Netsilik and the Copper Eskimo; the Iglulik banned such marriages. To account for the disparity, Damas turned to the practice of female infanticide. The Netsilik and Copper people often killed infant females, an institution which presumably had group survival value for them. The Iglulik did not engage in it, apparently, because their economic circumstances were not as straitened. Infanticide skewed the sex ratio and lowered the population. For Netsilik and Copper Eskimo males to have a chance at getting a spouse, the stretching of the definition of incest was useful.

That similar traits appeared in both the Iglulik and Netsilik was vexing and raised some question about ecological relationships. Damas, however, recognized that his attempt to use ecology as an explanatory device might appear to be superficial. Research, he thought, using caloric intake and expenditure, careful censusing of animals, and daily climatic conditions might have revealed ecological causes. But these refined techniques were no longer possible for the Central Canadian region because of changing cultures and technology. Even if it were possible, Damas suggested that a consideration of historical factors—migration, diffusion, cultural drift—would strengthen ecological analyses, serving both as a control and a supplement to explicate more fully the connections between societies and their physical, cultural, and social universes.[7]

While hunters and gatherers drew the most attention, culture patterns of others also prompted investigation. The intriguing and exotic Northwest Coast potlatch received its share of anthropological investigations and speculations. Potlatching was the showering of food and expensive gifts upon guests from other villages, or in some cases, clans, in return for their recognition of their host's social rank and prestige. Initial interpretations of the institution ignored or denied any relationships between it and the environment. Drucker and Heizer, for example, asserted that shortages in food and other resources were most uncommon along the Northwest Coast and the idea of starvation was absurd.[8] For them, the potlatch was a "formal procedure for social integration; its prime purpose being to identify publicly the membership of a group and to define the social

[7]David Damas, "Environment, History, and Central Eskimo Society," in *Cultural Ecology*, B. Cox, ed. pp. 269–301. For a discussion and critique of Damas and Balikei, see David Riches, *Northern Nomadic Hunter-Gatherers*. (New York: Academic Press, 1982), pp. 82–89.

[8]Philip Drucker and Robert F. Heizer, *To Make My Name Good*. (Berkeley: University of California Press, 1967), p. 39.

status of this membership."[9] Rosman and Rubel, in the same vein said of the Kwakiutl potlatch that it took place among kin groups who exchanged wives, thus it reflected the combination of hostility and solidarity typical of the relationship between in-laws.[10] These kinds of explanations were based upon structure-function theory.

Ecologically minded scholars who, while not dismissing such analyses, found ecological explications more satisfying. Wayne Suttles was among the first to search for connections between the "irrational" potlatch and the environment. Among the Salish people, he wrote, the potlatch was one of a number of ways to redistribute resources to adjust to local annual or longer term shortages which were due to environmental variations.[11] About Kwakiutl potlatching, Piddocke said that although their territory was rich and abundant, local regions fluctuated in resources and threatened inhabitants with famine. Potlatching between village chiefs effected exchanges of food and wealth thus insuring a level of subsistence for the total population. He added that whatever the origins, the hunger for prestige and consequent status rivalry between chiefs directly prompted potlatching and indirectly kept their followers producing goods beyond those needed for survival.[12]

Leland and Mitchell, using early historic records on salmon runs, were able to demonstrate statistically a correlation between salmon resources and prestige ranking of southern Kwakiutl villages. Local groups or winter villages having the richest resource bases enjoyed the highest prestige in the potlatch system. This in turn led to larger villages, which of course had an advantage over others in that they had more labor available for the production of food and goods.[13] While their work did not illustrate a one-to-one relationship between potlatching and environment, it showed a correlation between village size and prestige within the potlatch network and so supported the value of ecological hypotheses.

Although Elizabeth Colson did not treat the issue of potlatch and environment, she lent credence to the ecological tenet that resources were not always constant or abundant in the Northwest coast culture area. Aged Makah Indians living on the shores of Cape Flattery told her dismal stories of hard times when extreme deprivation threatened the lives of their parents and grandparents.[14]

[9]Ibid., p. 8.

[10]Abraham Rosman and Paula Rubel, *Feasting with Mine Enemy*. (New York: Columbia University Press, 1971).

[11]Wayne Suttles, "Coping with Abundance," in *Man the Hunter*, pp. 56–67.

[12]Stuart Piddocke, "The Potlatch System of the Southern Kwakiutl: A New Perspective," *The Southwest Journal of Anthropology* 21(1965):245–259.

[13]Donald Leland and Donald H. Mitchell, "Some Correlates of Local Group Rank Among the Southern Kwakiutl," *Ethnology* 14(1975):325–345.

[14]Elizabeth Colson, "In Good Years and Bad: Food Strategies of Self Reliant Societies," *Journal of Anthropological Research* 35(1979):18–29.

The disparate explanations of the potlatch are not "either/or" propositions. Potlatches had diversionary values: They validated social rank, and they reaffirmed cultural and social values. But they also motivated production, reallocated goods, stimulated social and economic cooperation under hereditary leaders, and emphasized continuity of chiefly rights in basic resources.

Meticulous cultural ecological studies on other Native Americans are few for reasons that are clear. Apart from arctic and subarctic peoples, most of the others have lived on reservations for a century or more; traditional subsistence patterns and technologies were long ago abandoned. Even with good historical records, accurate reconstructions of the fit between cultures and their environments are difficult, but the southwest did afford some opportunities. Richard I. Ford examined the eastern Pueblos through an ecological perspective.

Contrary to many ethnographic contentions about the security of the Pueblo economic system, Ford asserted that from pueblo to pueblo environmental conditions—rain, snowfall, frost, soil fertility, and animal depredations—varied. In fact, within a pueblo these factors often affected fields differently. After calculating calories needed and calories produced by San Juan Pueblo in 1890, he found that there was less than a two month's surplus. But more important, while the village may have had a surplus, individual households may have had more or far less than the average.[15] From information contained in early reports on the various villages, he found that such circumstances prevailed and famine or near starvation jeopardized some families.

How, then, in the absence of a leader empowered to commandeer food and distribute it to the needy, did the Pueblos cope with shortages? Ford postulated that rituals, both calendric and critical, (those attending individuals—births, initiations, illness, marriage, and death), served to diminish hardships. For any service performed for individuals by nonkin, people paid with food: corn meal, bread, or in some cases meat. Persons celebrating their Saint's day in Santo Domingo and other Keres villages prepared feasts for guests; these, of course were calendrical but they were individually sponsored and occurred throughout the year.

But it was in the dramatic and symbolically complex seasonal sacred pageants that the greatest quantity of food was offered. Although these ceremonial dramas took place year-round they were most numerous during the winter when shortages were most likely to plague people. All of them were characterized by the accumulation of food and its subsequent redistribution. Ford remarked that these rituals were examples of time-dependent regulation; they operated regardless of the needs of any indi-

[15]Richard I. Ford, "An Ecological Perspective on the Eastern Pueblos," in *New Perspectives on the Pueblos*, Alfonso Ortiz, ed. (Albuquerque: University of New Mexico Press, 1972), pp. 6–7.

vidual members of the pueblo. Sometimes, then, the redistribution function was only symbolic; at others it was very significant for assisting impecunious villagers.[16]

Pueblo survival was at times precarious. Because microenvironmental factors affected households differently, devices were needed to buttress stressed families. The numerous ritual events, some critical, some calendrical, provided this function.[17]

As I noted, apart from these studies and a few others, exacting ecological analyses of Native North American societies are few. Most accounts, including this volume, attempt to demonstrate linkages between cultures or features of cultures and their environments in general terms. Some stress the instrumental nature of culture, almost as if culture were a totally rational and sentient phenomenon, singling out technology as the key to adaptation. Others describe the relationship between culture and environment as one of mutual interaction and note that adaptations to the environment have consequences for most areas of life. Van Stone's *Athapaskan Adaptations* is an excellent example.[18]

True, a few descriptions come close to uttering truisms or stating the obvious: Hunters "pray" for game; farmers "pray" for crops. Yet, of course, less superficial inferences can be drawn. It is clear that foragers who use several microenvironments in their annual food quest alter their basic band organizations, coming together at one time, dispersing into smaller units at others. Colin Turnbull refers to this as flux, "the recurrent fission and fusion which affects the composition of local bands."[19] It is a social organizational response to hunting and gathering, regardless of whether the environment might be utilized differently.

Flux is related to several hunter-gatherer cultural characteristics. It implies a precise knowledge about environments and their seasonal opportunities; to congregate or divide without some assurance of food resources would be hazardous. Because of fluctuation in food supplies and equally as significant, inability to preserve quantities, sharing is a norm. Flux militates against the formation of institutionalized political authority. How can people be governed when they never "sit still?" The fluidity instead encourages the development of informal leadership which frequently shifts from one person to another. Indeed, power and authority often evoke ambivalence. Without centralized authority, social control relies upon diffuse mechanisms—often invoking "supernatural intervention"—and flux. Disputants, to avoid open hostility, frequently move to another group thus resolving

[16]Ibid., p. 14.

[17]Ibid., pp. 16–17.

[18]James van Stone, *Athapascan Adaptations: Hunters and Fishermen of the Subarctic Forests.* (Chicago: Aldine Publishing Co., 1974).

[19]Colin Turnbull, "The Importance of Flux in Two Hunting Societies," in *Man the Hunter,* p. 132.

conflict. Such nonrandom coming and going also creates a social environment ill-suited to the creation of corporate clans.

Less obvious, perhaps, is the relationship between environment subsistence and social organization and ideology. Yet it is there. Foragers' beliefs about the universe—usually perceived as the territory they travel—and the space above and below it, are forged from elements, some of them inexplicable, within it. This is, to be sure, not unique to them. Conceptions of the supernatural vary, of course, but they centered on life's exigencies, most often the capriciousness of animals and illness. Because of the seminomadic life and shifting of personnel, beliefs were not woven into well-formed theologies; individuals or small groups held idiosyncratic ideas. Likewise, most rituals were carried out by individuals or in small groups and were prompted by immediate circumstances. Shamans were the only mediators between this world and the other.

The Netsilik, the Cree, and the Washo, although they adapted to different environments, fit the general profile of hunter-gatherers and differed in major respects from people who combined foraging with gardening.

Societies which merged hunting and gardening seldom appear as subsistence types in the literature on Native North Americans, probably because the mode was so common in the New World after plant domestication. Yet the dual economy, usually featuring transhumancy, produced cultural characteristics which differentiated these peoples from hunter-gatherers, from the "opulent" nonfarmers, and from intensive gardeners. Because of this, some scholars have depicted their cultures as transitional between the others types, but it seems unlikely that they were transitional in any simple sense. Even with the example of the Pueblo farmers before them, the Havasupai and the Western Apache showed little inclination to give up their traditional economic cycle in favor of permanent village life supported by cropping. Yet adopting and adapting Pueblo technology to their specific physical circumstances would have allowed the change. The opposite question can be asked: Why did not the Pueblo people assume the Apachean life way? Did the "freedom" have no appeal for them? Would their gods have deserted them? There is more at work here than delayed cultural evolution and/or environmental constraints or stimuli. History and tradition, deep satisfactions with a way of life, and worldview must be part of ecological explanations or hypotheses.

Not only did cultural configurations of people engaged in a combined subsistence differ from other economic types, they differed in many dimensions from one another, yet they had characteristics in common.

Unilineal kinship systems resulting in lineages and/or clans were typical. Leaders or chiefs, either of lineages or villages, directed activities. Although their power and authority were limited, they lectured the people ex cathedra. Among the Apache, even more so among the Mandan, there was a trend toward differences in family or lineage prestige. Social control was effected both through informal techniques and more structured mechanisms. Supernatural beliefs differed in detail, but doctrines were fairly well systematized. Individuals practiced private rites (not uncommon in the most sophisticated of societies), but large community ceremonies figured prominently in the ritual life of these peoples.

To construct a cultural model to accommodate the part-time gardeners is not nearly so simple as it was for the semiisolated foragers who lived in marginal areas. A variety of factors influenced the ultimate shape of farming-hunting societies.

Although they employed broadly similar subsistence patterns, where they did so had important ramifications for each. Some of the differences among them can be attributed to the dissimilarities in their homelands. When we examine the ecological differences between the prairie-plains, the semiarid Arizona plateau, and the gentle Cataract canyon floor we can see how apparent their effects were on the people's adaptations. Yet environment and technology cannot directly account for the cultural diversity. Intervening variables, too, had their repercussions. Population size was one. The Havasupai never had more than several hundred people; there were a thousand or more Mandan; four thousand comprised the Apache. We can surmise that some of the cultural variations can be credited to group numbers. Historical events also had formative effects. Where did the people originate? What were their cultural antecedents? With whom did they come into contact? Some culture patterns can be traced to diffusion of ideas and objects; for example, the arrival of the horse was pivotal for the Mandan and the Apache.

Unsnarling the intertwined variables in a search for the most potent is a formidable and probably fruitless assignment. In our current state of knowledge, we can only ascribe the differences as well as the similarities to a complex skein of variables and history in an interplay with environment. We can conclude, as well, that they did constitute one of the cultural types of Native North Americans.

It has been an ethnographic custom to include the "affluent" hunters and fishermen in the hunter-gatherer category. Sociocultural differences, however, were so substantial that they demand a separate taxonomy. To do otherwise is comparable to lumping apples, oranges, and baseballs. To be sure, one might argue that pairing the Cheyenne and the Nootka is equally as grievous. Although they do differ from one another in many specifics, the richness of their cultures was a fundamental departure from both the foraging and the part-time hunting models.

Like the Apache, the Havasupai, and the Mandan, the Nootka were organized into clans and lineages; the Cheyenne, however, were bilateral as were the Cree, the Netsilik, the Washo, and modern Americans. Additional likenesses were few. The flux concept could be applied to the Cheyenne as they harmonized their yearly social and economic cycle with the feeding habits of the bison. When the animals congregated in large herds, the Cheyenne bands assembled. The Council of Fourty-four met; dramatic tribal rituals were performed; and the great orderly buffalo hunts took place. When the animals drifted away in smaller groups, the diaspora of the Cheyenne bands followed. But any resemblance to the peregrinations of the Cree, Netsilik, and Washo is superficial. Cheyenne bands did not divide into the smaller clusters typical of the other three. Tribal and band governance remained firmly in place; people never lost their awareness of their tribal affiliation.

Nootkan fortunes depended largely on salmon runs; other fishes, marine mammals, and berries and plants augmented their food supplies. The presence of winter villages and smaller summer villages was a response to salmon biology as well as to the weather. Reversing the Cheyenne pattern, Nootkans separated in the summer and congregated in the winter. Their impressive and startling ritual plays dissipated winter boredom. Whatever the function of potlatching and widespread feasting, they maintained the hereditary privileges of chiefs and gave them power to be used judiciously.

Distinctions between family or lineage prestige was well-established in both Cheyenne and Nootkan social structure. Nootkan, of course was hereditary, primogeniture was the deciding factor. Cheyenne distinctions were based upon wealth in horses, male courage, and female honor and dignity. These and many other traits clearly segregate the two from the simpler foragers and the part-time farmers in whom some of the characteristics were incipient.

Environmental factors are demonstrable in their effects on Cheyenne and Nootkan culture. Buffalo was the central resource of the Cheyenne, they provided food, clothing, shelter, and ritual focus. Man and animal were in a symbiotic relationship. The Cheyenne adaptation to the vast plains was, however, recent. Before they acquired horses they lived in villages, farming and hunting much like the Mandan-Hidatsa. With the mobility provided by horses, the great open land became a magnet. Abandoning sedentary life, they moved to the plains. Horses had a major imprint on Cheyenne culture.[20] An egalitarian society was replaced by one with social classes; intertribal raiding and warfare for horses and glory burgeoned. Regardless of whether their sophisticated political institutions were in place prior to the exodus, they reached their apogee on the open land. Contacts with the many other prairie and plains people had consequences too. All coalesced in the plains culture of the Cheyenne and provided a superb adaptation.

Nootkan life revolved around the river and sea. To harvest the riches

---

[20]Symmes Oliver, *Ecology and Cultural Continuity as Contributing Factors in the Social Organization of the Plains Indians.* (Berkeley: University of California Publications in American Archaeology and Ethnology, 1962).

they developed a marine technology. Weirs, nets, and a complex of fishing devices captured migrating salmon and other fishes. The capacity to preserve the fish released the people from food searches during cold inclement winters. Harpoons, lines, and drags brought great whales down. Carpentering, too, was a decisive skill in their technological baggage. Nootka men constructed large seaworthy canoes and erected huge houses from the tall timber fringing the beaches. Ritual and ideological beliefs received their inspiration from forest and ocean.

Where or why the system of hereditary chieftains developed cannot be uncovered; other political forms might have served as well. Kinship systems of some of their close neighbors differed from the Nootka. The roots of potlatching are obscure, too. Ecological analyses are limited in their ability to discover origins. But it is fair to claim that the Northwest Coast environment was a creative force in Nootkan culture.

The complex social structure and organization, the political institutions, the rich communal rituals combined to create a cultural grandeur far removed from all other native lifeways, except for some full-time farmers. They constitute an identifiable culture form.

Why did farmers farm? Farming is labor intensive; it is hard work. To claim dogmatically that environment favored it is implausible. Environment allowed, but did not create, a farming adaptation.

We may never know with any confidence why the Cherokee embraced it. Game appeared to be plentiful in the territory they claimed and wild edible plants flourished. What we do know is that knowledge of plant domestication entered the southeast from Mexico, probably traveling up the Mississippi River valley. Beginning in about 1500 BC it fanned outward and the native peoples slowly added it to their coping repertoire. By 1500 AD, the Cherokee depended upon their crops for their major food supply.

Horticulture seemed an even more unlikely choice for the semiarid Colorado plateau people. To do it successfully demanded technological ingenuity, especially in water control. Without irrigation, farming was impossible in most of the area. But here, wild food resources were not abundant. It may be that a more or less reliable food source, despite the arduous labor needed to produce it, outweighed trailing after elusive fauna and flora. In any case, Mexico was also the donor of agriculture to the southwest. It filtered in through southern Arizona and New Mexico reaching the Anasazi about 100 BC. By 700 AD, the typical Pueblo culture patterns had appeared and the people were dedicated farmers.[21]

Agriculture impinges forcefully and directly on human life: Residence patterns, social organization, political institutions, and sacred beliefs all respond to its influences. What specific form these institutions take,

[21]See Alice B. Kehoe, *North American Indians* (Englewood Cliffs, NJ: Prentice-Hall, 1961), pp. 151–166, for an account of the prehistoric events in the southeast. Pages 112–114 describe the course of agriculture in the southwest.

which distinguishes farmers from others, depends upon environmental characteristics working in concert with other variables less easy to tease out.

The Cherokee and Santo Domingans were farmers who exhibited some of the same cultural patterns: permanent villages occupied year around; matrilineal clans and lineages; theocratic political systems; and symbolically rich communal rituals directed by priests. Unlike the Nootka and the Cheyenne, neither evolved social classes. Was this because their primitive farming techniques did not allow individual families to produce wealth in food surpluses? Was it because the value of sharing and generosity discouraged acquisitiveness, or was it an interplay between the two?

In spite of the similarities one might expect in farming societies, there were differences, too. Santo Domingo men tended the fields; as far as we know, Pueblo warfare was mainly defensive. Keres governance was controlling. Cherokee government relied heavily on persuasion and affection for the aged. Cherokee women gardened; their men absented themselves on hunting expeditions and aggressive raiding, but only after the harvest; men could have done the cultivation. The dissimilarities in environment, culture development, and the history of the spread of agriculture in the two areas no doubt account for the differences. But we have no clear idea of their comparative influence.

The variation in water sources, however, may be responsible for the contrasting political systems. Ditch irrigation requires at least a minimum of cooperation; cooperation usually calls for coordination; coordination in turn requires some authority.[22] There is reason to think that authority was institutionalized among the people before they migrated to the Rio Grande valley, but we might suspect that the need to control water enhanced it. Because water meant success or failure, plenty or paucity, it is understandable that water was a major focus of religious behavior. To direct the communal sacred rituals concerned with water, the Pueblos vested authority in their sacred officers. Ultimately the power associated with their sacred status extended to other dimensions of village life.

Water in the cascading mountain rivers was precious to the Cherokee, too. But because it was a constant there was never a need to shepherd it; nor was it vital to their fields. It did, however, have a role in the governmental ideology. The roots of the Cherokee nonauthoritarian political system are shrouded by the distant past, but the rivers helped to maintain its form. In their waters, concealed animosities and interpersonal hostilities were ritually carried away each autumn, symbolically preparing the townspeople for another year of harmony.

In the preface, I somewhat boldly suggested that classifying cultures by their subsistence mode, thus implying an ecological turn of mind, ap-

---

[22]Karl Wittfogel in *Oriental Despotism: A Comparative Study of Total Power* (New Haven: Yale University Press, 1957) contended that "Oriental Despotism" developed from the need for bureaucratic organization required to control water resources.

peared to be as rational as employing the culture area concept for the purpose. The fundamental assumption was that common modes of earning a living would generate sufficient cultural similarities to justify speaking of culture "types," although some divergence from the model was to be expected. Using this approach to classify North American aboriginal societies yielded four cultural forms: foragers, part-time farmers, "affluent hunters and fishermen," and agriculturalists. Each was a distinctive adaptation which produced the cultural diversity among Native North Americans; their cultures were creative responses to their world as they conceived it to be. How lamentable that what required thousands of years to develop was almost totally obliterated in four hundred.

The haunting question, incapable of an answer is: What would have been the outcome if the People had had another century to themselves to continue their cultural adaptations?

References
Cited

ALLEN, JOHN LOGAN, *Passing Through the Garden: Lewis and Clark and the Image of the American Northwest*. Urbana: University of Illinois Press, 1975.

ALSBERG, HENRY G., and HARRY HANSEN, eds. *Arizona*. New York: Hastings House, 1966.

ASHE, GEOFFREY, "Analysis of the Legends," in *The Quest For America*, Geoffrey Ashe, ed. New York: Praeger Publishers, 1971.

BALIKCI, ASEN, *The Netsilik Eskimo*. Garden City, NY: Natural History Press, 1970.

BANDELIER, ADOLPH F., *The Southwestern Journals, 1880–1882*, Charles H. Lange and Carroll L. Riley, eds. Albuquerque: University of New Mexico Press, 1966.

BANDELIER, ADOLPH F. and EDGAR L. HEWETT, *Indians of the Rio Grande Valley*. New York: Cooper Square Publishers, Inc., 1973.

BASSO, KEITH H., *The Gift of Changing Woman*. Bulletin of the Bureau of American Ethnology No. 196, Washington, D.C., Smithsonian Institution, 1966.

BASSO, KEITH H., *Western Apache Witchcraft*. Anthropological Papers of the University of Arizona No. 15, Tucson: University of Arizona Press, 1971.

BASSO, KEITH H., *The Cibecue Apache*. Case Studies in Anthropology. New York: Holt, Rinehart and Winston, 1970.

BASSO, KEITH H., "To Give Up On Words: Silence in Western Apache Culture," in *Apachean Culture History and Ethnology*, Keith H. Basso and Morris E. Opler, eds. Anthropological Papers of the University of Arizona No. 21, 1971.

BENNETT, JOHN W., *The Ecological Transition: Cultural Anthropology and Human Adaptation*. New York: Pergamon Press, 1976.

BIRKET-SMITH, KAJ, *Ethnographic Collections From the Northwest Passage, Report of the Fifth Thule Expedition 1921–1924*, vol. 6. New York: Ams Press (Reprint 1976).

BIRKET-SMITH, KAJ, *The Eskimos*. New York: E. P. Dutton and Co., 1935.

BOAZ, FRANZ, *The Central Eskimo*. Lincoln: University of Nebraska Press, 1964. Original publication part of 6th Annual Report of the Bureau of American Ethnology, Washington, D.C., Smithsonian Institution, 1888.

BORDEN, CHARLES E., "Peopling and Early Cultures of the Pacific Northwest," *Science* 203(1979):963–971.

BOWERS, ALFRED W., *Mandan Social and Ceremonial Organization*, Chicago: The University Press, 1950.

BRUNER, EDWARD M., "Mandan," in *Perspectives in American Indian Culture Change*, Edward H. Spicer, ed. Chicago: University of Chicago Press, 1961.

CARTER, GEORGE F., *Earlier Than You Think: A Personal View of Man in America*. College Station: Texas A & M Press, 1980.

CATLIN, GEORGE E., *O-Kee-Pa: A Religious Ceremony and Other Customs of the Mandan*, John Ewers, ed. New Haven: Yale University Press, 1967.

COHEN, YEHUDI, *Man in Adaptation: The Cultural Present*. Chicago: Aldine Publishing Co., 1968.

COLE, GLEN, "Of Land Bridges, Ice Free Corridors, and Early Man in the Americas," *Bulletin of the Field Museum of Natural History*, Jan., 1979.

COLSON, ELIZABETH, *The Makah Indians*. Minneapolis: University of Minnesota Press, 1953.

COLSON, ELIZABETH, "The Good Years and Bad: Food Strategies of Self Reliant Societies," *Journal of Anthropological Research* 35(1979):18–29.

CRAVEN, MARGARET, *I Heard The Owl Call My Name*. Garden City, NY: Doubleday & Co., 1973.

DAMAS, DAVID, "The Diversity of Eskimo Societies," in *Man The Hunter*, Richard B. Lee, Irven DeVore, eds. Chicago: Aldine Publishing Co., 1968.

DAMAS, DAVID, "Environment, History, and Central Eskimo Society," in *Cultural Ecology: Readings on the Canadian Indians and Eskimos*, Bruce Cox, ed. Toronto: McClelland and Steward, LTD., Carleton Library Series, 1973.

D'ASEVEDO, WARREN L., ed. *The Washo Indians of California and Nevada*. University of Utah Anthropological Papers 67, 1963.

DENSMORE, FRANCES, *Mandan and Hidatsa Music*. Bureau of American Ethnology Bulletin No. 80, Smithsonian Institution, 1923.

DENSMORE, FRANCES, *Music of Santo Domingo Pueblo, New Mexico*. Southwest Museum Papers #12, 1938.

DORSEY, GEORGE, *The Cheyenne*. Field Columbian Museum Anthropological Series IX, 1903. New York: Kraus Reprint Co., 1971.

DOWNS, JAMES, *The Two Worlds of the Washo: Case Studies in Cultural Anthropology*. New York: Holt, Rinehart and Winston, 1966.

DOZIER, EDWARD, "Rio Grande Pueblos," in *Perspectives in American Indian Culture Change*, Edward H. Spicer, ed. Chicago: University of Chicago Press, 1961.

DRIVER, HAROLD, *Indians of North America*, 2nd ed. Chicago: University of Chicago Press, 1969.

DRUCKER, PHILIP, *The Northern and Central Nootkan Tribes*. Bureau of American Ethnology Bulletin 144, 1951.

DRUCKER, PHILIP, *Cultures of the North Pacific Coast*. San Francisco: Chandler Publishing Co., 1965.

DRUCKER, PHILIP and ROBERT F. HEIZER, *To Make My Name Good*. Berkeley: University of California Press, 1967.

DUTTON, BERTHA P., *The Pueblos*. Englewood Cliffs, NJ: Prentice-Hall, Inc., 1976.

DUTTON, BERTHA P., *The Rancheria, Utes, and Southern Paiute Peoples*. Englewood Cliffs, NJ: Prentice-Hall, Inc., 1976.

EGGAN, FRED, *The American Indian*. Chicago: Aldine Publishing Co., 1966.

EKHOLM, GORDON, "Diffusion and Archaeological Evidence," in *Man Across The Sea: Problems of Pre-Columbian Contacts*, Carroll J. Riley, Charles Kelly, Campbell W. Pennington, and Robert L. Rands, eds. Austin: University of Texas Press, 1971.

ERNEST, ALICE HENSON, *The Wolf Ritual of the Northwest Coast*. Eugene: University of Oregon Press, 1952.

EVERETT, MICHAEL, "Drinking As A Measure of Proper Behavior: The White Mountain Apache," in *Drinking Behavior Among Southwestern Indians*, Jack O. Waddell and M. Everett, eds. Tucson: University of Arizona Press, 1980.

EWERS, JOHN C., The Horse Complex in Plains Indian History," in *The North American Indians*, Roger C. Owen, James J. F. Deetz, and Anthony Fisher, eds. New York: MacMillan Co., 1967.

FEIT, HARVEY, "The Ethno-Ecology of the Waswanipi Cree; or How Hunters Can Manage Their Resources," in *Cultural Ecology: Readings on the Canadian Indian and Eskimo*, Bruce Cox ed. Toronto: McClelland and Stewart, Ltd., Carleton, Library Series, 1973.

FENNEMAN, NEVIN, *Physiography of Western United States*. New York: McGraw-Hill Book Co., 1931.

FISHER, ANTHONY D., "The Cree of Canada: Some Ecological and Evolutionary Considerations," in *Cultural Ecology: Readings on the Canadian Indians and Eskimo*. Bruce Cox, ed. Toronto: McClelland and Steward Ltd., Carleton Library Series, 1973.

FLANNERY, REGINA, "The Position of Women Among the Eastern Cree," *Primitive Man* 8(1935):81–86.

FLANNERY, REGINA, "Cross Cousin Marriage Among the Cree and Montagnais of James Bay," in *Primitive Man* 11(1938):29–33.

FLANNERY, REGINA, "The Shaking Tent Rite among the Montagnais of James Bay," in *Primitive Man* 12(1939):11–16.

FLINT, RICHARD FOSTER, *Glacial and Quaternary Geology*. New York: John Wiley and Sons, 1971.

FOGELSON, RAYMOND D., *The Cherokee Ball Game: A Study in Southeastern Ethnology*. PhD. Dissertation, University of Pennsylvania, 1962. University MicroFilms, Ann Arbor.

FORD, RICHARD I., "An Ecological Perspective on the Eastern Pueblos," in *New Perspectives on the Pueblos*, Alfonso Ortiz, ed. Albuquerque: University of New Mexico Press, 1972.

FOX, RUBIN, "Some Unsolved Problems of Pueblo Social Organization," in *New Perspectives on the Pueblos*, Alfonso Ortiz, ed. Albuquerque: University of New Mexico Press, 1972.

FREED, STANLEY A., *Changing Washo Kinship*. University of California Anthropological Records 14, 1960.

FREED, STANLEY A., "A Reconstruction of Aboriginal Washo Social Organization," in *The Washo Indians of California and Nevada*, Warren L. d'Asevedo, ed. University of Utah Anthropological Papers 67, 1963.

FREED, STANLEY A., and RUTH S. FREED, "A Configuration of Washo Culture" in *The Washo Indians of California and Nevada*, Warren L. d'Asevedo, ed. University of Utah Anthropological Papers 67, 1963.

GEARING, FRED, *Priests and Warriors: Social Structures for Cherokee Politics in the 18th Century*. American Anthropological Association vol. 64, memoir 93, 1962.

GETTY, HARRY T., *The San Carlos Indian Cattle Industry*. Anthropological Papers of the University of Arizona No. 7, 1963.

GILBERT, WILLIAM H., *The Eastern Cherokees*. Bureau of American Ethnology Bulletin 133, Smithsonian Institution, 1943.

GOODWIN, GRENVILLE, "The Characteristics and Function of Clan in a Southern Athapascan Culture," *American Anthropologist* 30(1937):394–407.

GOODWIN, GRENVILLE, *The Social Organization of the Western Apache*. Chicago: University of Chicago Press, 1942.

GOODWIN, GRENVILLE, *Western Apache Raiding and Warfare*, Keith H. Basso, ed. Tucson: University of Arizona Press, 1971.

GORDON, CYRUS H., *Before Columbus: Links Between the Old World and Ancient America*. New York: Crown Publishers, 1971.

GRIFFIN, JAMES B., "The Origin and Dispersion of American Indians in North America," in *The First Americans: Origins, Affinities, and Adaptations*. William S. Laughlin and Albert B. Harper, eds. New York: Gustav Fisher, 1979.

GRINNELL, GEORGE BIRD, *The Fighting Cheyenne*. Norman: University of Oklahoma Press, 1956.

GRINNELL, GEORGE BIRD, *The Cheyenne Indians: Their History and Ways of Life*, vols. 1 & 2. New York: Cooper Square Publishers, 1962.

HAAG, WILLIAM, "The Bering Strait Land Bridge," *Scientific American* 206(1962):112–123.

HARRIS, MARVIN, *The Rise of Anthropological Theory*. New York: Crowell Co., 1968.

HARRIS, MARVIN, *Cultural Materialism: The Struggle For A Science of Culture*. New York: Random House Vintage Books, 1980.

HAYNES, C. VANCE, JR., "Carbon 14 Dates and Early Man in the New World," in *Pleistocene Extinctions: The Search for a Cause*. Proceedings of the VIIth Congress of the International Association for Quaternary Research. New Haven: Yale University Press, 1967.

HAYNES, C. VANCE, JR., "Ecology of Early Man in the New World," in *Geoscience and Man*, vol. XIII, Ecology of the Pleistocene. R. C. West and William Haag, eds. Baton Rouge: Louisiana State University, 1976.

HESTER, JAMES J., "The Agency of Man in Animal Extinction," in *Pleistocene Extinctions: The Search for a Cause*. Proceedings of the VIIth Congress of the International Association for Quaternary Research. New Haven: Yale University Press, 1967.

HEYERDAHL, THOR, "Isolationist or Diffusionist," in *The Quest for America*. Geoffrey Ashe, ed. New York: Praeger Publishers, 1971.

HOEBEL, E. ADAMSON, *The Cheyennes: Indians of the Great Plains*. Case Studies in Anthropology. New York: Holt, Rinehart and Winston, Inc., 1960.

HOIG, STAN, *The Peace Chiefs of the Cheyenne*. Norman: University of Oklahoma Press, 1980.

HOIJER, "The Southern Athabascan Languages," *American Anthropologist* 30(1938).

HONIGMANN, JOHN J., *The Athawapiskat Swampy Cree: An Ethnographic Reconstruction*. Anthropological Papers of the University of Alaska 5, 1956.

HONIGMANN, JOHN J., "Interpersonal Relations and Ideology in a Northern Canadian Community," *Social forces* 35(1957):366–370.

HONIGMANN, JOHN J., "Indians of Nouveau, Quebec" in *Le Nouveau Quebec*, J. Malarie and J. Rousseau, eds. Paris: Mouton, 1964.

HOPKINS, DAVID, "Landscape and Climate of Beringia During Late Pleistocene and Holocene Time," in *The First Americans: Origins, Affinities, and Adaptations*. William S. Laughlin and A. B. Harper, eds., New York: Gustav Fisher, 1979.

HOWAY, FREDERICK W., ed., *Voyages of the "Columbia" to the Northwest Coast 1787–1790 and 1790–1793*. Massachusetts Historical Society Collections, LXXIX. Cambridge: Harvard University Press, 1941.

HUDDLESTON, LEE ELDRIDGE, *Origins of the American Indians*. Austin: University of Texas Press, 1967.

HUDSON, CHARLES. *The Southeastern Indians*. Knoxville: University of Tennessee Press, 1976.

JABLOW, JOSEPH, *The Cheyenne in Plains Indian Trade Relations: 1795–1840*. American Ethnological Society Monograph #19. Seattle: University of Washington Press, 1950.

JEFFREYS, M.D.W., "Pre-Columbian Maize in Asia," in *Man Across The Sea: Problems of Pre-Columbian Contacts*. Carroll J. Riley, Charles Kelley, Campbell W. Pennington, Robert Rands, eds. Austin: University of Texas Press, 1971.

JELINEK, ARTHUR J., "Man's Role in the Extinction of Pleistocene Faunas," in *Pleistocene Extinctions, The Search for a Cause*. Proceedings of the VIIth International Association for Quaternary Research. New Haven: Yale University Press, 1967.

JENNESS, DIAMOND, *Indians of Canada*, 7th ed. Toronto: University of Toronto Press, 1977.

JEWITT, JOHN R., *A Narrative of the Adventures and Sufferings of John R. Jewitt, 1815*. The Garland Library of Narratives of North American Indian Captives, Wilcomb E. Washborn, arranger. New York: Garland Publishing Co., 1976.

KEHOE, ALICE B., "Small Boats Upon the Atlantic," in *Man Across The Sea: Problems of Pre-Columbian Contacts*, Carroll J. Riley, Charles Kelley, Campbell W. Pennington, and Robert Rands, eds. Austin: University of Texas Press, 1971.

KEHOE, ALICE B., *North American Indians*. Englewood Cliffs, NJ: Prentice-Hall, Inc., 1981.

KNIGHT, ROLF, "A Re-examination of Hunting, Trapping, and Territoriality Among the North Eastern Algonkian Indians," in *Man, Culture and Animals*, Anthony Leeds and Andrew P. Vayda, eds. Washington, D.C., American Association for the Advancement of Science, 1965.

KROEBER, ALFRED L., "Demography of the North American Indians" in *The North American Indians*, Roger C. Owen, James D. F. Deetz, and Anthony D. Fischer, eds. New York: MacMillan Co., 1967.

KUPFERER, HARRIET J., "Material Change in a Conservative Pueblo," *El Palacio* 69 (1962):248–251.

KUPFERER, HARRIET J., *The Principal People, 1960: A Study of the Cultural and Social Groups of the Eastern Cherokee*. Bureau of American Ethnology Bulletin 196, Smithsonian Institution, 1966.

KUPFERER, HARRIET J., "Impotency and Power: A Cross Cultural Comparison of the Effect of Alien Rule," in *Political Anthropology*, Marc J. Swartz, Victor W. Turner, and Arthur Tuden, eds. Chicago: Aldine Publishing Company, 1966.

LAL, CHAMAN, *Hindu America*. New York: Chaman Lal, 1966.

LAUGLIN, WILLIAM S. and SUSAN WOLF, "Introduction," in *The First Americans: Origins, Affinities, and Adaptations*. William S. Laughlin and Albert B. Harper, eds. New York: Gustav Fisher, 1979.

LEIS, PHILIP E., "Washo Witchcraft: A Test of the Frustration-Aggression Hypothesis," in *The Washo Indians of California and Nevada*, Warren L. d'Asevedo, ed. University of Utah Anthropological Papers 67, 1963.

LELAND, DONALD and DONALD H. MITCHELL, "Some Correlates of Local Group Rank Among the Southern Kwakiutl," *Ethnology* 14(1975):325–345.

LLEWELLYN, K. N. and E. ADAMSON HOEBEL, *The Cheyenne Way*, Norman: University of Oklahoma Press, 1941.

LOWIE, ROBERT H., "Ethnographic Notes on the Washo," University of California Publications in American Archaeology and Ethnology 36, 1965.

MACNEISH, RICHARD, "Early Pleistocene Adaptations: A New Look at Early Peopling of the New World as of 1976," *Journal of Anthropological Research* 34(1978):474–496.

MANNERS, ROBERT, HENRY F. DOBYNS, ROBERT C. EULER, *Havasupai Indians*. New York: Garland Publishing Co., 1974.

MARTIN, PAUL, "The Discovery of America," *Science* 179(1973):969–974.

MATSCH, CHARLES L., *North America and the Great Ice Age*. Earth Science Paperback Series. New York: McGraw-Hill Book Co., 1976.

MEGGERS, BETTY, CLIFFORD EVANS, and EMELIO ESTRADA, *Early Formative Period of Coastal Ecuador*. Washington D.C.: Smithsonian Contributions to Anthropology, I, 1965.

MEGGERS, BETTY, "Contacts From Asia," in *Quest For America*, Geoffrey Ashe, ed. New York: Praeger Publishers, 1971.

MEYER, ROY WILLARD, *The Village Indians of the Upper Missouri*. Lincoln: University of Nebraska Press, 1971.

MISHKIN, BERNARD, *Rank and Warfare Among the Plains Indians*. American Ethnological Society Monograph #3. Seattle: University of Washington Press, 1940.

MOONEY, JAMES, *Myths of the Cherokee*. Bureau of American Ethnology, Nineteenth Annual Report, 1897–1898, Part 1, Smithsonian Institution.

MOONEY, JAMES, *The Swimmer Manuscript, Cherokee Sacred Formulas and Medicinal Prescriptions*, Franz M. Olbrect, ed. Bureau of American Ethnology Bulletin 99, Smithsonian Institution, 1932.

MORAN, EMELIO F., *An Introduction to Ecological Anthropology*. Boulder, CO: Westview Press, 1982.

MOZIÑO, JOSE MARIANO, *Noticias de Nutka: An Account of Nootka Sound in 1792*, rev. ed. Translated by Iris Higbie Wilson. The American Ethnological Society Monograph #50. Seattle: University of Washington Press, 1970.

MÜLLER-BECK, HANSGURGEN, "Paleohunter in America: Origins and Diffusions," *Science* 152(1966):1191–1210.

NETTING, ROBERT McC., *Cultural Ecology*. Cummings Modular Program in Anthropology. Menlo Park, CA: Cummings Publishing Co., 1977.

NEUMANN, GEORGE K., "Archaeology and Race in the American Indian," in *Archaeology of Eastern United States*, James B. Griffin, ed. Chicago: University of Chicago Press, 1952.

NEUMANN, GEORGE K., "Origins of the Indians of the Middle Mississippi Area," in *Proceedings of the Indiana Academy of Sciences* 60(1960).

NEWMANN, MARSHALL T., "Evolutionary Changes in Body Size and Head Form in American Indians," *American Anthropologist* 64(1962):237–257.

OLIVER, SYMMES, *Ecology and Cultural Continuity as Contributing Factors in the Social Organization of the Plains Indians*. Berkeley: University of California Publications in American Archaeology and Ethnology, 1962.

ORTIZ, ALFONSO, *The Tewa World: Space, Time, Being, and Becoming in a Pueblo Society*. Chicago: The University of Chicago Press, 1969.

ORTIZ, ALFONSO, "Ritual Drama and the Pueblo World View," in *New Perspectives on the Pueblos*, Alfonso Ortiz, ed. Albuquerque: University of New Mexico Press, 1972.

PIDDOCKE, STUART, "The Potlatch System of the Southern Kwakiutl: A New Perspective," *The Southwest Journal of Anthropology* 21(1965):245–259.

PRESTON, RICHARD J., III, "Cree Reticence and Self Expression: A Study of Style in Social Relationships," *Proceedings of the Seventh Algonkian Conference*, W. Cowan ed., 1976.

PRICE, JOHN A., "Some Aspects of Washo Life Cycle," in *The Washo Indians of California and Nevada*, Warren L. d'Asevedo, ed. University of Utah Anthropological Papers 67, 1963.

PRICE, JOHN A., "Washo Pre-History: A Review of Research," in *The Washo Indians of California and Nevada*, Warren L. d'Asevedo, ed. University of Utah Anthropological Papers 67, 1963.

RASMUSSEN, KNUD, *The Netsilik Eskimos, Social Life and Spiritual Culture*. Report of the Fifth Thule Expedition, 1921–1924, vol. 8. New York: AMS Press (Reprint 1976).

RICHES, DAVID, *Northern Nomadic Hunter-Gatherers*. New York: Academic Press, 1982.

ROGERS, EDWARD S., "Natural Environment-Social Organization-Witchcraft: Cree vs Ojibwa-a Test Case," National Museum of Canada Bulletin No. 230, 1969.

ROSMAN, ABRAHAM and PAULA RUBEL, *Feasting With Mine Enemy*. New York: Columbia University Press, 1971.

RUBEL, ARTHUR J. and HARRIET J. KUPFERER, "Perspectives on the Atomistic Type Society," *Human Organization* 27(1968):189–190.

SAHLINS, MARSHALL, "Notes on the Affluent Society," in *Man The Hunter*, Richard B. Lee and Irven DeVore, eds. Chicago: Aldine Publishing Co., 1968.

SAHLINS, MARSHALL, "Culture and Environment," in *Horizons of Anthropology*, 2nd ed., Sol Tax and Leslie G. Freeman, eds. Chicago: Aldine Publishing Co., 1977.

SERVICE, ELMAN, R., *Profiles in Ethnology*. New York: Harper and Row, Publishers, 1963.

SLAUGHTER, BOB H., "Animal Ranges as a Clue to Pleistocene Extinctions," in *Pleistocene Extinctions: The Search for a Cause*. Proceedings of the VIIth Congress of the International Association for Quaternary Research. New Haven: Yale University Press, 1967.

SMITHSON, CARMA LEE, *The Havasupai Woman*. Anthropological Papers, University of Utah 38, 1959.

SPECK, FRANK, "The Family Hunting Band as the Basis of Algonkian Social Organization," *American Anthropologist* 17(1915):289–305.

SPECK, FRANK and LOREN C. EISELEY, "The Significance of the Hunting Territory Systems of the Algonkian in Social Theory," *American Anthropologist*, 41(1939):269–280.

SPECK, FRANK and LEONARD BROOM, *Cherokee Dance and Drama*. Berkeley: University of California Press, 1951.

SPIER, LESLIE, "Problems Arising From the Cultural Position of the Havasupai," *American Anthropologist* 31(1919).

SPIER, LESLIE, *Havasupai Ethnography*. Anthropological Papers, American Museum of Natural History 29, 1928.

STANDS IN TIMBER, JOHN and MARGOT LIBERTY, *Cheyenne Memories*. New Haven: Yale University Press, 1967.

STEWARD, JULIAN, "Determinism in Primitive Society," in *Cultural Ecology: Readings on the Canadian Indians and Eskimos*, Bruce Cox, ed. Toronto: McClelland and Steward Ltd., Carleton Library Series, 1973.

STEWARD, JULIAN, *The Theory of Culture Change*. Urbana: University of Illinois Press, 1955.

SUTTLES, WAYNE, "Coping with Abundance," in *Man The Hunter*, Richard B. Lee, Irven DeVore, eds. Chicago: Aldine Publishing Co., 1968.

SZATHMARY, EMÖKE, J. E. and NANCY OSSENBERG, "Are the Biological Differences between North American Indians and Eskimos Truly Profound?" in *Current Anthropology*, 19(1978):673–685.

TANNER, ADRIAN, *Bringing Home Animals*. New York: St. Martins Press, 1979.

TERRAL, RUFUS, *The Missouri Valley: Land of Drought, Flood, and Promise*. New Haven: Yale University Press, 1947.

THOMAS, DAVIS AND KARIN RONNEFELDT, *People of the First Man: Life Among the Plains Indians in Their Final Days of Glory*. New York: E. P. Dutton, 1976.

TURNBULL, COLIN, "The Importance of Flux in Two Hunting Societies," in *Man The Hunter*. Richard B. Lee, Irven DeVore, eds. Chicago: Aldine Publishing Co., 1968.

VAN SERTIMA, IVAN, *They Came Before Columbus*. New York: Random House, 1976.

VAN STONE, JAMES, *Athapaskan Adaptations: Hunters and Fishermen of the Subartic Forests*. Chicago: Aldine Publishing Co., 1974.

VAYDA, ANDREW P. and ROY RAPPAPORT, "Ecology: Cultural and Non-Cultural," in *Introduction to Cultural Anthropology*, James A. Clifton, ed. Boston: Houghton Mifflin Company, 1968.

WAUCHOPE, ROBERT, *Lost Tribes and Sunken Continents*. Chicago: University of Chicago Press, 1962.

WEBB, PRESCOTT, *The Great Plains*. Boston: Ginn & Co., 1931.

WHITAKER, THOMAS, "Endemism and Pre-Columbian Migrations" in *Man Across The Sea: Problems of Pre-Columbian Contacts*, Carroll J. Riley, Charles Kelley, Campbell W. Pennington, and Robert L. Rands, eds. Austin: University of Texas Press, 1971.

WHITE, LESLIE A., *The Pueblo of Santo Domingo, New Mexico*. Memoirs of the American Anthropological Association #43, 1935. Kraus Reprint Co., 1974.

WHITE, LESLIE A., *The Evolution of Culture*. New York: McGraw-Hill, 1959.

WINTERHALDER, BRUCE, "History and Ecology of the Boreal Zone in Ontario," in *Boreal Adaptations*, A. T. Steegman, Jr., ed. New York: Plenum Press, 1983.

WINTERHALDER, BRUCE, "Boreal Forest Strategies," in *Boreal Adaptations*, A. T. Steegman, Jr., ed. New York: Plenum Press, 1983.

WISSLER, CLARK, "Influence of the Horse in Plains Culture," in *American Anthropologist* 16(1914):1–25.

WITTFOGEL, KARL, *Oriental Despotism: A Comparative Study of Total Power*. New Haven: Yale University Press, 1957.

WRIGHT, H. E., JR., "Pleistocene Ecology, Some Current Problems," *Geoscience and Man*, vol. XIII, Ecology of the Pleistocene, R. C. West and William Haag, eds. Baton Rouge: Louisiana State University, 1976.

Index